ScottForesman Spanish Program

PASO A PASO

1

Unas molas de San Blas, Panamá

ScottForesman Spanish Program

PASO A PASO

1

Myriam Met
Coordinator of Foreign Languages
Montgomery County Public Schools
Rockville, MD

Richard S. Sayers
Niwot High School
Longmont, CO

Carol Eubanks Wargin
Glen Crest Junior High School
Glen Ellyn, IL

ScottForesman

A Division of HarperCollinsPublishers

Editorial Offices: Glenview, Illinois

Regional Offices: San Jose, California • Atlanta, Georgia
Glenview, Illinois • Oakland, New Jersey • Dallas, Texas

Visit ScottForesman's Home Page at http://www.scottforesman.com

Contributing Writers

Eduardo Aparicio
Miami, FL

Margaret Juanita Azevedo
Stanford University
Palo Alto, CA

Thomasina Pagán Hannum
Albuquerque, NM

Mary de López
University of Texas
El Paso, TX

Reader Consultants

The authors and editors would like to express our heartfelt thanks to the following team of reader consultants. Each of them read the manuscript, chapter by chapter, offering suggestions and providing encouragement. Their contribution has been invaluable.

Rosario Martínez-Cantú
Northside Health Careers High School
San Antonio, TX

Greg Duncan
InterPrep
Marietta, GA

Walter Kleinmann
Sewanhaka Central High School District
New Hyde Park, NY

Bernadette M. Reynolds
Parker, CO

Rudolf L. Schonfeld, Ph.D.
Brooklawn Middle School
Parsippany, NJ

Marcia Payne Wooten
Starmount High School
Boonville, NC

Tabla de materias

EL PRIMER PASO

CAPÍTULO 1

Y tú, ¿cómo eres?

CAPÍTULO 2

¿Qué clases tienes?

Capítulo 3

Los pasatiempos

Capítulo 4

¿Qué prefieres comer?

CAPÍTULO 5

¿Cómo es tu familia?

CAPÍTULO 6

¿Qué desea Ud.?

CAPÍTULO 11

¿Qué te gustaría ver?

CAPÍTULO 12

¡Vamos a un restaurante mexicano!

CAPÍTULO 13

Para proteger la Tierra

CAPÍTULO 14

¡Vamos a una fiesta!

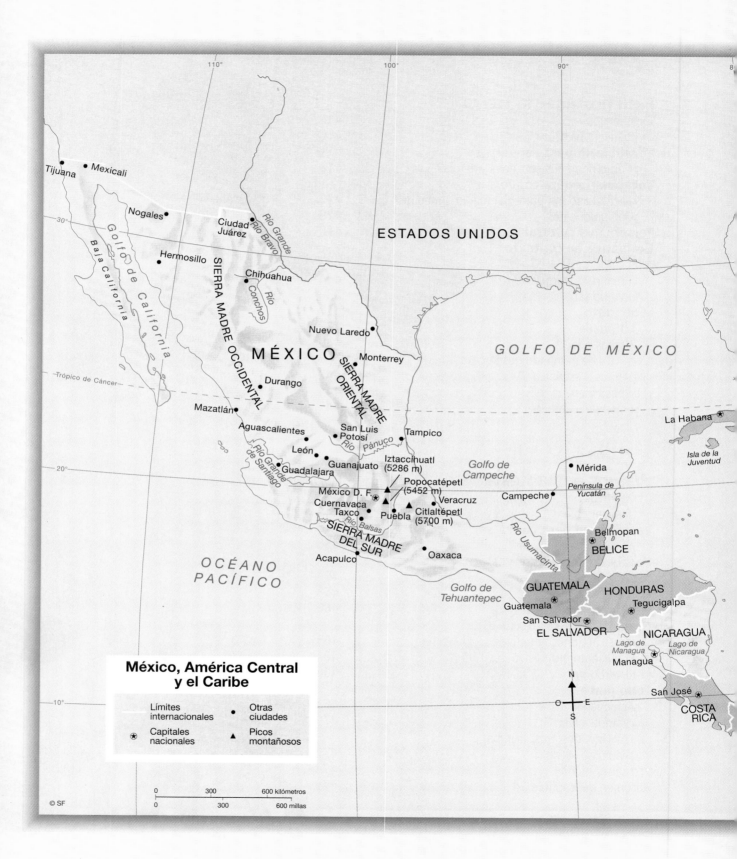

México, América Central y el Caribe

Límites internacionales
Capitales nacionales
Otras ciudades
Picos montañosos

0   300   600 kilómetros
0   300   600 millas

© SF

XIV

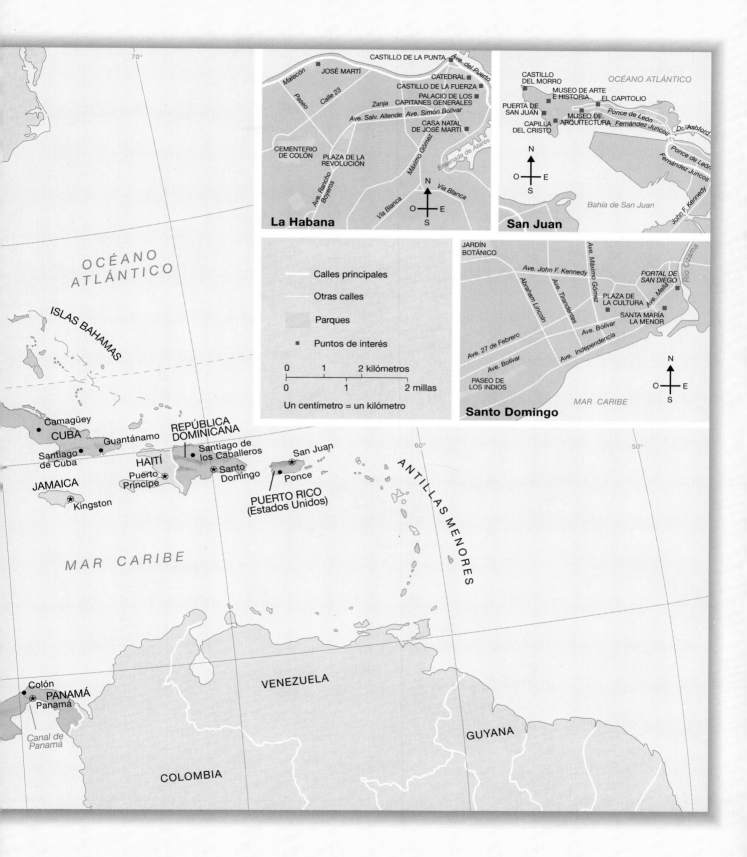

La Habana

CASTILLO DE LA PUNTA
JOSÉ MARTÍ
Malecón
Paseo
Calle 23
Zanja
Ave. Salv. Allende
Ave. del Puerto
CATEDRAL
CASTILLO DE LA FUERZA
PALACIO DE LOS CAPITANES GENERALES
Ave. Simón Bolívar
CASA NATAL DE JOSÉ MARTÍ
CEMENTERIO DE COLÓN
PLAZA DE LA REVOLUCIÓN
Ave. Rancho Boyeros
Máximo Gómez
Ensenada de Atarés
Vía Blanca
Vía Blanca
N
O E
S

San Juan

OCÉANO ATLÁNTICO
CASTILLO DEL MORRO
MUSEO DE ARTE E HISTORIA
EL CAPITOLIO
PUERTA DE SAN JUAN
MUSEO DE ARQUITECTURA
Ponce de León
Fernández Juncos
Dr. Ashford
CAPILLA DEL CRISTO
Ponce de León
Fernández Juncos
John F. Kennedy
Bahía de San Juan
N
O E
S

Calles principales

Otras calles

Parques

Puntos de interés

0   1   2 kilómetros
0   1   2 millas

Un centímetro = un kilómetro

Santo Domingo

JARDÍN BOTÁNICO
Ave. John F. Kennedy
Ave. Máximo Gómez
Abraham Lincoln
Ave. Tiradentes
PORTAL DE SAN DIEGO
Río Ozama
PLAZA DE LA CULTURA
Ave. Mella
SANTA MARÍA LA MENOR
Ave. 27 de Febrero
Ave. Bolívar
Ave. Independencia
Ave. Bolívar
PASEO DE LOS INDIOS
MAR CARIBE
N
O E
S

OCÉANO ATLÁNTICO

ISLAS BAHAMAS

Camagüey
CUBA
Guantánamo
Santiago de Cuba
JAMAICA
Kingston

REPÚBLICA DOMINICANA
Santiago de los Caballeros
HAITÍ
Puerto Príncipe
Santo Domingo

San Juan
Ponce
PUERTO RICO
(Estados Unidos)

ANTILLAS MENORES

MAR CARIBE

VENEZUELA

GUYANA

Colón
PANAMÁ
Panamá
Canal de Panamá

COLOMBIA

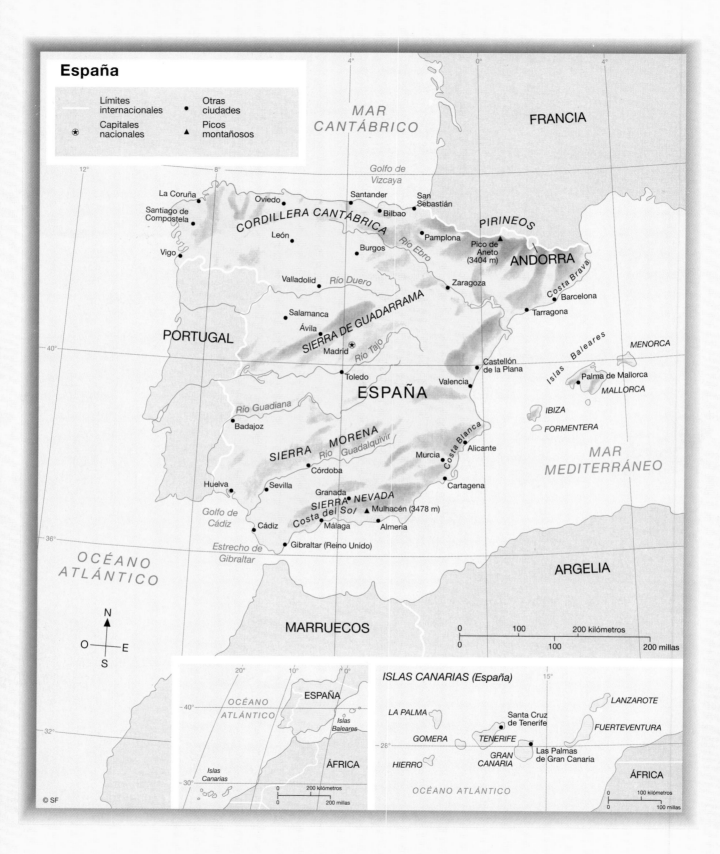

España

Límites internacionales
Capitales nacionales
Otras ciudades
Picos montañosos

MAR CANTÁBRICO

FRANCIA

Golfo de Vizcaya

La Coruña
Santiago de Compostela
Oviedo
Santander
San Sebastián
Bilbao
CORDILLERA CANTÁBRICA
PIRINEOS
León
Pamplona
Río Ebro
Pico de Aneto (3404 m)
ANDORRA
Vigo
Burgos
Zaragoza
Costa Brava
Valladolid
Río Duero
Barcelona
Salamanca
Tarragona
Ávila
SIERRA DE GUADARRAMA
Madrid
Río Tajo
Castellón de la Plana
Islas Baleares
MENORCA
Toledo
Valencia
PORTUGAL
ESPAÑA
Palma de Mallorca
MALLORCA
Río Guadiana
IBIZA
FORMENTERA
Badajoz
SIERRA MORENA
Río Guadalquivir
Costa Blanca
MAR MEDITERRÁNEO
Córdoba
Murcia
Alicante
Huelva
Sevilla
Granada
SIERRA NEVADA
Cartagena
Golfo de Cádiz
Costa del Sol
Mulhacén (3478 m)
Cádiz
Málaga
Almería
Estrecho de Gibraltar
Gibraltar (Reino Unido)
ARGELIA
OCÉANO ATLÁNTICO

N
O E
S

MARRUECOS

0   100   200 kilómetros
0   100   200 millas

© SF

OCÉANO ATLÁNTICO
ESPAÑA
Islas Baleares
ÁFRICA
Islas Canarias
0   200 kilómetros
0   200 millas

ISLAS CANARIAS (España)

LA PALMA
LANZAROTE
Santa Cruz de Tenerife
GOMERA
TENERIFE
FUERTEVENTURA
HIERRO
GRAN CANARIA
Las Palmas de Gran Canaria
OCÉANO ATLÁNTICO
ÁFRICA
0   100 kilómetros
0   100 millas

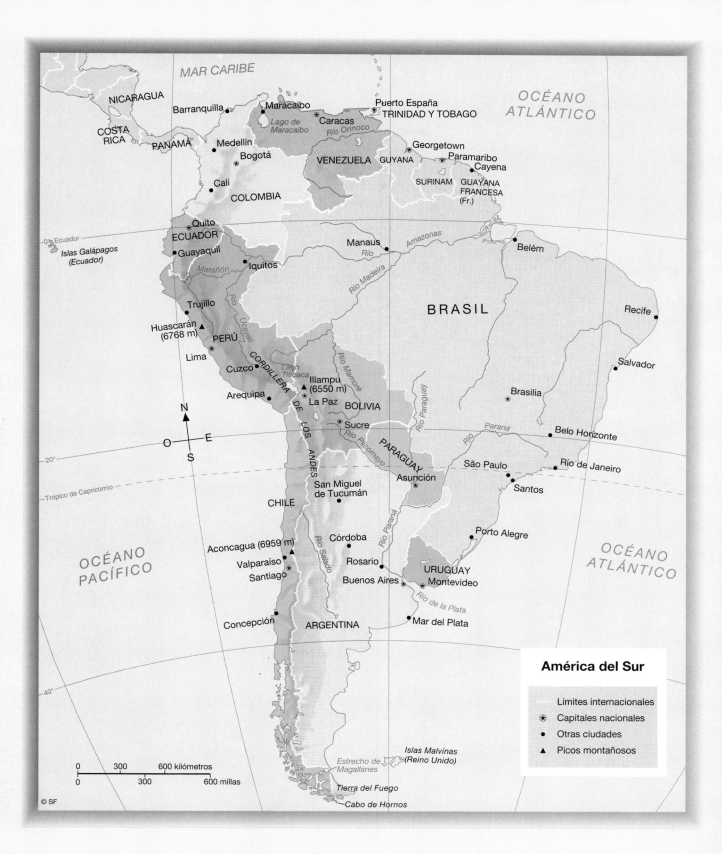

MAR CARIBE

OCÉANO
ATLÁNTICO

NICARAGUA

Barranquilla

Maracaibo

Caracas

Puerto España
TRINIDAD Y TOBAGO

COSTA
RICA

Lago de
Maracaibo

Río Orinoco

PANAMÁ

Medellín

Georgetown

Bogotá

VENEZUELA

GUYANA

Paramaribo
Cayena

Cali

SURINAM

GUAYANA
FRANCESA
(Fr.)

COLOMBIA

Quito

0° Ecuador

ECUADOR

Manaus

Río Amazonas

Belém

Islas Galápagos
(Ecuador)

Guayaquil

Marañón

Iquitos

Trujillo

Río Ucayali

Río Madeira

B R A S I L

Recife

Huascarán
(6768 m)

PERÚ

Lima

CORDILLERA

Salvador

Cuzco

Lago
Titicaca

Río Marmoré

Illampu
(6550 m)

DE

Arequipa

La Paz

BOLIVIA

Brasilia

LOS

Sucre

Río Pilcomayo

Río Paraguay

Belo Horizonte

20°

ANDES

PARAGUAY

Río Paraná

São Paulo

Río de Janeiro

Trópico de Capricornio

Asunción

Santos

San Miguel
de Tucumán

CHILE

Porto Alegre

OCÉANO
PACÍFICO

Aconcagua (6959 m)

Córdoba

Río Salado

Río Paraná

Valparaíso

Rosario

URUGUAY

OCÉANO
ATLÁNTICO

Santiago

Buenos Aires

Montevideo

Concepción

ARGENTINA

Mar del Plata

Río de la Plata

40°

Islas Malvinas
(Reino Unido)

Estrecho de
Magallanes

Tierra del Fuego

Cabo de Hornos

0   300   600 kilómetros
0   300   600 millas

© SF

América del Sur

—— Límites internacionales

✳ Capitales nacionales

● Otras ciudades

▲ Picos montañosos

EL PRIMER PASO

You are about to embark on a wonderful journey through the Spanish-speaking world as you begin to learn the language. Think of the possibilities! By the end of this chapter, *El primer paso*, you will have experienced:

P resentations of some of the rich and varied aspects of Hispanic cultures

A cquisition of key vocabulary so that you can start speaking Spanish right away

S trategies and suggestions to help you learn more quickly and effectively and evaluate your progress—and have fun while doing it

O pportunities to increase your job and career choices, as well as improve your English-language skills and college entrance exam scores

EL PRIMER PASO

OBJECTIVES

At the end of this chapter, you will be able to:

- understand the widespread influence of the Spanish language and Hispanic cultures

- greet people and introduce yourself

- ask how someone is feeling and tell how you are feeling

- ask where someone's from and tell where you are from

- say good-by

- use the Spanish alphabet to spell

- use numbers to count and tell your age, your phone number, and the date

- ask questions and respond to requests in the classroom

- use your textbook to help you learn Spanish

3

In this section you will learn about the widespread influence of the Spanish language and Hispanic cultures.

Countries with the largest Spanish-speaking populations

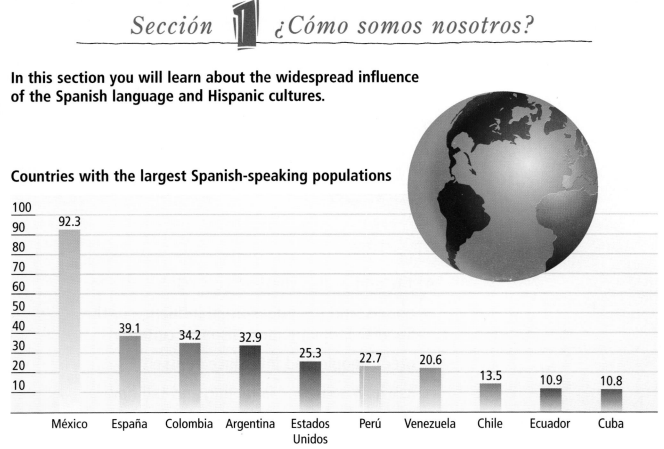

Numbers shown in millions

Cities with the largest Spanish-speaking populations

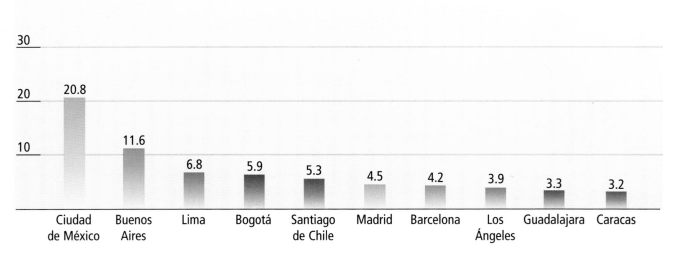

Numbers shown in millions

A Look at the graph of the countries with the largest Spanish-speaking populations. Where does the United States fall in rank order?

Now look at the graph of the cities. Where does a U.S. city fall in rank order?

B Discuss the information with a partner. Which fact was most surprising to you? Which facts did you know before you saw these graphs?

C There are many words we use every day that come from Spanish. You probably already know how to pronounce a few of these words and phrases. See how many more you can add:

ANIMALS: armadillo, pinto, . . .
BUILDINGS: adobe, patio, . . .
CLOTHING: poncho, sombrero, . . .
EXPRESSIONS: adiós, hasta la vista, . . .
FAMOUS PEOPLE: *(past and present, real or fictional)*: Andy García, Don Quijote, . . .
FOODS: tacos, tamales, . . .
GAMES / SPORTS: piñata, jai alai, . . .
GEOGRAPHY: chaparral, mesa, . . .
MUSIC / DANCE: mariachi, tango, . . .
PEOPLE: matador, señor, . . .
PLACE NAMES: Nevada, Santa Fe, . . .

D Spanish is a Romance language, meaning that it comes from Latin, the language of the Romans. Because of the great influence of Latin on the English language, there are also many words in Spanish that look and / or sound similar to English words. These are called cognates. Take advantage of this!

Can you guess the meaning of these Spanish words?

- *carnaval*
- *comunicación*
- *delicioso*
- *fabuloso*
- *farmacia*
- *libertad*
- *limón*
- *parque*
- *oficina*

E Look at these photos and read the captions.

Can you guess what these professions are in English? Here is an additional list for you to practice with:

el actor / la actriz
el arquitecto / la arquitecta
el / la astronauta
el banquero / la banquera
el carpintero / la carpintera
el / la chofer
el científico / la científica
el ingeniero / la ingeniera
el mecánico / la mecánica
el médico / la médica
el piloto / la pilota
el político / la política
el presidente / la presidenta
el profesor / la profesora
el secretario / la secretaria
el supervisor / la supervisora

"Soy dentista y soy de Miami."

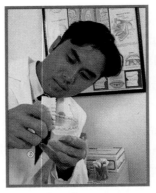

"Soy fotógrafa y soy de Costa Rica."

"Soy veterinario y soy de Ecuador."

"Soy policía y soy de la Ciudad de México."

- With a partner, discuss why knowing Spanish would be valuable in these careers. What career(s) are you considering? How will knowing Spanish help you with your goals?

- With your partner, make a list of the six most popular jobs or volunteer positions that students might have. If you were hiring a teenager, would you prefer one who spoke Spanish? Why? Are there summer jobs in which knowing Spanish would be especially helpful?

You have made a great decision to study Spanish. Let's take it *PASO A PASO*, step by step. You'll be communicating in Spanish very soon.

¡OJO!

Did you know that, according to research, high-school students with two years of a foreign language score up to 12% higher on the S.A.T. verbal exam—and their scores continue to rise by at least 5% for each additional year of foreign-language study?

Vocabulario para conversar

In the next four sections you will find some study notes to help you learn about the various parts of each chapter. Here are some words you will need to greet people and introduce yourself.

También necesitas . . .

Mucho gusto.	*Pleased / Nice to meet you.*
Igualmente.	*Likewise.*
Muy bien.	*Very well.*
Así, así.	*So-so.*

Here's a list of common names in Spanish. You might want to choose one that is equivalent to yours, or another name that you prefer to use in class.

NOMBRES DE MUCHACHOS

Adán
Agustín
Alejandro (Ale)
Andrés
Antonio (Toño)
Armando
Arturo
Benito
Benjamín
Bernardo
Carlos (Chacho, Cacho)
Cristóbal
Daniel (Dani)
David
Eduardo (Edu)
Emilio
Enrique (Quique)
Esteban
Federico
Felipe
Francisco (Paco)
Gerardo (Gérar)
Gregorio
Guillermo (Guille)
Ignacio (Nacho)
Jaime
Jesús
Jorge
Jorge Luis
José (Pepe)
José Eduardo

José Emilio
José Luis
Juan (Juancho)
Juan Carlos (Juanca, Juaca)
Julio
Julio César
Luis (Lucho)
Luis Miguel
Manuel (Manolo)
Marco Antonio
Marcos
Mario
Mateo
Miguel
Miguel Ángel
Nicolás (Nico)
Pablo
Patricio
Pedro
Rafael (Rafa)
Ramón
Raúl
Ricardo
Roberto (Beto)
Samuel
Santiago (Santi)
Timoteo (Timo)
Tomás (Tomi)
Vicente
Víctor

NOMBRES DE MUCHACHAS

Alicia
Ana
Ana Luisa
Ana María
Ángela
Bárbara
Carmen (Mamen)
Carolina (Caro)
Catalina (Cata)
Cecilia (Ceci)
Clara
Claudia
Cristina (Tina)
Diana
Dolores (Lola)
Elena
Elisa
Emilia
Esperanza
Eva
Gloria
Guadalupe (Lupe)
Guillermina
Inés
Irene
Isabel (Chabela, Isa)
Josefina
Juana
Julia
Laura
Lourdes

Lucía
Luisa
Luz
Margarita
María
María del Carmen
María Elena
María Eugenia
María José (Marijó)
María Luisa
María Soledad
María Teresa (Maite, Marité)
Mariana
Marisol
Marta
Mónica (Moni)
Patricia (Pati)
Pilar
Raquel
Rebeca
Reina
Rocío
Rosa (Rosi)
Sara (Saruca)
Soledad
Susana (Susa)
Teresa (Tere)
Verónica (Vero)
Victoria
Virginia

Empecemos a conversar

In these exercises you will create conversations according to a model. With a partner, take turns at being *Estudiante A* and *Estudiante B.* Use the words that are cued or given in the balloons to replace the underlined sections in the model.  means you can make your own choices for that item or exercise.

¡OJO!

You might want to scan the exercise first in order to get the gist of doing it. If you need help, review the *Vocabulario para conversar* or *También necesitas . . .* sections.

1 Estudiante A —¡Hola! Me llamo <u>María</u>. ¿Cómo te llamas?
　Estudiante B —Me llamo <u>Rafael</u>.
　Estudiante A —Mucho gusto, <u>Rafael</u>.
　Estudiante B —Igualmente, <u>María</u>.

　　　　Y ahora Uds.

　　　(This is the cue for you and your partner to begin the exercise.)

Estudiante A　　　　Estudiante B

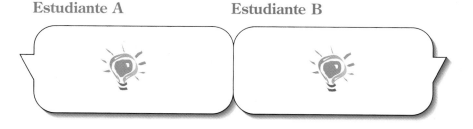

Did you use your own name in the conversation? Now redo it with five other classmates. Play both roles. Your teacher may ask you to tell your classmates' names, so remember their answers.

2 A —Buenos días. ¿Cómo estás, <u>Pilar</u>?
　B —Muy bien, gracias. ¿Y tú?
　A —Así, así.

　　　Y ahora Uds.

Estudiante A　　　　Estudiante B

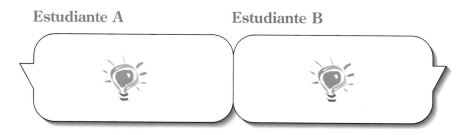

Did you keep using the same answers for how you feel? Repeat this conversation with four other classmates and vary your answers.

Vocabulario para conversar

Here are some more words and expressions you will
need to greet people and tell where you are from.

¡OJO!

Do you remember *¿Y tú?* and *¿Cómo estás?* There is another way to say "How are you?" in Spanish. We use *usted* to show respect when speaking to an older person.

Buenas tardes,
Señora García.
¿Cómo está Ud.?*

Bien, gracias, ¿y tú?

Buenas noches.
Me llamo Anita. ¿Qué tal?

Me llamo Miguel.
Muy bien, gracias.

¡OJO!

Look at the words in the section titled *¿Y qué quiere decir . . . ?* You will see this section often. These are cognates, or are closely related to words you have already learned.

También necesitas . . .

¿De dónde eres (tú)?	*Where are you from?*
(Yo) soy de ___.	*I am from ___.*
¿Y usted?	*And you?*
Hasta luego.	*See you later.*

¿Y qué quiere decir . . . ?

sí	o	señor (Sr.)	señorita (Srta.)
no	Adiós.	señora (Sra.)	

* *Usted* is often abbreviated *Ud.* in writing.

Empecemos a conversar

For Exercise 1, refer to the map below.

1 A — *¡Hola! Me llamo <u>Benito</u>. ¿Y tú?*
B — *Me llamo <u>Luisa</u>. ¿De dónde eres?*
A — *Soy de <u>Costa Rica</u>. ¿Y tú?*
B — *Soy de <u>Bolivia</u>.*

Y ahora Uds.

Estudiante A   **Estudiante B**

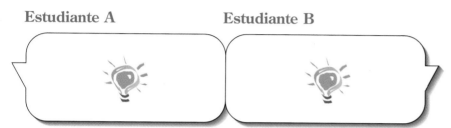

Did you use your own name and country? Now repeat this
dialogue with three classmates. Pretend to be someone else,
and use different names and countries.

2 Now repeat the conversation with five classmates, using a city
name from page 4.

Empecemos a escribir

Write your answers in Spanish.

3 List four ways to greet someone.

4 What are two ways to say "good-by"?

5 ¿Cómo te llamas?

6 ¿Cómo estás?

7 ¿De dónde eres?

¡OJO!

In this section you will write your answers and ideas in Spanish. Above all, communicate the message. After you finish, you can refer to *Vocabulario para conversar* and *También necesitas . . .* or the *Resumen* at the end of the chapter to check your spelling.

Empecemos a escribir y a leer

In this section you will write your answers and also do some reading.

Write your answers in Spanish.

8 How do you greet an older person and ask how he or she is feeling?

9 Read the following conversation, then answer the questions with *sí* or *no*.

> PROFESORA: Buenas tardes. Me llamo Señora Guzmán. ¿Y tú?
> ESTUDIANTE: Me llamo Ana María Hernández. Mucho gusto.
> PROFESORA: Igualmente. ¿De dónde eres? ¿De los Estados Unidos?
> ESTUDIANTE: No, soy de Costa Rica. ¿Es usted de Argentina o de Chile?
> PROFESORA: Soy de Uruguay. Adiós, Ana María. Hasta luego.
> ESTUDIANTE: Adiós, profesora.

a. The people in the dialogue know each other.
b. The teacher is a woman.
c. We know the last names of both people.
d. The student is from the United States.

¡OJO!

You might want to read the passage twice, once to get the general meaning, and a second time to try to figure out words you don't know. Many times you can guess the meaning of a word just by how it is used. YOU DON'T HAVE TO UNDERSTAND EVERY WORD TO GET THE OVERALL MEANING.

Vocabulario para conversar

la sala de clases

la pizarra

el profesor

la profesora

pl. los estudiantes

la estudiante

el estudiante

pl. los compañeros

el compañero

la compañera

el pupitre

la hoja de papel

la mesa

el libro

el bolígrafo

También necesitas . . .

¿Cómo se dice ___ en español?	*How do you say ___ in Spanish?*
¿Cómo se escribe ___?	*How do you spell ___?*
Se escribe ___.	*It's spelled ___.*

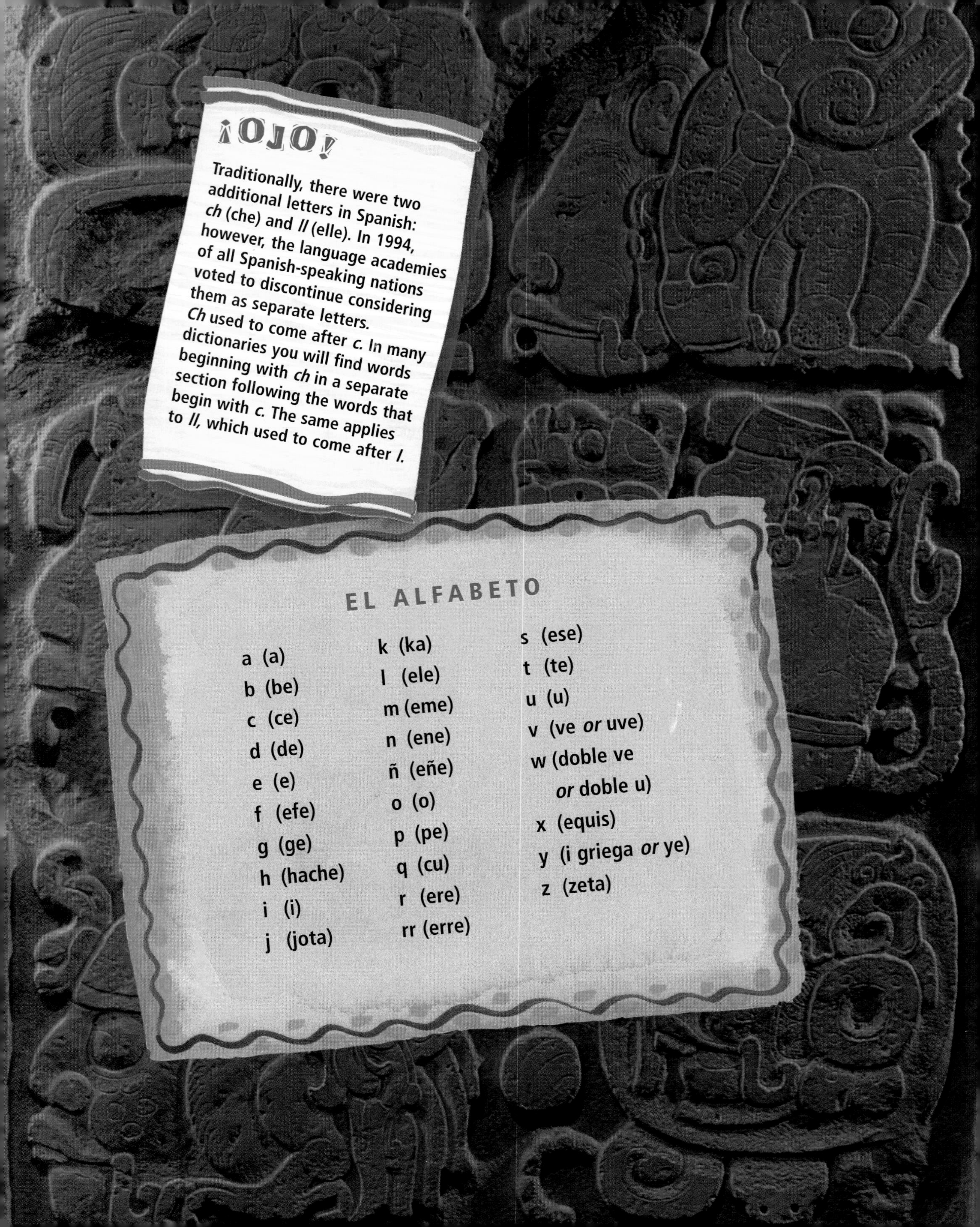

¡OJO!

Traditionally, there were two additional letters in Spanish: *ch* (che) and *ll* (elle). In 1994, however, the language academies of all Spanish-speaking nations voted to discontinue considering them as separate letters. *Ch* used to come after *c.* In many dictionaries you will find words beginning with *ch* in a separate section following the words that begin with *c.* The same applies to *ll,* which used to come after *l.*

EL ALFABETO

a (a)
b (be)
c (ce)
d (de)
e (e)
f (efe)
g (ge)
h (hache)
i (i)
j (jota)
k (ka)
l (ele)
m (eme)
n (ene)
ñ (eñe)
o (o)
p (pe)
q (cu)
r (ere)
rr (erre)
s (ese)
t (te)
u (u)
v (ve *or* uve)
w (doble ve *or* doble u)
x (equis)
y (i griega *or* ye)
z (zeta)

Empecemos a conversar

1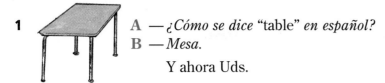
A — *¿Cómo se dice "table" en español?*
B — *Mesa.*
  Y ahora Uds.

Estudiante A   **Estudiante B**

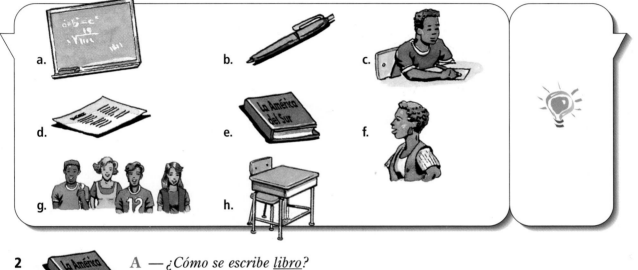

2
A — *¿Cómo se escribe <u>libro</u>?*
B — *Se escribe <u>ele-i-be-ere-o</u>.*
  Y ahora Uds.

Estudiante A   **Estudiante B**

Empecemos a escribir

Write your answers in Spanish.

3 Your teacher will spell some names. Listen carefully and
write them down. Later, compare your paper with a partner's.

Vocabulario para conversar

¡OJO!
Spanish calendars begin the week with Monday *(lunes)* and end with Sunday *(domingo).*

el mes

E N E R O

la semana

el día

LUNES	MARTES	MIÉRCOLES	JUEVES	VIERNES	SÁBADO	DOMINGO
						1 UNO
					7 SIETE	8 OCHO
			5 CINCO	6 SEIS	14 CATORCE	15 QUINCE
2 DOS	3 TRES	4 CUATRO	12 DOCE	13 TRECE	21 VEINTIUNO	22 VEINTIDÓS
9 NUEVE	10 DIEZ	11 ONCE	19 DIECINUEVE	20 VEINTE	28 VEINTIOCHO	29 VEINTINUEVE
16 * DIECISÉIS	17 DIECISIETE	18 DIECIOCHO	26 VEINTISÉIS	27 VEINTISIETE		
23 VEINTITRÉS	24 VEINTICUATRO	25 VEINTICINCO				
30 TREINTA	31 TREINTA Y UNO					

Mi cumpleaños es el 6 de junio.

¿Cuándo es tu cumpleaños?

* You will also see the numbers 16–19 spelled *diez y seis, diez y siete, diez y ocho, diez y nueve.* The numbers 21–29 may also be written *veinte y uno, veinte y dos,* and so on.

los meses

También necesitas . . .

¿Cuántos(as) ___ hay? *	*How many ___ are there?*
¿Cuántos años tienes?	*How old are you?*
Tengo ___ años.	*I'm ___ years old.*
el año	*year*
¿Cuál es tu número de teléfono?	*What's your phone number?*
¿Cuándo es ___?	*When is ___?*
¿Cuál es la fecha de hoy?	*What's the date today?*
Hoy es ___.	*Today is ___.*
Mañana es ____.	*Tomorrow is ___.*
¿Qué día es hoy?	*What day is today?*
Mi / Tu cumpleaños	*My / Your birthday*
el 6 de febrero	*the 6th of February / February 6*
el primero de mayo	*the first of May / May 1*

¡OJO!

We form dates using *el* + number + *de* + month. We use *primero* for "first," but we use the regular numbers for the rest of the dates. Notice, too, that the days of the week and the months of the year are not capitalized.

por favor	*please*
Hay	*There is / are*
Mi	*My*

¿Y qué quiere decir . . . ?
cero
en

---

* We use *cuántos* with masculine nouns and *cuántas* with feminine nouns.

Empecemos a conversar

1 0, 2, 4, . . .   A — *cero, dos, cuatro,* . . .
        B — *seis, ocho, diez,* . . .

        Y ahora Uds.

a. 5, 10, . . .
b. 1, 3, 5, . . .
c. 0, 3, 6, . . .

2   A — *¿Cuántos bolígrafos hay?*
        B — *Hay tres bolígrafos.*

        Y ahora Uds.

Estudiante A   Estudiante B

Empecemos a escribir y a leer

Write your answers in Spanish.

3 Find out when these popular Hispanic holidays occur and write down the dates for each of them: *el Año Nuevo* (New Year's Day), *el Día de los Reyes* (Twelfth Night / Epiphany), *el Día de la Raza* (Columbus Day), *el Día de los Muertos* (Day of the Dead / All Souls' Day), *la Navidad* (Christmas).

4 Count the items listed below and write the answer in Spanish. Compare your answer with a partner's.

a. books on your desk
b. girls in the class
c. countries in Latin America
d. people wearing jeans
e. letters in your teacher's last name

5 Read the following sentences and rewrite them, making the necessary corrections:

a. Mi cumpleaños es el 15 de diciembre.
b. El cumpleaños de Martin Luther King, Jr. es en octubre.
c. El Día de San Patricio es el 14 de enero.
d. El Día de San Valentín es en junio.
e. Chanukah es en febrero.

6 ¿Cuál es la fecha de hoy? ¿Y de mañana?

7 ¿Cuándo es tu cumpleaños?

8 ¿Qué día es hoy? ¿Y mañana?

9 ¿Cuál es tu número de teléfono? ¿Y el número de teléfono de tu compañero(a) de clase?

¡Comuniquemos!

This is another opportunity for you to use the vocabulary you've just learned.

1 Find out when your classmates' birthdays are. Then tally the results to find out which month has the most birthdays.

A — *¿Cuándo es tu cumpleaños?*
B — *Es el cinco de julio.*

2 Role-play a conversation with a partner in which you:

- greet each other
- find out each other's names
- ask and answer how you are
- say good-by

3 With a partner, role-play a meeting between you and a new student in which you:

- greet each other and ask each other's names
- say that you are glad to meet each other
- ask each other your ages and where you are from
- ask for each other's phone numbers
- give the information and then say good-by

¡OJO!

In the ¡Comuniquemos! section, you are free to use the language you already know. Try to use different expressions for the same ideas. Are you aware that you are now REALLY COMMUNICATING IN SPANISH?

Los cumpleaños

enero	febrero	marzo
₩₩₩ I	I	II

abril	mayo	junio
I	II	I

julio	agosto	septiembre
₩₩₩	III	₩₩₩

octubre	noviembre	diciembre
I	III	I

Expresiones para la clase

Por favor

Here is a list of requests and instructions. You will need to know what to do when your teacher says them, but you will **not** need to know how to say or write them.

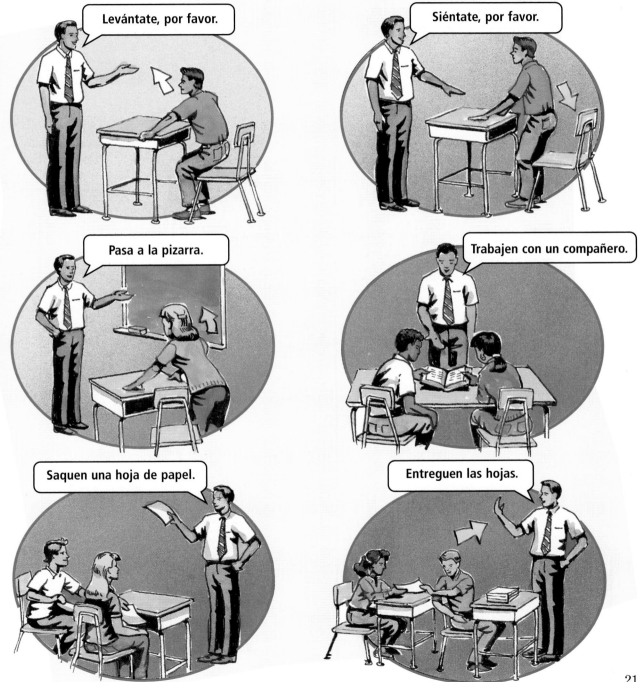

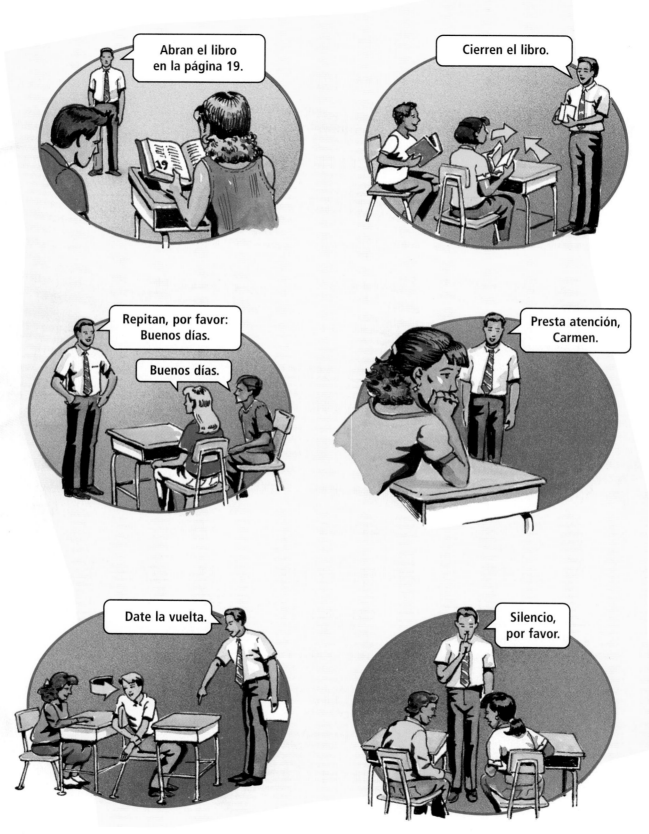

Profesor(a), ¿puedo . . . ?

When you need to ask for permission to do something, you should ask in Spanish. Here are some questions that you may frequently ask in class, and some of the expected answers.

Your teacher may respond to your requests in any of the following ways:

Sí / No.	*Yes / No.*
Sí, ve (al baño, a tu armario, etc.).	*Yes, go ahead (to ___).*
Sí, ábrela / ciérrala.	*Yes, open / close it.*
Claro.	*Of course.*
Ahora no.	*Not now.*
No, lo siento.	*No, I'm sorry.*

23

¿Lo sabes bien?

This section will help you organize your studying for the proficiency test, where you will be asked to do similar, though not identical, tasks. There will not be any models on the test.

Listening

Can you understand a brief conversation between two students who have just met? Listen as your teacher reads a sample similar to what you will hear on the test. What do the students find out about each other in this conversation?

Reading

Can you read a note and find out some information about that person? Read the following description about Arturo. Does he have any friends who speak Spanish? How many students are there in his class? What other information does he give?

Me llamo Arturo. Soy de Boston, Massachusetts. Tengo dieciséis años. Mi cumpleaños es el 20 de noviembre. En mi sala de clases hay veintinueve estudiantes. El profesor es de la República Dominicana. En la sala de clases tengo dos compañeras de Venezuela.

Writing

Can you put the words in the list under the appropriate categories: Classroom objects, Months of the year, Numbers, and Greeting or Saying good-by?

agosto

bolígrafo

Buenas noches.

cuatro

enero

Hasta luego.

pizarra

quince

Culture

What influences have the Spanish language and Hispanic cultures had on the United States? Can you give some examples?

Speaking

Can you and your partner play the roles of a teacher and a student greeting and introducing yourselves? Here is a sample dialogue:

A — *Buenos días. ¿Cómo está usted?*
B — *Muy bien, gracias. Y tú, ¿qué tal?*
A — *Así, así. Me llamo Miguel. ¿Y usted?*
B — *Me llamo Alfonso Beltrán.*
A — *Mucho gusto, Señor Beltrán.*

Resumen: El primer paso

Use the vocabulary from this chapter to help you:

- greet people and ask how they are feeling
- talk about classroom items
- use the Spanish alphabet to spell and tell numbers and dates

to greet people and say good-by
Buenos días.
Buenas tardes.
Buenas noches.
¿Cómo está usted?
¿Cómo estás?
¡Hola!
¿Qué tal?
Adiós.
Hasta luego.

to tell how you feel
Así, así.
(Muy) bien.

to ask someone's name and tell your name
¿Cómo te llamas?
(Yo) me llamo ___.

to acknowledge introductions
Mucho gusto.
Igualmente.
señor / señora / señorita

to ask for and give information
¿Cómo se dice ___ en español?
Se dice ___.
¿Cómo se escribe ___?
¿Cuál es la fecha de hoy?
Hoy es ___.
Mañana es ___.

¿Cuál es tu número de
   teléfono?
Mi / Tu (cumpleaños)
¿Cuándo es ___?
el año
¿Cuántos años tienes?
Tengo ___ años.
¿Cuántos, -as ___ hay?
Hay
¿De dónde eres?
(Yo) soy de ___.
¿Qué día es hoy?
es
¿Y tú?
¿Y usted?
no
sí
o

to say when something takes place
el día / el mes / la semana
en
el + *number* + de + *month*
lunes   viernes
martes   sábado
miércoles   domingo
jueves

enero   julio
febrero   agosto
marzo   septiembre
abril   octubre
mayo   noviembre
junio   diciembre

to count or give dates
el primero de
cero, uno, dos, tres, cuatro,
   cinco, seis, siete, ocho, nueve,
   diez
once, doce, trece, catorce,
   quince, dieciséis, diecisiete,
   dieciocho, diecinueve, veinte
veintiuno, veintidós, veintitrés,
   veinticuatro, veinticinco,
   veintiséis, veintisiete,
   veintiocho, veintinueve,
   treinta
treinta y uno

to say please and thank you
por favor / gracias

to talk about the classroom
el bolígrafo
el compañero,
   la compañera
   pl. los compañeros
el / la estudiante,
   pl. los estudiantes
la hoja de papel
el libro
la mesa
la pizarra
el profesor, la profesora
el pupitre
la sala de clases

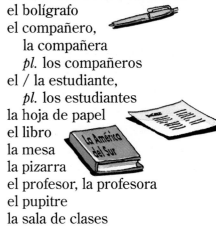

CAPÍTULO 1

Y tú, ¿cómo eres?

OBJECTIVES

At the end of this chapter, you will be able to:

■ describe yourself and tell about some of your likes and dislikes

■ find out what other people are like

■ compare your likes and dislikes with other people's

■ talk about teen activities and the concept of friendship in Spanish-speaking countries

Grupo de atletas de Esmeraldas, Ecuador

¡Piénsalo bien!

Look at the photographs.
In the captions these teens tell us something about themselves.

"Soy de Madrid. Me gusta mucho estar con mis amigos."

What is this group of friends doing?

"Soy de Barcelona. Me gusta hablar por teléfono con mis amigos."

What do you think the girl is saying in the caption?

"Me llamo Raúl y soy de Toluca, México. A mí me gusta ir al cine."

What do you think Raúl means when he talks about *cine*?

Vocabulario para conversar

¿Qué te gusta hacer?

Here are some new words and expressions you will need to talk about your likes and dislikes. Read them several times, then turn the page and practice with a partner.

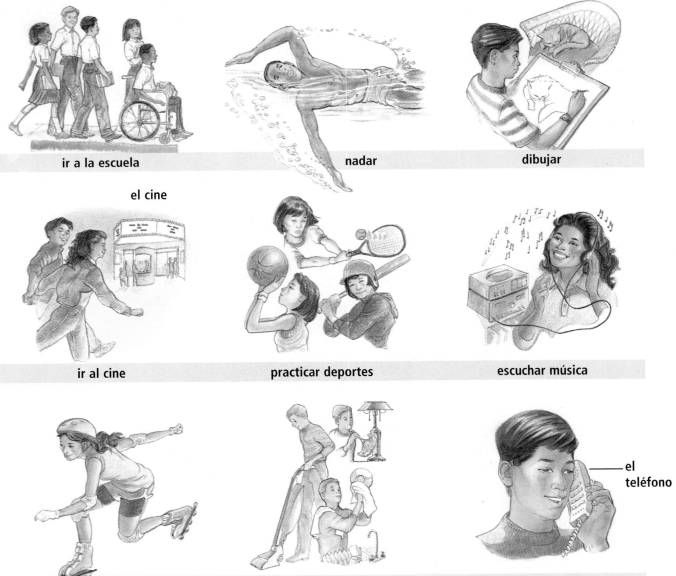

ir a la escuela

nadar

dibujar

el cine

ir al cine

practicar deportes

escuchar música

el teléfono

patinar

ayudar en casa

hablar por teléfono

estudiar

ver la televisión (la tele)

cocinar

leer

tocar la guitarra

También necesitas . . .

¿Qué te gusta (hacer)?	*What do you like (to do)?*
¿Te gusta ___?	*Do you like ___?*
estar con amigos	*to be with friends*
(A mí) me gusta ___.	*I like ___.*
más ___.	*___ better. (I prefer.)*
mucho ___.	*___ a lot.*
¿Y a ti?	*And you?*
(A mí) sí me gusta ___.	*I <u>do</u> like ___.*
A mí también.	*I do (like it) too.*
(A mí) no me gusta ___.	*I don't like ___.*
mucho ___.	*___ very much.*
nada ___.	*___ at all.*
___ tampoco.	*___ either.*
¿De veras?	*Really?*
Pues	*Well . . .*
y	*and*

Empecemos a conversar

With a partner, take turns being *Estudiante A* and *Estudiante B*.
Use the words that are cued or given in the balloons to replace
the underlined sections in the model. 💡 means you can make
your own choices.

1
A —¿Qué te gusta hacer? ¿Te gusta <u>nadar</u>?
B —<u>Sí, me gusta</u>.

　　　Y ahora Uds.

Estudiante A　　　　　　　　　　　　　　　　　　　　**Estudiante B**

a.　　　　　　　　b.　　　　　　　　c.

d.　　　　　　　　e.　　　　　　　　f.

Sí, me gusta.

o: No, no me gusta.

o: No, no me gusta nada.

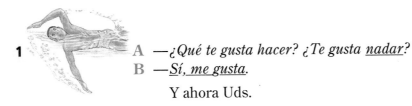

2
A —¿Qué te gusta más, <u>practicar deportes</u> o <u>hablar por teléfono</u>?
B —Pues, me gusta más <u>hablar por teléfono</u>.

　　　Y ahora Uds.

Estudiante A　　　　　　　　　　　　　　　　　　　　**Estudiante B**

a.　　　　　　　　　　　　　b.

c.　　　　　　　　　　　　　d.　　　　　　　　e.

3 A — *No me gusta mucho <u>ver la televisión</u>.*
   B — *<u>A mí no me gusta tampoco</u>.*

   Y ahora Uds.

Estudiante A   Estudiante B

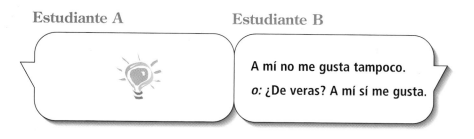

A mí no me gusta tampoco.

o: ¿De veras? A mí sí me gusta.

4 A — *A mí me gusta <u>tocar la guitarra</u>. ¿Y a ti?*
   B — *Pues, a mí me gusta <u>practicar deportes</u>.*
      o: *Pues, a mí también.*

   Y ahora Uds.

Estudiante A   Estudiante B

También se dice

People in different English-speaking countries often use different words to refer to the same thing. For example, what we call an "apartment" the English call a "flat." Similarly, in various Spanish-speaking countries, there are sometimes different words for the same thing

mirar la televisión (la tele)

Empecemos a escribir

Write your answers in Spanish.

5 Categorize the activities on pages 30–31 either as entertainment or as duties. Make two lists. Put a check next to any duties you enjoy.

6 Make a list of all those activities that you do on a normal school day.

7 ¿Qué te gusta hacer?

8 ¿Qué no te gusta hacer?

9 ¿Qué te gusta más, leer o ver la tele?

Vocabulario para conversar

¿Cómo eres?

Here's the rest of the vocabulary you will need to describe yourself and others.

generoso generosa   tacaño tacaña   impaciente   paciente

deportista   artístico artística   atrevido atrevida   prudente

ordenado   ordenada   **desordenado   desordenada**

trabajador   trabajadora   **perezoso   perezosa**

gracioso   graciosa   serio   seria

También necesitas . . .

¿Cómo eres?	*What are you like?*	callado, -a	*quiet*
(Yo) soy ___.	*I am (I'm) ___.*	pero	*but*
(Tú) eres ___.	*You are (You're) ___.*	a veces	*sometimes, at times*
muy	*very*		
amable	*nice, kind*		

¿Y qué quiere decir . . . ?
sociable

Empecemos a conversar

10 A —¿*Cómo eres, <u>ordenado(a)</u> o <u>desordenado(a)</u>?*
    B —*Soy <u>ordenado(a)</u>, pero a veces soy <u>desordenado(a)</u>.*

Y ahora Uds.

Estudiante A   Estudiante B

a.

b.

c.

d.

e.

11 A — ¿*Eres <u>serio(a)</u>?*
    B — *Sí, y soy <u>callado(a)</u> también.*
        o: *No, no soy <u>serio(a)</u>.*

Y ahora Uds.

Estudiante A   Estudiante B

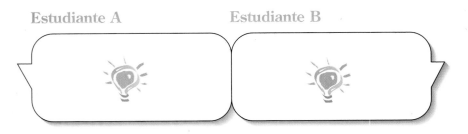

12

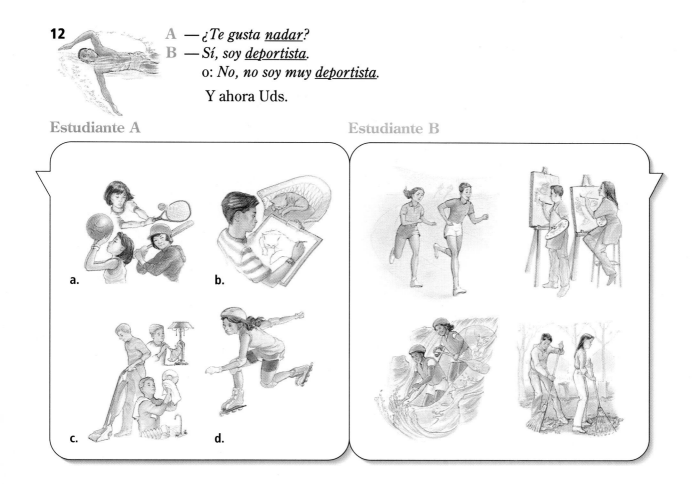

A — ¿*Te gusta nadar?*
B — *Sí, soy deportista.*
    o: *No, no soy muy deportista.*

    Y ahora Uds.

Estudiante A

a.

b.

c.

d.

Estudiante B

Empecemos a escribir y a leer

Write your answers in Spanish.

13 Look at the vocabulary on pages 34–35 and write down three
words that describe you.

14 Make a list of the words that you would use to describe:
- the ideal student
- the ideal teacher
- the ideal parent
- the ideal friend

15 ¿Cómo eres? ¿Eres amable? ¿Sociable? ¿Trabajador(a)?

16 ¡Hola! Me llamo Esteban. A mí me gusta nadar y patinar. También
me gusta estar con mis amigos o hablar por teléfono. No me gusta
ni cocinar ni ayudar en casa. ¿Cómo soy?

Eres . . .

¡Comuniquemos!

Here's another opportunity for you to use the vocabulary you've just learned.

1 Find out how many of these activities both you and your partner enjoy. Take turns asking the questions. Be sure to choose only those activities you really like.

A —*A mí me gusta escuchar música. ¿Y a ti?*
B —*A mí me gusta también.*
    o: *A mí no me gusta.*

a.
b.
c.
d.
e.
f.
g.
h.
i.
j.
k.
l.
m.

2 Now take turns finding out if you and your partner dislike the same things. Use the pictures in Exercise 1, and this time choose only those activities you <u>don't</u> like.

A —*No me gusta cocinar. ¿Y a ti?*
B —*A mí no me gusta tampoco.*
    o: *A mí sí me gusta.*

3 You are going to be an exchange student in Costa Rica and your host family wants to know what you are like. Write a few sentences telling them what you are like and some things you like to do. Then, with a partner, compare what you wrote about yourselves.

¿Qué sabes ahora?

Can you:

■ ask someone what he or she likes to do?
   —¿Qué ____ hacer?

■ tell someone what you like or do not like to do?
   —____ ir a la escuela.

■ ask someone what he or she is like?
   —¿Cómo ____?

■ tell someone what you are like?
   —Soy ____.

Perspectiva cultural

Te gusta estar con tus amigos, ¿no? ¿Qué te gusta hacer con tus amigos? ¿Les gusta ir al cine? ¿Hablar por teléfono? ¿Practicar deportes? Sí, probablemente. Pero, ¿qué quiere decir esa palabra mágica, "amigo"?

Estudiantes mexicanos en la escuela

Look at the people in the photos. How can you tell that they might be friends?

"Mike, this is my friend Luis." That is how my classmate introduced me to another boy in our class. It was my first day of school here. I was in the seventh grade. My family had come from El Salvador in July, so I had not met any English speakers my age. And here was someone introducing me as his friend when we had just met that morning! What a strange place I was in!

By the end of that year, I did have friends, friends in the Spanish sense. They are still my friends. I think that they will always be, because that is what we mean by *amigo,* a friend for life.

Where I came from, people didn't move around a lot. You would probably grow up in one neighborhood or town and might even live there your whole life. Yes, you might miss out on a few things, but you would form deep friendships and keep them. You would know people well, and would usually see your friends every day. You'd also get to know each other's families well.

And we share a lot. We share our true feelings and thoughts with our friends. We also share what we have. If a friend borrows money from me, I don't keep track or get an I.O.U. Or if I do a favor for a friend, I don't think any more about it. I know that my friend will always help me out. In the long run, it will probably turn out even.

Of course, we are warm and welcoming to people we don't

know very well, people we might call friends but whom we would call *conocidos* (acquaintances). We may get along quite well, but they are not *amigos.* Perhaps some day they will be, but that takes time. An *amigo* is someone you can count on all your life.

La cultura desde tu perspectiva

1 What are some similarities and differences between who is considered a friend in a Spanish-speaking country and in the United States?

2 What could you expect to occur if you became friends with someone in a Spanish-speaking country?

"Soy de Chile. Me gusta tocar la guitarra."

Gramática en contexto

Here is a descriptive poem entitled "Yo." What kind of information would you expect to find in such a poem?

Now read the poem.

Yo

Yo . . .
Yo no . . .
Yo no soy . . .
ni sociable ni callada,
ni generosa ni tacaña.
Yo . . .
Yo no . . .
Yo no soy . . .
ni atrevida ni prudente,
ni ordenada ni desordenada;
pero yo . . .
Yo soy . . .
Yo soy ¡YO!

A Think about the predictions you made before you read the poem. Did you find the information that you thought you would find in the poem? What did you find out about the person who wrote it?

B Is the poet male or female? How do you know? Find at least three words that give you that information.

C *Ni . . . ni* appears four times in the poem. What do you suppose it means?

D Think of a guideline that could help you decide whether to use the words *generoso* or *generosa* and *serio* or *seria* to describe a person. Are there any adjectives (descriptive words) on pages 34–35 that your rule does not cover? Which ones?

Los adjetivos

Words describing people and things are called adjectives.

- In Spanish, adjectives describing females usually end in -*a*.

- Adjectives describing males usually end in -*o*. However, there are some exceptions, such as *deportista,* which can describe both males and females.

- Adjectives that end in -*e* can describe either females or males, for example: *amable*.

Here are the adjectives you already know:

amable	impaciente
artística	ordenada
artístico	ordenado
atrevida	paciente
atrevido	perezosa
callada	perezoso
callado	prudente
deportista	seria
desordenada	serio
desordenado	sociable
generosa	tacaña
generoso	tacaño
graciosa	trabajador
gracioso	trabajadora

1 Students are preparing a who's who that describes each member of the class. Ask your partner what he or she is like. Each of you should choose four or more words from the list on the right to describe yourselves.

A — *¿Cómo eres?*
B — *Soy graciosa, artística, paciente y sociable.*
   o: *Soy gracioso, artístico, paciente y sociable.*

2 How similar are you and your partner? For each of the following pictures, say whether you have that personality trait. Then find out whether your partner has it too.

A — *Yo soy deportista. ¿Y tú?*
B — *Yo soy deportista también.*
   o: *No, yo no soy deportista.*

o: A — *Yo no soy deportista. ¿Y tú?*
   B — *Yo no soy deportista tampoco.*
    o: *Yo soy (muy) deportista.*

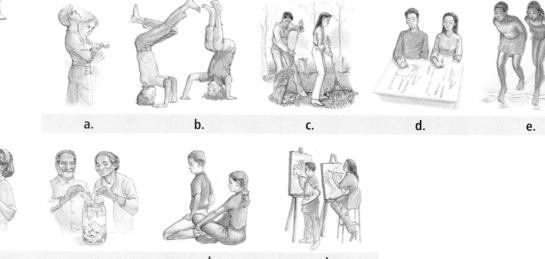

a.   b.   c.   d.   e.

f.   g.   h.   i.

Ni . . . ni

- If you want to say that you do not like either of two choices, use *ni . . . ni* to mean "neither . . . nor" or "not . . . or."
  For example:
  No me gusta **ni** nadar **ni** dibujar.

- Use *ni . . . ni* to say that neither of two descriptions fits you.
  No soy **ni** deportista **ni** artístico.

3 Imagine that these are new students in your Spanish class. Tell what each person might say about his or her likes and dislikes.

María

Me gusta dibujar y tocar la guitarra, pero no me gusta ni cocinar ni patinar.

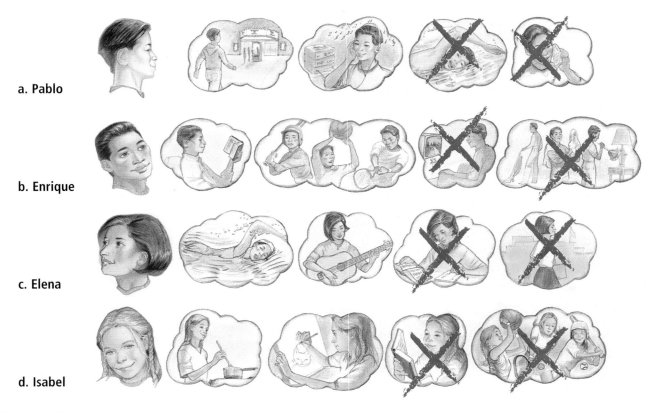

a. Pablo

b. Enrique

c. Elena

d. Isabel

4 Take turns asking and answering questions to find out what your partner is like. Discuss whether your partner is *sociable* or *callado(a)*, *paciente* or *impaciente*, *prudente* or *atrevido(a)*, and *trabajador(a)* or *perezoso(a)*.

A — *¿Eres generoso(a) o tacaño(a)?*
B — *Soy (muy) generoso(a).*
    o: *Soy tacaño(a).*
    o: *No soy ni generoso(a) ni tacaño(a).*

Sí / Tampoco

- Use *sí + me gusta* to contrast something you like with something you or someone else dislikes. For example:
  —A mí no me gusta hablar por teléfono. ¿Y a ti?
  —A mí **sí me gusta.**

- Use *no me gusta + tampoco* to agree with someone who dislikes something. For example:
  —A mí no me gusta practicar deportes. ¿Y a ti?
  —A mí **no me gusta tampoco.**

5 You and your partner are discussing activities that you like and don't like. Choose some activities that you don't like, and find out whether or not your partner agrees.

A — *A mí no me gusta patinar. ¿Y a ti?*
B — *Pues, a mí sí me gusta.*
    o: *A mí no me gusta tampoco.*

Ahora lo sabes

Can you:

- **describe yourself or someone else?**
  —Yo soy ___, pero tú eres ___.
- **say that you do not like either of two choices?**
  —No me gusta ___ ver la tele ___ ir al cine.
- **say that neither of two descriptions fits you?**
  —No soy ___ perezoso(a) ___ sociable.

- **emphasize that you do like something?**
  —¿No te gusta? ¡A mí ___!
- **say that you do not like something either?**
  —A mí ___.

Para decir más

Here is some additional vocabulary that you might find useful for activities in this section.

cariñoso, -a
affectionate

comprensivo, -a
understanding

dinámico, -a
energetic

estudioso, -a
studious

simpático, -a
nice, friendly

sincero, -a
sincere

cuidar niños
to baby-sit

jugar básquetbol
to play basketball

jugar videojuegos
to play video games

montar en bicicleta
to ride a bicycle

montar en monopatín
to skateboard

Actividades

Here's an opportunity for you to expand your use of Spanish by putting together the material you learned in this chapter.

1 In order to get a job at a summer camp, you must convince the camp supervisor that you are the best person for the job. As part of your application, tell what you are like, and list some of the things you like to do.

Jugando básquetbol en San Miguel de Allende, México

Muchachas sacando fotos en Ambato, Ecuador

2 In four or more sentences, describe yourself, including your personality traits and interests. Your sentences should include:

- some words that describe you and some that do not
- some things you do and don't like to do
- contrasts of things you like to do with things you don't like to do

3 Take a poll to find out which activities your classmates like to do. On a sheet of paper, list across the top the activities mentioned in this chapter. In the left-hand column, write these words: *me gusta mucho, me gusta, no me gusta, no me gusta nada.* Then interview four classmates, asking about all the activities on the list. Mark the answers on your chart and total the number of votes for each activity under each heading.

Músicos en Madrid

	NADAR	PATINAR	VER LA TELE	IR AL CINE
ME GUSTA MUCHO	//		/	
ME GUSTA		///		//
NO ME GUSTA	/		///	
NO ME GUSTA NADA	//	/		//

¡Vamos a leer!

Antes de leer

STRATEGY ➤ Using prior knowledge

We usually make new friends through personal acquaintances, but sometimes we meet people through correspondence. For example, you might want to look through a pen pal column in a Spanish-language magazine to start a correspondence with someone from another country.

You can help yourself read in Spanish by using certain strategies. One strategy is using what you know to predict what a reading might contain. For example, you already know the kinds of information you might find in the various sections of a newspaper or magazine.

Buscando amigos is the name of the pen pal section in the Mexican magazine *15 a 20*.

1 What do you think the title *15 a 20* refers to?

2 List three things you might expect to find in a pen pal section.

BUSCANDO AMIGOS

Jaime Muñoz Pardo
Insurgentes Sur Nº 2938
Torre 3, Suite 410
14000 México D.F.
Edad: 18
Pasatiempos: escuchar música,
coleccionar estampillas y leer

Vanessa Salinas Garza
Calle 52 Nº 2420
entre 42 y 47
San Nicolás, La Habana, Cuba
Edad: 18
Pasatiempos: ajedrez, nadar,
acampar, fútbol

Luz María Arévalo Huerta
Juan de Toledo Nº 218
Jardines de la Asunción
20260 Aguascalientes, Ags.
Estados Unidos Mexicanos
Edad: 20
Pasatiempos: escuchar
música y tocar la guitarra

Santiago R. Flores
Emiliano Sánchez Nº 1932
Col. Álamo
44890 Guadalajara, Jal.
Estados Unidos Mexicanos
Edad: 16
Pasatiempos: karate, leer,
música rock

Marisol Toledo Vega
Ret. 2, Oriente 269 Nº 9
Col. Agrícola Oriental
07500 México D.F.
Edad: 15
Pasatiempos: ver películas,
básquetbol, acampar

Fausto Salcedo Gómez
Costeñas Nº 129
Col. Benito Juárez, 3º sec.
5800 México D.F.
Edad: 17
Pasatiempos: leer, acampar, escuchar
música, coleccionar postales

Estudia con nosotros: **¡Entonces ven! Juez**
- Diseño de Modas
- Modista en alta Costura
- Industria de la Moda
- Tecnico en Modelaje Profesional

VEN Y PIDE INFORMACION COMPLETA
PLANTEL MEXICO: JALAPA 94 COL. ROMA TEL: 525 86 47
PLANTEL PUEBLA: 37 PTE. 312 COL. GABRIEL PASTOR TEL: 37 20 45

Mira la lectura

STRATEGY ➤ Scanning

Look at this pen pal section. Does it include the three things you expected to find? What, if anything, is missing? What additional types of information did you find?

Infórmate

STRATEGY ➤ Scanning

Scanning is another strategy you can use. When you scan you only look for certain information. You do *not* have to read and understand every word.

1 Look at the first listing, for Jaime Muñoz Pardo. In what order does Jaime provide the following information?

address	age	hobbies	name

2 Look at the first names of the people seeking pen pals. On a separate sheet of paper, list them in the three categories shown below. How many are girls? How many are boys? What clue(s) did you use to help you decide?

Boys	Girls	Not sure

3 Read about each person's pastimes.

a. List the pastimes that two or more of them share.

b. List five pastimes that are not shared.

c. Are there any pastimes whose meaning you cannot guess? If so, you and a partner should choose two that you can't figure out. Each of you should find out the meaning of one of the words and share it with the class.

Muchacho ecuatoriano de Quito

Aplicación

Imagine that you are seeking a pen pal. Provide information about yourself that you think is important to share. You may want to use the following categories:

- Nombre
- Dirección
- Edad
- Pasatiempos

"Me gusta mucho leer y estudiar."

¡amos a escribir!

Write a poem about yourself similar to the one on page 42. Follow these steps:

1 Read the poem on page 42 again.

2 Look at the vocabulary on pages 34–35 and write down five adjectives that apply to you and five that don't. Use the headings *Soy* and *No soy.*

Then, using the vocabulary on pages 30–31, write down at least three things that you like to do and three things that you don't like to do. Use the headings *Me gusta mucho* and *No me gusta nada.*

3 Write your poem based on the lists that you made. Focus on arranging your ideas in a way that you like.

4 Now show your poem to a partner. Ask which parts of the poem he or she likes and which ones might be changed. Decide whether or not you agree, then rewrite your poem, making any changes that you have decided on.

5 Check to make sure that everything is spelled correctly. Are capital letters used where they are needed? Are accents used correctly? Did you use question marks and exclamation points at the beginning and end of a sentence?

6 Now recopy your corrected poem. Add drawings or pictures if you like.

"¡Hola! Soy de Guatemala."

"Soy de Argentina. Soy seria y paciente."

"Soy colombiano y soy muy amable."

"A mí me gusta estar con mis amigos."

¿Lo sabes bien?

This section will help you organize your studying for the proficiency test, where you will be asked to do similar, though not identical, tasks. There will not be any models on the test.

Listening

Can you understand when someone talks about personality traits and interests? Listen as your teacher reads you a sample similar to what you will hear on the test. Would the person making the statements be more likely to participate in a school play or read at home?

Reading

Can you understand a written description of a person's traits and interests? Scan the paragraph below. What is the person like? Is it a description of a boy or a girl?

> Me gusta mucho patinar. También me gusta ir al cine. A veces soy impaciente, pero soy amable y generoso.

Writing

Can you write a letter describing your personality and interests? Here is an example of an appropriate letter.

> ¡Hola, Alfredo!
>
> Soy trabajador y me gusta ayudar en casa. También me gusta ir a la escuela y tocar la guitarra. No soy prudente. No soy callado tampoco. Y tú, ¿cómo eres?
>
> Saludos,
> Antonio

Culture

Can you explain what the word *amigo* might mean to a person from a Spanish-speaking country?

En Otavalo, Ecuador

Speaking

Can you describe yourself and tell what you like to do? Here is one example of a good response:

—*Pues, yo soy seria y callada, pero no soy ni deportista ni artística. Me gusta mucho leer y estar con amigos. No me gusta nada hablar por teléfono.*

Resumen del capítulo 1

Use the vocabulary from this chapter to help you:
- describe yourself and tell about some of your likes and dislikes
- find out what other people are like
- compare your likes and dislikes with other people's

to talk about activities
ayudar en casa
cocinar
dibujar
escuchar música
estar con amigos
estudiar
hablar por teléfono
   el teléfono
ir a la escuela
ir al cine
   el cine
leer
nadar
patinar
practicar deportes
tocar la guitarra
ver la televisión (la tele)

to say what you like
(A mí) me gusta ___.
           más ___.
           mucho ___.
(A mí) sí me gusta ___.
A mí también.

to say what you do not like
(A mí) no me
  gusta ___.
      mucho ___.
      nada ___.
      ___ tampoco.

to say what you or someone else is like
(Yo) soy ___.
(Tú) eres ___.

to ask someone what he or she likes
¿Qué te gusta (hacer)?
¿Te gusta ___?
¿Y a ti?

to ask someone what he or she is like
¿Cómo eres?
¿Eres (tú) ___?

to describe yourself or others
amable
artístico, -a
atrevido, -a
callado, -a
deportista
desordenado, -a
generoso, -a
gracioso, -a
impaciente
ordenado, -a
paciente
perezoso, -a
prudente
serio, -a
sociable
tacaño, -a
trabajador, -a

to ask if a statement is accurate
¿De veras?

other useful words and expressions
a veces
muy
ni . . . ni
pero
pues
también
tampoco
y

CAPÍTULO 2

¿Qué clases tienes?

OBJECTIVES

At the end of this chapter, you will be able to:

- describe your class schedule
- list some school supplies you use
- find out about someone else's schedule
- compare your school experience with that of a student in a Spanish-speaking country

Unos estudiantes delante de su escuela en Barcelona, España

¡Piénsalo bien!

Look at the pictures.
In the captions these teens talk about school.

"A mí me gusta mucho jugar fútbol después de las clases."

What do you think *fútbol* means in this picture? What do you think the expression *fútbol americano* might mean? Which is more popular in your school: *fútbol* or *fútbol americano*?

En España

"Los miércoles tengo inglés en la primera hora. La clase empieza a las siete y media."

Which of your classes is most like this *clase de inglés?*

"Los estudiantes de mi clase tienen un 10 . . ."

What do you think getting a grade of 10 in a Spanish-speaking school means?

En una escuela secundaria en México

Vocabulario para conversar

¿Qué clases tienes?

Here are some new words and expressions you will need to talk about your class schedule and school supplies. Read them several times, then turn the page and practice with a partner.

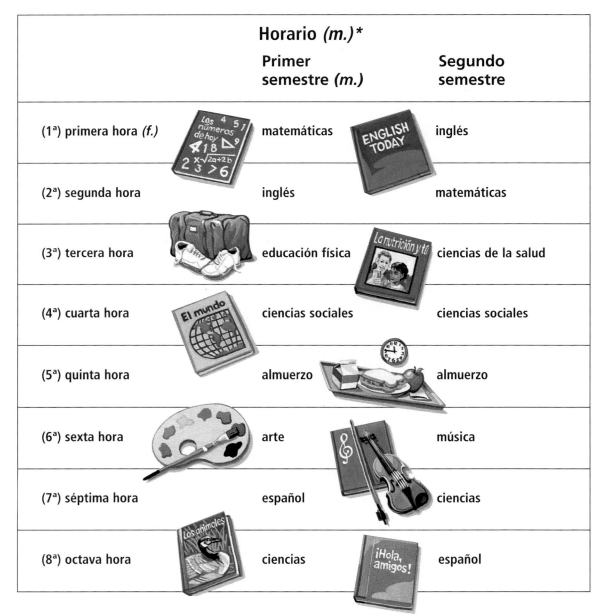

	Horario (m.)*	
	Primer semestre (m.)	Segundo semestre
(1ª) primera hora (f.)	matemáticas	inglés
(2ª) segunda hora	inglés	matemáticas
(3ª) tercera hora	educación física	ciencias de la salud
(4ª) cuarta hora	ciencias sociales	ciencias sociales
(5ª) quinta hora	almuerzo	almuerzo
(6ª) sexta hora	arte	música
(7ª) séptima hora	español	ciencias
(8ª) octava hora	ciencias	español

* The letters in parentheses indicate the gender of the noun: masculine (m.) or feminine (f.).

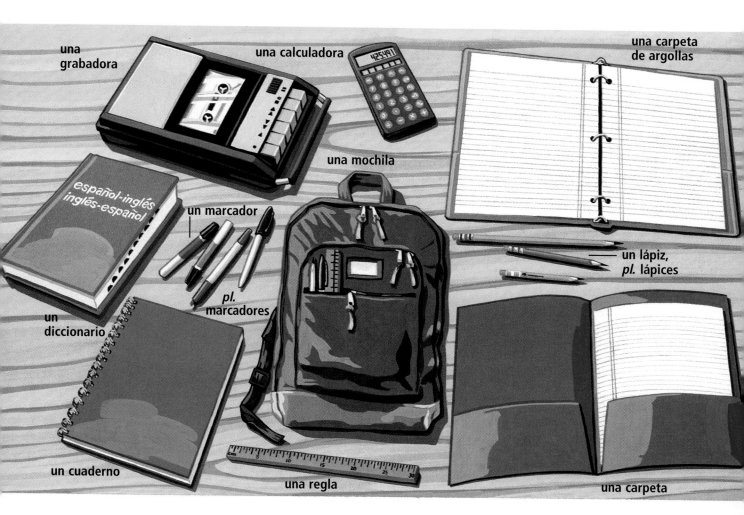

una grabadora

una calculadora

una carpeta de argollas

una mochila

español-inglés inglés-español

un marcador

pl. marcadores

un diccionario

un lápiz, pl. lápices

un cuaderno

una regla

una carpeta

También necesitas . . .

la clase de ____	____ class	para	for
difícil	difficult, hard	tu	your
fácil	easy	¿Qué?	What?
la tarea	homework	Lo siento.	I'm sorry.
aprender: (yo) aprendo	to learn: I learn	A ver . . .	Let's see . . .
(tú) aprendes	you learn	Aquí / Allí está.	Here / There it is.
necesitar: (yo) necesito	to need: I need		
(tú) necesitas	you need		
tener: (yo) tengo	to have: I have		
(tú) tienes	you have		

¿Y qué quiere decir . . . ?
mucho, -a

Empecemos a conversar

With a partner, take turns being *Estudiante A* and *Estudiante B.* Use the words that are cued or given in the balloons to replace the underlined sections in the model. 💡 means you can make your own choices.

1

A — *¿Tienes mucha tarea en tu clase de <u>ciencias</u>?*
B — *Sí, tengo mucha tarea.*
     o: *No, no tengo mucha tarea.*

     Y ahora Uds.

Estudiante A   Estudiante B

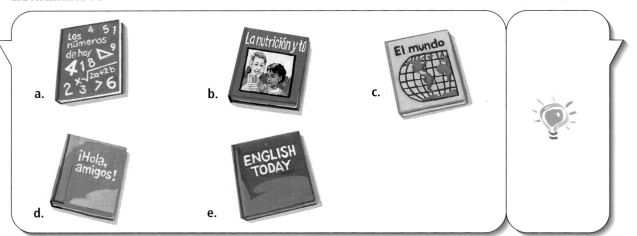

a.   b.   c.

d.   e.

2 A — *¿Tienes <u>una calculadora</u>?*
B — *A ver . . . Sí, aquí está.*
     o: *Sí, allí está.*
     o: *A ver . . . No, lo siento.*

     Y ahora Uds.

Estudiante A   Estudiante B

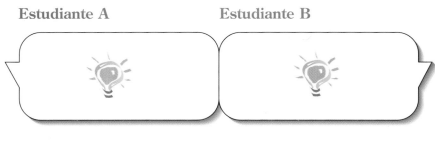

3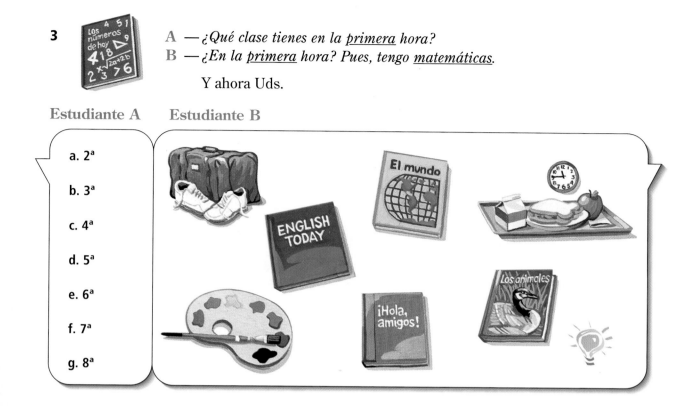

A — *¿Qué clase tienes en la <u>primera</u> hora?*
B — *¿En la <u>primera</u> hora? Pues, tengo <u>matemáticas</u>.*

Y ahora Uds.

Estudiante A   **Estudiante B**

a. 2ª

b. 3ª

c. 4ª

d. 5ª

e. 6ª

f. 7ª

g. 8ª

Empecemos a escribir

Write your answers in Spanish.

4 List the school supplies you have with you right now. Next to each item, write the name of at least one class in which you use it.

5 In two columns, under the headings *Fácil* and *Difícil*, list the subjects you are taking this year.

6 ¿Qué necesitas para tu primera clase?

7 ¿Qué te gusta más, hacer la tarea de español o hablar con tus compañeros(as) en la clase de español?

8 ¿Qué tienes en tu mochila?

También se dice

el lapicero
la pluma
el boli

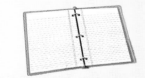

la carpeta de anillas
el archivador

Vocabulario para conversar

¿Qué hora es?

Here's the rest of the vocabulary you will need to talk about your class schedule.

Es la una.

Son las dos.

Son las tres.

Son las cuatro.

Son las cinco.

Son las seis.

Son las siete.

Son las ocho.

Son las nueve.

Son las diez.

Son las once.

Son las doce.

Son las dos
y cinco.

Son las dos y
cuarto. (Son las
dos y quince.)

Son las dos
y veinte.

Son las dos y
media. (Son las
dos y treinta.)

Son las dos
y cuarenta
y cinco.

Son las dos
y cincuenta
y ocho.

32 treinta y dos
33 treinta y tres
34 treinta y cuatro
35 treinta y cinco
36 treinta y seis
37 treinta y siete
38 treinta y ocho
39 treinta y nueve
40 cuarenta
41 cuarenta y uno ...
49 cuarenta y nueve
50 cincuenta
51 cincuenta y uno ...
59 cincuenta y nueve

¡NO OLVIDES!

You worked with the numbers 0 to 31 in *El primer paso*.

El reloj del Parque Hundido,
Ciudad de México

También necesitas ...

enseñar:
  enseña
	to teach:
	  (he / she) teaches
		terminar: termina	*to end: it ends*

a	*at*	es	*he / she / it is*
¿A qué hora _____?	*At what time _____?*	¿Qué hora es?	*What time is it?*
empezar: empieza	*to begin: it begins*	¿Quién?	*Who? Whom?*

Empecemos a conversar

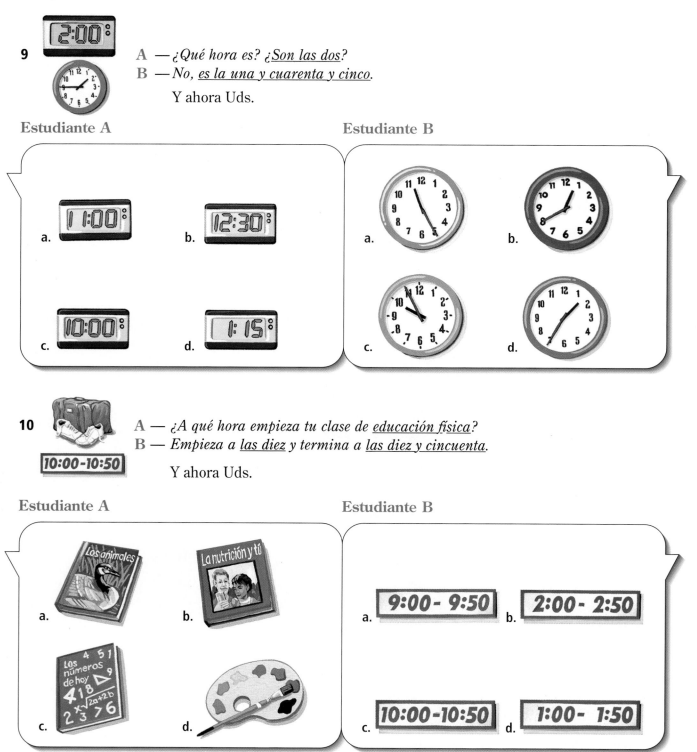

9

A — *¿Qué hora es? ¿Son las dos?*

B — *No, es la una y cuarenta y cinco.*

Y ahora Uds.

Estudiante A

a. b.

c. d.

Estudiante B

a. b.

c. d.

10

A — *¿A qué hora empieza tu clase de educación física?*

B — *Empieza a las diez y termina a las diez y cincuenta.*

Y ahora Uds.

Estudiante A

a. Los animales   b. La nutrición y tú

c. Los números de hoy   d.

Estudiante B

a. 9:00 - 9:50   b. 2:00 - 2:50

c. 10:00-10:50   d. 1:00 - 1:50

11 A —*¿Cuándo tienes la clase de <u>ciencias</u>?*
   B —*A ver... A <u>las ocho y diez</u>.*
   A —*¿Quién es tu profesor(a)?*
   B —<u>*La profesora González*</u>.

   Y ahora Uds.

Estudiante A   **Estudiante B**

¡NO OLVIDES!

Remember that when using *señor(a), profesor(a)* or any other title to talk about a person, we need to add the definite article to the title: *El señor López enseña inglés.* However, when addressing a person, we do not use the article: *¿Cómo está, señor López?*

Empecemos a escribir y a leer

Write your answers in Spanish.

12 Redesign your school schedule. You decide when classes begin and end and how long each period lasts.

13 ¿A qué hora es el almuerzo? ¿Cuándo termina?

14 ¿Quién es tu profesor(a) favorito(a)? ¿Qué enseña? ¿A qué hora empieza la clase? ¿Cuándo termina?

15 Federico dice: "Yo soy artístico. Me gusta mucho dibujar," pero Ernesto responde: "A mí no me gusta nada dibujar, pero me gusta mucho practicar deportes, especialmente nadar y patinar." Ana dice: "A mí me gusta más leer libros de historia," pero Susana responde: "A mí no me gusta mucho leer, pero sí me gustan los números y los cálculos."

¿Quién dice...
a. "Mi clase favorita es matemáticas"?
b. "Mi clase favorita es educación física"?
c. "Mi clase favorita es arte"?

¡Comuniquemos!

Here's another opportunity for you to use the vocabulary you've just learned.

¡NO OLVIDES!

To say that you don't like either of two things, use *ni . . . ni.* See page 44.

1 Find out which classes your partner prefers.

A — *¿Qué clase te gusta más, ciencias o ciencias sociales?*
B — *Me gusta más la clase de ciencias.*

2 You are planning to go shopping for school supplies with a friend. Find out from each other what supplies you need for each class you are taking.

A — *¿Qué necesitas para tu clase de ciencias sociales?*
B — *A ver . . . Necesito un cuaderno y un bolígrafo.*

Estudiante A   **Estudiante B**

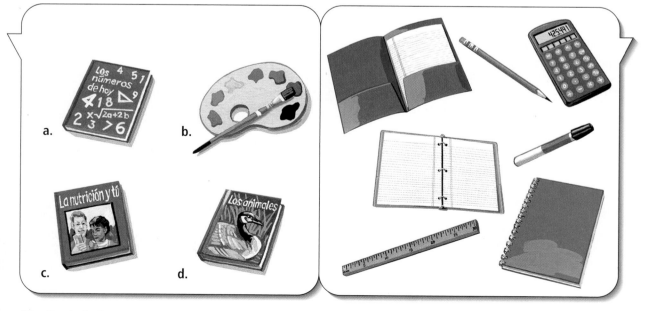

¿Qué sabes ahora?

Can you:

- ask someone what he or she needs for a certain class?

  —¿Qué ___ para la clase de inglés?

- tell someone what you need for a class?

  —___ un bolígrafo o ___ lápiz y ___ cuaderno.

- ask someone what classes he or she has?

  —¿Qué clases ___ el primer semestre?

- tell someone what classes you have?

  —___ ciencias, español y matemáticas.

Perspectiva cultural

Los estudiantes en los países hispanos tienen muchas clases. Y tú, ¿qué clases tienes? ¿Qué clases te gustan más? ¿Qué clases no te gustan?

Look at the photo of public school students and the school schedule below. What do you notice that you didn't expect?

Although an *escuela secundaria* in Mexico City has a lot in common with a high school in the United States, there are some striking differences. And even though there are differences among Mexican schools, you might find that any or all of these things happen:

- In most schools, when a teacher enters the classroom, the students stand.
- The teacher probably calls the students by their last name.
- The students, on the other hand, are more likely to address their teacher simply as *maestro* or *maestra,* without a last name.
- The average amount of time students spend on homework ranges from 15 to 30 minutes per class.
- Teachers usually collect the homework the next day rather than reviewing it in class.

- The grading scale in Mexico ranges from a low of 1 to a high of 10, with 6 being the lowest passing grade. A grade of 6 or 7 is roughly equivalent to a C, 8 to a B, and 9 and 10 to an A.
- Grades are based much more on test results and homework than on class participation.
- Class time is generally spent with the teacher lecturing rather than with class discussion.
- Many public schools require uniforms at least four days a week.

La cultura desde tu perspectiva

1 If you attended school in Mexico City, what might you find that might be familiar to you? What would you have to adjust to?

2 Based on what you now know about schools in Mexico City, list five suggestions that might help an exchange student from Mexico City adjust to your school's system.

HORA	HORAS	LUNES	MARTES	MIÉRCOLES	JUEVES	VIERNES
1a	7:30 a 8:15	Ciencias naturales	Educación física	Inglés	Ciencias sociales	Ciencias naturales
2a	8:15 a 9:00	Ciencias naturales	Tecnología	Español	Ciencias sociales	Ciencias naturales
3a	9:00 a 9:45	Inglés	Tecnología	Ciencias sociales	Matemáticas	Español
4a	9:45 a 10:30	Ciencias sociales	Ciencias sociales	Ciencias sociales	Ciencias naturales	Matemáticas
	10:30 a 10:50			R E C E S O		
5a	10:50 a 11:35	Español	Ciencias sociales	Matemáticas	Ciencias naturales	Tecnología
6a	11:35 a 12:20	Matemáticas	Inglés	Ciencias naturales	Educación artística	Tecnología
7a	12:20 a 13:05	Tecnología	Educación artística	Tecnología	Educación física	Orientación vocacional
8a	13:05 a 13:50	Tecnología	Español	Tecnología	LIBRE	LIBRE

Estudiantes en la Ciudad de México

Gramática en contexto

This is a letter that a science teacher sent home before school started. What information would you expect to find in a letter like this?

ESCUELA SECUNDARIA FEDERAL • FRANCISCO VILLA • VALLE NACIONAL Y JAZMINAL • CHIHUAHUA, CHIH.

28 de agosto

Estimados padres y estudiantes:

En mi clase de ciencias tengo a los estudiantes del 9° grado. Es una clase importante y muy interesante. Los estudiantes preparan experimentos en el laboratorio y trabajan mucho en la clase; pero también necesitan estudiar mucho en la casa.

Para la clase de ciencias, los estudiantes necesitan lápices, papel y una carpeta. También usamos frecuentemente una calculadora y una regla en la clase.

Si Uds. necesitan más información, favor de llamar al 222–89-67 durante la tercera hora, que empieza a las 10 y termina a las 10:50.

Atentamente,

Rosalba Hernández de Mejía

A Find all the words in the letter that end in *-an*. Why do you think they end in those two letters? (Hint: *Necesito* and *tengo* both end in *-o*. Think about what the *o* might tell you. *Necesitas* and *tienes* also have similar endings. What might their *-s* ending tell you?)

B Now look at the word *usamos* in the second paragraph. Can you guess at the meaning of this word?

Los pronombres personales

We often use people's names to tell who is doing an action.
We also use what we call subject pronouns.

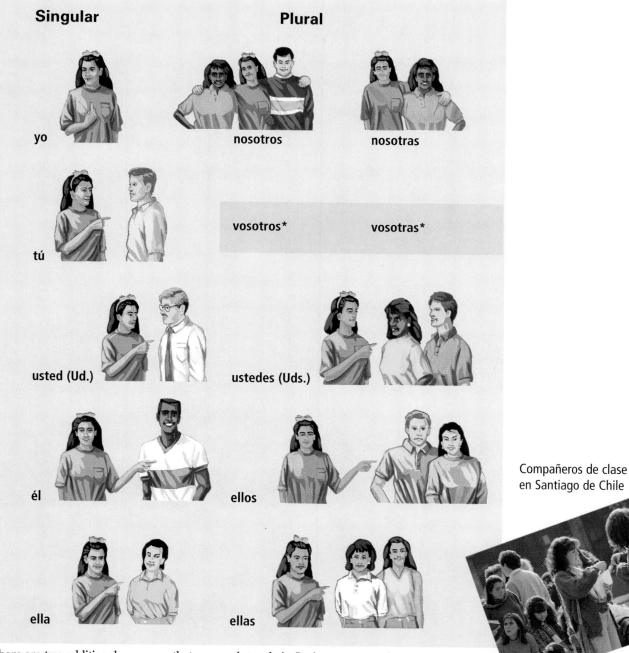

Singular	Plural
yo	nosotros / nosotras
tú	vosotros* / vosotras*
usted (Ud.)	ustedes (Uds.)
él	ellos
ella	ellas

Compañeros de clase
en Santiago de Chile

*There are two additional pronouns that are used mostly in Spain: *vosotros* and *vosotras.* They are used when speaking to two or more people whom you would call *tú* individually: *tú* + *tú* = *vosotros* or *vosotras.* We will include these pronouns when we present new verb forms, and we will use them occasionally in situations that take place in Spain. So you should learn to recognize them.

- Yo means "I."

- *Tú, usted,* and *ustedes* mean "you."
  a. Use *tú* with family members, close friends, people around your age or younger, and anyone you call by a first name.
  b. Use *usted* with adults and anyone you would address with a title of respect, such as *señor, señora,* etc. *Usted* is usually written as *Ud.*
  c. Use *ustedes* when speaking to two or more people, even if you would call them *tú* individually. We usually write it as *Uds.*

- There are two forms for "we" in Spanish: *nosotras* for females, and *nosotros* for males or for a mixed group of males and females.

- There are also two forms for "they." *Ellos* refers to a group of males or to a mixed group of males and females. *Ellas* refers to a group of females only.

- In Spanish, subject pronouns may be omitted because most verb forms indicate who the subject is: ***Tengo** ciencias en la primera hora.*

- Subject pronouns are usually used for emphasis or contrast, or if the subject is not clear: ***Él** es trabajador, pero **ella** es perezosa.*

1 With your partner, take turns telling which subject pronouns Ana would use to speak to or about these people.

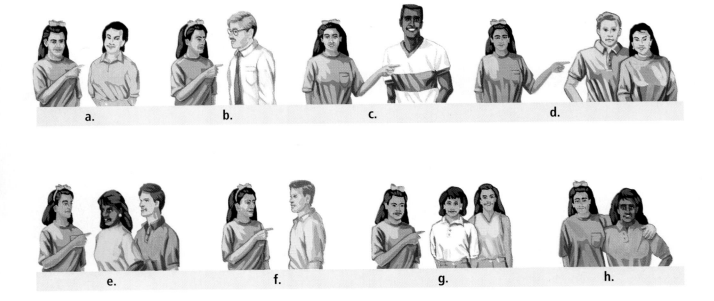

a.   b.   c.   d.

e.   f.   g.   h.

2 Now tell which form of "you" you would use if you were speaking to these people.

a. your father
b. the principal
c. the girl next door
d. your teacher
e. your mother and sister
f. your cousin
g. an older person sitting next to you on the bus
h. three classmates

Verbos que terminan en *-ar*

A verb usually names the action in a sentence. We call the verb form that ends in *-r* the infinitive. It is the form you would find in a Spanish dictionary. It means "to ___." On the right are some of the infinitives you already know. We call these *-ar* verbs.

ayudar	nadar
cocinar	necesitar
dibujar	patinar
enseñar	practicar
escuchar	terminar
estudiar	tocar
hablar	

- In Spanish, the last letter or letters of the verb tell you who does the action.

- To change an infinitive to a form that tells who is doing the action, remove the *-ar* and add the appropriate ending.

		ESTUDIAR	
Singular		**Plural**	
(yo)	estud**io**	(nosotros) (nosotras)	estudi**amos**
(tú)	estudi**as**	(vosotros) (vosotras)	estudi**áis***
Ud. (él) (ella)	estudi**a**	Uds. (ellos) (ellas)	estudi**an**

* Verb forms ending in *-áis*, such as *estudiáis*, are used mainly in Spain. We will use them occasionally and you should learn to recognize them.

- The verb forms in the chart are in the present tense. They are the equivalent of both "I study, you study, he or she studies" and "I'm studying, you're studying, he's or she's studying," and so on.

- When you want to say that you do *not* do something, use *no* before the verb form.

    Yo **no cocino** en la clase de educación física.

- When we ask a question in Spanish, we usually put the subject after the verb or sometimes at the end of the sentence.
    ¿Cocina **Juan** en la clase de ciencias?
    ¿Estudia mucho **Paulina?**

3   Imagine that someone from Colombia has just arrived at your school. Which of these statements could you use to tell this student what you personally do and what you need at school?

   a. Necesitamos bolígrafos y marcadores.
   b. Hablo inglés.
   c. Practico deportes.
   d. Necesitan un cuaderno para la clase de español.
   e. Tocamos la guitarra en la clase de música.
   f. Habla inglés.
   g. Necesito una mochila.
   h. Estudian mucho para la clase de ciencias.
   i. Cocinamos en la clase de ciencias sociales.
   j. Dibuja en la clase de arte.
   k. Estudia inglés.
   l. Necesita un diccionario para la clase de inglés.
   m. Habla inglés y español.
   n. Nadamos en la clase de educación física.
   o. Escuchan música en la clase de inglés.

4 Which sentences in Exercise 3 could you use to tell about your friend Tomás? Which could you use to tell about Tomás and yourself? Which ones could you use to tell about two friends?

5 What school supplies do you and your classmates need for different classes? Talk about the students listed below.

a. what Sandra and David need
b. what Carlos and you need
c. what you need
d. what your friend Norma needs

6 Tell what these people are studying.

Ramón estudia matemáticas.

Ramón

a. Roberto

b. Max, Ana y yo

c. Samuel y Josefina

d. María y Linda

e. Ángela

f. Julia y yo

Los sustantivos

Nouns refer to people, animals, places, and things. In Spanish, nouns have gender. They are either masculine or feminine.

- Most nouns that end in *-o* are masculine. Most nouns that end in *-a* are feminine. For example:

  el libro   la calculadora

  There are a few exceptions. You know one: *el día.*

- Other Spanish nouns end in *-e* or a consonant. Some of these are masculine, and some are feminine. For example:

  el cine   el marcador
  la clase   la televisión

- A few nouns can be both masculine and feminine. For example: *el / la estudiante.*

- *El* and *la* are called definite articles and are the equivalent of "the" in English. We use *el* with masculine nouns, *la* with feminine nouns.

- *Un* and *una* are indefinite articles, like "a" and "an" in English. We use *un* with masculine nouns, *una* with feminine nouns.

It is a good idea to learn a noun with its definite article, *el* or *la,* because that will usually tell you the gender.

7 Take turns finding out which of these things you and your partner have with you right now.

A — *¿Tienes un libro?*
B — *Sí, tengo. Aquí está.*
   o: *Sí, tengo. Allí está.*
   o: *No, lo siento.*

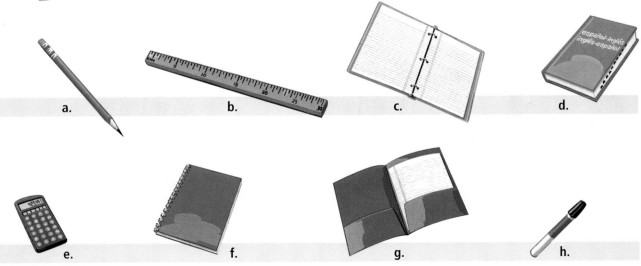

a.   b.   c.   d.

e.   f.   g.   h.

Ahora lo sabes

Can you:

- state who is doing an action without using people's names?

  —¿Practican deportes Marta y Teresa?

  —Sí, ___ nadan y patinan.

- use the correct verb form to tell what you and others do regularly?

  —¿Estudian Uds. para la clase de matemáticas?

  —No, (nosotros) ___ para la clase de ciencias.

- say that you do *not* do something?

  —(Yo) ___ cocino en la clase de matemáticas.

- use the appropriate subject pronouns when addressing someone?

  —Miguel, ¿tocas ___ la guitarra?

  —Señora, ¿habla ___ inglés?

  —Jorge y Juan, ¿practican ___ deportes?

Todo Junto

Para decir más

Here is some additional vocabulary that you might find useful for activities in this section.

la biología
biology

la computadora
computer

la historia
history

la literatura
literature

la química
chemistry

la física
physics

la economía doméstica
home economics

la geometría
geometry

la clase de computación
computer class

Actividades

Here's an opportunity for you to expand your use of Spanish by putting together the material you learned in this chapter with what you learned earlier.

1 Ask a partner:
- which classes he or she is taking
- who the teacher is
- what time each class begins
- when each class ends
- whether or not he or she likes the class

Afterward you can create a class schedule for each other, showing teachers' names and times.

2 Find out which class your partner likes the most and which one he or she does not like at all. Say whether or not you too like or dislike those classes. When possible, tell why you like or dislike a given class.

A — *¿Qué clase te gusta más?*
B — *Me gusta más la clase de ciencias.*
A — *A mí también. ¿Y qué clase no te gusta nada?*
B — *Pues, la clase de inglés. No me gusta mucho leer.*
A — *¿De veras? A mí sí me gusta.*

3 Make a schedule in Spanish for a family member to follow at Open House at your school. Use your regular schedule, but make each period only 20 minutes long. Include the name of each class, who teaches it, which period, and when it begins and ends. When you have finished, compare your schedule with that of a partner.

Muchachos y muchachas
jugando hockey sobre hierba

¡Vamos a leer!

Antes de leer

STRATEGY ➤ Using prior knowledge

Depending on the kind of document we are reading, we can often predict the kind of information it will include. For example, in a menu we expect to find the names and prices of different dishes. In a bus schedule, we look for the time of arrival and departure of buses throughout the week, as well as ticket prices.

Here is a report card for a student in Mexico. Make a list of four things you might expect to find in a report card.

Mira la lectura

STRATEGY ➤ Scanning

Remember that scanning is a strategy to help you look for certain information.

Of the four things you listed, how many can you find on the report card shown here?

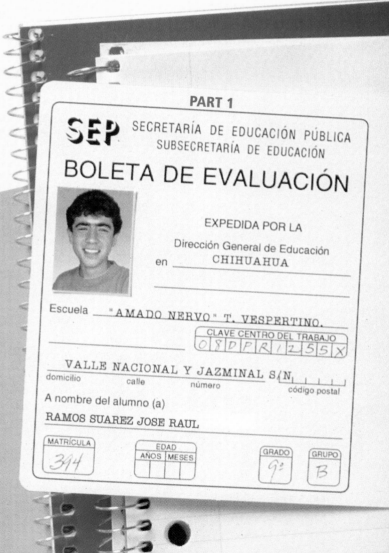

PART 1

SEP SECRETARÍA DE EDUCACIÓN PÚBLICA
SUBSECRETARÍA DE EDUCACIÓN

BOLETA DE EVALUACIÓN

EXPEDIDA POR LA

Dirección General de Educación
en   CHIHUAHUA

Escuela   "AMADO NERVO" T. VESPERTINO.

CLAVE CENTRO DEL TRABAJO
| 0 | 8 | D | P | R | 1 | 2 | 5 | 5 | X |

VALLE NACIONAL Y JAZMINAL S/N
domicilio   calle   número   código postal

A nombre del alumno (a)
RAMOS SUAREZ JOSE RAUL

MATRÍCULA	EDAD		GRADO	GRUPO
	AÑOS	MESES		
394			9º	B

Infórmate

STRATEGY Scanning

As you read, match what you expected to find with the information given.

1 Study Part 1 of the *Boleta de evaluación.*

a. What is the name of the school?

b. Where is it located?

c. What is the name of the student?

d. What grade is he in? How old do you think he is?

2 Examine Part 2, *Resultados del aprendizaje.*

a. How many subjects did the student take?

b. How many grading periods were there during the school year?

c. Did the student's grades generally improve or decline during the year? In which subject(s) did he improve the most? In which was he most consistent? In which subject did he receive his lowest mark?

d. Using the scale explained in the *Escala de evaluación,* which words would you use to describe the student's overall academic work?

3 Read Part 3, *Asistencia.*

a. How many school days were there? How many days was the student absent?

b. In which month were there the fewest days of instruction?

4 Look at Part 4, *Resultado final.* Were you surprised by the student's final results for the year? Why or why not?

Aplicación

Design a report card in Spanish for your classes this year.

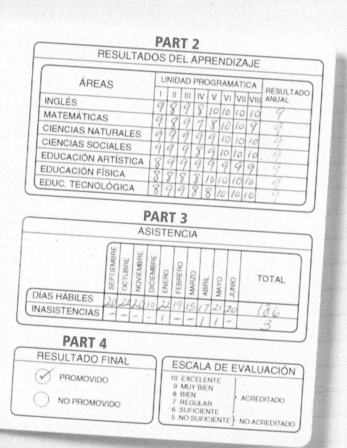

PART 2
RESULTADOS DEL APRENDIZAJE

ÁREAS	UNIDAD PROGRAMÁTICA								RESULTADO ANUAL
	I	II	III	IV	V	VI	VII	VIII	
INGLÉS	9	8	9	8	10	10	10	10	9
MATEMÁTICAS	9	8	9	7	8	10	10	9	9
CIENCIAS NATURALES	9	9	9	9	9	10	10	10	9
CIENCIAS SOCIALES	9	9	9	8	9	10	10	10	9
EDUCACIÓN ARTÍSTICA	8	9	9	9	9	9	9	9	9
EDUCACIÓN FÍSICA	8	8	8	8	10	10	10	10	9
EDUC. TECNOLÓGICA	8	9	9	8	8	10	10	10	9

PART 3
ASISTENCIA

	SEPTIEMBRE	OCTUBRE	NOVIEMBRE	DICIEMBRE	ENERO	FEBRERO	MARZO	ABRIL	MAYO	JUNIO	TOTAL
DÍAS HÁBILES	20	24	20	10	22	19	15	17	21	20	186
INASISTENCIAS	–	–	–	–	1	–	–	1	1	–	3

PART 4

RESULTADO FINAL	ESCALA DE EVALUACIÓN
✓ PROMOVIDO	10 EXCELENTE 9 MUY BIEN 8 BIEN } ACREDITADO 7 REGULAR 6 SUFICIENTE
◯ NO PROMOVIDO	5 NO SUFICIENTE } NO ACREDITADO

¡Vamos a escribir!

Write a letter to a Spanish-speaking friend about your school day. Follow these steps.

1 Write out your class schedule. Put a check mark beside those classes in which you have a lot of homework. Underline the classes that you like a lot.

2 Write your letter using the class schedule and the information you've added to it. On the right is an outline that will help you get started.

3 Now show your letter to a partner. Ask which parts might be changed. Decide whether or not you agree, then rewrite your letter, making any changes that you have decided on.

4 Check your letter for spelling and punctuation, including accents. Did you begin with the date and the greeting *Hola?* Did you end with a closing expression and your name?

5 Make any corrections and recopy. You might send your letter to:

- a new pen pal
- a student of Spanish in another school
- a student in another Spanish class at your school
- a student in your Spanish class

___ de _____ de 19__

Hola, ___:

_____

_____

_____

Saludos,

(name)

"¡Hola! A mí me gustan muchas clases, pero me gusta más la clase de ciencias sociales."

Una estudiante prepara su tarea para las clases.

¿Lo sabes bien?

This section will help you organize your studying for the proficiency test, where you will be asked to do similar, though not identical, tasks. There will not be any models on the test.

Listening

Can you understand when people talk about their class schedules? Listen as your teacher reads you a sample similar to what you will hear on the test. Would you say the student making the statement is talking about his morning or afternoon schedule?

Reading

How well can you understand a person's written schedule? Scan the paragraph below. Can you chart out Mauricio's schedule based on this description?

Mauricio tiene muchas clases. En la primera hora tiene clase de inglés, su clase favorita. En la segunda hora tiene clase de matemáticas. La clase de ciencias es a las 10:00. La clase de educación física empieza a las 11:00 y termina a las 11:50. El almuerzo es a las 12:00.

Writing

Can you write a list of supplies you need for school? Your parents want to discuss the school supplies you need to buy. To prepare for the discussion, list under the headings provided below the supplies and the classes you need the supplies for. For example:

¿Qué?	¿Para qué clases?
regla	matemáticas, arte

Culture

Can you list some possible differences between your school and one in Mexico City?

Speaking

Ask a partner which classes he or she likes better, and which ones he or she doesn't like at all. Do you and your partner like and dislike the same classes? Here is a sample dialogue:

A — ¿Qué clase te gusta más?

B — Me gusta mucho la clase de música. También me gustan mucho la clase de ciencias y las matemáticas.

A — ¿Qué clase no te gusta nada?

B — La clase de educación física. Yo soy muy perezosa. ¿Y tú?

Resumen del capítulo 2

Use the vocabulary from this chapter to help you:

- describe your class schedule
- list some school supplies you use
- find out about someone else's schedule

to talk about school subjects
el almuerzo
el arte (f.)
las ciencias
las ciencias
   de la salud
las ciencias sociales
la clase de ___
la educación física
el español
el inglés
las matemáticas
la música
difícil
fácil
enseñar: enseña
la tarea

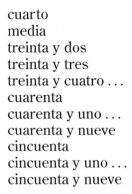

to talk about school supplies
la calculadora
la carpeta (de argollas)
el cuaderno
el diccionario
la grabadora
el horario
el lápiz, pl. los lápices
el marcador, pl. los marcadores
la mochila
la regla

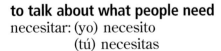

to talk about what people need
necesitar: (yo) necesito
     (tú) necesitas

to say what something is for
para

to express possession
tener: (yo) tengo
     (tú) tienes
tu

to express quantity
mucho, -a
un, -a

to ask for information
¿Qué?

to ask and tell when something takes place
a
¿A qué hora ___?
empezar: empieza
terminar: termina
es
la hora
   la primera hora
   la segunda hora
   la tercera hora
   la cuarta hora
   la quinta hora
   la sexta hora
   la séptima hora
   la octava hora
el semestre
   el primer semestre
   el segundo semestre

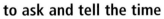

to ask and tell the time
¿Qué hora es?
Es la una (y ___).
Son las ___ (y ___).

cuarto
media
treinta y dos
treinta y tres
treinta y cuatro ...
cuarenta
cuarenta y uno ...
cuarenta y nueve
cincuenta
cincuenta y uno ...
cincuenta y nueve

to express regret
Lo siento.

to express hesitation, to consider
A ver ...

to talk about location
aquí
   Aquí está.
allí
   Allí está.

to tell who performs an action
yo
tú
usted (Ud.)
él, ella
nosotros, -as
vosotros, -as
ustedes (Uds.)
ellos, -as
¿Quién?

Capítulo 3

Los pasatiempos

OBJECTIVES

At the end of this chapter, you will be able to:

- talk about some of your leisure-time activities
- make plans with friends
- extend, accept, or decline invitations
- compare leisure-time activities in Spanish-speaking countries with those in the United States

En la piscina en Taxco, México

¡Piénsalo bien!

Look at the photos and read the captions. How do the leisure activities of these teens compare to what you and your friends do? Which of these activities would you be most likely to do with your friends?

"Me encanta celebrar los días festivos y bailar sevillanas."

What are these teens celebrating? By looking at the photo, how do you think teens participate in the celebration? Do you have similar festivals in your community?

En Sevilla, España

What do you think a "parque de diversiones" might be? And can you guess what the "montaña rusa" means?

"Me gusta mucho ir al parque de diversiones y montar en la montaña rusa. ¡Pero a mi amiga Lupe no le gusta nada!"

"En el verano, me encanta ir a la playa y jugar vóleibol."

En Gijón, España

89

Vocabulario para conversar

¿Cuándo vas al parque?

Here are some new words and expressions you will need to talk about your leisure-time activities. Read them several times, then turn the page and practice with a partner.

las estaciones
(*sing.,* la estación)

la primavera

el verano

el otoño

el invierno

También necesitas . . .

a	here: *to*
a la, al *(a+el)*	*to the*
el pasatiempo	*hobby, pastime*
el lunes, el martes . . .	*on Monday, on Tuesday . . .*
los lunes, los martes . . .	*on Mondays, on Tuesdays . . .*
los fines de semana	*on the weekends*
después (de)	*after*
después de las clases	*after school*
(por) la mañana	*(in) the morning*
la tarde	*the afternoon*
la noche	*the evening*
generalmente	*usually, generally*
todos los días	*every day*
¡No me digas!	*Really? You don't say!*
mi, mis	*my*
tus	*your*

¿Y qué quiere decir . . . ?
¿Dónde?
ir: (yo) voy
   (tú) vas
con
el amigo, la amiga
la familia
solo, -a

Empecemos a conversar

With a partner, take turns being *Estudiante A* and *Estudiante B*.
Use the words that are cued or given in the balloons to replace
the underlined sections in the model. 💡 means you can make
your own choices.

¡NO OLVIDES!

a + el = al

1

A —¿Cuándo vas *al parque*?
B —Voy *los viernes*.
  o: *Pues, generalmente no voy.*

  Y ahora Uds.

Estudiante A   **Estudiante B**

a. b. c.
d. e. f.

los lunes, los martes . . .

los fines de semana

todos los días

por la mañana /
  tarde / noche

después de las clases

2

A —¿Qué te gusta hacer en *el verano*?
B —Me gusta *nadar e* ir a la playa con*
  mis amigos.
A —¡No me digas! A mí también.

  Y ahora Uds.

Estudiante A   **Estudiante B**

a. b.
c. d.

* The Spanish word *y* becomes *e* before a word beginning with *i* or *hi*.

3 A —¿*Con quién vas <u>al parque de diversiones</u>?*
   B —*Generalmente voy <u>con mis amigos</u>.*
      o: *Generalmente voy <u>solo(a)</u>.*

   Y ahora Uds.

Estudiante A   Estudiante B

También se dice

la alberca
la pileta

el parque de atracciones

Empecemos a escribir

Write your answers in Spanish.

4   For each season write one activity that you enjoy doing.

5   Write questions to ask your partner about when and with
       whom he or she goes to three different places. Record your
       partner's answers.

6   ¿Te gusta más el verano o el invierno? ¿Qué estación no te
       gusta?

7   Generalmente, ¿adónde vas después de las clases? ¿Cuál es tu
       pasatiempo favorito?

Vocabulario para conversar

¿Te gustaría ir conmigo?

Here's the rest of the vocabulary you will need to talk about your leisure-time activities and to extend, accept, or decline invitations.

jugar vóleibol

jugar básquetbol*

jugar tenis

ir de compras

jugar fútbol

jugar béisbol

ir a una fiesta

jugar fútbol americano

ir de pesca

jugar videojuegos

* The names for the sports are all masculine, for example: *el básquetbol.*

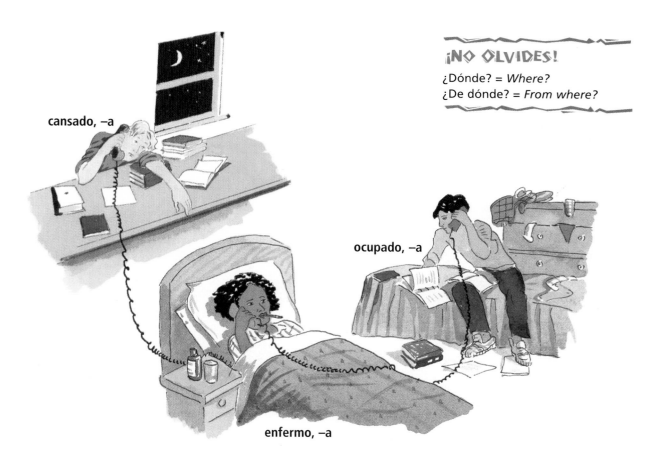

cansado, –a

ocupado, –a

enfermo, –a

¡NO OLVIDES!

¿Dónde? = *Where?*
¿De dónde? = *From where?*

También necesitas . . .

estar: (yo) estoy	*to be: I am*
(tú) estás	*you are*
¿Adónde?	*(To) where?*
conmigo, contigo	*with me, with you*
¿(A ti) te gustaría ___?	*Would you like ___?*
(A mí) me gustaría ___.	*I would like ___.*
poder: (yo) puedo	*can: I can*
(tú) puedes	*you can*
querer: (yo) quiero	*to want: I want*
(tú) quieres	*you want*
¡Claro que sí!	*Of course!*
¡Claro que no!	*Of course not!*
De nada.	*You're welcome.*
¡Genial!	*Great! Wonderful!*
¡Qué lástima!	*That's too bad! That's a shame!*

¿Y qué quiere decir . . . ?
hoy no
mañana*

* *Mañana* alone means "tomorrow"; *la mañana* means "morning."

Empecemos a conversar

√ **8** el lunes

A — ¿Adónde vas _el lunes_?
B — Voy _al parque_.
A — ¡No me digas! Yo también.

Y ahora Uds.

Estudiante A   **Estudiante B**

a. el martes
b. el miércoles
c. el jueves
d. el viernes
e. el sábado
f. el domingo
g. mañana

√ **9**

A — ¿Te gustaría _ir a una fiesta_ conmigo?
B — ¿Contigo? _Sí, me gustaría (mucho)_.

Y ahora Uds.

Estudiante A   **Estudiante B**

Pues, ¡claro que sí!

Lo siento, pero no puedo.

No puedo. Tengo mucha tarea.

¡Sí, genial! ¡Gracias!

¡Qué lástima! No puedo.

Sí, me gustaría (mucho).

10

A — *¿Puedes <u>ir al cine</u> conmigo?*
B — *Hoy no; lo siento. Estoy <u>ocupado(a)</u>.*
   o: *¡Claro que no! Estoy <u>enfermo(a)</u>.*

   Y ahora Uds.

Estudiante A

a.

b.

c.

d.

e.

f.

Estudiante B

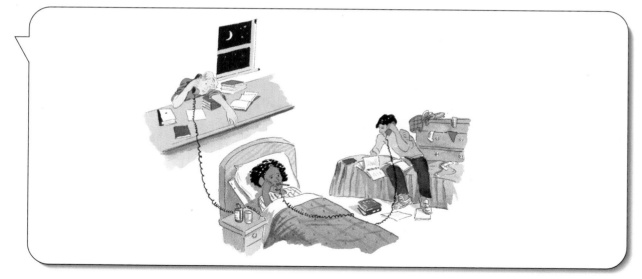

√**11**

A — *¿Quieres <u>jugar videojuegos</u>?*
B — *Quiero, pero no puedo. Necesito <u>ir de compras</u>.*
A — *¡Qué lástima!*

Y ahora Uds.

Estudiante A

a.

b.

c.

d.

e.

f.

g.

Estudiante B

Empecemos a escribir y a leer

Write your answers in Spanish.

12 Write full sentences telling when you do any four of the following activities. You can mention the season, the day of the week, or time of day. For example:

En el otoño, voy a la playa los fines de semana.

or: *En la primavera, voy al campo los domingos.*

13 Write three excuses that you have learned how to say in this chapter.

14 ¿Qué te gustaría hacer hoy después de las clases?

15 ¿Qué quieres hacer el sábado por la noche?

16 ¿Es lógico o no?

"No soy nada atrevido. Al contrario, soy muy prudente. Generalmente voy al parque de diversiones cuando estoy cansado."

"¡Qué lástima! Estoy enferma hoy y no puedo ir de compras contigo."

"Soy paciente y me gusta estar sola. En el verano, cuando no estoy ocupada los fines de semana, me gusta mucho ir de pesca."

También se dice

jugar baloncesto

jugar balonvolea

¡Comuniquemos!

Here's another opportunity for you to use the vocabulary you've just learned.

1   Ask a partner to join you in an activity.
He or she will refuse politely.

A— *¿Quieres patinar conmigo?*
B— *Me gustaría, pero hoy voy a la playa con mi familia.*

a.

b.

c.

d.

e.

2 Your partner wants to get together with you, but you are always busy.

A — *¿Estás ocupado(a) el sábado a las nueve?*
B — *Sí. Voy al parque para jugar béisbol.*
A — *¡Qué lástima!*

Estudiante A   **Estudiante B**

3 You're going to a party Friday night. Find out from a partner what time the party begins and with whom he or she is going. If your partner is going alone, ask if he or she would like to go with you.

¿Qué sabes ahora?

Can you:

■ say what you would like to do after class?

—___ ir al cine después de las clases.

■ say that you want to do an activity but cannot?

—___ ir a la playa, pero ___.

■ invite someone to do something with you?

—¿___ ir de compras conmigo?

■ accept or decline an invitation?

—¿Te gustaría ir al cine el sábado?
—Sí (No), ___.

Perspectiva cultural

Muchas personas, generalmente, van al parque los fines de semana. Van con la familia, con los amigos o van solas a practicar deportes, leer, visitar museos o a hacer un picnic y conversar.

Look at the photos. Why might a family often choose to spend time together in these places?

Mexico City's Chapultepec Park is one of the largest in the world. It has a castle, a zoo, a botanical garden, and a world-famous anthropological museum. It also contains an amusement park, which offers a variety of rides—*la montaña rusa* (roller coaster), *la rueda de feria* (Ferris wheel), *los carros locos* (bumper cars), and so on.

In the Retiro Park in Madrid you could visit the Crystal Palace, where numerous expositions are held, or row a boat in the *estanque* (lake).

However, most parks are not very big. In small cities and towns, the main outdoor gathering place would be a *plaza,* a small green area that usually includes a small playground. Like the park, the *plaza* is where people meet to exchange news and local gossip, and where vendors sell *paletas* (popsicles or ice cream bars) or *globos* (balloons). In many cities, the *plaza,* or town square, is truly the heart of town. Many families will often spend an entire Sunday afternoon in a *plaza* or a park.

La cultura desde tu perspectiva

1 In what ways are parks in Spanish-speaking countries similar to or different from parks that you know? Have you ever visited a park that has facilities similar to the ones in Chapultepec or El Retiro?

2 If you lived near El Retiro or Chapultepec, how often do you think you would go there? Why?

El parque del Retiro en Madrid, España

Una plaza en San Juan,
Puerto Rico

El parque de Chapultepec en la Ciudad de México

Gramática en contexto

Look at the brochure describing a family vacation camp. What kind of information would you expect to find in a brochure such as this?

¿Está Ud. cansado?
¿Necesita unas vacaciones?

El campamento Bella Vista está a su disposición.

Ud., su familia y sus amigos van a pasar unos días maravillosos con nosotros. El campamento Bella Vista está a dos kilómetros de la playa y es el lugar perfecto para sus vacaciones. Nosotros vamos a preparar un plan de actividades que les va a gustar.

Por la mañana van a nadar en la piscina olímpica o ir de pesca en la costa.

Por la tarde van a montar a caballo en el campo o tomar el sol en la playa.

Por la noche van a escuchar música o practicar deportes.

Para hacer reservas o para obtener más información, llame al 1-555-776-6181

A Find the sentence that tells where the camp is located. What verb is used? How many times does it appear in the brochure?

B What activities are planned for guests? What verb is used with each pair of activities? (HINT: You already know two forms of the verb *ir: voy* and *vas.*) What do you think the *ustedes* and *nosotros* forms of the verb *ir* might be?

C In the brochure, *van a* is always followed by a verb. What do you think *van a nadar* and *van a escuchar música* mean? Based on what you've seen here, could you create a rule for this?

El verbo *ir*

You know that verbs whose infinitives end in *-ar* follow a pattern. The endings show who is doing the action: *(yo) cocino, (tú) cocinas,* and so on.

- Verbs that follow certain patterns are called regular verbs. Those that do not follow those patterns are called irregular. The verb *ir,* "to go," is irregular. It is often followed by the word *a:* **Voy al** *cine.* Here are its present-tense forms.

(yo)	**voy**	(nosotros) (nosotras)	**vamos**
(tú)	**vas**	(vosotros) (vosotras)	**vais**
Ud. (él) (ella)	**va**	Uds. (ellos) (ellas)	**van**

1 There is a teachers' meeting today and you have the day off from school. Everyone is going to a different place. With a partner, take turns asking and answering questions about where the following people are going.

A — *¿Adónde va Carlos?*
B — *Va al parque.*

Carlos

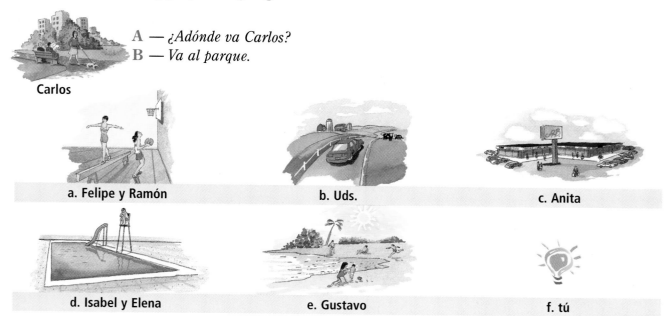

a. Felipe y Ramón

b. Uds.

c. Anita

d. Isabel y Elena

e. Gustavo

f. tú

Ir + *a* + infinitivo

We also use a form of the verb *ir* + *a* + infinitive to tell what someone is going to do.

> Yo **voy a nadar**. Y tú, ¿**vas a jugar** fútbol?

2 With a partner, take turns asking and answering whether or not you're going to do these things tomorrow.

ir al cine
A — *¿Vas a ir al cine mañana por la tarde?*
B — *Sí, voy a ir.*
    o: *No, voy a ir al centro comercial.*

a. estudiar
b. ayudar en casa
c. ir al centro comercial
d. ir a una fiesta

e. jugar básquetbol
f. jugar fútbol americano
g. jugar vóleibol
h. jugar béisbol

Niños paseando en bote en el estanque de la Plaza de España, Sevilla

3 Based on the answers your partner gave in Exercise 2, tell another student what your partner will and will not do tomorrow.

La preposición *con*

When you want to say that you do something with another person, use the word *con*. *Con* may be used with the names of people or in the following ways:

conmigo	**con nosotros / nosotras**
contigo	**con vosotros / vosotras**
con Ud. / él / ella	**con Uds. / ellos / ellas**

4 With a partner, take turns asking each other about doing these activities together.

estudiar

A —*¿Quieres estudiar conmigo después de las clases?*

B —*¿Contigo? ¡Claro que sí!*

o: *¿Contigo? Me gustaría, pero no puedo.*

a. ver la tele

b. practicar deportes

c. ir al gimnasio

d. ir de compras

e. jugar videojuegos

f. jugar tenis

g. jugar fútbol

h.

5 Take turns asking a partner with whom he or she would like to do these activities.

A —*¿Con quién te gustaría ir al cine el sábado?*

B —*Con Alicia.*

A —*¿Con ella?*

B —*Sí, con ella.*

Alicia

a. Susana y Julia

b. Marcelo y Graciela

c. Uds.

d. Marcos

e. Ana María

f. tú

El verbo *estar*

Estar ("to be") is an irregular verb. We use it to tell how someone feels or where someone is. Here are its present-tense forms.

(yo)	**estoy**	(nosotros) (nosotras)	**estamos**
(tú)	**estás**	(vosotros) (vosotras)	**estáis**
Ud. (él) (ella)	**está**	Uds. (ellos) (ellas)	**están**

- In writing, be sure to use the accent mark on all forms except *estoy* and *estamos*.

6 With a partner, take turns asking and answering where these people are.

A — *¿Dónde está Alejandro?*
B — *Está en el campo.*

Alejandro

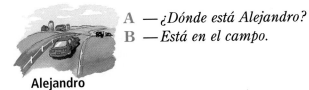

a. Rosa   b. José Antonio   c. Uds.

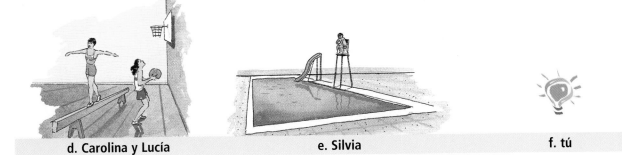

d. Carolina y Lucía   e. Silvia   f. tú

7 Find out from several classmates how they are feeling today. Take turns asking and answering using *bien, enfermo(a), ocupado(a),* or *cansado(a).*

¡NO OLVIDES!

Many adjectives end in -o in the masculine and in -a in the feminine. Those ending in -e can describe either masculine or feminine nouns.

Ahora lo sabes

Can you:

■ say where someone is going?

—Mariana y yo ___ a la piscina.

■ say what someone is going to do?

—Alejandro y Marta ___ jugar básquetbol mañana.

■ say who does an activity with you?

—Mis amigos estudian ___ después de las clases.

■ say how someone feels?

—Felipe ___ muy cansado hoy.

■ say where someone is?

—José y Ana ___ aquí.

Jugando béisbol en la República Dominicana

Para decir más

Here is some additional vocabulary that you might find useful for activities in this section.

jugar hockey
to play hockey

hacer gimnasia
to do gymnastics

ir a la iglesia
to go to church

ir al templo
to go to temple

ir a la mezquita
to go to the mosque

Actividades

Here's an opportunity for you to expand your use of Spanish by putting together the material you learned in this chapter with what you learned earlier.

1 Your teacher will designate certain parts of the room as favorite places to go when you are not in school. Choose your favorite place and go to that part of the room. With the other students who are there, discuss when you go to that place. Keep a tally of your group's responses.

A — *¿Cuándo vas a la playa?*
B — *Generalmente los sábados o los domingos.*

As a group, be prepared to report on the results of your poll.

A — *¿Cuándo van Uds. a la playa?*
B — *Tres estudiantes van a la playa los sábados.*
C — *Pablo y yo vamos a la playa en el verano.*

El ballet folklórico de México

2 Tell your partner at least four things that you are going to do this weekend. Mention either when or with whom you are going to do the activities. Your partner will ask about the missing information.

A —*Voy a ir a la piscina el sábado.*
B —*¿Con quién?*
A —*Voy con Enrique.*
  o: *Voy solo(a).*

A —*Voy a ir a la piscina con Enrique.*
  o: *Voy a ir a la piscina solo(a).*
B —*¿Cuándo (vas a ir allí)?*
A —*El sábado.*

**"Después de las clases,
  voy a la playa con mis amigos."**

3 With a partner, create a dialogue:
  • find out where your partner is going
  • ask if you can go with him or her
  • your partner accepts
    or declines politely

ENCIENDA SU IMAGINACIÓN

LEER,

TAN DIVERTIDO COMO VER TELEVISIÓN

ES RICO LEER
PLAN NACIONAL DE LECTURA
PRESIDENCIA DE LA REPÚBLICA

**"Cuando estoy sola,
  me gusta leer."**

¡Vamos a leer!

Antes de leer

 **STRATEGY** ➤ Using prior knowledge

Earlier you used your own experience with certain kinds of reading materials to predict the types of information you might find in a pen pal column or report card. If you are looking at a calendar of events, what types of information would you expect to find?

Remember that what you already know about a newspaper section like this in English can help you predict, look for, and even understand information in Spanish.

CALENDARIO

CIUDAD JUAREZ

VIERNES 16

TEATRO.- Festival de Teatro de la UACJ Verano 93 presenta a su compañía con "Si algo te debo" en el Teatro del Centro de Convenciones Universitario en P.E. Calles y Hnos Escobar. Admisión N$10.00. Funciones a las 20:00 horas.

SABADO 17

TEATRO.- Festival de Teatro de la UACJ Verano 93 presenta a su compañía con "Si algo te debo" en el Teatro del Centro de Convenciones Universitario en P.E. Calles y Hnos Escobar.
Admisión N$10.00./20:00 horas
FUTBOL con las Cobras en el inicio de temporada. Estadio Olímpico Benito Juárez a las 20:00 horas. Boletos en Superettes del Río.
MUSICA: Grupo Liberación, en los Jardines Carta Blanca a las 20:00 horas, costo $30 pesos nuevos.
Little Joe y la Familia, La Peluza y los Ases del Norte en la explanada de la Feria Juárez, desde las 20:00 horas. Costo $25 pesos nuevos.

DOMINGO 18

TEATRO.- Festival de Teatro de la UACJ Verano 93 presenta a su compañía con "Si algo te debo" en el Teatro del Centro de Convenciones Universitario en P.E. Calles y Hnos Escobar.
Admisión N$10.00. Funciones a las 20:00 horas.

ESTA VEZ VIENE CON SU PAPA

HARRISON FORD   SEAN CONNERY

INDIANA JONES 4
LA ULTIMA CRUZADA

Distribuida por United International Pictures.

Mira la lectura

STRATEGY ➤ Scanning

Look at the calendar of events, noting the title, format, illustrations, and boldface headings.

1 Which days of the week are featured?

2 Which day of the week offers the greatest selection of activities? What kinds of events are there?

3 Do you find the display ad effective? Does it contain all the information a reader would need to know? Did you find what you expected to find?

Infórmate

STRATEGY ➤ Scanning

Using the ad, make plans for Saturday night.

1 Look at the calendar of events and identify four places to go on Saturday, then choose the one you would like to go to.

2 Find the following information for the place you choose:

- Lugar (cine; concierto; partido de fútbol; teatro)
- Nombre de la película / del grupo musical / del equipo de fútbol / de la obra de teatro
- Dirección
- Hora
- Admisión

3 What seems unusual about some of the times given?
How else could you express 20:00?

The following movie times are based on the 24-hour clock. How would they read according to the 12-hour clock?

11:15   13:45   16:20   18:50   21:30

4 N$ means *nuevos pesos*. When the Mexican government revalued the peso in the spring of 1993, N$ 3 equaled US $1. Given this information, figure out the price of admission to the place you selected in United States dollars.

24
sábado
julio

| 8:00 |
| 8:30 |
| 9:00 |
| 9:30 |
| 10:00 |
| 10:30 |
| 11:00 |
| 11:30 |
| 12:00 |
| 1:00 |
| 1:30 |
| 2:00 |
| 2:30 |
| 3:00 |
| 3:30 |
| 4:00 |
| 4:30 |
| 5:00 |

205

sábado 24 ...

25
domingo
julio

| 8:00 |
| 8:30 |
| 9:00 |
| 9:30 |
| 10:00 |
| 10:30 |
| 11:00 |
| 11:30 |
| 12:00 |
| 1:00 |
| 1:30 |
| 2:00 |
| 2:30 |
| 3:00 |
| 3:30 |
| 4:00 |
| 4:30 |
| 5:00 |

206

domingo 25 de julio   159

Aplicación

Take a poll to see which of the activities mentioned in the calendar of events would be the most popular among your classmates.

¡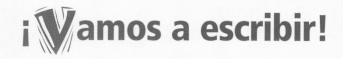amos a escribir!

You and a friend are giving a party. Plan your party and write the invitation you will send to your friends. Follow these steps.

1 Think about what you are going to do at the party. A checklist will help you plan. With a partner, write a list in Spanish of the activities and when each might begin. For example:

Actividad   Hora

Vamos a . . .   a las . . .

2 Next, write the invitation. Include the day and time, your names, the address, and what you are going to do. Here is a model blank invitation:

_____ y _____ te invitan a una

¡¡¡ **FiESTA** !!!

Cuándo: el _____ de _____ a la(s) _____

Dónde: _____

Actividades: En la fiesta vamos a _____

_____

¡¡¡La fiesta va a estar fantástica!!!

3 Exchange invitations with another group and share any suggestions for improvement. Is there enough information, or should something be added?

4 Think about their suggestions and any other changes you may want to make. Rewrite your invitation. Check it for spelling and punctuation, including accents. Let the other group check it too. Ask them if you have included all the necessary information.

5 Now recopy your corrected invitation. You may want to file it in a writing portfolio.

Te invito a una ¡fiesta!

Cuándo: el sábado 10 de octubre
Hora: 6:00
Dónde: la casa de María Elena, Calle Príncipes 436

¡Vamos a bailar, comer, escuchar música y divertirnos muchísimo! Favor de contestarme antes del 5 de octubre al 555-9341

¡¡¡La fiesta va a estar fantástica!!!

¿Lo sabes bien?

This section will help you organize your studying for the proficiency test, where you will be asked to do similar, though not identical, tasks. There will not be any models on the test.

Listening

Can you understand when people talk about their free-time activities? Listen as your teacher reads you a sample similar to what you will hear on the test. Is Margarita going to the movies with Luis or not?

Reading

Can you look at this letter and get an idea of how Ruth is planning to spend her weekend? In what city is Ruth spending the weekend?

Querida Isabel:

Voy a estar contigo tres días allí en Miami. El viernes me gustaría ir de compras todo el día. ¿Puedes ir conmigo? El sábado por la mañana quiero ir a la playa a nadar y por la noche quiero ir a patinar con mis amigos. El domingo necesito dormir. Soy muy perezosa, pero me gustaría ir al cine por la tarde. Y tú, ¿qué prefieres?

Saludos,
Ruth

Writing

Can you write a note to a classmate in which you decline an invitation and say why? You should also suggest other days when you are free and what you would like to do. Here is a sample:

Rebeca:

Me gustaría mucho ir de compras contigo el viernes, pero estoy ocupada. El sábado, claro que sí, no tengo ni clase ni tarea. Me gustaría ir a nadar por la mañana, y por la noche me gustaría ir al cine. También me gustaría ir contigo al campo el domingo. ¿Quieres ir?

Cecilia

Culture

Can you compare a *plaza* to a park such as El Retiro or Chapultepec?

El parque del Retiro en Madrid

"¿Te gustaría ir al parque conmigo?"

Speaking

Can you invite your partner to do an activity with you? You and your partner should agree on what to do, where, and when. For example:

A — *¿Te gustaría jugar básquetbol?*
B — *Sí, pero prefiero ir a patinar.*
A — *¡Genial! ¿Adónde vamos? ¿Al parque?*
B — *Sí. ¿A qué hora? ¿Puedes ir a las 9:00?*
A — *No, necesito ir de compras con mi familia. ¿Y a las 11:00?*
B — *Sí, a las 11:00.*

Resumen del capítulo 3

Use the vocabulary from this chapter to help you:

- talk about some of your leisure-time activities
- make plans with friends
- extend, accept, or decline invitations

to tell how someone feels or where someone is
¿Dónde?
estar: (yo) estoy
     (tú) estás

to tell where someone is going
¿Adónde?
ir: (yo) voy
    (tú) vas
a
a la, al *(a + el)*
el campo
el centro comercial
el gimnasio
el parque
el parque de diversiones
la piscina
la playa

to talk about activities
ir a una fiesta
ir de compras
ir de pesca
jugar básquetbol
jugar béisbol
jugar fútbol
jugar fútbol americano
jugar tenis
jugar videojuegos
jugar vóleibol
el pasatiempo

to say when you do an activity
la estación, *pl.* estaciones
    la primavera
    el verano
    el otoño
    el invierno
el lunes, el martes . . .
los lunes, los martes . . .
el fin (los fines) de semana
después de (las clases)
(por) la mañana
    la tarde
    la noche
generalmente
hoy no
mañana
todos los días

to say with whom you do an activity
con
conmigo, contigo
el amigo, la amiga
la familia
solo, -a

to extend, accept, or decline invitations
¿(A ti) te gustaría ___?
(A mí) me gustaría ___.
poder: (yo) puedo
      (tú) puedes
querer: (yo) quiero
      (tú) quieres
¡Claro que sí!
¡Claro que no!
De nada.
cansado, -a
enfermo, -a
ocupado, -a

to express surprise, enthusiasm, or disappointment
¡No me digas!
¡Genial!
¡Qué lástima!

to express possession
mi, mis
tus

CAPÍTULO 4

¿Qué prefieres comer?

OBJECTIVES

At the end of this chapter, you will be able to:

- describe what you like and don't like to eat and drink
- tell when you have meals
- say whether you are hungry or thirsty
- compare and contrast eating customs in Spanish-speaking countries and in the United States

Mercado al aire libre en Perú

¡Piénsalo bien!

Look at the photos. How is the food similar to or different from what you might eat? Now look at the teens gathered at a fast-food place. How does this restaurant compare to a similar place in your community? What do you think *hamburguesa* means?

"Me gustaría una hamburguesa."

A la hora del almuerzo en la Ciudad de México

Un desayuno en un hotel de Asunción, Paraguay

En Navidad, una familia dominicana a la hora de la cena

Vocabulario para conversar

¿Qué te gusta comer?

Here are some new words and expressions you will need to talk about mealtimes and foods you like and don't like to eat. Read them several times, then turn the page and practice with a partner.

El desayuno

el pan tostado
el cereal
el huevo
el jamón

El almuerzo

las frutas
las papas fritas
la hamburguesa
los sandwiches
el tomate
el queso
la ensalada
el sandwich de jamón y queso

La cena

el pan

la sopa de tomate

la sopa de pollo

la sopa de verduras

el bistec

el pescado

el arroz

las papas al horno

las verduras

el pollo

También necesitas . . .

comer: (yo) como	*to eat: I eat*	me encanta(n)	*I love*
(tú) comes	*you eat*	siempre	*always*
la comida	*meal*	nunca	*never*
más o menos	*more or less*		
¡Qué asco!	*Yuk! That's disgusting!*		
¿Por qué?	*why?*		
porque	*because*		
¿verdad?	*isn't that so? right?*		

¿Y qué quiere decir . . . ?
en el desayuno / el almuerzo / la cena
preferir: (yo) prefiero
        (tú) prefieres

Empecemos a conversar

With a partner, take turns being *Estudiante A* and *Estudiante B*. Use the words that are cued or given in the balloons to replace the underlined sections in the model. 💡 means you can make your own choices.

1

A — ¿Comes _jamón_?
B — _Sí, a veces._

Y ahora Uds.

Estudiante A

a.
b.
c.
d. 💡

Estudiante B

Sí, a veces.

Sí, todos los días

Sí, siempre.

No, nunca.

No, ¡qué asco!

2

A — Te gustan _las ensaladas_, ¿verdad?
B — _Sí, me encantan._

Y ahora Uds.

Estudiante A

a.
b.
c.
d.
e.
f.
g.

Estudiante B

Sí, me encantan.

Sí, más o menos.

No, no me gustan (mucho).

No, ¡qué asco!

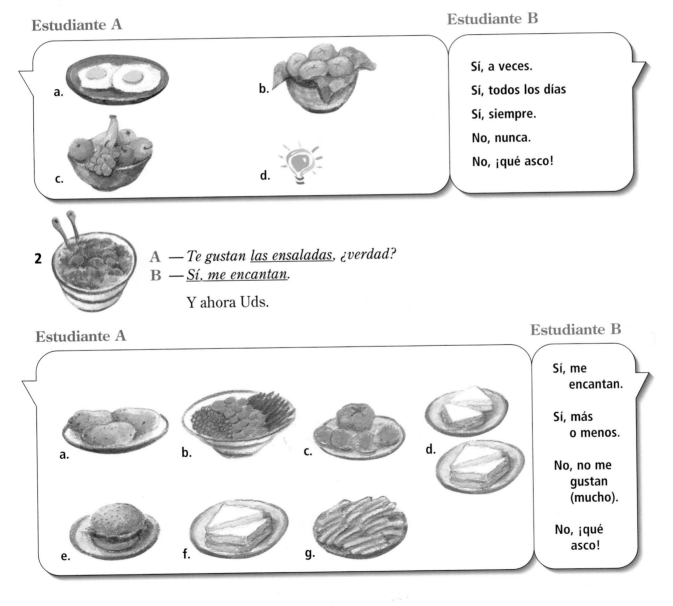

3 el desayuno A —¿*Qué comes en* <u>*el desayuno*</u>?
B —*Generalmente como* <u>*cereal y pan tostado*</u>.
Y ahora Uds.

Estudiante A

a. la cena

b. el almuerzo

c. el desayuno

Estudiante B

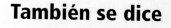

la tostada

los bocadillos
los emparedados

el bife
el biftec

Empecemos a escribir

Write your answers in Spanish.

4 Write the names of at least three foods under each of these headings: *Todos los días, A veces, Nunca*. Then write three complete sentences telling how often you eat those foods.

5 Copy the names of the soups you have learned. Using these as a model, choose other foods from the vocabulary and write the names of at least three other soups.

6 ¿Qué comida prefieres, el desayuno o la cena? ¿Por qué?

7 Generalmente, ¿qué comes en el almuerzo y con quién comes?

las legumbres
las hortalizas

los jitomates

Detalle de *La gran ciudad de Tenochtitlán* (1945), Diego Rivera

Vocabulario para conversar   125

Vocabulario para conversar

¿Tienes hambre?

Here's the rest of the vocabulary you will need to tell what you like and don't like to eat and drink and to say whether you are hungry or thirsty.

tener hambre

FRUTAS

VERDURAS

la lechuga

los guisantes

la naranja

las judías verdes

las zanahorias

la manzana

las cebollas

las papas

la uva

el plátano

tener sed

el agua *(f.)**

la leche

el café

el té

la limonada   los refrescos

el jugo
de naranja

el té helado

También necesitas . . .

beber: (yo) bebo, (tú) bebes	*to drink: I drink you drink*	deber: (yo) debo (tú) debes	*ought to, should*
bueno, -a (para la salud)	*good (for your health)*	son	*(they) are*
malo, -a (para la salud)	*bad (for your health)*	unos, unas	*some*
sabroso, -a	*delicious, tasty*		
Creo que sí.	*I think so.*		
Creo que no.	*I don't think so.*		
algo	*something*		

¿Y qué quiere decir . . . ?
horrible

*Note that *agua* is a feminine noun. However, we use the article *el* with feminine nouns beginning with stressed *a* or *ha*.

Empecemos a conversar

8

A — _Tengo sed. Necesito beber algo._
B — _¿Te gustaría un refresco?_

Y ahora Uds.

Estudiante A

Necesito beber algo.
Debo beber algo.

Necesito comer algo.
Debo comer algo.

Estudiante B

9

A — _Las verduras son buenas para la salud, ¿verdad?_
B — _Sí, y son sabrosas también._

Y ahora Uds.

Estudiante A

a. b. c.

d. e. f.

Estudiante B

Sí, y son sabrosas también.

Sí, pero no me gustan
mucho.

Sí, pero no son sabrosas.

Sí, pero son horribles.

Creo que sí.

No, creo que no.

No, son malas para
la salud.

Más o menos.

Empecemos a escribir y a leer

Write your answers in Spanish.

10 Imagine that you are waiting tables and need to write yourself a reminder. Write down what comes with the hamburgers, and at least four ingredients that are in the vegetable soup today.

11 ¿Qué bebida prefieres en el desayuno, en el almuerzo y en la cena? ¿Por qué?

12 ¿Qué verduras te gustan?

13 Unos animales hablan de lo que prefieren comer. ¿Qué dicen? (*What do they say?*)

el mono

el pato

el cerdo

la gallina

el conejo

¿Quién dice . . . ?

a. —A ver . . . Me encantan el pan y el agua. Sí, sí. Me gusta mucho beber agua, y como mucho pan en el parque.

b. —En el desayuno siempre como plátanos. En el almuerzo a veces como más plátanos. ¿Y en la cena? Pues . . . generalmente como plátanos también. Son muy buenos para la salud, ¿verdad?

c. —¿Comer huevos? ¡Ay, no! ¿Huevos? ¡Nunca!

d. —Como mucho todos los días. ¡Pero no puedo comer jamón! ¡Nunca voy a comer jamón!

e. —Yo como muchas zanahorias. ¡A mí me encantan las zanahorias! Me gustaría comer zanahorias en todas las comidas.

También se dice

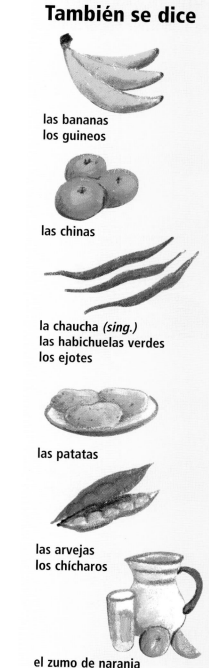

las bananas
los guineos

las chinas

la chaucha (*sing.*)
las habichuelas verdes
los ejotes

las patatas

las arvejas
los chícharos

el zumo de naranja

¡Comuniquemos!

Here's another opportunity for you to use the vocabulary you've just learned.

1 You and a friend are having dinner at a restaurant. Take turns asking each other about your food preferences.

¡NO OLVIDES!

If you need help spelling, ask ¿Cómo se escribe . . . ?

A — *¿Prefieres sopa de pollo o sopa de tomate?*
B — *Prefiero sopa de pollo, ¿y tú?*
A — *Yo prefiero sopa de pollo también.*
    o: Yo prefiero sopa de tomate.
    o: A mí no me gusta ni la sopa de pollo
      ni la sopa de tomate.

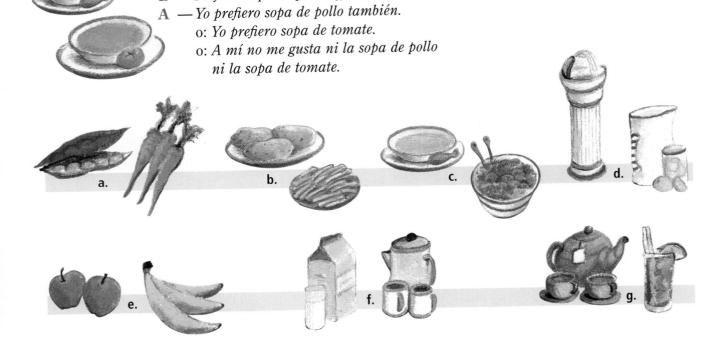

2 Help a friend prepare a shopping list. Ask what he or she needs, and write down the responses.

la sopa
    A — *¿Qué necesitas para la sopa?*
    B — *Necesito zanahorias, tomates y cebolla.*

Estudiante A   **Estudiante B**

a. los sandwiches
b. la ensalada de frutas
c. la ensalada de verduras
d. el desayuno
e. el almuerzo
f. la cena

3 Your family is having guests this weekend and you are expected to be at every meal. Find out at what time all of the meals are and what is going to be served. Your partner will play the role of a family member.

el almuerzo

A — *¿A qué hora es el almuerzo el sábado?*
B — *A las doce.*
A — *¿Qué vamos a comer?*
B — *Pollo y ensalada.*
A — *¡Pero siempre comemos pollo y ensalada!*
   o: *¡Me encantan!*

Estudiante A

desayuno   sábado

almuerzo   domingo

cena

Estudiante B

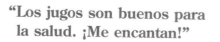

¿Qué sabes ahora?

Can you:

■ **tell someone that you are hungry / thirsty?**

—Tengo ___ / ___.

■ **tell someone what you like or do not like to eat and drink?**

—Me encanta comer ___ , pero (no) me gusta beber ___.

■ **say that you like certain foods because they are healthful or tasty?**

—Me gustan las uvas ___ son ___.

"Los jugos son buenos para la salud. ¡Me encantan!"

En una tienda de jugos en la Zona Rosa, Ciudad de México

Perspectiva cultural

¿A qué hora es el desayuno, el almuerzo y la cena en los Estados Unidos? ¿Qué comemos en el desayuno, por ejemplo? En las fotos, ¿a qué hora comen los hispanos?

Look at the mealtimes shown in the photos. Based on those times, do you think there might be another meal not pictured? Explain your answer.

In Spanish-speaking countries, as in the United States, there are three main meals—*el desayuno, el almuerzo,* and *la cena.*

El desayuno, which generally takes place between 7:00 and 8:30, is usually a light meal that consists of coffee or *café con leche,* which is half coffee and half hot milk, and bread or rolls with butter and jam. Children and teenagers sometimes drink hot chocolate or chocolate milk instead of coffee.

El almuerzo (called *la comida* in Spain and Mexico) is the largest and most important meal of the day. It is eaten between noon and 3:00. Many businesses and schools close so that families can enjoy *el almuerzo* together at home. Although this lengthy midday break is still common, more and more businesses are adopting a *jornada continua* or *horario continuado* (uninterrupted schedule) similar to working hours in the United States. This does not leave time for employees to go home for lunch.

La cena is the evening meal. It may start around 7:00 or much later, especially in countries that have a late midday meal. In Spain, *la cena* may start as late as 10:00 or 11:00, since most Spaniards enjoy going out after work or school and it is customary to wait until all family members are present before sitting down to eat. *La cena* is usually a light meal, and it may include leftovers from *el almuerzo.*

In some countries, there is also a late afternoon meal called *la merienda.* It may be like a *desayuno*, or it may resemble an English tea, with sandwiches, pastries, or rolls and *café con leche*, tea, or hot chocolate.

La cultura desde tu perspectiva

1 In what ways are mealtimes in Spanish-speaking countries similar to or different from those in the United States?

2 Why would a late-afternoon snack probably be necessary for someone from the United States who was visiting a Spanish-speaking country? Are there any other times of day when a snack might be needed?

2:00 PM

Málaga,
España

Ciudad de México,
México

5:00 PM

Unos amigos españoles a la hora del almuerzo

En México, a la hora de la merienda

Santiago,
Chile

9:30 PM

En Chile, familiares y amigos empiezan a cenar.

Perspectiva cultural   133

Gramática en contexto

Look at this ad for imported cheeses. Are most of the cheeses you expected to find there?

¿Sí? Pues, en LA CASA DE LOS QUESOS tenemos quesos deliciosos preparados especialmente para ti.

Tenemos quesos franceses, ingleses y suizos. También ofrecemos quesos finos de Holanda, Italia y Grecia. Para las personas que no deben o no quieren comer mucha grasa, tenemos una gran variedad de quesos dietéticos. El queso suizo es nuestra especialidad. Es muy sabroso.

¡Buen provecho! Bon appétit! Enjoy!

A Working with a partner, list all the words from the ad that describe cheese when it is written *quesos*.

- Find two words that describe cheese when it is written *queso*.
- When would you use *sabroso* or *sabrosos* to describe food?

B Look at the headline. How is this form of the expression for "Do you like …" different from the form you learned earlier? How would you explain this?

134   Capítulo 4

El plural de los sustantivos

- In Spanish, to make nouns plural, we generally add *-s* to words ending in a vowel (*libro → libros*) and *-es* to words ending in a consonant (*papel → papeles*).

- The plural definite articles are *los* and *las*. *Los* is used with masculine plural nouns, *las* with feminine plural nouns.

  los cereal**es**   **las** pap**as**

- *Los* is also used with a plural noun that includes both males and females.

  el profesor Sánchez y la profesora Romero
  = **los** profesor**es**

- Singular nouns that end in the letter *z* change the *z* to *c* in the plural.

  el lápi**z** → los lápi**ces**

- To keep the stress on the correct syllable, we sometimes have to add or remove an accent mark in the plural.

  el ex**amen** → los ex**ámenes**
  el jam**ón** → los jam**ones**

- The plural indefinite articles are *unos* and *unas*. They mean "some" or "a few."

  No tengo mucha hambre, pero voy a comer **unas** papas fritas.

- We use *me gustan* and *me encantan* to talk about a plural noun.

  No me gust**an** las manzanas pero me encant**an** las uvas.

¡NO OLVIDES!

The singular definite articles are *el* and *la*. The singular indefinite articles are *un* and *una*.

1 Discuss with a partner whether or not you like the
following foods.

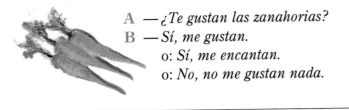

A — ¿*Te gustan las zanahorias?*
B — *Sí, me gustan.*
  o: *Sí, me encantan.*
  o: *No, no me gustan nada.*

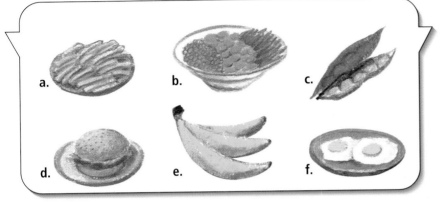

a.

b.

c.

d.

e.

f.

2 Now use the pictures in Exercise 1 to ask if your partner would
like to eat those foods.

A —¿*Te gustaría comer unas zanahorias?*
B —¡*Claro que sí! A mí me encantan.*
  o: *No, no tengo hambre. Gracias.*

**"Me encanta comer en un
restaurante con mis amigos."**

En un restaurante en la Ciudad de México

3 These foods might be served in your school cafeteria this week. Take turns with a partner telling whether you like them or not.

A —*Me gustan las papas al horno.*
B —*A mí también.*
   o: *A mí no.*

A —*No me gustan las papas al horno.*
B —*A mí tampoco.*
   o: *A mí sí.*

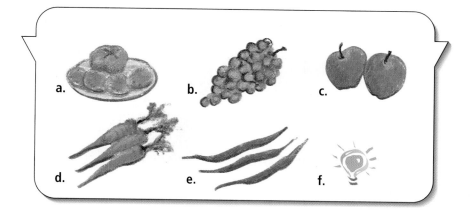

a.   b.   c.

d.   e.   f.

El plural de los adjetivos

You know that in Spanish most adjectives have different masculine and feminine singular forms: *La leche es sabrosa; el cereal es bueno para la salud.* If the noun is plural, the adjective too must be plural:

La**s** papa**s** frita**s** son sabrosa**s** pero no son buena**s** para la salud.

Lo**s** guisante**s** son bueno**s** para la salud.

- To make adjectives plural, add -*s* to the final vowel. If the adjective ends in a consonant, add -*es*.

horrible	horrible**s**
trabajador	trabajador**es**

- When an adjective describes both masculine and feminine nouns, use the masculine plural ending.

Los plátanos y las manzanas son sabros**os**.

4 For each of these adjectives, name two famous people or people in your class or school whom the adjective fits.

Carl Herrera y Gabriela Sabatini son deportistas.

artístico, -a
deportista
atrevido, -a
callado, -a
desordenado, -a
gracioso, -a
sociable
ordenado, -a
serio, -a
trabajador, -a

Verbos que terminan en *-er*

You know the pattern of present-tense endings for regular *-ar* verbs.

- Another group of regular verbs has infinitives that end in *-er*. Some that you know are *beber, comer, leer,* and *deber.*

- Here are the present-tense forms of the verb *comer.* How does this pattern differ from that of *-ar* verbs?

(yo)	como	(nosotros) (nosotras)	com**emos**
(tú)	com**es**	(vosotros) (vosotras)	com**éis**
Ud. (él) (ella)	come	Uds. (ellos) (ellas)	com**en**

- With *-er* verbs we use the vowel *-e* in all forms except *yo*. Remember that *-ar* verbs use the vowel *-a* except in the *yo* form.

- You also know the verb *ver*. It is regular except in the *yo* form, which is *veo*.

5 With a partner, take turns asking and answering what the
following people drink at different meals.

A —¿Qué beben tus amigos en el almuerzo?
B —Beben refrescos.

tus amigos / almuerzo

a. Anita / desayuno

b. Pilar y Pablo / almuerzo

c. Graciela y Juan / cena

d. Carlitos / desayuno

e. Uds. / cena

f. tú / almuerzo

6 These people do not eat certain foods. With your partner,
discuss why they should eat them.

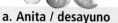

Juan Carlos

A —Juan Carlos no come judías verdes.
B —¡Pero debe comer judías verdes!
    Son buenas para la salud.

a. Víctor y Tomás

b. Inés

c. Raúl

d. Carmen y yo

e. Gloria y Victoria

f. yo

Sujetos compuestos

- When you talk about yourself and someone else, you really mean "we." Therefore, you should use the *nosotros* form of the verb.

  Alejandro y yo (nosotros) estudi**amos** por la noche.
  Tú y yo (nosotros) com**emos** a las doce.

- When speaking to more than one person—even if you call one of them *tú*—use the *ustedes* form of the verb.

  Tú y Tomás (ustedes) practic**an** deportes.

- When you talk about more than one person or thing, use the *ellos / ellas* form of the verb.

  Marta y él (ellos) beb**en** jugo de uva.
  Marta y ella (ellas) escuch**an** música.

7 Imagine that these students are talking about activities they usually do or activities they are planning to do. Choose the correct verb form to complete each of the following sentences.

a. Mis amigos y yo *(dibujamos / dibujan)* en el parque.

b. ¡No me digas! Pablo y ella *(practican / practicamos)* deportes también.

c. Esteban y tú *(hablan / hablamos)* por teléfono todos los días, ¿verdad?

d. Juan va a cocinar hoy. Él y yo siempre *(ayudan / ayudamos)* en casa.

e. Él y ella *(comemos / comen)* en casa los fines de semana.

f. Tú y yo *(deben / debemos)* ir de compras mañana por la mañana.

g. ¡Qué lástima! Patricia y yo no *(vamos / van)* a ir de pesca en el verano.

h. Elena nunca lee, pero mis amigos y yo *(leen / leemos)* todos los días.

i. José y mis amigas siempre *(hablamos / hablan)* después de las clases.

j. No veo la tele por la tarde, pero Juanita y tú *(ves / ven)* la tele todos los días por la tarde.

Ahora lo sabes

Can you:

■ tell that you like or don't like certain food groups?

—(No) _____ las frutas.

■ describe groups of people or things?

—Los huevos son ___, pero las verduras son ___.

■ say what you eat or drink at different meals?

—A ver . . . En el desayuno (nosotros) ___ cereal y ___ jugo de naranja.

■ make clear to or about whom you are talking when more than one person is referred to?

—Timoteo y tú ___ la televisión todos los días, ¿verdad?

TODO JUNTO

Para decir más

Here is some additional vocabulary that you might find useful for activities in this section.

la pera
pear

el durazno
peach

el tocino
bacon

los espaguetis
spaghetti

la mermelada
jam

la jalea
jelly

el helado
ice cream

el pastel
cake

el chocolate caliente
hot chocolate

la mantequilla de cacahuate
peanut butter

rico, -a
delicious

Actividades

Here's an opportunity for you to expand your use of Spanish by putting together the material you learned in this chapter with what you learned earlier.

1 People have different tastes in food. Tell your partner your opinion of different foods and drinks. He or she will agree or disagree.

A —*Las ensaladas son muy sabrosas. A mí me encantan.*

B —*¿Te encantan? Pues, a mí no me gustan nada. ¡Qué asco!*
o: *¡No me digas! A mí también me gustan las ensaladas.*

2 On the weekend our pattern of eating often changes. Find out what your partner's meals are usually like on the weekend. Ask:

- at what time he or she eats certain meals
- whether he or she eats alone or with family or friends
- what the meal usually consists of

Una paella típica de España

3 With a partner, talk about what you plan to eat. Include the following, but keep your conversation going as long as you can:

- Find out if your partner is hungry.
- Your partner answers affirmatively.
- Ask what he or she wants / prefers / would like to eat.
- Your partner answers.

¡amos a leer!

Antes de leer

STRATEGY ➤ Using prior knowledge

What you are about to read tells the history of chocolate, which was used by the Mayas and the Aztecs of Mexico over a thousand years ago. And they used it in a very different way! How do you think chocolate got to Europe and why did Europeans use it differently?

As you already know, you can use pictures and your own experience with certain kinds of reading materials to predict and understand the information you might find there.

Mira la lectura

STRATEGY ➤ Using cognates

As you read, try to use cognates (words that are similar to English words) to help you figure out the meaning.

1 What are some of the other products that the Europeans found when they came to America?

2 When did chocolate become one of the most popular drinks in Europe?

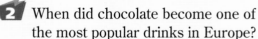

En el siglo XV los conquistadores llegan a América. Allí descubren muchos productos nuevos para la comida española y europea, por ejemplo: la papa, el tomate y el cacao. El cacao es uno de los ingredientes que los aztecas usan para hacer el *tchocolatl* (palabra azteca para chocolate).

Los aztecas preparan el *tchocolatl* con cacao, verduras y varios tipos de chiles. Es una bebida muy fuerte que los indios beben en sus ceremonias religiosas. Pero el *tchocolatl* azteca es muy diferente del chocolate que bebemos hoy.

En Europa, el *tchocolatl* se transforma en una bebida más líquida y más dulce. En los siglos XVI y XVII el chocolate es una de las bebidas más populares de Europa. El chocolate caliente se hace con cacao y agua o leche. Hoy, en España, hay chocolaterías, lugares donde sirven chocolate casi exclusivamente.

Infórmate

 STRATEGY ➤ Using context to get meaning

Using context to get meaning is another useful strategy. When you are reading and you run across a word you don't understand, look at the other words in the sentence. See if knowing those words can help you understand the one you don't know.

Read this selection again. Make a list of five words you don't understand. Then try to guess their meaning by looking at the surrounding words.

1 How and when was chocolate introduced in Europe?

2 How did the Aztecs prepare their *tchocolatl?* Was it an everyday drink or was it used on special occasions? Explain.

3 How was the chocolate the conquistadores brought to Europe different from the Aztecan *tchocolatl?*

Aplicación

List as many cognates as you can that you found in this reading.

¡**V**amos a escribir!

Your health class is studying nutrition and the teacher wants you to think about what, when, and where you eat. Write a short paragraph about your favorite meal of the day. Follow these steps.

1 Answer these questions, then use the answers to write your paragraph.
- ¿A qué hora comes tu comida favorita?
- ¿Dónde comes: en la casa, en la escuela o en un restaurante?
- ¿Con quién comes?
- ¿Qué comes y qué bebes?

2 Show your paragraph to a partner. Does he or she have any ideas to suggest? Did you use the answers to all the questions in your paragraph? Think about any changes you may want to make, then write a second draft.

3 Check for correct spelling and punctuation. Did you use the *yo* form of the verbs? Did you use *me gusta(n)* or *me encanta(n)*? Does your partner have any further suggestions?

Write your final draft. Add the corrected paragraph to your writing portfolio.

grasa *(fat)*
azúcar *(sugar)*

CRISPITOS

¿Lo sabes bien?

This section will help you organize your studying for the proficiency test, where you will be asked to do similar, though not identical, tasks. There will not be any models on the test.

Listening

Can you understand when people talk about food? Listen as your teacher reads you a sample similar to what you will hear on the test. Which meal is Eugenio talking about?

Reading

Can you quickly read through this ad and use the context to guess any word or words that you might not know? Who is this product recommended for and why?

La crema de cacao es un alimento especialmente indicado para adolescentes con una gran energía. Es un alimento nutritivo, ideal para la merienda.

Writing

Can you write the order for the customers you are waiting on? Here is a sample:

Cuenta

| CAMARERO | MESA | CLIENTES | NÚMERO DE CUENTA |
| | | | 14543 |

una hamburguesa
un sandwich de jamón

dos papas fritas

dos refrescos

IMPUESTO
TOTAL

Cuenta 210

Speaking

Can you discuss your food preferences with a partner? Do you like or dislike the same foods? For example:

A — *¿Te gusta el pescado?*
B — *No me gusta nada. ¿Y a ti?*
A — *No mucho. Mi madre siempre cocina pescado los viernes. Es horrible. ¿Te gustan las zanahorias?*
B — *Sí, pero prefiero las papas o las judías verdes. No me gustan nada las cebollas. ¡Qué asco!*
A — *Pues, a mí me encantan las cebollas. Son muy sabrosas.*

Culture

Can you describe the four meals that are typical of many Spanish-speaking countries?

"Me encantan los refrescos."

Resumen del capítulo 4

Use the vocabulary from this chapter to help you:

- describe what you like and don't like to eat and drink
- tell when you have meals
- say whether you are hungry or thirsty

to indicate hunger or thirst
tener hambre / sed

to describe meals
beber: (yo) bebo
      (tú) bebes
comer: (yo) como
      (tú) comes
la cena
la comida
el desayuno
en el desayuno / el almuerzo /
  la cena

to talk about foods
el arroz
el bistec
el cereal
la ensalada
las frutas
  la manzana
  la naranja
  el plátano
  la uva
la hamburguesa
el huevo
el jamón
el pan
  el pan tostado
la papa
  las papas al horno
  las papas fritas
el pescado
el pollo

el queso
los sandwiches
  el sandwich de
  jamón y queso
la sopa de pollo / de tomate /
  de verduras
las verduras
  la cebolla
  los guisantes
  las judías verdes
  la lechuga
  el tomate
  la zanahoria

to talk about drinks
las bebidas
  el agua *(f.)*
  el café
  el jugo de naranja
  la leche
  la limonada
  el refresco
  el té
  el té helado

to describe foods
bueno, -a (para la salud)
horrible
malo, -a (para la salud)
sabroso, -a

to express likes or preferences
más o menos
me encanta(n)

me gusta(n)
preferir: (yo) prefiero
      (tú) prefieres

to express an opinion
Creo que sí / no.
¡Qué asco!

to ask for an explanation
¿Por qué?

to give an explanation
porque

to elicit agreement
¿verdad?

to refer to obligation
deber: (yo) debo
      (tú) debes

to indicate frequency
nunca
siempre

to refer to something you cannot name
algo

other useful words
son
unos, unas

CAPÍTULO 5

¿Cómo es tu familia?

OBJECTIVES

At the end of this chapter, you will be able to:

- describe family members and friends
- tell what someone's age is
- say what other people like and do not like to do
- explain how names are formed in Spanish-speaking countries

Una familia mexicana

¡Piénsalo bien!

Look at the two photos and compare the families to your own. How many people are in your family? Which family members do you think make up a family? Do you consider your grandparents, uncles, aunts, and cousins as your "family" or are they just "relatives"? Do you all get together sometimes?

"Aquí estoy con mis primos. Siempre voy a nadar con ellos."

En la República Dominicana

"Me llamo Maricarmen y estoy con mi familia para celebrar el cumpleaños de mi abuelo. Tiene 67 años."

Who did you think the "abuelo" is? How did you know?

Una familia en Santiago, Chile

Vocabulario para conversar

¿Cómo se llama tu hermano?

Here are some new words and expressions you will need to talk about your family, to tell what someone's age is, and to say what other people like and do not like to do. Read them several times, then turn the page and practice with a partner.

mis abuelos

mi abuelo
Pedro, 80 años

mi abuela
Carmen, 75 años

mis padres

mis tíos

mi madre
María, 46 años

mi padre
Luis, 52 años

mi tía
Verónica, 50 años

mi tío
Tomás, 48 años

mis hermanos*

mis primos

mi hermano
José, 19 años

mi hermana
Gabriela, 23 años

yo
Mariana, 15 años

mi primo
Carlos, 16 años

mi prima
Ana, 18 años

* *Hermanos* can mean either "brothers" or "brothers and sisters."

60 sesenta
61 sesenta y uno . . .
70 setenta
71 setenta y uno . . .
80 ochenta
81 ochenta y uno . . .
90 noventa
91 noventa y uno . . .
100 cien

También necesitas . . .

el hijo / la hija	*son / daughter*
el hijo único / la hija única	*only child (m.) / only child (f.)*
¿Cómo se llama?	*What is his / her name?*
¿Cómo se llaman?	*What are their names?*
Se llama(n) ___.	*His / her (their) name(s) is (are) ___.*
¿Cuántos años tiene ___?	*How old is ___?*
Tiene ___ años.	*He / she is ___ years old.*
su	*his, her*
de	*of*
(A + *person*) le gusta(n) / le encanta(n) ___.	*(He / she) likes / loves ___.*
¿Cuántos, -as?	*How many?*
sólo	*only*

> **¿Y qué quiere decir . . . ?**
> los hijos

Empecemos a conversar

With a partner, take turns being *Estudiante A* and *Estudiante B.* Use the words that are cued or given in the balloons to replace the underlined sections in the model. 💡 means you can make your own choices.

For Exercises 1 and 2, refer to the family tree on page 154.

1 la tía
　　　A —*¿Cómo se llama la tía de Mariana?*
　　　B —*Se llama Verónica.*

　　　　　Y ahora Uds.

Estudiante A　　　　　　　　　　　Estudiante B

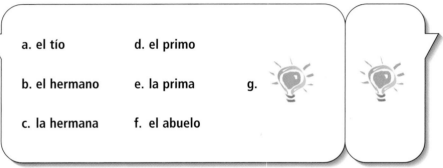

a. el tío　　　　d. el primo

b. el hermano　　e. la prima　　g. 💡

c. la hermana　　f. el abuelo

2 José
　　　A —*¿Cuántos años tiene José?*
　　　B —*Tiene diecinueve años.*

　　　　　Y ahora Uds.

Estudiante A　　　　　　　　　　　Estudiante B

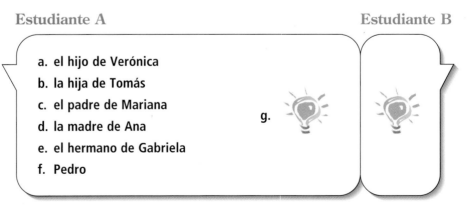

a. el hijo de Verónica
b. la hija de Tomás
c. el padre de Mariana　　g. 💡
d. la madre de Ana
e. el hermano de Gabriela
f. Pedro

In Exercises 3 and 4, ask each other about your own family
members or create ideal families to talk about.

3 A —*¿Tienes hermanos?*
  B —*Sí, tengo un hermano y una hermana.*
    o: No, no tengo hermanos.
    o: No, no tengo. Soy hijo(a) único(a).
  A —*¿Cómo se llama(n)?*
  B —*Mi hermano se llama Daniel y mi hermana se llama Laura.*

  Y ahora Uds.

Estudiante A   **Estudiante B**

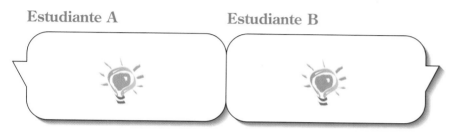

4 A —*¿Qué le gusta hacer a tu primo?*
  B —*Le gusta dibujar.*
    o: Le encanta dibujar.

  Y ahora Uds.

Estudiante A   **Estudiante B**

Empecemos a escribir

Write your answers in Spanish.

5 Mention at least three interests you share
  with other family members. For example:
  *A mi hermana le gusta practicar
  deportes. A mí también.*

6 Give the name and age of your favorite
  relatives: *Mi tía favorita se llama Gloria.
  Tiene cuarenta años (más o menos).*

7 ¿Eres hijo(a) único(a)?

8 ¿Cuántos primos tienes?

Vocabulario para conversar

¿Cómo es tu abuelo?

Here's the rest of the vocabulary you will need to describe family members and friends.

el hombre
Juan

el pelo castaño

la mujer
Gloria

el pelo rubio

el muchacho
Marcos

la muchacha
Adela

baja

alto

pelirrojos

bonito

feo

el perro

los gemelos
Paco y Pepe

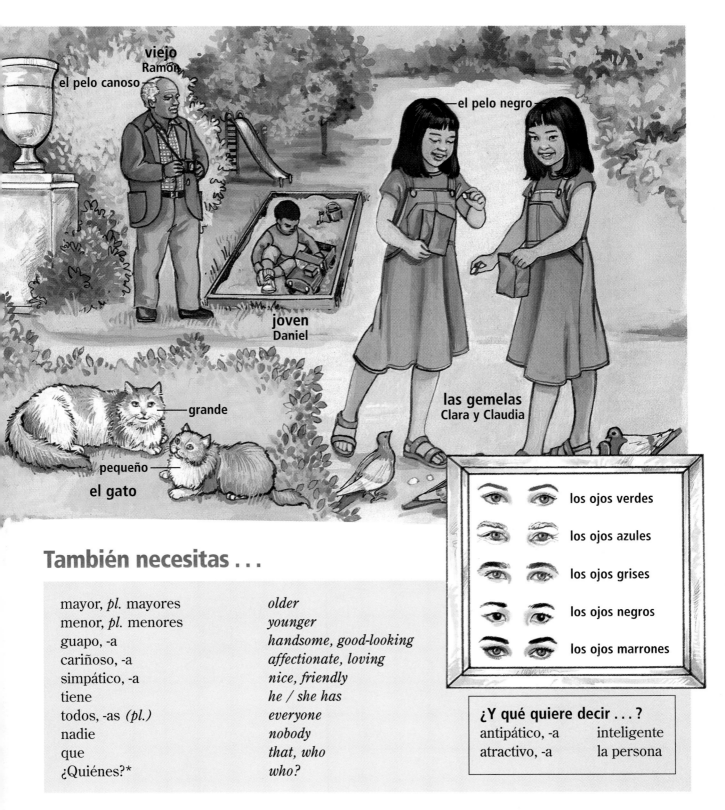

viejo
Ramón

el pelo canoso

el pelo negro

joven
Daniel

grande

pequeño

el gato

las gemelas
Clara y Claudia

los ojos verdes

los ojos azules

los ojos grises

los ojos negros

los ojos marrones

También necesitas . . .

mayor, *pl.* mayores	*older*
menor, *pl.* menores	*younger*
guapo, -a	*handsome, good-looking*
cariñoso, -a	*affectionate, loving*
simpático, -a	*nice, friendly*
tiene	*he / she has*
todos, -as *(pl.)*	*everyone*
nadie	*nobody*
que	*that, who*
¿Quiénes?*	*who?*

¿Y qué quiere decir . . . ?

antipático, -a	inteligente
atractivo, -a	la persona

* We usually use *¿Quiénes?* instead of *¿Quién?* if we know or expect that the answer will be more than one person.

Empecemos a conversar

For Exercise 9, refer to the pictures on pp. 158–159.

9

A —*¿Cómo se llama <u>el hombre que tiene</u>*
<u>el pelo castaño?</u>

B —*Se llama <u>Juan.</u>*

Y ahora Uds.

Estudiante A   **Estudiante B**

a.   b.   c.   d.

10

A —*En la clase, ¿quién <u>tiene ojos verdes</u>?*

B —*<u>Diana y Jeff.</u>*
   o: *Todos.*
   o: *Nadie.*

Y ahora Uds.

Estudiante A   **Estudiante B**

a.   b.

11

gemelos

A —¿Hay *gemelos en la clase?*
B —*Sí, James y John.*
   o: *No, no hay.*

Y ahora Uds.

Estudiante A

a. personas altas
b. personas rubias
c.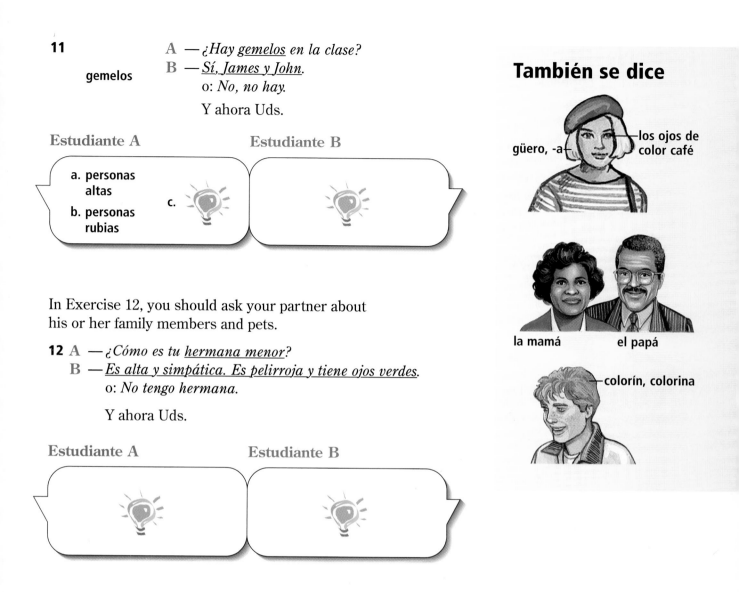

Estudiante B

También se dice

güero, -a
los ojos de color café

la mamá   el papá

colorín, colorina

In Exercise 12, you should ask your partner about his or her family members and pets.

12 A —¿*Cómo es tu hermana menor?*
B —*Es alta y simpática. Es pelirroja y tiene ojos verdes.*
   o: *No tengo hermana.*

Y ahora Uds.

Estudiante A

Estudiante B

Empecemos a escribir y a leer

Write your answers in Spanish.

13 You are going to the airport to meet someone you haven't seen before. How would you describe yourself to that person?

14 Now describe your best friend.

15 On a separate piece of paper, write *sí* or *no* in response to the statements about the following paragraph.

¡Hola! Me llamo Cristina. Soy la hermana mayor. Tengo pelo castaño y ojos marrones. Tengo dos hermanas gemelas. Son altas y tienen ojos verdes.

a. Cristina es hija única.
b. Ella es la hermana mayor.
c. Cristina tiene ojos verdes.
d. En la familia de Cristina hay gemelas.

¡Comuniquemos!

Here's another opportunity for you to use the vocabulary you've just learned.

1 These pictures of members of the football team are for the school yearbook. Before you can write the captions, you must identify the people in the pictures. Call the coach for help. Take turns with your partner playing the roles of the yearbook writer (A) and the coach (B).

Raja Patel

A — *¿Cómo es Raja Patel?*
B — *Tiene ojos negros y pelo negro.*
A — *¡Ah! Raja es el número sesenta y tres.*

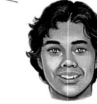

a. George King   **b. Juan Enríquez**   **c. John Green**

d. Hal Jensen   **e. Sean Morrow**   **f. Felipe del Castillo**   **g. Matt Brown**

2 Choose either the cat or the dog and describe him to your partner. To make sure your partner is listening, make two or three untrue statements. Your partner will correct you. Then your partner will describe the other animal to you. For example:

Se llama . . .   (No) es . . .   (No) le gusta . . .   Tiene . . .

Chispa

Michi

3 An exchange student from Ecuador is going to spend the next year with your family. Describe his or her family to your partner.

¿Qué sabes ahora?

Can you:

■ **describe what members of your family look like?**

—¿Es pelirrojo tu hermano mayor?

—No, tiene pelo ___ y ojos ___ .

■ **describe the personalities of family members?**

—Mi abuela es ___ y ___ .

■ **tell how old people in your family are?**

—Mi primo ___ años.

■ **tell what members of your family like to do?**

—A mi tía ___ gusta ___ .

Perspectiva cultural

Look at the names on the wedding invitation and the passport. In what ways do the names resemble or not resemble those you are used to? Can you identify the last names?

In Spanish-speaking countries a person's full name consists of a first name *(nombre)*, a middle name, and two surnames—the father's family name *(apellido paterno)* followed by the mother's family name *(apellido materno)*.Take, for example, the bride's mother's name on the wedding invitation:

> María Luisa González Prado de Enciso

González is her *apellido paterno.* Prado is her *apellido materno.* Enciso is her husband's last name. Now look at her husband's name. What are his *apellido paterno* and *apellido materno?*

Although a person's full name is used on all official documents, such as birth certificates, school records, passports, and identification cards, in daily life they usually use only one first name and one last name, most often the father's.

When a woman marries, she may keep her full name unchanged, or she may add her husband's last name to her own. For example, Gloria Luisa Enciso González may add *de* and her husband's last name, Ayala. Her *nombre completo* will then be Gloria Luisa Enciso González de Ayala. You would address her either as Señora Ayala or Señora Enciso de Ayala. But she would never be called Señora <u>Hugo</u> Ayala. Her children's last names will be Ayala Enciso.

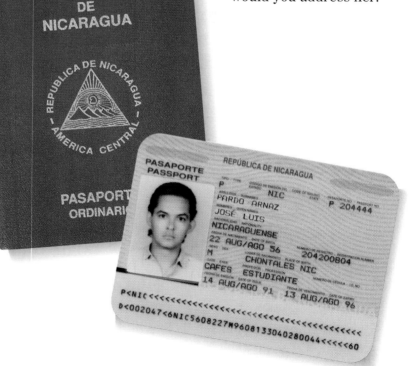

La cultura desde tu perspectiva

1 Explain how names in Spanish-speaking countries are different from names in the United States. Based on the Spanish naming convention, what would your *nombre completo* be? Your father's? Your mother's?

2 You need to telephone *Ana Cristina Padilla Sánchez de Irujo.* Under what letter would you look in the phone book? When she answers the phone, how would you address her?

En Pátzcuaro, México

Una boda en
Xochimilco, México

El Sr. Roberto Manuel Enciso Cuevas

y

la Sra. María Luisa González Prado de Enciso

El Sr. Antonio Miguel Ayala Arévalo

y

la Sra. Ana Clara Pérez Soler de Ayala

invitan cordialmente a la celebración del matrimonio de sus hijos

Gloria Luisa   y   Hugo Eduardo

Gramática en contexto

Look at this page from a Mexican magazine article about TV star Sara Sánchez. Now read the captions.

Sarita es muy seria y trabajadora. A veces es graciosa y perezosa, dice la madre de Sara, la señora María Sánchez.

Sara Sánchez, estrella de telenovelas mexicanas: Me gusta la comida de mi mamá. Sus enchiladas son deliciosas.

Tiene 24 años y hoy está en la casa de su madre: Me gusta estar aquí con mi mamá. Somos madre e hija, pero también somos muy buenas amigas.

A Sara's age is one fact that is given in the captions. How old is she? Look at the verb in the expression that tells her age. What is the difference between expressing age in English and in Spanish?

B You already know the verb forms *soy, eres, es,* and *son.* They are all forms of the verb *ser.* Using what you know about verb endings, read the captions and find the form of *ser* that we use with *nosotros.*

C Find the expression that tells about Sara's mother's cooking *(comida)*. Find two other places where an expression with *de* is used. What explanation can you give for this use of *de*?

El verbo *tener*

The verb *tener*, "to have," follows the pattern of other *-er* verbs. However, some forms of this verb are irregular. Here are all of its present-tense forms.

(yo)	**tengo**	(nosotros) (nosotras)	**tenemos**
(tú)	**tienes**	(vosotros) (vosotras)	**tenéis**
Ud. (él) (ella)	**tiene**	Uds. (ellos) (ellas)	**tienen**

You have already seen some of these verb forms. In what ways is *tener* irregular?

• As you know, *tener* is sometimes used where in English we use a form of the verb "to be": *tener sed / hambre / años.*

1 A class is getting ready to start a project. Several students have gathered the supplies they need. Find out who has them and how many they have.

carpetas
de argollas

A —*¿Quién tiene las carpetas de argollas?*
B —*Miguel.*
A —*¿Cuántas carpetas de argollas tiene?*
B —*Cuatro.*

a. marcadores
b. reglas
c. diccionarios
d. cuadernos
e. lápices
f. carpetas
g. bolígrafos

Miguel (4) Marcos, Yo (16) Carlos, Jorge (14) Victoria (6) Yo (3) Pilar, Sofía (8) Anita (10) Andrés (5)

2 Find out the ages and the number of family members of different students in your class. On a sheet of paper, copy the table below. As you ask students the questions, write their names and the information you receive. While talking to them, observe their hair and eye color and write this information in the appropriate columns.

A — *¿Cuántos años tienes?*
B — *Tengo 15 años.*
A — *¿Cuántos primos tienes?*
B — *Tengo nueve primos.*
    o: *No tengo primos.*

Estudiante	Años	Familia	Ojos	Pelo
Daniel	15	9 primos	azules	rubio

3 Using the information from Exercise 2, compare yourself with your classmates. Write as many statements as you can about similarities in age, number of family members, and appearance. Then report to the class.

Daniel y yo tenemos 15 años.
Tenemos el pelo rubio.

El verbo *ser*

The verb *ser*, "to be," is also an irregular verb. We use *ser* with adjectives to tell what someone or something is like.

- You already know some forms of *ser*. Here are all of its present-tense forms.

(yo)	**soy**	(nosotros) (nosotras)	**somos**
(tú)	**eres**	(vosotros) (vosotras)	**sois**
Ud. (él) (ella)	**es**	Uds. (ellos) (ellas)	**son**

¡NO OLVIDES!

Remember that adjectives agree in gender and number with the nouns they describe.

4  In each of these groups, two persons are alike in some way and the third is different. Describe their similarities and differences.

Ángela y Mónica son graciosas, pero Gregorio es serio.

Ángela y Mónica / Gregorio

a. José / Miguel y tú

b. Carolina / Luisa y yo

c. Juanito y David / tú

d. Barrabás / Turquesa y Condesa

e. Claudia y Marisol / yo

f. Jorge / Samuel y yo

g. Coqui / Napoleón y Sultán

5 Think of pairs of people in your class who are alike in at least one way. Your partner should tell you how these two classmates are alike. You may want to use the list on the right to help you.

A — *¿Cómo son Pablo y Pedro?*
B — *Son altos.*

Now ask your partner in what way you and various classmates are alike or different.

A — *¿Cómo somos Ignacio y yo?*
B — *Uds. son trabajadores.*
    o: *Ignacio es trabajador, pero tú eres perezoso.*

alto, -a	impaciente
amable	inteligente
artístico, -a	joven
atrevido, -a	ordenado, -a
bajo, -a	paciente
bonito, -a	perezoso, -a
callado, -a	prudente
cariñoso, -a	serio, -a
deportista	simpático, -a
desordenado, -a	sociable
generoso, -a	tacaño, -a
gracioso, -a	trabajador, -a
guapo, -a	viejo, -a

Los adjetivos posesivos

To tell what belongs to someone or to show relationships, we use *de* + noun. For example:

Tengo el cuaderno **de** Felipe.
La hermana **de** María es amable.

• Another way to tell what belongs to someone and to show relationships is to use possessive adjectives. You already know some of them.

mi hermano	**mis** hermanos
tu abuela	**tus** abuelas
su hijo	**sus** hijos

• The possessive adjective must be singular if the noun is singular and plural if the noun is plural.

Mi prima es alta.   Todas mi**s** prima**s** son alta**s**.

— ¿Son rubios los hermanos de Rafael?
— No, su**s** herman**os** son pelirroj**os**.

6 Using the family tree on page 154, make three true and false statements about Mariana's family to your partner. Your partner will look at the family tree and answer *sí* if a statement is correct. If a statement is incorrect, your partner will answer *no* and correct it.

A —*La hermana de Mariana tiene 23 años.*
B —*Sí, su hermana tiene 23 años.*
A —*Los abuelos de Mariana se llaman Pedro y Carolina.*
B —*No, sus abuelos se llaman Pedro y Carmen.*

7 Work in groups of three. Each of two students will choose three classroom items that they can "lose" for a moment. These students will turn their backs while their partner puts these objects out of sight. Then, when they turn around, one of them should ask where their things are.

A —*¿Dónde está mi carpeta?*
B —*¿Tu carpeta? Aquí está.*
A —*¿Dónde están sus libros?*
  o: *¿Dónde están los libros de Antonio?*
B —*¿Sus libros? Aquí están.*

Ahora lo sabes

Can you:

■ **tell what someone has?**

—Tomás y Mariana ___ doce libros.

■ **tell what a person's age is?**

—El abuelo de Celeste ___ 74 años.

■ **tell what someone or something is like?**

—Mi hermano ___ guapo.

■ **tell what belongs to someone or show relationships?**

—¿Dónde está el cuaderno ___ Luis?

—___ cuaderno está aquí.

El virrey José de Iturrigaray y su familia
(alrededor de 1805), (anónimo)

Para decir más

Here is some additional vocabulary that you might find useful for activities in this section.

el esposo, la esposa
husband, wife

el nieto, la nieta
grandson, granddaughter

**el hermanastro,
la hermanastra**
stepbrother, stepsister

el padrastro, la madrastra
stepfather, stepmother

el padrino, la madrina
godfather, godmother

calvo, -a
bald

largo, -a
long (hair)

corto, -a
short (hair)

las pecas
freckles

las trenzas
braids

Actividades

Here's an opportunity for you to expand your use of Spanish by putting together the material you learned in this chapter with what you learned earlier.

1 Write a brief description of your ideal family, including the number of grandparents, parents, aunts and uncles, cousins, and brothers and sisters that you have. Do not include their names.

¡NO OLVIDES!

Remember that *tú* with an accent means "you." *Tu* without an accent means "your."

Tengo dos abuelos y dos padres. También tengo tres tíos. Tengo una hermana.

Exchange papers with your partner. Find out about the members of your partner's ideal family by asking about their names, ages, and appearance or personalities. Write down the information you receive.

A —*¿Cómo se llaman tus abuelos?*
B —*Mi abuelo se llama Frank y mi abuela se llama Dorothy.*
A —*¿Cuántos años tienen?*
B —*Mi abuelo tiene 63 años y mi abuela tiene 59 años.*
A —*¿Cómo son?*
B —*Mi abuelo es muy alto y mi abuela también es alta. Él tiene pelo rubio y ojos azules, y ella es pelirroja y tiene ojos marrones. Mis abuelos son muy cariñosos.*

2 Report to your teacher the information you found out about your partner's ideal family.

Andrew tiene dos abuelos. Su abuelo se llama Frank. Tiene 63 años, es muy alto, es rubio y tiene ojos azules. Su abuela se llama Dorothy. Tiene 59 años, es alta, pelirroja y tiene ojos marrones. Sus abuelos son cariñosos.

Una familia a la hora de la cena en Santiago, Chile

Unos padres mexicanos

Unos abuelos en Madrid

3 Work in pairs to talk about each other's class schedules.

Write down the information you receive in order to report it later.

A —*¿Tienes matemáticas?*
B —*Sí, tengo. Empieza a las nueve y media y termina a las diez y media.*

A —*¿Cómo se llama tu profesora?*
B —*Mi profesora es la señora Pereda.*
A —*¿Y te gusta la clase?*
B —*Sí, me encanta.*

4 Now you and your partner should work with another pair of students. Take turns reporting to the other pair what you two found out. After each statement you make, a member of the other pair should tell how the information is similar to or different from his or her schedule. Keep the conversation flowing as long as you can.

A —*Alice tiene matemáticas a las doce y cuarto.*
B —*Yo también.*
    o: *Yo no. Tengo matemáticas a las nueve y media.*

A —*Su profesora de matemáticas es la señora Rodríguez.*
B —*Mi profesora de matemáticas es la señora Rodríguez también.*

¡Vamos a leer!

Antes de leer

STRATEGY ➤ Using prior knowledge

What are some important considerations when choosing a family pet? What kinds of information would you hope to find in an article offering advice about pet choices?

Mira la lectura

STRATEGY ➤ Using titles and context clues for meaning

1 Does the title give a good idea about the subject of the article?

2 Look at the listings in the column entitled *mascota*. How many animals are considered here?

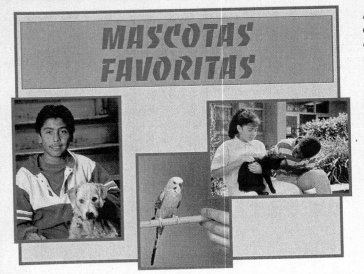

MI PRIMERA MASCOTA

MASCOTAS FAVORITAS

A los niños les gusta casi cualquier animal. Sin embargo, algunos animales no son recomendables para ellos. Es conveniente que los padres escojan una mascota de acuerdo a la edad de sus hijos. Los niños de entre cinco y diez años pueden tener un perro, por ejemplo, un pastor alemán, un dálmata o un collie. También pueden escoger otras clases de mascotas: gatos, conejos, periquitos, peces, tortugas, hámsters (ratoncillos domésticos), etc. Cuando escojan una mascota deben tener en consideración los siguientes aspectos: la longevidad, los cuidados y la alimentación.

Mascota	Gatos	Perros	Hámsters	Periquitos
Longevidad	15 años	15 años	2 años	5 años
Cuidados	Agua y comida todos los días. Vitaminas. Bañarlo con agua tibia una vez al mes.	Agua y comida todos los días. Vitaminas. Collar para pulgas. Bañarlo una vez a la semana.	Agua y comida especial todos los días. Limpiar la jaula cada cinco días.	Agua y comida todos los días. Lechuga, plátano y semillas. Limpiar la jaula una vez por semana.

Infórmate

STRATEGY ➤ Scanning

Column and row headings identify the main categories. We can scan the entries relating to them for the specific information we need.

Scanning, or reading for specific information, is useful because charts and tables offer an efficient way to condense information in order to make quick comparisons.

1 Scan the long paragraph and find the age range of children for whom these pets are recommended. Using what you know about cognates, can you identify the names of some of the dog breeds? From what you know, do you agree that these are good pets for children in this age range?

2 Turning to the table, scan the information in the row entitled *Longevidad*. Do you know an English equivalent for *longevidad*? Does this information correspond to your own experience with pets? What do you think the row next to *Cuidados* is about?

Dos hermanas con armadillos en Taxco, México

Aplicación

The recommendations given below are described in the table as necessary for the care of *los perros.* Can you figure out what these recommendations are? To which of these family members would you assign each of the first two tasks: *hijo mayor (10 años), hija menor (5 años), los padres?*

- bañarlo una vez a la semana
- comida y agua todos los días
- collar para pulgas
- vitaminas

¡ amos a escribir!

You have a new pen pal and you want to tell your new friend about your family. Write a letter about your family in which you are going to include 3 to 5 photos or drawings. Follow these steps.

1 Think about how you would describe the people in your photos or drawings: Who are they? What do they look like? What type of personality do they have? List your answers under each of these categories. Number your pictures so that you can refer to them easily.

2 Write a first draft of your letter describing three or four people in your family as completely as you can.

Un abuelo con su nieta en Madrid

Hola, _____:

Las fotos que ves son de mi familia. En la foto #1 están mi hermana y mi mamá. Mi hermana se llama _____.

Es _____ y _____.

Saludos,

_____

Una familia en México

Show your letter to a partner and ask if he or she would make any changes. Do you give enough information about each person? Think about any changes your partner suggests as well as others you may want to make. Then rewrite your letter.

 Check for accuracy in spelling, accents, and punctuation. Did you use the correct forms of the adjectives? Does your partner have any further suggestions?

Make a clean copy of your letter and attach the pictures. Add the letter to your writing portfolio. You may send it to a "pen pal" in another Spanish class in your school.

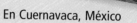
En Cuernavaca, México

Con su mascota favorita

Hermanas en Guatemala

¿Lo sabes bien?

This section will help you organize your studying for the proficiency test, where you will be asked to do similar, though not identical, tasks. There will not be any models on the test.

Listening

Can you understand when someone describes family members and friends? Listen as your teacher reads you a sample similar to what you will hear on the test. What color is Enrique's hair? Does any other member of his family have the same color hair?

Culture

What version of her name would Ana Carmen most likely use to introduce herself to a new friend?

Reading

Can you quickly glance through this chart and get an idea of its content? Now look at the information under the column entitled *Color de ojos*. What is the dominant color of eyes? Is there any common color of eyes missing?

Nombre	Edad	Color de pelo	Color de ojos
Rosalba	19	castaño	marrones
José Miguel	18	pelirrojo	verdes
Carlos	21	castaño	verdes
Maribel	19	rubio	azules

Writing

Can you write an ad for actors for a school play? Here is a sample:

Necesito una mujer
50-60 años
alta
pelo canoso
———
para representar
a la madre

Speaking

Can you talk with a partner about your families? For example:

A — *Tengo tres hermanos mayores. ¿Y tú?*

B — *Yo tengo una hermana mayor y una hermana menor. Mariana tiene dieciocho años y Roxana cinco.*

A — *Mis hermanos se llaman Roberto, Ramiro y Rafael. Todos son muy deportistas.*

B — *Mis hermanas son pelirrojas y tienen ojos verdes. Son muy simpáticas.*

Resumen del capítulo 5

Use the vocabulary from this chapter to help you:

- describe family members and friends
- tell what someone's age is
- say what other people like and do not like to do

to talk about family members

los abuelos: el abuelo,
          la abuela
los hermanos: el hermano,
          la hermana
los hijos: el hijo,
          la hija
los padres: el padre,
          la madre
los primos: el primo,
          la prima
los tíos: el tío,
          la tía
el hijo único, la hija única
los gemelos, las gemelas

to tell someone's name

¿Cómo se llama(n) ___?
Se llama(n) ___.

to ask and tell how old someone is

¿Cuántos años tiene ___?
Tiene ___ años.
sesenta (sesenta y uno ...)
setenta (setenta y uno ...)
ochenta (ochenta y uno ...)
noventa (noventa y uno ...)
cien

to talk about people

el hombre
el muchacho, la muchacha
la mujer
la persona
¿Quiénes?

to describe people, animals, and things

alto, -a
antipático, -a
atractivo, -a
bajo, -a
bonito, -a
cariñoso, -a
feo, -a
grande
guapo, -a
inteligente
joven
mayor, *pl.* mayores
menor, *pl.* menores
pequeño, -a
simpático, -a
viejo, -a
ser + *adjective*
el pelo: canoso
          castaño
          negro
          rubio
pelirrojo, -a

los ojos: azules
          grises
          marrones
          negros
          verdes

to name animals

el gato
el perro

to indicate possession

de
su, sus
tener

to talk about what someone likes

(A + *person*) le gusta(n) / le encanta(n)

to indicate number

¿Cuántos, -as?
nadie
sólo
todos, -as

other useful word

que

CAPÍTULO 6

¿Qué desea Ud.?

OBJECTIVES

At the end of this chapter, you will be able to:

- describe the color, fit, and price of clothes
- ask about and buy clothes
- tell where and when you bought clothes and how much you paid for them
- compare where people shop for clothes in Spanish-speaking countries and in the United States

Un muchacho buscando ropa en Chichicastenango, Guatemala

¡Piénsalo bien!

Look at the photographs and read the captions.

"¡Qué bonito!"

En Buenos Aires

En la Ciudad de México

How do the stores in these pictures compare
with those in a mall that you know?

"¡Me encanta la ropa de esta tienda!"

"¿Cuándo vas a las zapaterías?"

En España

Vocabulario para conversar

¿Cuánto cuesta la camisa?

Here are some new words and expressions you will need to
talk about clothes and colors. Read them several times, then
turn the page and practice with a partner.

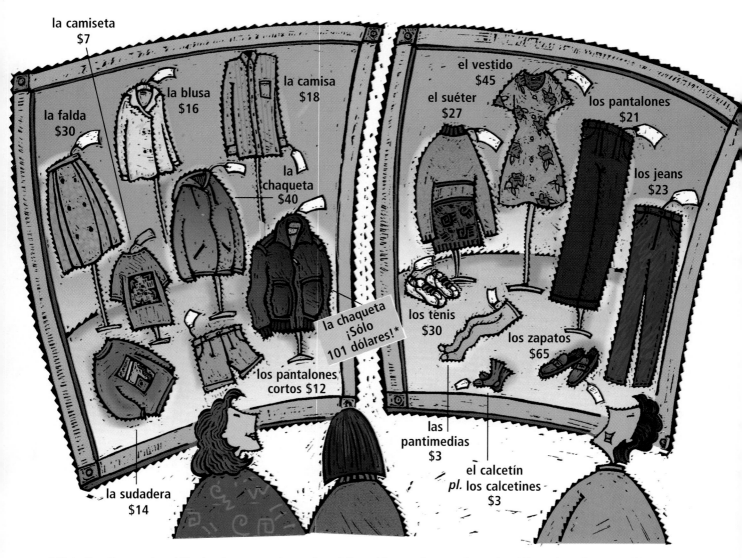

la camiseta
$7

la blusa
$16

la camisa
$18

la falda
$30

la chaqueta
$40

el vestido
$45

el suéter
$27

los pantalones
$21

los jeans
$23

la chaqueta
¡Sólo
101 dólares!*

los tenis
$30

los zapatos
$65

los pantalones
cortos $12

las
pantimedias
$3

el calcetín
pl. los calcetines
$3

la sudadera
$14

* Note that the number 100, *cien*, becomes *ciento* when followed by another number: *cien dólares,* but *ciento un dólares.*
  If followed by a feminine noun, we use *ciento una: ciento una camisas.*

Los colores

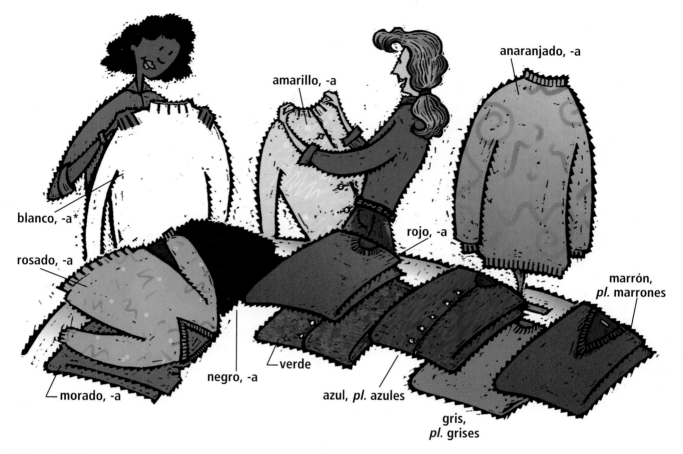

blanco, -a*

rosado, -a

morado, -a

amarillo, -a

negro, -a

verde

anaranjado, -a

rojo, -a

azul, *pl.* azules

gris, *pl.* grises

marrón, *pl.* marrones

También necesitas . . .

¿Cómo te queda(n)?	*How does it (do they) fit you?*	¿Cuánto?	*How much?*
		Cuesta(n) . . .	*It costs (They cost) . . .*
Me queda(n) bien.	*It fits (They fit) me well.*	¿Qué desea (Ud.)?	*May I help you?*
		el / la joven, *pl.*	*young man, sir, young lady;*
¿De qué color?	*What color?*	los jóvenes	pl. *young people*
buscar	*to look for*	perdón	*excuse me*
comprar	*to buy*		
llevar	*to wear*		
para mí / ti	*for me / you, to me / you*		
este, esta; ese, esa	*this; that*		
lo, la	*it*		
los, las	*them*		

> ### ¿Y qué quiere decir . . . ?
>
> el dólar

* When talking about individual colors, we use the masculine definite article: *Me gustan el rojo y el amarillo.*

Empecemos a conversar

With a partner, take turns being *Estudiante A* and *Estudiante B.* Use the words that are cued or given in the balloons to replace the underlined sections in the model. 💡 means you can make your own choices.

1
A — *Perdón, ¿cuánto cuesta(n) <u>la(s) camisa(s)</u>?*
B — *Cuesta(n) <u>veintidós</u> dólares.*
    Y ahora Uds.

Estudiante A   Estudiante B

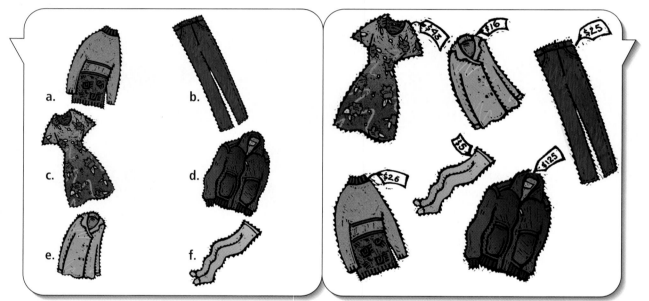

2
A — *¿Qué desea, señor (señora / joven / señorita)? ¿<u>Una camisa</u>?*
B — *Sí, busco <u>una camisa amarilla</u> para mí y <u>una camisa rosada</u> para mi hermana.*
    Y ahora Uds.

Estudiante A   Estudiante B

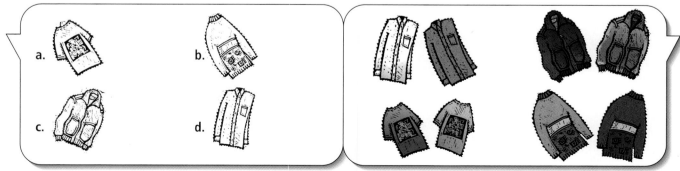

3

A —*Me encanta esa <u>camiseta</u> azul. ¿La tiene en amarillo?*
B —*¿Esta <u>camiseta</u>? Sí, aquí la tiene.*
   o: *No, no la tenemos en amarillo.*

   Y ahora Uds.

Estudiante A   **Estudiante B**

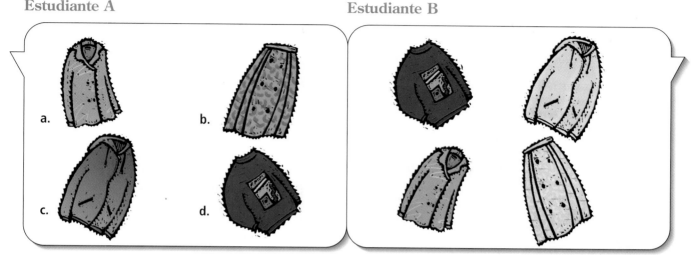

a.   b.   c.   d.

4

A —*¿Cómo te quedan <u>los zapatos</u>?*
B —*<u>Me quedan bien.</u> Los compro.*
   o: *No me quedan bien. Son muy grandes (pequeños).*

   Y ahora Uds.

Estudiante A   **Estudiante B**

a.   b.   c.   d.

Empecemos a escribir

Write your answers in Spanish.

5 The seasons affect how we dress. List a couple of clothing items you wear in each season of the year.

6 Choose three of the following items and say which colors you prefer for each one: *la chaqueta, los tenis, las pantimedias, la sudadera, los jeans, los pantalones cortos.*

7 ¿Qué ropa vas a llevar mañana?

8 ¿Qué colores te gustan más?

9 ¿Qué ropa compras para ti?

Unos jóvenes chilenos en la playa

Unos jóvenes en una plaza en México

Una zapatería en Madrid

En la Sierra Nevada en España

el jersey
la chompa

el vaquero

la pollera

la remera
la franela
la playera

la chamarra
la campera

el short

las medias

las zapatillas (deportivas)
los zapatos de tenis

de color café

Vocabulario para conversar

¿Cuánto pagaste por el suéter?

Here's the rest of the vocabulary you will need to talk about where and when you bought clothes.

el almacén

la tienda de ropa

la ropa

la tienda de descuentos

la zapatería

¡Gangas!

También necesitas . . .

la ganga	*bargain*	pagar:	*to pay:*
barato, -a	*inexpensive*	(yo) pagué	*I paid*
caro, -a	*expensive*	(tú) pagaste	*you paid*
nuevo, -a	*new*	por	*for*
¡Qué + *adjective!*	*How ___!*	estos, estas; esos, esas	*these; those*
comprar:	*to buy:*	otro, -a	*another, other*
(yo) compré	*I bought*	hace + *time expression*	*___ ago*
(tú) compraste	*you bought*	por aquí	*around here*

Empecemos a conversar

10

A — *¿Dónde compraste esos pantalones nuevos?*
B — *Los compré en el almacén Gómez y Caló.*

Y ahora Uds.

Gómez y Caló

Estudiante A   **Estudiante B**

El Calzado Elegante

La Casa de las Gangas

Loma Verde

Ramírez y Hermanos

a.   b.

c.   d.

11

A — *¿Cuánto pagaste por el suéter?*
B — *Pagué veintiséis dólares.*
A — *¡Qué caro!*
  o: *¡Qué barato!*

Y ahora Uds.

Estudiante A   **Estudiante B**

a.   b.

c.   d.

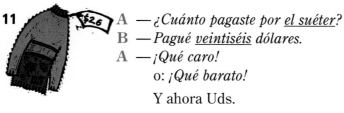

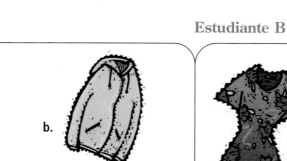

12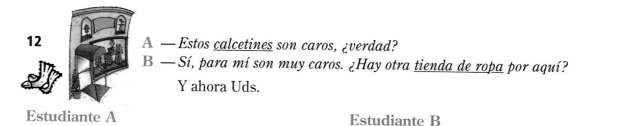

A — *Estos <u>calcetines</u> son caros, ¿verdad?*

B — *Sí, para mí son muy caros. ¿Hay otra <u>tienda de ropa</u> por aquí?*

Y ahora Uds.

Estudiante A

Estudiante B

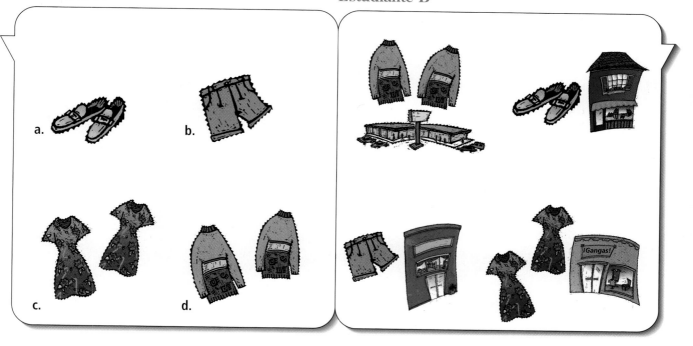

a.

b.

c.

d.

13

A — *Esa <u>blusa</u> es muy bonita. ¿Es nueva?*

B — *Más o menos. La compré <u>hace dos días</u>.*

Y ahora Uds.

Estudiante A

Estudiante B

a.

b.

c.

d.

Empecemos a escribir y a leer

Write your answers in Spanish.

14 Choose three of your favorite clothing items, and tell in what kinds of stores you bought them.

15 Describe your three favorite items of clothing.

16 Cuando vas de compras, ¿buscas gangas o no?

17 ¿Compraste algo hace dos semanas? ¿Qué? ¿Y hace un mes?

"¿A qué tienda quieres ir ahora?"

Dos jóvenes en un centro comercial en México

18 Lee este diálogo.

SILVIA   Hola, Marta. ¡Qué bonito tu vestido!

MARTA   ¿Te gusta?

SILVIA   Sí, me gusta mucho. ¿Es nuevo?

MARTA   Pues, lo compré hace una semana.

SILVIA   ¿Dónde lo compraste?

MARTA   En la tienda de descuentos Nosotras.

SILVIA   ¿Y cuánto pagaste?

MARTA   ¡Diez dólares!

SILVIA   ¡No me digas! ¡Qué ganga! Yo también necesito comprar un vestido nuevo. ¿Quieres ir de compras mañana?

MARTA   ¡Claro que sí!

a.   ¿Quién tiene un vestido nuevo?

b.   ¿Quién necesita un vestido nuevo?

c.   ¿Qué es "Nosotras"?

d.   En tu opinión, ¿la ropa en los almacenes es barata o cara? ¿Es necesario comprar ropa cara? ¿Por qué?

¡Comuniquemos!

Here's another opportunity for you to use the vocabulary you've just learned.

1 Find out what your partner wears to different places.

A — *¿Qué ropa llevas cuando vas al parque?*
B — *Generalmente llevo . . .*
  o: *Nunca voy al parque.*

¡NO OLVIDES!
a + el = al

a.

b.

c.

d.

e.

f.

2 Find out how much your partner paid for his or her school supplies. You may use real prices or the prices suggested below.

A — *¿Cuánto pagaste por tu diccionario?*
B — *Pagué cinco dólares.*
  o: *No compré un diccionario.*

$5

a. $16

b. $15

c. $7

d. $1

e. $4

f. $3

g. $25

h. $2

3 Plan your next shopping trip for clothes. Decide on three items you need and what colors they should be. Your partner will estimate how much money you will need.

A —*Necesito una blusa azul.*
B —*Vas a necesitar quince dólares.*

¿Qué sabes ahora?

Can you:

- describe what clothes you wear?
  —Hoy llevo ___.

- tell where you bought something?
  —___ mis jeans en ___.

- tell how much you paid for something?
  —___ veinte dólares ___ la camisa.

- ask how much something costs?
  —¿Cuánto ___ esa camisa?

Perspectiva cultural

¿Te gusta ir de compras en los almacenes o los centros comerciales? ¿Qué compras?

Look at the photos on these pages. What kinds of stores do you think are shown here?

In big cities in Spanish-speaking countries, you can usually find a variety of malls or shopping centers. The idea of the shopping mall originated in the United States, and other countries have adopted the concept by creating malls of great beauty. However, there are also tailors and dressmaking stores where people can have their clothes custom-made at affordable prices.

Teenagers in Spanish-speaking countries like to window-shop at malls and clothing stores, just as they do here. And, just as in other countries, there is a wide variety of materials, styles, and fashions to choose from. Teens in Spanish-speaking countries tend to be fashion-conscious and stylish in the way they dress, and many like to wear custom-made formal clothes on special occasions.

La cultura desde tu perspectiva

1 What do you think are some of the advantages and disadvantages of shopping in a mall rather than in separate stores within several blocks?

2 Do you think you would be able to find some clothing brands that you are familiar with in the stores pictured? Why or why not?

Una joven en un centro comercial en Córdoba, Argentina

De compras en una tienda en Caracas, Venezuela

Tienda de ropa en la Ciudad de México

Centro comercial en Zaragoza, España

Plaza de las Américas en San Juan, Puerto Rico

Gramática en contexto

Here is an ad for a store. What kinds of information would you expect to find in an ad for a discount clothing store?

¿Por qué la Tienda de Descuentos Bolívar?

¿Por qué pagar los precios altos de un almacén por camisas, blusas y faldas cuando nosotros las tenemos a precios mucho más bajos?

La Tienda de Descuentos Bolívar tiene ropa espectacular, y ahora Ud. la puede comprar a un precio razonable. Esta ropa es nueva y elegante pero muy barata. Este mes Ud. debe visitar la Tienda de Descuentos Bolívar para ver las muchas gangas que ofrecemos.

Calle Colón 356, Bogotá • lunes a sábado, 9:00—18:00

A You know that *estos* and *estas* mean "these." Look at the ad. Which word is used before *ropa? Mes?* Which form of the word would be used before *gangas?* Can you explain the difference?

B You know that *lo* and *la* can mean "it," and *los* and *las* can mean "them." In the question that begins *"¿Por qué pagar los precios altos ... cuando nosotros las tenemos ... ,"* what does *las* refer to? In the sentence that begins *"La Tienda de Descuentos Bolívar tiene ... y ahora Ud. la puede comprar ... ,"* why do you think *la* is used, and not *lo?* If you were talking about a shirt *(camisa),* would you say *lo compro* or *la compro?*

La posición de los adjetivos

In Spanish, adjectives usually come after the noun they describe.

Me gusta más la camisa **blanca.**

Tenemos un perro **grande y feo.**

1 You and your partner are going shopping for clothing. Look at the items pictured and tell your partner which you would like to buy. Your partner will respond with his or her choice.

A —*Me gustaría comprar una camiseta blanca.*
B —*A mí también.*
    o: *A mí no. Prefiero una camiseta roja.*

¡NO OLVIDES!

Adjectives agree in number (singular / plural) and gender (masculine / feminine) with the nouns they describe.

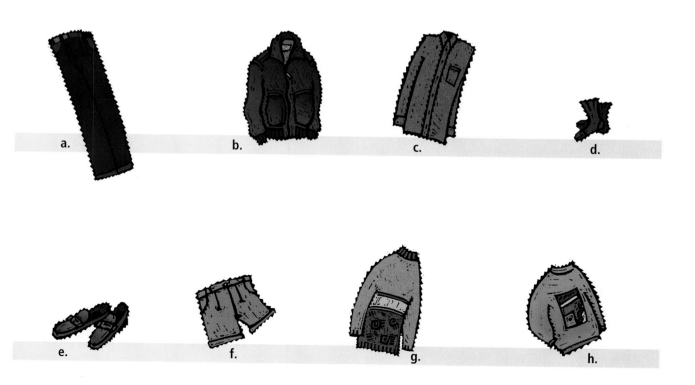

a.   b.   c.   d.

e.   f.   g.   h.

2 Take turns with your partner playing the roles of a salesperson and a customer. The salesperson should find out what item the customer is looking for and for whom. The items can be for a family member or a person of your choice.

A — *¿Qué desea, señor (señora / joven / señorita)?*
B — *Busco unos calcetines blancos.*
A — *¿Para Ud.?*
B — *Sí, para mí.*
    o: *No, para mi madre (padre).*

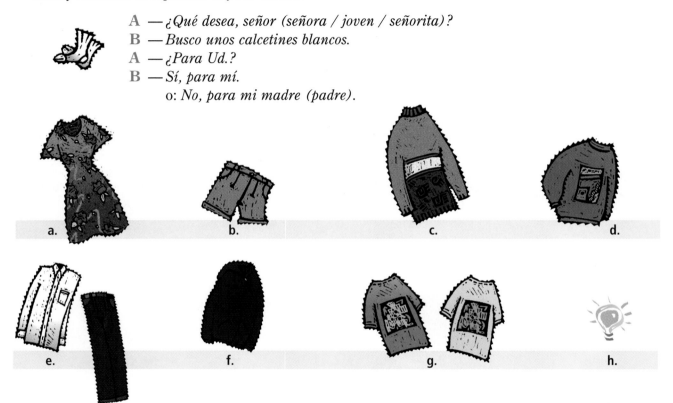

a.   b.   c.   d.

e.   f.   g.   h.

Los adjetivos demostrativos

We use demonstrative adjectives to point out people and things. You've already seen these forms: *este, esta, estos, estas* (this, these), and *ese, esa, esos,* and *esas* (that, those).

Demonstrative adjectives come before the noun. They have the same gender and number as the nouns that follow them.

SINGULAR	PLURAL
este vestido (**this** dress)	**estos** vestidos (**these** dresses)
esta blusa (**this** blouse)	**estas** blusas (**these** blouses)
ese suéter (**that** sweater)	**esos** suéteres (**those** sweaters)
esa sudadera (**that** sweatshirt)	**esas** sudaderas (**those** sweatshirts)

3 You are at a party and you want to get to know the guests.
Find out from your partner their names and ages.

A — *¿Cómo se llama esa muchacha alta y rubia?*
B — *Marta.*
A — *¿Cuántos años tiene?*
B — *Quince.*

Marta

Lucía, 28

Pilar y Conchita, 17

Carlitos, 9

Marta, 15

Javier, 35

Eva, 75

Miguel y Mateo, 14

4 While shopping with a friend, you pick up and look at several items.
Ask if your partner likes them.

A — *¿Te gusta este suéter azul?*
B — *Sí, me gusta mucho.*
    o: *No, no me gusta nada.*

a.

b.

c.

d.

e.

f.

El complemento directo: Los pronombres

A direct object tells who or what receives the action of the verb.

Quiero **esa falda.**

Compré **unos zapatos.**

To avoid repeating a direct object noun, we often replace it with a direct object pronoun ("it" or "them").

— ¿Cuándo compraste **la falda?**
— **La** compré hace cinco días.

— Isabel, ¿tienes **mi suéter?**
— No, no **lo** tengo.

	SINGULAR		PLURAL
lo	*it* (masculine)	**los**	*them* (masculine)
la	*it* (feminine)	**las**	*them* (feminine)

- The direct object pronoun usually comes right before the verb. If the verb is negative, the pronoun is placed between *no* and the verb.
  — ¿Compras **esos pantalones?**
  — No, no **los** compro.

- When we have a verb followed by an infinitive, the direct object pronoun is usually placed right before the main verb (not the infinitive).
  — ¿Quieres comprar **esa falda?**
  — Sí, **la** quiero comprar.

- Direct object pronouns have the same gender and number as the nouns they are replacing. When the pronoun replaces both a masculine and a feminine direct object noun, we use *los*.
  — ¿Cuándo compraste **la falda y el vestido?**
  — **Los** compré el sábado.

5 Today is November 28 and you recently went shopping for
clothes. Use the calendar to answer your partner's questions.

A — *Tu camisa es nueva, ¿no?*
B — *Sí, la compré hace tres semanas.*

6 You're trying to help your partner clean out a messy locker.
Ask whether or not he or she needs the objects pictured.

A —*¿Necesitas la calculadora?*
B —*¡Claro que sí! La necesito para mi clase de matemáticas.*
  o: *No, no la necesito.*

7 It's the first day of class and you're talking to a friend about the supplies you need to buy. With a partner, take turns asking and answering based on the pictures from the previous exercise.

A — *Necesito comprar una calculadora.*
B — *¿Cuándo la quieres comprar?*
A — *Mañana.*

Ahora lo sabes

Can you:

■ **identify and describe articles of clothing?**

—Necesito un(a) ____.

■ **point out people and things?**

—¿Qué bolígrafo prefieres?

—Prefiero ____ bolígrafo.

■ **avoid reusing a noun by replacing it with** *lo, la, los,* **or** *las?*

—¿Tienes la calculadora y la regla?

—Sí, ____ tengo.

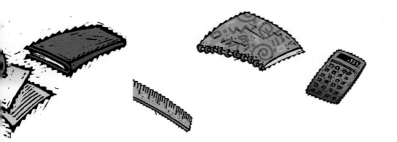

Para decir más

Here is some additional vocabulary that you might find useful for activities in this section.

el abrigo
overcoat

las botas
boots

el cinturón
belt

la gorra
cap

gastar
to spend

ahorrar
to save

el dinero
money

el sombrero
hat

Actividades

Here's an opportunity for you to expand your use of Spanish by putting together the material you learned in this chapter with what you learned earlier.

1 With your partner, play the roles of a store clerk and a customer who wants to buy an item of clothing:

- Get the clerk's attention
- The clerk will ask how he or she can help you
- Tell the clerk that you want to see an item
- The clerk will clarify which item you are talking about
- Find out the price of the item
- Find out if they have it in another color
- Tell the clerk whether you will buy it or not

2 Your partner is getting ready to fix dinner and is asking if you have different foods and drinks that he or she might need. Unfortunately, you forgot to buy them.

A — ¿Tienes cebollas y tomates?

B — A ver . . . No, no los tengo.

A — ¿Pero, no los compraste? ¿Y qué voy a cocinar para la cena?

B — Podemos comer un sandwich de . . .

3 Role-play a scene in which you try to convince your parent(s) that you need to buy some new clothing. As the adult, your partner will try to convince you that you don't need the clothing. For example:

A — Mamá, necesito una blusa nueva.

B — Pero, hija. Tienes tres blusas blancas y una blusa amarilla.

A — Ay, no, mamá. ¡Esas blusas son viejas!

B — ¡Viejas! ¡Pero las compraste hace sólo un mes!

¡Vamos a leer!

Antes de leer

STRATEGY ➤ Using titles and pictures to predict

Look at the title and pictures to predict what the story is about.

Mira la lectura

STRATEGIES ➤ Skimming
Identifying the main idea

Skimming is another useful strategy. By quickly glancing through a reading selection, you can often get a general idea of the subject and content.

This story tells of a decision a boy has to make. Skim through it quickly to get the main ideas.

a. What is Juanito's problem?
b. What does he decide to do?
c. What is the grandmother's reaction?

EL PROBLEMA DE LAS DOS CAMISAS

Juanito es un muchacho amable y sociable. Para su cumpleaños, Juanito recibe muchos regalos y muchísima ropa de su familia. Le encanta la ropa, pero una semana después de su cumpleaños, recibe una invitación para ir a cenar a la casa de su abuela.

Ahora tiene un problema: Su abuela le regaló dos camisas, una gris y otra amarilla. ¿Cuál va a llevar? Habla con su mamá.

Juanito: Mamá, ¿qué voy a llevar? Tengo las dos camisas nuevas de la abuela.

La mamá: Bueno, hijo, ¿por qué no llevas la camisa que te gusta más?

Juanito: Es que no quiero ofender a la abuela. Ella es un poco difícil a veces.

La mamá: Pues, hijo, puedes llevar una de las camisas para esta cena, y otro día puedes llevar la otra camisa.

Juanito decide llevar la camisa gris. Cuando él entra en la casa, la abuela le dice: "Y, ¿qué pasa? No llevas la camisa amarilla. ¿No te gusta?"

La mamá le dice a Juanito: "No te preocupes. Es imposible contentarles a todos."

¡Feliz cumpleaños!

Infórmate

STRATEGY > Using context to get meaning

Remember that when you are reading and you come across a word you don't understand, you should look at the other words in the sentence to see if they will help you understand.

As you read the story again, make a list of five words or phrases you don't understand.

a. What type of boy is Juanito? What words or phrases tell you that?
b. What do you think of the mother's advice? Would you have given the same advice? Why or why not?
c. What would you have done in Juanito's place?
d. What do you think the last line means?

Aplicación

Think of a similar situation where it seemed impossible to please someone. Create a short dialogue with a partner and end it with a solution that pleases both of you.

¡Vamos a escribir!

Many teens love to shop. They read fashion magazines and browse in stores to learn about the newest fashions, styles, and colors. Create an ad for an article of clothing to appear in a teen magazine or catalog.

1 First, think about what might appeal to you and your friends. What article of clothing are you going to sell? What colors does it come in? Where can you buy it? How much does it cost? Write out the answers to these questions in Spanish.

2 Invent a brand name for your clothing. Use it and the answers to the questions in Part 1 to help you design your ad. Be sure to give all the information and arrange it in a way that will catch the eye.

3 Show your ad to a partner. Does he or she want to suggest changes or additions? Think about any changes you might want to make, and rewrite your ad.

4 Check the ad for spelling, accents, and punctuation. Did you use the correct forms of the adjectives? If necessary, make a clean copy and add drawings or magazine pictures to illustrate your ad.

5 You can file your ad in your writing portfolio, or the entire class can collect the ads into a catalog ("ROPA DE PRIMAVERA / VERANO / OTOÑO / INVIERNO 19___").

LOS NUEVOS **PAREDES** ¡ya están en las zapaterías!

Con éstos, de base de POLIURETANO no sentirás el frío ni el calor, son ISOTÉRMICOS. Su base es totalmente ANATÓMICA. Caminar con ellos, es un auténtico placer.

GRAND-PRIX

...y, si te gusta cosido,

Ésta, es la nueva versión (mejorada) del legendario modelo COMPETICIÓN.

Su piel, es napa y está cosida a una estudiada suela de caucho de gran agarre. Se le ha incorporado una entresuela de EVA para que amortigüe y absorba los impactos que se producen en el talón durante un partido de tenis.

PAREDES la estrella

DISEÑO:

ZAPATOS

¿Buscas zapatos de tenis?

En la tienda Suárez, tenemos muchos colores

y estilos para ti. Tenemos también los colores

atractivos de este año: verde y rojo.

Los tenis de Suárez:

¡SÓLO $25!

¿Lo sabes bien?

This section will help you organize your studying for the proficiency test, where you will be asked to do similar, though not identical tasks. There will not be any models on the test.

Listening

Can you understand when people talk about clothes? Listen as your teacher reads a sample similar to what you will hear on the test. How many items is the person planning to buy? Approximately how much money is he or she going to spend?

Reading

Can you understand a description about shopping and clothes? Read through this paragraph to get the main idea. What kind of store does Inés prefer to go to, and why?

"A mí me gusta ir de compras en todas partes, pero lo que más me gusta es ir a los centros comerciales. Es agradable también ir a los almacenes, y a veces puedes comprar ropa buena y barata en las tiendas de descuentos. Pero hay muchas tiendas de todo tipo en los centros comerciales. También hay restaurantes allí, y si estás cansada puedes ir a beber un refresco y descansar."

Writing

Can you write a letter to your parents similar to the one an exchange student might write home asking for money to buy school clothes? Here is an example:

Queridos papá y mamá:

Necesito comprar ropa nueva. Me gustaría comprar tres o cuatro camisetas. Hay camisetas muy bonitas y baratas. Sólo cuestan 10 dólares. No tengo pantalones cortos ni tenis. Necesito también unos pantalones y dos camisas. Los necesito para ir a fiestas. La ropa aquí es muy barata. Voy a necesitar sólo . . . 150 dólares.

Su hijo,
Luis

Culture

If you were visiting a Spanish-speaking country, would you prefer to buy clothes at a shopping center or go to a tailor or dressmaker? Why?

Centro comercial en Buenos Aires, Argentina

Speaking

Can you and a partner play the roles of a salesperson and a customer in a store? For example:

A — *¿Qué desea, señora (joven / señor / señorita)?*

B — *Busco un suéter blanco.*

A — *Sí, señora. Tenemos unos suéteres muy bonitos.*

B — *¿Cuánto cuestan?*

A — *Sólo 165 dólares.*

B — *¿Sólo 165 dólares? Perdón, señor . . . ¿hay otra tienda de ropa por aquí?*

Resumen del capítulo 6

Use the vocabulary from this chapter to help you:

■ describe the color, fit, and price of clothes
■ ask about and buy clothes
■ tell where and when you bought clothes and how much you paid for them

to talk about articles of clothing
la blusa
el calcetín, *pl.* los calcetines
la camisa
la camiseta
la chaqueta
la falda

los jeans
los pantalones (cortos)
las pantimedias
la ropa
la sudadera
el suéter
los tenis
el vestido
los zapatos

to describe clothes
la ganga
barato, -a
caro, -a
nuevo, -a
¿Cómo te queda(n)?
Me queda(n) bien.
¡Qué + *adjective!*

to talk about colors
el color
¿De qué color?
amarillo, -a
anaranjado, -a
azul, *pl.* azules
blanco, -a
gris, *pl.* grises
marrón, *pl.* marrones
morado, -a
negro, -a
rojo, -a
rosado, -a
verde

to talk about places to shop for clothing
el almacén
la tienda de descuentos
la tienda de ropa
la zapatería

to talk about shopping
buscar
comprar: (yo) compré
      (tú) compraste
llevar
pagar: (yo) pagué
    (tú) pagaste
para mí / ti
por

to indicate a specific item or items
ese, -a, esos, -as
este, -a, estos, -as
lo, la, los, las
otro, -a

to talk about prices
ciento un(o), una . . .
¿Cuánto?
Cuesta(n) . . .
el dólar, *pl.* los dólares

to assist customers in a store
¿Qué desea (Ud.)?

to address people
el / la joven, *pl.* los jóvenes

to start a conversation
perdón

to talk about when something happened
hace + *time expression*

to indicate location
por aquí

CAPÍTULO 7

¿Adónde vas a ir de vacaciones?

OBJECTIVES

At the end of this chapter, you will be able to:

- describe vacation choices and activities
- talk about the weather
- discuss what to take on a trip
- talk about how teens in Chile spend their vacations

Pirámide maya en Uxmal, México

¡Piénsalo bien!

Look at these photographs of four vacation destinations in Mexico, Colombia, Ecuador, and Uruguay. Which place would you most like to visit? Why?

"Quisiera ver la cancha de juego de Chichén Itzá en Yucatán . . .

In what ways is this playing field like or different from a football field or a basketball court that you know?

. . . o visitar el Museo del Oro
en Bogotá, Colombia . . .

. . . o explorar las islas Galápagos en Ecuador. . .

The Galápagos Islands are
located off the coast of
Ecuador. What do you
know about these islands?
Do you know the name of
a famous British scientist
who visited the islands in
the nineteenth century?

. . . o descansar en las playas de Punta del Este, Uruguay."

Vocabulario para conversar

¿Qué puedes hacer en México?

Here are some new words and expressions you will need to talk about vacation choices and activities. Read them several times, then turn the page and practice with a partner.

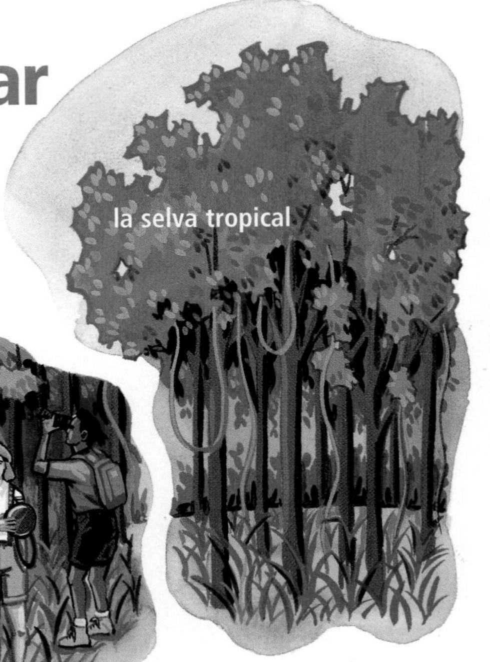

la selva tropical

explorar la selva

pasear en bote

el bote

el lago

los recuerdos

el museo

las montañas

sacar fotos

la foto

esquiar

las cataratas

la pirámide
subir la pirámide

tomar el sol

las ruinas

la catedral

bucear

el mar

También necesitas . . .

la ciudad	*city*
el país	*country*
los lugares de interés	*places of interest*
descansar	*to rest*
quisiera	*I'd like*
ir: (yo) fui	*to go: I went*
(tú) fuiste	*you went*
pasado, -a	*last (year, month, week)*
no . . . ninguna parte	*nowhere, not anywhere*
para + *inf.*	here: *in order to*

¿Y qué quiere decir . . . ?
cuando*
las vacaciones *(pl.)*
ir de vacaciones
visitar

* When question words are used as conjunctions to join two parts of a sentence, we do not use
the accent mark: *¿Cuándo?* → *cuando, ¿Dónde?* → *donde,* etc.

Empecemos a conversar

With a partner, take turns being *Estudiante A* and *Estudiante B.* Use the words that are cued or given in the balloons to replace the underlined sections in the model. ⚡ means you can make your own choices.

1

A — *Cuando voy de vacaciones a <u>las montañas</u>, ¿qué puedo hacer?*

B — *Puedes <u>esquiar</u>. (También puedes . . .)*

Y ahora Uds.

Estudiante A **Estudiante B**

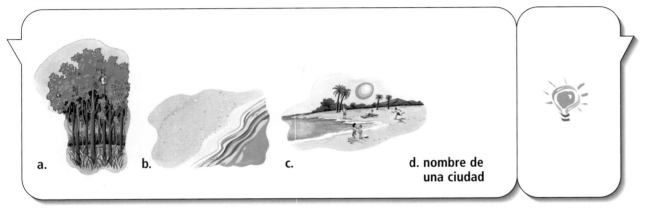

a. b. c. d. nombre de una ciudad

2 el verano pasado

A — *¿Adónde fuiste <u>el verano pasado</u>?*

B — *Fui a <u>Los Ángeles</u>.*

o: *No fui a ninguna parte.*

Y ahora Uds.

Estudiante A **Estudiante B**

a. el año pasado

b. el mes pasado

c. la semana pasada

d. el invierno pasado

e. el fin de semana pasado

3

A — *¿Adónde vas a ir este verano?*
B — *Quisiera ir a la playa para tomar el sol.*
   Y ahora Uds.

Estudiante A

Estudiante B

a.

b.

c.

d.

Empecemos a escribir

Write your answers in Spanish.

4 List three things that you would like to do on vacation.

5 Using *fui*, name a place you went to last week, one you went to last month, and one you went to last year.

6 ¿Adónde te gustaría ir de vacaciones?

También se dice

los suvenires

tomar fotos

Vocabulario para conversar

¿Qué tiempo hace?

Here's the rest of the vocabulary you will need to talk about the weather and to discuss what to take on a trip.

el viento

la lluvia

Llueve.

Hace viento.

Hace fresco.

el abrigo

el gorro

la bufanda

la nieve

los guantes

las botas

Hace frío.

Nieva.

el traje de baño

los anteojos de sol

el bronceador

Hace calor.

Hace mal tiempo.

Hace sol.

el sol

Hace buen tiempo.

el impermeable

la maleta

el paraguas

También necesitas . . .

llevar	here: *to take, to carry along*
salir*	*to leave*
regresar	*to come back, to return*
pensar + *inf.*: (yo) pienso	*to plan: I plan*
(tú) piensas	*you plan*
¿Qué tiempo hace?	*What's the weather like?*
¡Vaya!	*My goodness! Gee! Wow!*
Menos mal que ___.	*It's a good thing that ___.*

> **¿Y qué quiere decir . . . ?**
> la cámara
> fantástico, -a
> el pasaporte

*Salir has an irregular *yo* form: *salgo.*

Empecemos a conversar

7

A — *¿Qué tiempo hace en <u>San Antonio</u> en <u>noviembre</u>?*
B — *<u>Un tiempo fantástico</u>. <u>Hace sol</u>.*

San Antonio / noviembre

Y ahora Uds.

Estudiante A

a. Miami / julio

b. Denver / enero

c. San Francisco / noviembre

d. Chicago / octubre

e. Washington, D.C. / abril

f.

Estudiante B

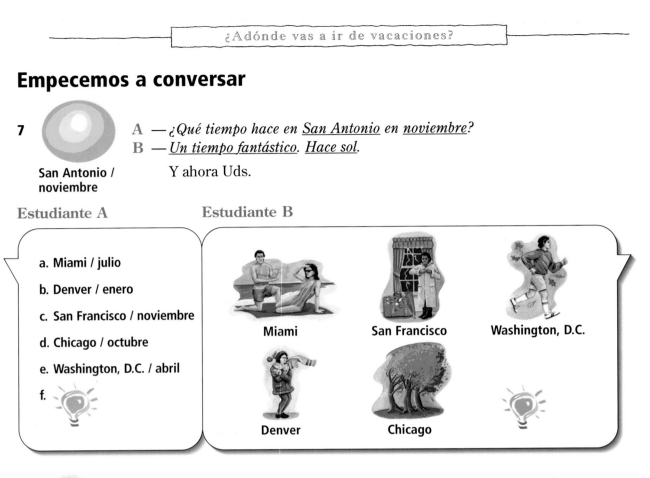

Miami   San Francisco   Washington, D.C.

Denver   Chicago

8

A — *¡Vaya! <u>Hace frío</u> hoy.*
B — *Menos mal que tienes <u>tu abrigo</u>.*

Y ahora Uds.

Estudiante A

Estudiante B

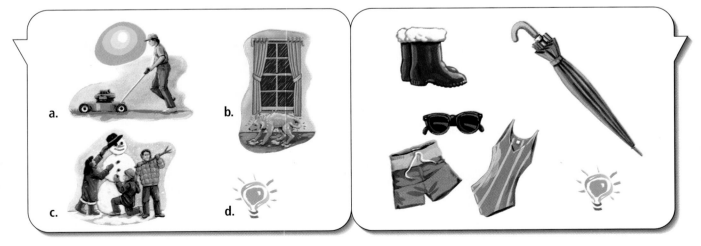

a.

b.

c.

d.

9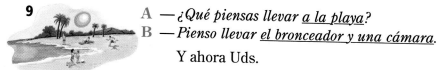
A — *¿Qué piensas llevar <u>a la playa</u>?*
B — *Pienso llevar <u>el bronceador y una cámara</u>.*
    Y ahora Uds.

Estudiante A   Estudiante B

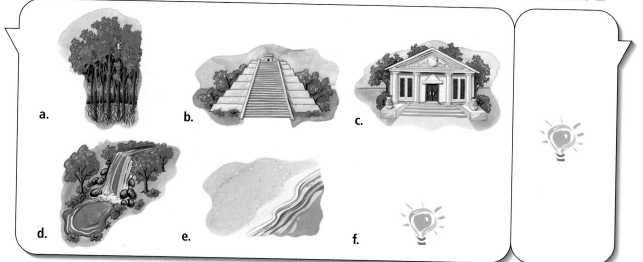

a.   b.   c.

d.   e.   f.

Empecemos a escribir y a leer

Write your answers in Spanish.

10 Describe what the weather is like in your community in all four seasons. *En el invierno . . .*

11 Choose three types of weather and tell one activity you like to do in each one. *Cuando hace mal tiempo, . . .*

12 ¿Vas a ir de vacaciones este año? ¿Cuándo piensas salir? ¿Y regresar?

13 Cuando una persona va a esquiar, ¿qué ropa lleva en su maleta?

14 ¿Es lógico o no?

¡Vaya! Hace frío hoy. Me gustaría ir a la playa para tomar el sol.

¿Piensas ir a Argentina? Debes llevar tu pasaporte y una cámara para sacar fotos de los lugares de interés.

El año pasado no fui a ninguna parte. Este año voy a ir a la selva tropical para pasear en bote.

También se dice

la loción bronceadora
la crema para el sol

las gafas de sol
los lentes de sol

la máquina fotográfica

el bañador
la malla
la trusa
la ropa de baño

¡Comuniquemos!

Here's another opportunity for you to use the vocabulary you've just learned.

1 Read the sentences in the first column. Your partner will give
you the appropriate response from the second column.

a. ¡Vaya! no tengo paraguas.
b. No voy a tener vacaciones este año.
c. No llevo mis anteojos de sol.
d. No tengo botas.
e. Necesito ir a Colombia en dos semanas.
f. Vamos a ir a la playa esta tarde.

Menos mal que no hace mucho sol.
Menos mal que no nieva mucho.
Menos mal que tienes tu impermeable.
Menos mal que compraste un traje de baño la
   semana pasada.
Menos mal que fuiste a Cancún el año pasado.
Menos mal que tienes tu pasaporte.

2 With a partner, take turns asking and telling
what activities you like to do in different
kinds of weather. The list of verbs on the right
will help you answer.

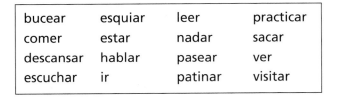

bucear	esquiar	leer	practicar
comer	estar	nadar	sacar
descansar	hablar	pasear	ver
escuchar	ir	patinar	visitar

A — *¿Qué te gusta hacer cuando llueve?*
B — *Pues, me gusta leer o ver la televisión.*

a.   b.   c.   d.

e.   f.   g.   h.

3 You and your partner are planning your vacations. Take turns asking and answering where and with whom you would like to go, and what activities you would like to do there. Don't forget to say when you are leaving and when you are planning to come back.

¿Qué sabes ahora?

Can you:

- tell what you can see or do on a vacation?

  —En México puedo ___.

- tell what you plan to do on a vacation?

  —En las vacaciones ___ visitar museos.

- tell what you will take on your vacation?

  —Pienso llevar ___ a España.

- describe the weather at your vacation destination?

  —___ en San Antonio en el invierno.

Perspectiva cultural

En el verano, muchas personas van de vacaciones. A muchos jóvenes les gusta ir a la playa. A otros les gusta ir a las montañas. Y a ti, ¿qué te gusta hacer?

The large photo was taken in Chile. In which months might the activities be taking place? Would that be during the school year or vacation time?

January and February are summer months in Chile. Because of Chile's long coastline along the Pacific Ocean, going to the beach is very popular.

A Chilean teen reports, "I like to go to Viña del Mar with my family. In the daytime, we swim in the ocean or in a pool, and we sunbathe. We rest in the afternoon, and in the evening we can play tennis, go to a movie, or go dancing. There are a lot of people my age there."

In July, Chilean students have a short winter vacation. Some may go to a ski resort in the Andes, but it is much more common for them to visit relatives and friends.

In Chile, most high-school students do not get a summer job. However, some may bag groceries at a supermarket or work at one of the growing number of fast-food restaurants.

La cultura desde tu perspectiva

1 How is your vacation similar to or different from that of Chilean teens?

2 How does the geography affect vacation options for Chilean students? How does the geography of your area affect your vacation options?

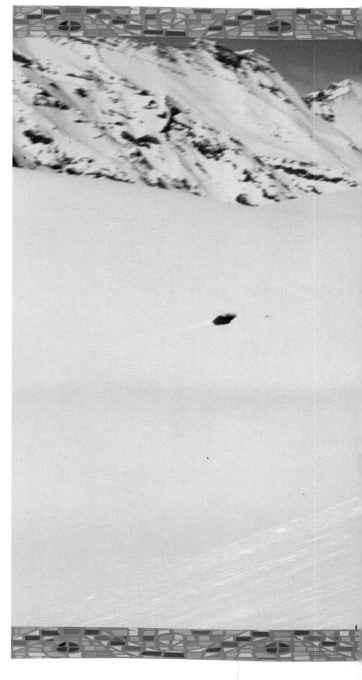

Esquiando en Le Grand Mur, Valle Nevado, Chile

Trabajando durante las vacaciones

En una playa de Chile

Gramática en contexto

Look at this ad for a travel agency. How does a travel agency attract new clients?

¿Qué piensa hacer
Ud. este invierno?

¿Adónde puede ir Ud. para hacer
todo esto y mucho más?

¡A la República Dominicana, el
paraíso de las vacaciones!

¿Piensa llevar a la familia? Pues,
debe ir a Puerto Plata, donde hay
muchas actividades que sus hijos
pueden hacer. ¿Piensa llevar un
suéter o su abrigo? Pues, no los
necesita. En Puerto Plata nunca hace
frío. Hace buen tiempo todo el año.

Aquí en la Agencia de Viajes Cristal
estamos para ayudar a nuestros
clientes. Queremos y pensamos
hacer de sus vacaciones algo
fabuloso. Visite nuestra oficina
en la Quinta Avenida 578,
o llame al número 1-555-523-3493.

La República Dominicana, donde el
verano nunca termina...

¿Quiere tomar el sol?

¿Quiere jugar tenis?

¿Quiere pasear en bote?

A Can you find in the ad at least one other form of each of these verbs: *puedo / puedes, quiero / quieres,* and *pienso / piensas?* What do these verb forms mean? How is the *nosotros* form of *pensar* different from its other forms?

B Look at the question in red that begins with *¿Adónde . . . ?* and the first sentence of paragraph 3. What form of the verb follows *para?*

C In paragraph 2, look at the two questions that begin, *¿Piensa llevar . . . ?* What are the direct objects? In which question is the direct object a thing? In which question is the direct object people? What word comes before the direct object that refers to people?

El verbo *poder*

Puedo and *puedes* come from the infinitive *poder,* "can, to be able to."

(yo)	**puedo**	(nosotros) (nosotras)	**podemos**
(tú)	**puedes**	(vosotros) (vosotras)	**podéis**
Ud. (él) (ella)	**puede**	Uds. (ellos) (ellas)	**pueden**

- When we drop the *-er* of the infinitive, the part that remains is called the stem. Notice that in four forms of *poder*, the *o* of the stem changes to *ue*. We call *poder* an *o → ue* stem-changing verb.

- The endings follow the pattern of regular *-er* verbs.

- When the forms of *poder* are followed by another verb, the second verb is always in the infinitive. For example:

  No **puedo ir** al cine contigo el viernes.

Artesanía maya

1 With a partner, take turns telling what these people cannot do and why.

Marta no puede tomar el sol porque hace fresco.

Marta

a. Felipe   b. Alejandro y María Teresa   c. Margarita

d. Pablo y tú   e. Esteban y yo   f. Ud.

2 While you are on vacation your friend asks if you can do these activities together. Tell your friend you can't because you don't have the necessary items.

A —*¿Puedes ir a nadar conmigo?*
B —*No, no puedo. No tengo traje de baño.*

a.   b.   c.   d.   e.

Para + infinitivo

You know that *para* means "for" or "in order to." Whenever *para* is followed by a verb, the verb is in the infinitive form. For example:

Vamos a México **para bucear** y **tomar** el sol.

3 With a partner, take turns telling what you need these things for.

cuaderno   *Necesitamos un cuaderno para estudiar.*

a. piscina	d. papas
b. hoja de papel	e. cámara
c. libro	f. 💡

cocinar	leer
sacar fotos	dibujar
nadar	💡

4 With a partner, take turns telling why these young people are going to a friend's house.

A —*Antonio va a la casa de Felipe, ¿verdad?*
B —*Sí, va allí para escuchar música.*

Antonio / Felipe

Estudiante A   **Estudiante B**

a. Marisol / Yolanda

b. Eduardo y Raúl / David

c. Tú / Manuel

d. Lourdes / Andrea

e. Armando y tú / Sergio

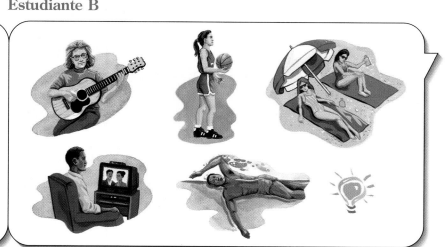

Los verbos *querer* y *pensar*

You know that we use *quiero* and *quieres* to tell what we want to do, and we use *pienso* and *piensas* to tell what we plan to do. These verb forms come from the infinitives *querer* and *pensar*. Here are their present-tense forms:

(yo)	pienso quiero	(nosotros) (nosotras)	pensamos queremos
(tú)	piensas quieres	(vosotros) (vosotras)	pensáis queréis
Ud. (él) (ella)	piensa quiere	Uds. (ellos) (ellas)	piensan quieren

- Notice that there is a stem change from *e* to *ie* in all except the *nosotros* and *vosotros* forms. *Querer* and *pensar* are called *e → ie* stem-changing verbs.

- The endings follow the pattern of regular -*ar* and -*er* verbs.

- When the forms of *querer* and *pensar* are followed by another verb, the second verb is always in the infinitive. For example:
  — ¿Quieres **estudiar** conmigo?
  — No, pienso **ver** la tele.

5 Take turns asking and answering where these tourists plan to go tomorrow.

Javier

A — *¿Adónde va a ir Javier mañana?*
B — *Piensa ir al museo.*

Estudiante A

a. Mariana

b. Enrique y tú

c. Miguel y Julia

d. Ud.

e. Juan Carlos

f. tú

g. Clara y Teresa

Estudiante B

La *a* personal

You know that the direct object is the person or thing that receives the action of a verb. In Spanish, when the direct object is a specific person or group of people, we use *a* before it. That's why it's called the personal *a*.

Quiero visitar **a** mis abuelos.
Quiero visitar **al** señor López.

• To ask who receives the action of a verb, we use *¿A quién?*

— **¿A quién** quieres visitar?
— Quiero visitar **a** mis primos.

• We can also use the personal *a* when the direct object is an animal, especially a pet.

Busco **a mi perro**.

• We usually do not use the personal *a* after the verb *tener.*

Tengo muchos tíos.

6 Imagine that the members of the Ramírez family live in different parts of the country. They all want to visit each other. Ask your partner which family member each person wants to visit. Your partner's answers will be based on the family tree.

Andrea y Armando

Graciela y Gustavo

Dolores y Ernesto

Anita y Claudia

Marta y Paco

Claudia /
Marta y Paco

A — *¿A quién quiere visitar Claudia?*
B — *Quiere visitar a sus primos.*

a. Anita y Claudia / Armando y Andrea
b. Armando y Andrea / Ernesto
c. Paco y Marta / Anita y Claudia

d. Paco / Gustavo y Graciela
e. Graciela / Armando y Andrea
f. Ernesto / Graciela

7 Find out what or whom each of these tourists is looking for.

Pedro / Elena

    A — *¿A quién busca Pedro?*
    B — *Busca a Elena.*
        o:

Pedro / el paraguas

    A — *¿Qué busca Pedro?*
    B — *Busca el paraguas.*

a. Ana María / sus hijos
b. Juan y Enrique / la catedral
c. Carmen / la maleta
d. Pablo / su hermana

e. Eugenio y Cristóbal / Diana
f. Clara y Bárbara / las ruinas
g. Ud. / el museo
h. Elisa y tú / Raquel

Ahora lo sabes

Can you:

■ **tell what someone can do, plans to do, and wants to do?**

  —Yo ___ nadar.

  —Julio ___ visitar la selva tropical.

  —Ellas ___ subir la pirámide.

■ **tell the reason for doing something?**

  —Luz va a la playa para ___.

■ **use the personal *a* correctly?**

  —¿___ quién ves?

  —Veo ___ Antonio.

¿Esquías o trabajas?

Si te gusta el esquí y puedes permitirte dejar el trabajo unos días, ven a esquiar a Andorra.
En Andorra, de lunes a viernes, esquiarás tranquilo y a tu aire. Podrás practicar toda clase de deportes de nieve en cualquiera de las 97 pistas de sus cinco estaciones.
Además, en Andorra el après-ski es tan excitante como el esquí. Actividades deportivas y de salud, compras increíbles y la vida nocturna que sólo Andorra te ofrece. Haz como algunos. Déjalo todo y ven a esquiar a Andorra entre semana.
¿Y tú, esquías o trabajas?

ANDORRA
Fiesta de Nieve

Infórmate en tu agencia de viajes más próxima.

TODO JUNTO

Para decir más

Here is some additional vocabulary that you might find useful for activities in this section.

Está nublado.
It's cloudy.

el cielo
sky

las manoplas
mittens

el esquí acuático
waterskiing

dar una caminata
go hiking

ir de camping
go camping

visitar a los parientes
visit relatives

Actividades

Here's an opportunity for you to expand your use of Spanish by putting together the material you learned in this chapter with what you learned earlier.

1 Find out where your partner plans to go on Saturday and what he or she plans to do. Also find out with whom your partner is going.

A — *Jaime, ¿adónde piensas ir el sábado y qué piensas hacer?*
B — *Pienso ir al gimnasio para practicar deportes.*
A — *¿Con quién vas a ir?*
B — *Voy a ir con Federico.*

When you finish, report the results to another classmate.

El sábado, Jaime piensa ir al gimnasio para practicar deportes. Va a ir con su amigo Federico.

2 With your partner, role-play an interview with a travel agent and discuss a place your family can visit, activities you can do there, when you plan to go, and anything you might need to take along. For example:

A — *Queremos ir de pesca en el mar.*

B — *Pues, Uds. pueden ir a Puerto Rico.*

A — *¿También podemos bucear allí?*

B — *Sí, pueden bucear y nadar. ¿Cuándo quieren ir Uds.?*

A — *Pensamos ir en julio. Queremos salir el dos de julio y regresar el veinticinco. ¿Qué necesitamos llevar?*

B — *Pues, necesitan ropa de verano, traje de baño y una cámara. En julio hace sol y hace calor en Puerto Rico.*

3 In a group, find out when and how frequently your classmates visit family members on their vacations. Ask about *primos, abuelos, tíos,* and other family members. On a piece of paper make tally marks under the following headings: *Muchas veces, A veces, Nunca.* When you finish, report the results to your class.

A — *En las vacaciones, ¿visitas a tus abuelos?*

B — *Sí, los visito muchas veces.*

El Aeropuerto Internacional Luis Muñoz Marín en San Juan, Puerto Rico

Con la familia en Xochimilco, México

Actividades 241

¡Vamos a leer!

Antes de leer

STRATEGY ➤ Using prior knowledge

Advertisements can give us lots of ideas about things to do in unknown locales. What kinds of information might you expect to find in this travel advertisement? Name three or four different kinds of activities that you would expect to find.

Mira la lectura

Look at the title, photograph, and coupon.
- What country is advertised?
- What two tourist attractions does the photograph suggest it offers?
- What aspect of Mexico is mentioned in the coupon heading?
- What would you receive if you sent the coupon?

DEJA DE SOÑAR Y HAZ LA MALETA.

México.

México, un tesoro de 3,000 años de antiguas civilizaciones. Olmecas, Aztecas, Mixtecas y Mayas. Sus monumentos se encuentran por todas partes: Pirámides y templos, murales y frisos e, incluso, ciudades totalmente amuralladas. Todo en México es increíble.

Ven a México, tendrás mucho que recordar. Sus nobles ciudades coloniales, 10,000kms. de soleadas playas. Sus alegres mariachis. Su arte y escultura. Sus fiestas y folklore.

Tiendas de piel, plata, laca, tejidos. Y sus gentes que te reciben cordialmente, dándote siempre la bienvenida para que te sientas como en casa.

En México, vas a encontrar lo más moderno, elegante, lujoso y confortable. Con todo su pasado milenario a tu alrededor, México todavía sigue siendo México. Todavía sigue siendo mágico.

Visita México este año. Vas a tener las vacaciones que tú siempre has deseado. Ahora está a tu alcance. 14 días desde 123,050. pts.

Informate en tu agencia de viajes o envía este cupón a: Oficina de Turismo de México en España. Velázquez, 126. 28006 Madrid. Tel:261.18.27.

VENGA. VIVA LA HOSPITALIDAD DE MÉXICO.

Sírvase enviarme más información.   HO.2

Nombre _____

Dirección _____

_____

Código postal _____

SECRETARÍA DE TURISMO DE MÉXICO.

Chac-Mool, Yucatán Peninsula.

Infórmate

STRATEGIES ➤ Identifying
main ideas
Coping with
unknown words

If you run across a word you don't know, there are several things you can do. You can keep reading and discover that you don't need to know its meaning. You may discover that you can figure out its meaning from the surrounding words or the following sentence. Or you may find out that you *do* need to know its meaning and must either look it up or ask someone. Use this strategy when you run across a word you don't understand.

1 Look at each paragraph to find the main idea, then tell in which paragraph (1–6) each of the following ideas is featured.

Mapa del mundo de 1589

    Affordable vacation package

    Monuments of ancient civilizations

    Modern and traditional features

    Places and things to see

    How to get more information

    Opportunities for shopping

2 Which of the first four paragraphs describes the attractions that you find most appealing? Why do they appeal to you?

3 Scan the last paragraph to discover the country where this advertisement appeared.

Aplicación

List at least three words you did not know or need to know in order to understand this ad.

Montando en bicicleta en el
Zócalo de la Ciudad de México

¡Vamos a escribir!

Imagine that the government of Puerto Rico is offering a free vacation in San Juan to the student who writes the best short essay in Spanish on vacationing in Puerto Rico. Write an entry for this contest. Follow these steps.

1 First, think about what you want to say. Use the postcards to help you brainstorm some ideas. You may want to list your ideas under the headings Weather, Sights, Recreation, and Clothing.

2 Write a first draft of your essay. Focus on communicating your ideas clearly.

San Juan

El Capitolio, San Juan

El Parque Nacional de Luquillo, Puerto Rico

3 Show your first draft to a partner. Ask what he or she likes about it and what should be changed. Think about any changes that you want to make, then revise it.

4 Check your work for spelling, accents, and question and exclamation marks at the beginning and end of sentences.

5 Make a clean copy. You can file your work in your writing portfolio, or you can share it with your classmates, who can vote on the most interesting, the most complete, and the one that most makes them want to visit Puerto Rico.

La Plaza de Colón, San Juan

La Casa de España, San Juan

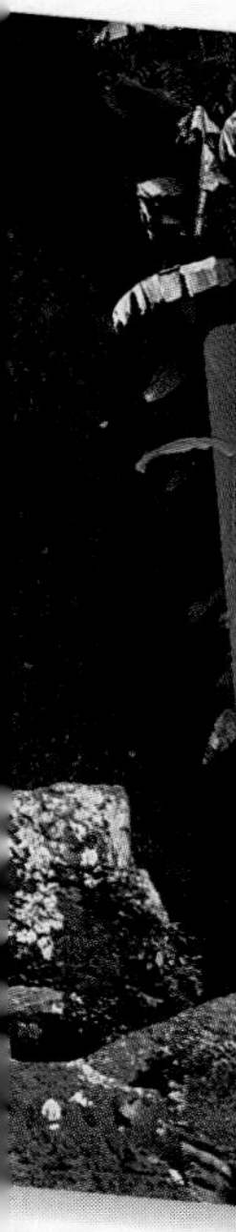

San Juan

El Castillo del Morro, San Juan

¿Lo sabes bien?

This section will help you organize your studying for the proficiency test, where you will be asked to do similar, though not identical, tasks. There will not be any models on the test.

Listening

Can you understand when people talk about their vacation activities? Listen as your teacher reads a sample similar to what you will hear on the test. Can you name, in Spanish, at least two items that Tomás may need today? What do you think the weather was like yesterday? Is Tomás definitely going to the waterfalls tomorrow?

Reading

Can you scan this travel ad and identify its author's main idea?

En Isla Mujeres en México

El mar es azul y las playas son blancas. En diciembre hace calor, hace sol y nunca llueve. Si no le gusta un invierno frío, venga a Isla Mujeres. Sólo necesita llevar su traje de baño, sus anteojos de sol y su pasaporte.

Writing

Can you write a postcard telling about your vacation at a ski resort? Here is an example:

Hola, Marisol:

Hace mucho frío aquí, pero también hace sol. Mañana quiero ir a la tienda para comprar unos anteojos de sol. Esta tarde voy a visitar a mis nuevos amigos. El sábado pienso ir a esquiar con ellos.

Tu amiga,

Susana

Culture

Based on what you know about vacation time in Chile, how would that affect the time of year you would visit that country?

Speaking

Can you discuss vacation choices and activities with a partner? For example:

A — ¿Adónde te gustaría ir este verano?

B — A mí me gustaría visitar las ruinas en Guatemala. ¿Y a ti?

A — Yo prefiero ir a una ciudad grande. Me gusta mucho visitar museos y comprar recuerdos. ¿Con quién piensas ir a Guatemala?

B — Con mi familia. Mi padre es de Guatemala. Y tú, ¿con quién piensas ir?

A — Con mi madre. A ella le gustan las ciudades grandes también.

Resumen del capítulo 7

Use the vocabulary from this chapter to help you:

- describe vacation choices and activities
- talk about the weather
- discuss what to take on a trip

to talk about vacation
las vacaciones *(pl.)*
ir de vacaciones

to talk about places to visit on vacation
las cataratas
la catedral
la ciudad
el lago
los lugares de interés
el mar
las montañas
el museo
el país
la pirámide
las ruinas
la selva tropical

to talk about things to do on vacation
bucear
los recuerdos
descansar
esquiar
explorar (la selva)
llevar
pasear (en bote)
el bote
sacar fotos
la foto *(f.)*
subir (la pirámide)
tomar el sol
visitar

to talk about planning a vacation
pensar (e → ie) + *inf.*
regresar
salir

to name items to take on vacation
el abrigo
los anteojos de sol
las botas
el bronceador
la bufanda
la cámara
el gorro
los guantes
el impermeable
la maleta
el paraguas *(sing.)*
el pasaporte
el traje de baño

to ask about or describe weather
¿Qué tiempo hace?
fantástico, -a
Hace buen tiempo.
Hace calor.
Hace fresco.
Hace frío.
Hace mal tiempo.
Hace sol.
Hace viento.

la lluvia
la nieve
el sol
el viento
Llueve.
Nieva.

to say that you want or would like something
querer (e → ie)
quisiera

to say where you went
ir: (yo) fui
    (tú) fuiste
no . . . ninguna parte

to say when events occur
cuando
pasado, -a

to indicate use or purpose
para + *inf.*

to express amazement
¡Vaya!

to express satisfaction
menos mal que

to express ability or permission
poder (o → ue)

CAPÍTULO 8

¿Qué haces en tu casa?

OBJECTIVES

At the end of this chapter you will be able to:

- tell where you live
- describe your home
- name household chores
- compare and contrast the use of outdoor space in a home in Spain and in the United States

Una casa en Maracaibo, Venezuela

¡Piénsalo bien!

Look at the photographs.

Una casa de Segovia, España

**In what ways is this house similar to and different
from homes that you know?**

In the captions, find the Spanish names for the rooms shown in the photographs. What do you think *dormitorio* might mean? What Spanish word do you know that is related to *la cocina*?

En Caracas, Venezuela

"Nuestro dormitorio no es muy grande, pero hay espacio para todo."

"Me gustan las cocinas modernas. ¡Puedo preparar de todo!"

Vocabulario para conversar

¿Cómo es tu casa?

Aquí tienes palabras y expresiones necesarias para hablar sobre dónde vives, cómo es tu casa y algunas cosas que tienes que hacer en casa. Léelas varias veces y practícalas con un(a) compañero(a) en las páginas siguientes.

una casa de dos pisos

el segundo piso

el primer piso*

el baño

el cuarto

el dormitorio

la sala

el comedor

la cocina

el coche

el lavadero

la sala de estar

el garaje

el sótano

hacer la cama

sacudir los muebles

lavar los platos

quitar la mesa

pasar la aspiradora

limpiar el baño

arreglar el cuarto

lavar la ropa

poner la mesa

cortar el césped

sacar la basura

el apartamento

También necesitas . . .

cerca (de)	*near*	hacer: (yo) hago	*to do, to make:*
lejos (de)	*far (from)*	(tú) haces	*I do / make,*
vivir: (yo) vivo	*to live: I live,*		*you do / make*
(tú) vives	*you live*	el quehacer	*(household) chore*
el piso	*floor*	(de la casa)	
bastante	*rather, quite*	tener que + *inf.*	*to have to ___*
nuestro, -a	*our*	más	*here: else*

* In a multistory building, we usually call the ground floor *la planta baja,* the second floor *el primer piso,* the third floor *el segundo piso,* the fourth floor *el tercer piso,* and so on. Note that for "first" and "third," we use *primer* and *tercer* in front of a masculine singular noun.

Empecemos a conversar

Túrnate con un compañero(a) para ser *Estudiante A* y *Estudiante B*.
Reemplacen las palabras subrayadas con las palabras representadas o
escritas en los recuadros. 💡 quiere decir que puedes escoger tu propia
respuesta. Para el Ejercicio 1, ve *(see)* el dibujo de la casa en la página 252.

1

A — ¿Dónde está *la cocina*?
B — Está en *el primer piso*.

Y ahora Uds.

Estudiante A   Estudiante B

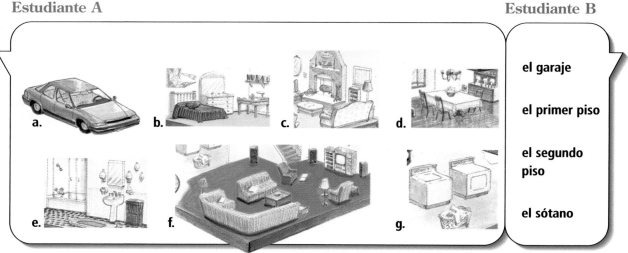

el garaje

el primer piso

el segundo
piso

el sótano

2

A — ¿Vives cerca de *un almacén*?
B — *Sí, bastante cerca.*
o: *No, vivo lejos.*

Y ahora Uds.

Estudiante A   Estudiante B

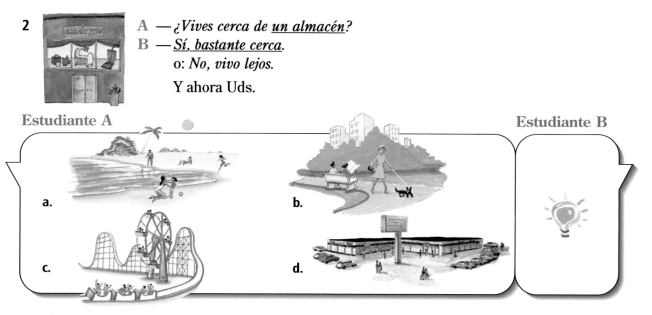

3

A —*¿Qué más tengo que hacer hoy? ¿Tengo que <u>lavar los platos</u>?*

B —*Sí, y también tienes que <u>sacar la basura</u>.*

Y ahora Uds.

También se dice

el living

la recámara
la habitación (de dormir)
la alcoba
la pieza
el cuarto

Estudiante A   **Estudiante B**

a.   b.   c.   d.   e.

el carro
el auto
la máquina

Empecemos a escribir

Escribe tus respuestas en español.

4   ¿Cuántos pisos y cuántos cuartos hay en tu casa o apartamento?

Nuestra casa / Nuestro apartamento tiene . . .

5   ¿En qué cuarto de la casa prefieres . . .

jugar videojuegos?
ver la tele?
leer?
estudiar?
escuchar música?

el zacate
la hierba
el pasto
la grama

6   ¿Te gusta más cortar el césped, pasar la aspiradora o sacudir los muebles? ¿Por qué?

7   ¿Qué quehaceres tienes para este fin de semana? ¿Qué más vas a hacer?

Vocabulario para conversar

¿Cómo es tu dormitorio?

Aquí tienes el resto del vocabulario necesario para hablar sobre las cosas que hay en una casa.

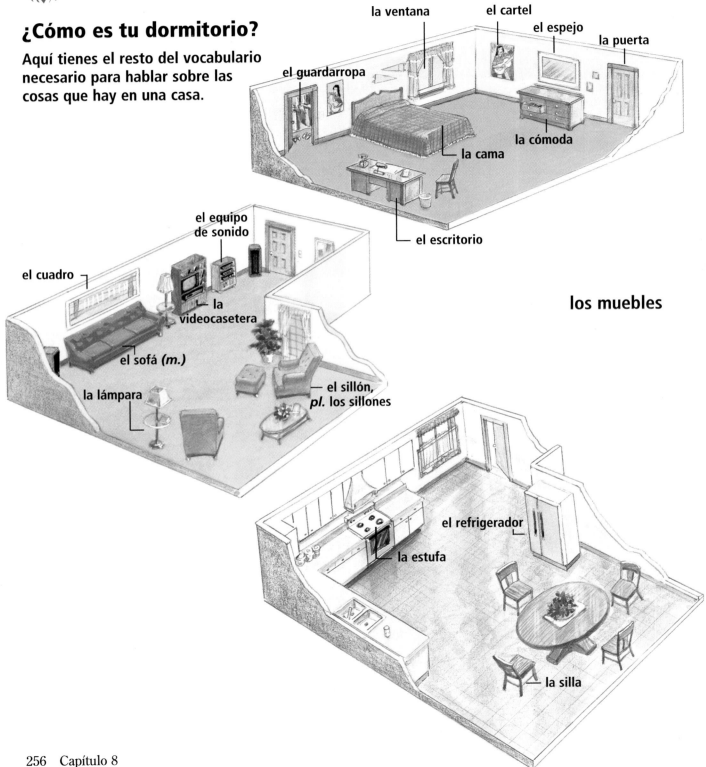

la ventana

el cartel

el espejo

la puerta

el guardarropa

la cómoda

la cama

el escritorio

el equipo de sonido

el cuadro

los muebles

la videocasetera

el sofá *(m.)*

el sillón, *pl.* los sillones

la lámpara

el refrigerador

la estufa

la silla

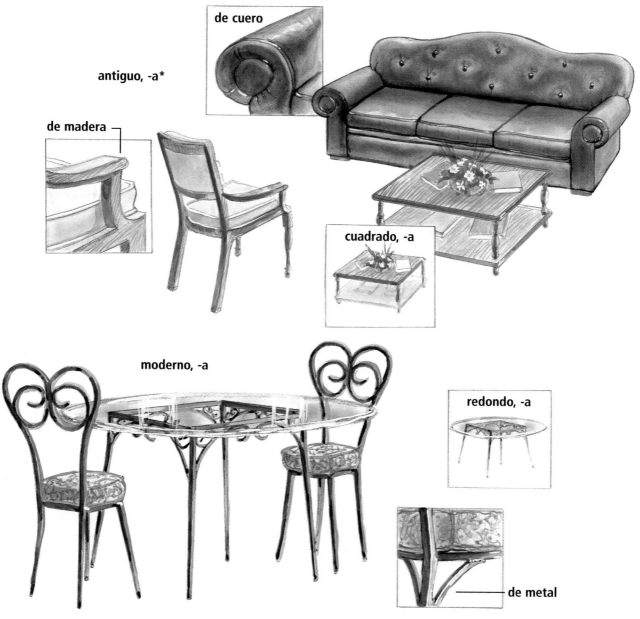

de cuero

antiguo, -a*

de madera

cuadrado, -a

moderno, -a

redondo, -a

de metal

También necesitas . . .

las cosas	*things*	poner: (yo) pongo	*to put (I put, you put),*
cómodo, -a	*comfortable*	(tú) pones	*to place, to set*
incómodo, -a	*uncomfortable*	(no) tener razón	*to be right (wrong)*
limpio, -a	*clean*	(no) estar de acuerdo	*to (dis)agree*
sucio, -a	*dirty*		

* In general, we use the adjective *antiguo, -a* for things, whereas we can use *viejo, -a* for either people or things. *Antiguo, -a* can imply value, as in *muebles antiguos.*

Empecemos a conversar

8   la cocina

A —¿Qué hay en <u>la cocina</u> de tu casa (apartamento)?

B —A ver...hay <u>una estufa y un refrigerador</u>.

Y ahora Uds.

Estudiante A

a. **el dormitorio**
b. **la sala**
c. **la sala de estar**
d. **el comedor**

Estudiante B

9

A —¿Qué vas a poner en <u>la sala</u>?

B —Voy a poner <u>un sofá muy cómodo</u>.

Y ahora Uds.

Estudiante A   **Estudiante B**

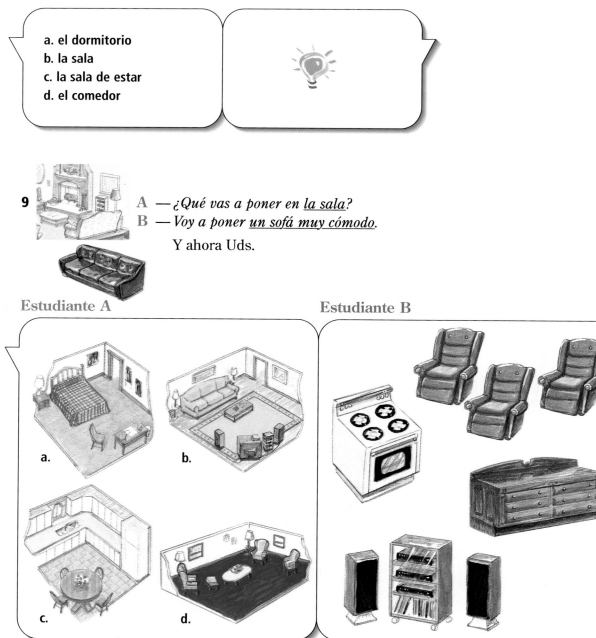

a.

b.

c.

d.

10

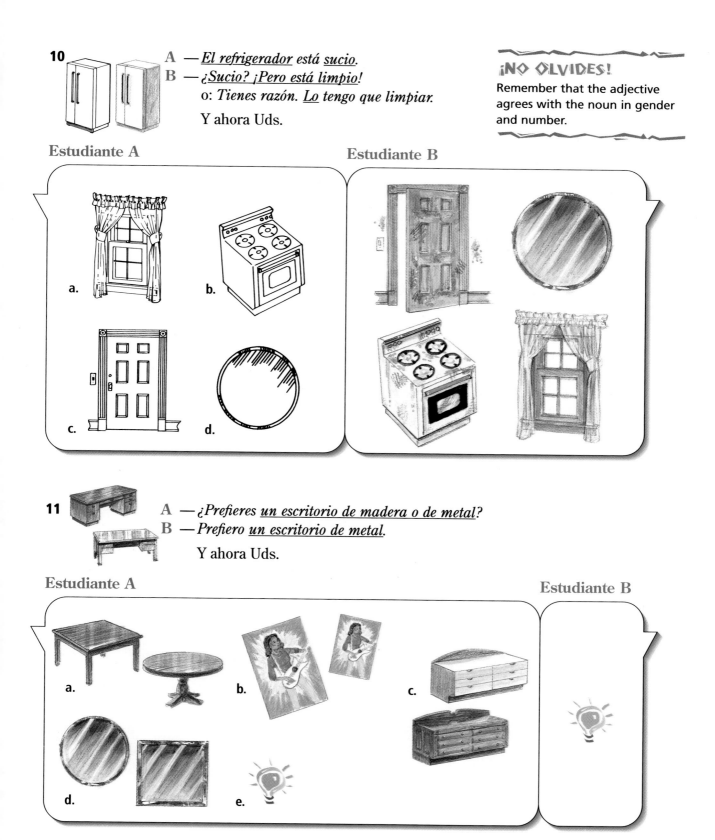

A — *El refrigerador* está *sucio.*
B — *¿Sucio? ¡Pero está limpio!*
  o: *Tienes razón. Lo tengo que limpiar.*

  Y ahora Uds.

¡NO OLVIDES!

Remember that the adjective agrees with the noun in gender and number.

Estudiante A

a.
b.
c.
d.

Estudiante B

11

A — *¿Prefieres un escritorio de madera o de metal?*
B — *Prefiero un escritorio de metal.*

  Y ahora Uds.

Estudiante A

a.
b.
c.
d.
e.

Estudiante B

Empecemos a escribir y a leer

Escribe tus respuestas en español.

12 Describe los muebles de un cuarto en tu casa. Di *(tell)* de qué colores son y si *(if)* son cómodos o incómodos.

En nuestra sala de estar hay dos sofás. Son . . .

13 ¿Cómo es tu dormitorio? ¿Hay muchas ventanas? ¿Cuadros? ¿Qué más hay?

14 ¿Estás de acuerdo con que todos tienen que ayudar con los quehaceres de la casa? ¿Por qué?

15 Lee este párrafo y dibuja la casa descrita aquí.

Nuestra casa tiene dos pisos, pero no tiene sótano. En el primer piso hay una cocina, un baño pequeño, una sala grande, un comedor y una sala de estar. En el segundo piso hay otro baño y tres dormitorios: dos bastante grandes y uno muy pequeño. También tenemos en el primer piso un lavadero moderno y muy práctico y un garaje para dos coches. Los muebles que más me gustan son un sofá antiguo pero cómodo, y ¡la videocasetera!

En el patio de una casa
en la Ciudad de México

Usando el
lavaplatos en
Zaragoza

Cortando el césped en la
Ciudad de México

También se dice

el gavetero
el buró

el afiche
el póster

la refrigeradora
la nevera
el frigorífico
la heladera

la cocina

el armario
el clóset
el ropero
el placard

¡Comuniquemos!

Aquí tienes otra oportunidad para usar el vocabulario de este capítulo.

1 Antes de *(before)* hacer planes con tus amigos, tienes que hacer otras cosas. Usa los dibujos y túrnate *(take turns)* con un(a) compañero(a) para hacer y aceptar invitaciones.

A — *¿Por qué no vamos al cine?*
B — *¿A qué hora? Tengo que limpiar el baño primero.*
A — *¿Puedes ir a las dos?*
B — *No, pero puedo ir a las cuatro.*

Estudiante A

Estudiante B

2 Tu familia acaba de mudarse *(has just moved)* a una casa nueva. Con un(a) compañero(a), di dónde están los muebles y los aparatos *(appliances)* y dónde quieres ponerlos. Después, tu compañero(a) va a decir *(say)* si *(if)* está de acuerdo o no.

A —*¿Dónde está la videocasetera?*
B —*Creo que está en el dormitorio de mamá.*
A —*Sí, aquí está. La pongo en la sala de estar.*
B —*No estoy de acuerdo. La debemos poner en el dormitorio.*

¿Qué sabes ahora?

Can you:

■ **tell where you live?**
—Vivo en un(a) ___ cerca de ___.

■ **name the rooms in your house?**
—Mi casa tiene una cocina, ___, ___ y ___.

■ **describe some furnishings?**
—Las sillas que están en el comedor son ___.

■ **name some household chores?**
—Yo tengo que ___ y mis hermanos tienen que ___.

Perspectiva cultural

**En España hay casas y apartamentos muy diferentes.
También hay diversos tipos de patios.**

What family members might use the part of the house pictured, and for what purpose? What might some people call it in English?

In the large cities of Spain, neighbors often visit each other's apartments in the same building. In small towns, you might see neighbors talking to each other through the windows that open onto the *patio*.

When you hear the English word "patio" you probably think of a small patch of concrete in a backyard. In Spanish, however, it can mean different things. For example, in a modern apartment building in a large city like Madrid, the *patio* is an air shaft in the center of the building. The kitchen may have a window that opens onto it.

However, in the south, in towns such as Sevilla and Córdoba, some *patios* are gardens with flowers, chairs, and perhaps caged birds. Some *patios* in Sevilla are in the front of the house and lead visitors in. More often, they are in the middle of the house, with big doors leading into the rooms. A *patio* in Sevilla is a place for friends and family to gather and talk.

Even though a *patio* in an apartment building in Madrid looks very different from a traditional one in Sevilla, they still have similar functions. A *patio* is a space that opens to the sky where friends and neighbors can spend time together chatting.

La cultura desde tu perspectiva

1 Many houses in the United States have patios in back. They are usually made of concrete. In what ways is the design and function of a patio in the United States similar to and different from one in Spain?

2 In the United States, most open spaces are in front or in back of the house, while in Spain you might find them in the middle. What advantages do you see to having an open space in the middle of a house? If you were building a home, would you include a Spanish-style patio in your plans? Why or why not?

Un patio en Córdoba, España

Una familia en su patio, Santiago de Chile

Gramática en contexto

Look at this page out of a student's photo album made during her trip to Cuernavaca, Mexico. From the photographs you see here, what do you think she will remember as she looks at this page?

Aquí estamos Marcia y yo con nuestra familia mexicana. Los señores Ortiz y sus hijos, Julia y Ramón.

Nuestra mamá mexicana cocina y pone la mesa. Al señor Ortiz también le gusta cocinar. Nosotros arreglamos nuestros cuartos y hacemos las camas.

Los abuelos Ortiz viven cerca. Su casa es muy grande y tienen un patio con alberca.

Yo prefiero tomar el sol por la mañana, pero Marcia prefiere tomar el sol por la tarde. ¡Qué buena vida!

A In the photo captions, you find *nuestra* and *nuestros*. What words determine whether *-a* or *-os* is used at the end?

B In the sentence *"Su casa es muy grande . . . ,"* the word *su* indicates the house belongs to someone. Whom do you believe it belongs to?

Los verbos *poner* y *hacer*

The forms of *poner* ("to put, to place, to set") and *hacer* ("to make, to do") follow the pattern of other *-er* verbs in all except the *yo* forms, *pongo* and *hago*.

Here are all the present-tense forms of *poner* and *hacer*.

(yo)	**pongo** **hago**	(nosotros) (nosotras)	pon**emos** hac**emos**
(tú)	pon**es** hac**es**	(vosotros) (vosotras)	pon**éis** hac**éis**
Ud. (él) (ella)	pon**e** hac**e**	Uds. (ellos) (ellas)	pon**en** hac**en**

1 Estas personas ayudan a una amiga a mudarse. Di en qué cuarto ponen las cosas.

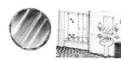

Teresa pone el espejo en el baño.

Teresa

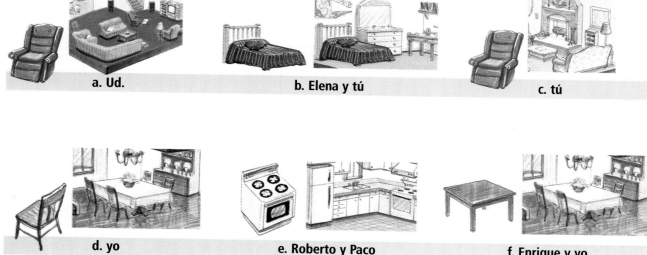

a. Ud. b. Elena y tú c. tú

d. yo e. Roberto y Paco f. Enrique y yo

2 ¿Qué tareas tienen que hacer estos estudiantes todos los días?

A — *¿Qué tarea hacen Carlos y Javier todos los días?*
B — *Generalmente hacen la tarea de matemáticas.*

Carlos y Javier

a. Felipe

b. Fabiola y tú

c. Irene y Bárbara

d. Ud.

e. Lupe y Raúl

f. tú

Los verbos que terminan en *-ir*

You already know the pattern of endings of present-tense *-ar* and *-er* verbs. There is one other group of regular verbs, those that end in *-ir*. *Vivir* ("to live") is a regular *-ir* verb. Here are all its present-tense forms.

(yo)	vi**vo**	(nosotros) (nosotras)	viv**imos**
(tú)	vi**ves**	(vosotros) (vosotras)	viv**ís**
Ud. (él) (ella)	vi**ve**	Uds. (ellos) (ellas)	viv**en**

• Notice that the pattern of endings for -ir verbs is identical to that of -er verbs, except for the nosotros and vosotros forms.

• Notice that *salir* is a regular *-ir* verb in the present tense except for its *yo* form: *(yo) salgo.*

3 Mira *(look at)* el dibujo de este pueblo *(town)*. Di a tu compañero(a) si estas personas viven cerca o lejos de ciertos lugares *(places)*.

David y Agustín
A — *¿Dónde viven David y Agustín?*
B — *Viven cerca del centro comercial.*
    o: *Viven lejos de la escuela.*

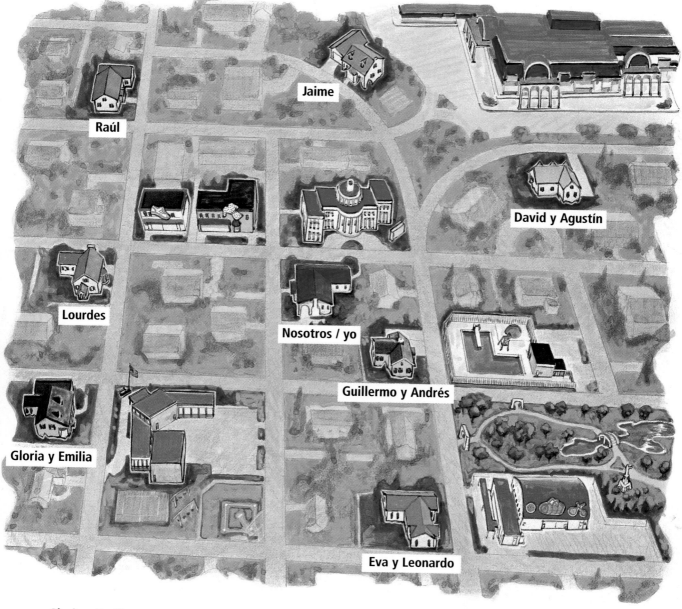

a. Gloria y Emilia
b. Uds.
c. Eva y Leonardo
d. Raúl
e. tú
f. Jaime
g. Lourdes
h. Guillermo y Andrés

El verbo *preferir*

Preferir "to prefer" is an *e → ie* stem-changing verb, similar to *querer* and *pensar*. Here are all its present-tense forms.

(yo)	prefiero	(nosotros) (nosotras)	preferimos
(tú)	prefieres	(vosotros) (vosotras)	preferís
Ud. (él) (ella)	prefiere	Uds. (ellos) (ellas)	prefieren

- Notice that the endings of *preferir* follow the pattern of regular *-ir* verbs, like *vivir*.

4 Con un(a) compañero(a), túrnate para preguntar y contestar *(asking and answering)* sobre las preferencias de estas personas.

A —¿Qué prefiere tu hermana, jugar fútbol o tenis?
B —Mi hermana prefiere jugar tenis.

tu hermana

a. tu abuelo b. tu papá c. tus amigos(as)

d. tus primos e. ustedes f. tu amiga

5 Di que las personas prefieren hacer estos pasatiempos y por qué.

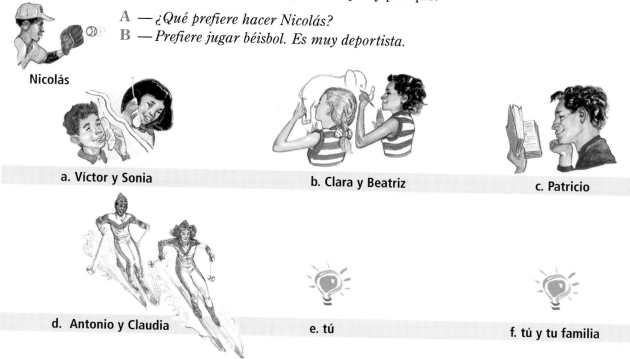

A — ¿Qué prefiere hacer Nicolás?
B — Prefiere jugar béisbol. Es muy deportista.

Nicolás

a. Víctor y Sonia

b. Clara y Beatriz

c. Patricio

d. Antonio y Claudia

e. tú

f. tú y tu familia

Los adjetivos posesivos: *Su* y *nuestro*

You already know that when we want to tell what belongs to
someone and to show relationships, we can use *mi(s)*, *tu(s),* and
su(s). Here are the other possessive adjectives.

nuestro primo **nuestros** primos	**nuestra** prima **nuestras** primas
***vuestro** tío **vuestros** tíos	**vuestra** tía **vuestras** tías
su hermano **sus** hermanos	**su** hermana **sus** hermanas

*Vuestro, -a, -os, -as is used mainly in Spain. We will use it occasionally and you
should learn to recognize it.

• Like other adjectives, the possessive adjectives agree in number
with the nouns that follow them. Only *nuestro* and *vuestro* have
different masculine and feminine endings.

6 Describe parte de tu casa o de otra casa. Usa las palabras *(words)* de abajo *(below)*.

casa / azul
Nuestra casa (no) es azul.
dormitorios / grandes
Nuestros dormitorios (no) son grandes.

    a. mesa / de metal
    b. sillas / de madera
    c. sillones / antiguos
    d. sofá / de cuero
    e. equipo de sonido / moderno
    f. cuadros / bonitos
    g. garaje / para dos coches
    h. sala de estar / cómoda
    i.

7 Intercambia *(exchange)* tu hoja del Ejercicio 6 con un(a) compañero(a). Usa esta información para describir su casa a otro(a) estudiante.

Una casa típica en Ushuaia, Tierra del Fuego, Argentina

La casa de los Johnson es azul. Sus dormitorios son muy grandes.

Ahora lo sabes

Can you:

- tell where someone puts something?

  —Generalmente (yo) ___ mis papeles en mi carpeta.

- say what someone makes or does?

  —Ana María y yo ___ las camas todos los días.

- tell where a person lives?

  —Mis abuelos ___ en Los Ángeles.

- tell what someone prefers?

  —Mis hermanos y yo ___ ir al cine el sábado.

- describe possession using *su* and *nuestra?*

  —___ mesa es redonda pero ___ mesa es cuadrada.

Unas casas en La Boca,
una zona de Buenos Aires

Una casa en Bolivia

Para decir más

Aquí tienes vocabulario
adicional que te puede ayudar
para hacer las actividades de
esta sección.

la mecedora
rocking chair

la alfombra
rug

la escalera
stairway

el pasillo
hallway

el balcón
balcony

el jardín
garden, yard

el patio
patio, yard

el garaje para dos coches
two-car garage

**el tocadiscos de
discos compactos**
CD player

el walkman
personal stereo

Actividades

**Esta sección te ofrece la oportunidad de aumentar
tus conocimientos de español al integrar lo que
aprendiste en este capítulo con lo que aprendiste
en capítulos anteriores.**

1 Usando el dibujo de la página 269, escoge una casa
e imagina que vives allí. Tu compañero(a) va a adivinar
(guess) dónde vives con preguntas como las siguientes.

¿Vives cerca o lejos del centro comercial?
¿Es amarilla tu casa?

2 ¿Qué prefieren hacer tu compañero(a) y sus amigos
cuando hace frío o calor? Pregunta y contesta según
(according to) el modelo y luego anota *(then note)* las
actividades más populares.

A — *¿Qué prefieren hacer Uds. cuando hace fresco?*
B — *Preferimos practicar deportes.*

3 Con un(a) compañero(a), haz *(make)* una lista de algunos quehaceres. Pregunta y contesta cuáles Uds. tienen que hacer.

A —*¿Tienes que . . . ?*

B —*Sí. ¿Y tú?*

    o: *No. ¿Y tú?*

A —*Yo también.*

    o: *Yo no.*

    o: *Yo tampoco.*

Luego haz un informe *(report)* para la clase.

A —*Yo tengo que . . . , pero Mateo no.*

    o: *Mateo y yo tenemos que . . .*

    o: *Ni Mateo ni yo tenemos que . . .*

Tus compañeros van a preguntar qué quehaceres prefieren Uds.

Clase —*¿Prefieres (Prefieren) . . . o . . . ?*

A o **B** —*Prefiero (Preferimos) . . .*

4 Con un(a) compañero(a) inventa este diálogo:

- pregunta si tu compañero(a) quiere hacer algo
- él (ella) no puede y explica *(explains)* lo que *(what)* tiene que hacer en casa
- tú tienes que sugerir *(suggest)* otro plan
- tu compañero(a) dice si está de acuerdo o no

¡Vamos a leer!

Antes de leer

 Using prior knowledge

Remember the story of Cinderella? Did you ever wonder what it would be like to be in her shoes? In this reading, a young man is about to find out. Use the pictures and what you know about Cinderella to predict what this reading might be about.

Mira la lectura

STRATEGY > Skimming

Skim through the story. Is it what you expected?

Esteban es un muchacho de 18 años. Vive en una casa más o menos grande con su padre, su madrastra y un hermanastro y una hermanastra. Pero su padre está frecuentemente fuera del país. ¿Y quién hace todos los quehaceres de la casa? Esteban, ¡claro! Los hace, pero no está nada contento.

2

UN DÍA . . .

TV: . . . La princesa Gabriela de Xilá está de visita aquí. Hay una gran fiesta en su honor.

MADRASTRA: ¡Claro que vamos a la fiesta!

1

MADRASTRA: Tienes que lavar los platos y pasar la aspiradora . . . y cortar el césped.

ESTEBAN: Pero . . .

3

MADRASTRA: Tú no puedes ir a la fiesta. Tienes que preparar nuestra ropa.

4

LA NOCHE DE LA FIESTA . . .

HERMANASTRO Y HERMANASTRA: Hasta luego, Esteban.

Infórmate

Using prior knowledge
Recognizing word families

Often you can use Spanish words you know to figure out the meaning of new words. For example: *madrastra, hermanastra,* and *hermanastro.* What names for family members do you recognize as parts of these words? Then think about the characters in Cinderella. Use this information to figure out the meaning of the three words. What do you think *madrina* means?

 Compare the story with Cinderella. How are they alike and how are they different?

 What is the turning point in the story? What happens?

 Do you agree with the way the story ends? Why or why not?

Aplicación

What do you think *padrastro* means?

6

Pero
¿quién es?
¡Qué guapo!
¡Debe ser un príncipe! ¡Mira los zapatos de vidrio!

5

MADRINA: Hola, Esteban. Soy la madrina de la Cenicienta. Y tú también vas a ir a la fiesta. A ver, ¿dónde están tu perro y la aspiradora? Los voy a convertir en un chófer y una limosina.

7

HERMANASTRA: Mamá . . .
¡Es Esteban!
HERMANASTRO: Pero ¿qué hace aquí?
MADRASTRA: No sé, hijo . . .

8

UNA SEMANA MÁS TARDE . . .
ESTEBAN: Voy a ser el asistente personal de la princesa. Y ¡no voy a hacer nunca más los quehaceres!

¡Vamos a escribir!

**Everyone can picture an ideal home—the perfect dream house.
How would you describe your dream house? Write an ad in Spanish
for a dream house for sale.**

 First, think about the house plan and list the rooms. Is it a one- or two-story house? Name three or four special features.

 Then write at least five sentences describing the house as if you were trying to sell it. You can start with the phrase *Se vende casa* (House for sale).

 Show your description to a partner. Then revise and edit it. Recopy your corrected description. You might want to add a sketch of the floor plan with the rooms labeled.

 Now you are ready to share your work. You can:

- collect all the ads into a book called *Se venden casas* and exchange books with another class
- display the ads on a bulletin board for each student to choose the house he or she would like to buy
- keep your ad in your writing portfolio

Casa moderna en Los Ángeles

En la zona de Chapultepec,
Ciudad de México

Una casa al estilo
de Gaudí en
Los Ángeles

¿Lo sabes bien?

This section will help you organize your studying for the proficiency test, where you will be asked to do similar, though not identical, tasks. There will not be any models on the test.

Listening

Can you understand when people talk about their household chores? Listen as your teacher reads a sample similar to what you will hear on the test. This is a note from Marina's mother explaining what Marina has to do on Saturday. What could you do to help Marina? How long do you think it would take you to do two of these chores? What are you going to do when you finish?

Reading

Can you understand a description of a dream house? Read the text that follows. Do you agree with some of the things María Elena wants?

"Quiero tener una casa no muy grande y amueblarla con cosas que me gustan— prácticas pero bonitas. Y me gusta vivir cómodamente. Quiero un equipo de sonido, una videocasetera, una piscina, una cancha de tenis, . . . ¡y otra persona para hacer todos los quehaceres!"

Writing

Can you write a letter to a friend describing the new house or apartment you've just moved into? Here is a sample:

> Querido Ernesto:
>
> Vivo con mi madre en un apartamento de Manhattan. Tenemos dos dormitorios, un baño, una cocina y una sala. Nuestro apartamento es pequeño, pero tenemos muchos muebles. En la sala hay una mesa con ocho sillas, un sofá con dos sillones, tres mesitas, un escritorio, tres lámparas, diez cuadros y dos espejos. Menos mal que en mi cuarto no hay muchas cosas. Tengo sólo una cama y una cómoda. Me gusta donde vivo, pero quisiera tener una casa más grande.
>
> Tu amiga,
>
> Magdalena

Culture

Can you describe a patio in Sevilla and in Madrid and its uses?

Speaking

Can you talk about household chores? Create a dialogue with your partner. Do you and your friend like and dislike the same chores? Here is a sample dialogue:

A —*¿Tienes quehaceres de la casa para el sábado?*

B —*Sí. Por la mañana tengo que cortar el césped, lavar los platos y sacar la basura.*

A —*A mí no me gusta ni sacar la basura ni limpiar el baño, pero lo hago todos los sábados. Prefiero hacer las camas.*

Resumen del capítulo 8

Use the vocabulary from this chapter to help you:

- tell where you live
- describe your home
- name household chores

to talk about where someone lives
cerca (de)
lejos (de)
vivir: (yo) vivo
(tú) vives

to talk about houses or apartments
el apartamento
el baño
la casa (de ... pisos)
el césped
la cocina
el comedor
el cuarto
el dormitorio
el garaje
el lavadero
el (primer) piso
la sala
la sala de estar
el sótano

to name household items
la cama
el cartel
el coche
la cómoda
las cosas
el cuadro
el equipo de sonido
el escritorio
el espejo

la estufa
el guardarropa
la lámpara
los muebles
la puerta
el refrigerador
la silla
el sillón, *pl.* los sillones
el sofá *(m.)*
la ventana
la videocasetera

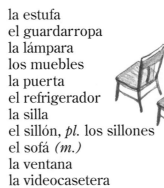

to describe household items
antiguo, -a
bastante
cómodo, -a
cuadrado, -a
de cuero
de madera
de metal
incómodo, -a
limpio, -a
moderno, -a
redondo, -a
sucio, -a

to indicate possession
nuestro, -a
su, -s (here: *their*)

to name chores around a home
arreglar
cortar (el césped)

hacer: (yo) hago
(tú) haces
hacer la cama
lavar la ropa / los platos
limpiar el baño
pasar la aspiradora
poner: (yo) pongo
(tú) pones
poner / quitar la mesa
el quehacer (de la casa)
sacar la basura
sacudir los muebles

to indicate preferences
preferir (e → ie)

to indicate obligation
tener que + *inf.*

to indicate that someone is right or wrong
(no) tener razón

to indicate whether you agree with someone or something
(no) estar de acuerdo

other useful expressions
más (here: *else)*

¿Cómo te sientes?

OBJECTIVES

At the end of this chapter, you will be able to:

- describe how you are feeling
- tell what parts of your body hurt
- suggest things you or others can do to feel better
- discuss attitudes toward health and health practices in the Spanish-speaking world

La medicina antigua y la moderna (1953), Diego Rivera

¡Piénsalo bien!

Look at the pictures and read the captions.

"Me duele la garganta. ¿Qué puedo tomar?"

In the photo, what do you think this person is saying to the pharmacist?

En una farmacia en Chile

"Pero mamá, no me gusta ir al médico."

What do you think a *Centro Pediátrico* is? What are the specialties of the doctors in this medical center?

Clínica del Centro Pediátrico de Isla Verde, Puerto Rico

"Me lastimé el pie."

What do you think *Cruz Roja* means? What do you think might have happened to the boy? How might it have happened?

Ayudando a un niño en Cali, Colombia

Vocabulario para conversar

¡Ay! ¡Me duele el pie!

Aquí tienes palabras y expresiones necesarias para hablar sobre las partes del cuerpo que te duelen y para sugerir *(suggest)* qué puedes hacer para sentirte mejor. Léelas varias veces y practícalas con un(a) compañero(a) en las páginas siguientes.

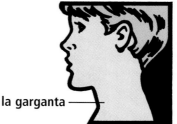

la garganta

El cuerpo

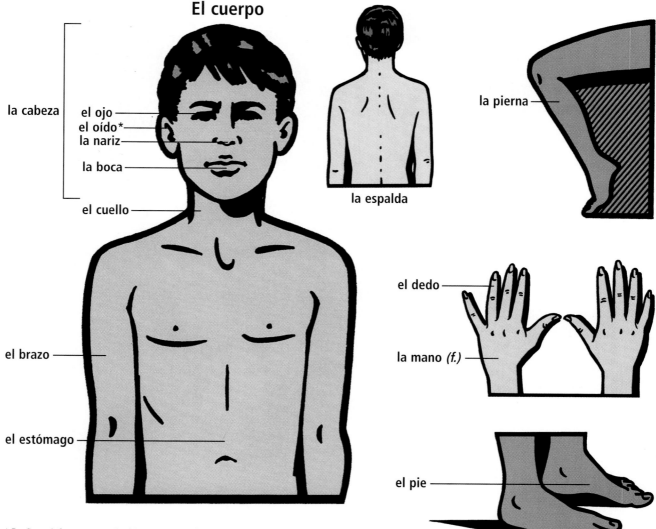

la cabeza

el ojo
el oído*
la nariz

la boca

el cuello

la espalda

la pierna

el brazo

el dedo

la mano *(f.)*

el estómago

el pie

* In Spanish we use *el oído* to mean the inner ear and *la oreja* to mean the outer ear. It is usually the inner ear that hurts.

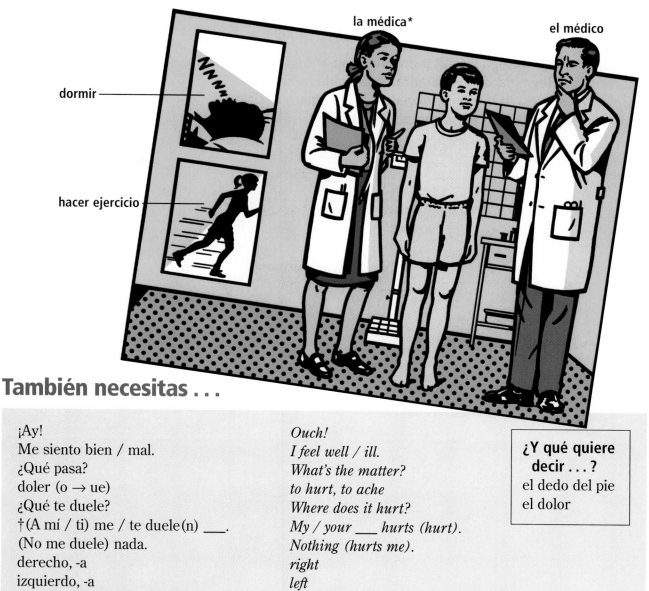

dormir

hacer ejercicio

la médica*

el médico

También necesitas . . .

¡Ay!	*Ouch!*
Me siento bien / mal.	*I feel well / ill.*
¿Qué pasa?	*What's the matter?*
doler (o → ue)	*to hurt, to ache*
¿Qué te duele?	*Where does it hurt?*
†(A mí / ti) me / te duele(n) ___.	*My / your ___ hurts (hurt).*
(No me duele) nada.	*Nothing (hurts me).*
derecho, -a	*right*
izquierdo, -a	*left*
¿Cuánto (tiempo) hace que ___?	*How long has it been since ___? /*
	(For) how long ___?
Hace + *time expression* + que ___.	*It's been* + time expression + *since ___. /*
	___ for + time expression
(Yo) creo que ___.	*I think that ___.*
Debes quedarte en la cama.	*You should stay in bed.*
llamar	here: *to call*

¿Y qué quiere decir . . . ?
el dedo del pie
el dolor

---

* To refer to or address a physician, we use the term *doctor(a)*.
  —*Doctor, me duele mucho la cabeza.*

† With expressions like *me / te duele(n)*, we usually use the definite article when
  talking about body parts: *Me duele el brazo.*

Empecemos a conversar

Túrnate con un(a) compañero(a) para ser *Estudiante A* y
Estudiante B. Reemplacen las palabras subrayadas con palabras
representadas o escritas en los recuadros. 💡 quiere decir que
puedes escoger *(choose)* tu propia respuesta.

1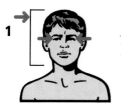

A — *¿Qué pasa? ¿Te duele la cabeza?*
B — *No, me duelen los ojos.*
    o: *No, no me duele nada. Me siento bien.*
    Y ahora Uds.

Estudiante A   **Estudiante B**

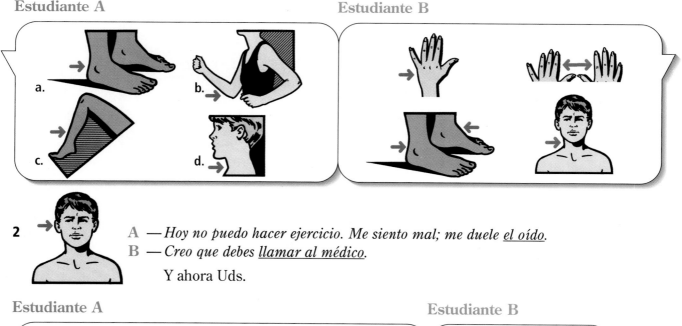

2

A — *Hoy no puedo hacer ejercicio. Me siento mal; me duele el oído.*
B — *Creo que debes llamar al médico.*
    Y ahora Uds.

Estudiante A   **Estudiante B**

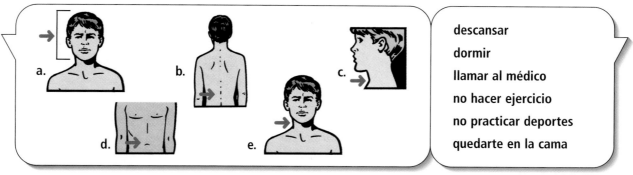

descansar
dormir
llamar al médico
no hacer ejercicio
no practicar deportes
quedarte en la cama

3 A —*¿Cuánto tiempo hace que te duele <u>la espalda</u>?*
   B —*Hace <u>una semana</u> que me duele.*

     Y ahora Uds.

Estudiante A   Estudiante B

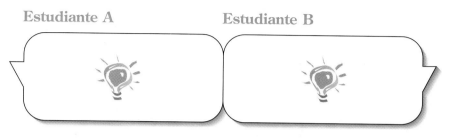

4 A —*¿Qué pasa? ¿Te duele <u>el oído</u>?*
   B —*Sí, <u>el derecho</u>.*
       o: *No, no me duele.*

     Y ahora Uds.

Estudiante A   Estudiante B

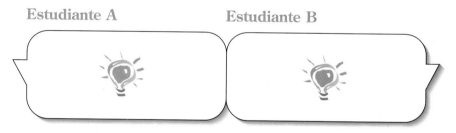

Empecemos a escribir

Escribe tus respuestas en español.

5 Dale *(give him / her)* dos consejos *(pieces of advice)* a un(a) amigo(a) que tiene dolor de garganta.

6 ¿Qué te duele cuando . . .

participas en un maratón? *Me duelen los pies.*

   a. estudias toda la noche para un examen?
   b. comes demasiado?
   c. lanzas la pelota *(pitch)* en un partido de béisbol?
   d. animas *(cheer)* mucho en un partido de básquetbol?
   e. tocas el piano por tres horas?

7 ¿Te duele algo? ¿Qué?

Vocabulario para conversar

¿Qué tienes?

Aquí tienes el resto del vocabulario necesario para describir cómo te sientes.

La enfermería

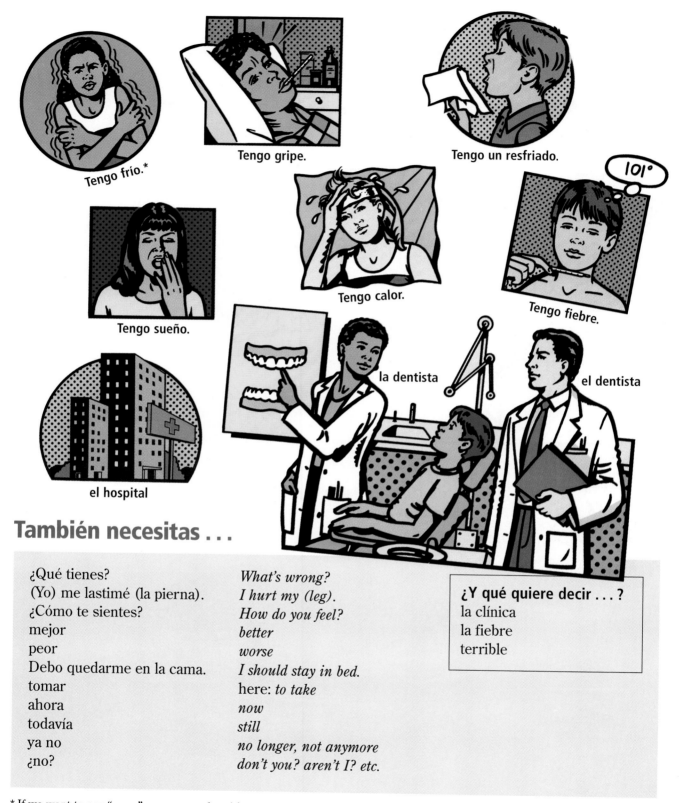

Tengo frío.*

Tengo gripe.

Tengo un resfriado.

Tengo sueño.

Tengo calor.

101°

Tengo fiebre.

la dentista

el dentista

el hospital

También necesitas . . .

¿Qué tienes? — *What's wrong?*
(Yo) me lastimé (la pierna). — *I hurt my (leg).*
¿Cómo te sientes? — *How do you feel?*
mejor — *better*
peor — *worse*
Debo quedarme en la cama. — *I should stay in bed.*
tomar — here: *to take*
ahora — *now*
todavía — *still*
ya no — *no longer, not anymore*
¿no? — *don't you? aren't I? etc.*

¿Y qué quiere decir . . . ?
la clínica
la fiebre
terrible

* If we want to say "very," we use *mucho* with *sueño*, *frío*, and *calor*, but *mucha* with *hambre* and *sed*: *Tengo mucho sueño*, but *Tengo mucha sed*.

Empecemos a conversar

8

A — ¿*Todavía tienes <u>sueño</u>?*
B — *Sí, todavía tengo <u>sueño</u>.*
   o: *No, ya no tengo <u>sueño</u>.*

   Y ahora Uds.

Estudiante A   **Estudiante B**

9

A — ¿*Cómo te sientes? ¿Está mejor <u>tu brazo</u>?*
B — *No, ahora está peor. Creo que debo <u>ir a la enfermería</u>.*

   Y ahora Uds.

Estudiante A   **Estudiante B**

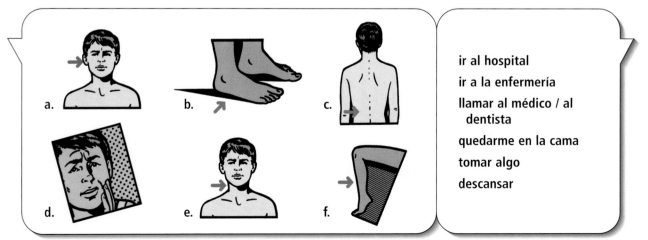

ir al hospital

ir a la enfermería

llamar al médico / al dentista

quedarme en la cama

tomar algo

descansar

10

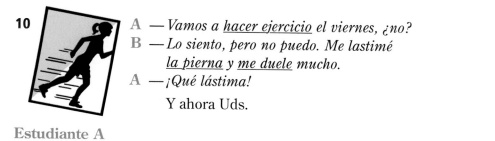

A — *Vamos a <u>hacer ejercicio</u> el viernes, ¿no?*
B — *Lo siento, pero no puedo. Me lastimé <u>la pierna</u> y <u>me duele</u> mucho.*
A — *¡Qué lástima!*

Y ahora Uds.

Estudiante A

a. b. c. d.

Estudiante B

Empecemos a escribir y a leer

Escribe tus respuestas en español.

11 ¿Cómo te sientes?

12 Escribe otras dos formas diferentes para decir *¿Cómo te sientes?*

13 Cuando tienes dolor de estómago, ¿qué debes hacer?

14 Marta dice: "Carolina, lo siento, pero hoy no puedo ir al cine contigo. Me siento mal. Tengo mucho frío y me duele la garganta. Tengo un terrible dolor de cabeza también. Creo que debo quedarme en la cama."

a. ¿Qué crees que tiene Marta?
b. ¿Qué más debe hacer?

También se dice

Tengo calentura.

Tengo gripa.

Tengo catarro.
Tengo resfrío.

¡Comuniquemos!

Aquí tienes otra oportunidad para usar el vocabulario de este capítulo.

1 Tu hermana menor no se siente bien. Cada vez *(each time)* que le preguntas le duele algo diferente. Túrnate con un(a) compañero(a) para preguntar y contestar.

> A — *¿Cómo te sientes? ¿Todavía tienes fiebre?*
> B — *Ya no. Ahora tengo dolor de cabeza.*

2 ¿Es lógica la tercera línea? Si no, escribe una solución lógica. Después, escribe un diálogo semejante *(similar)*. Un(a) compañero(a) va a escribir una buena solución.

A — *¿Por qué no quieres ir a nadar?*
B — *Porque llueve.*
A — *Ah, podemos ir a tomar el sol.*

A — *¿Por qué no vamos al cine?*
B — *Porque me duelen mucho los ojos.*
A — *Pues, podemos ver la tele aquí en tu casa.*

A — *¿Por qué no vamos al gimnasio?*
B — *Porque me lastimé la espalda.*
A — *¿Prefieres jugar golf?*

A — *¿Por qué no comes algo?*
B — *Todavía tengo este terrible dolor de estómago.*
A — *Yo creo que debes llamar al médico.*

3 Túrnate con un(a) compañero(a) para representar a una turista entusiasta y a su amiga que nunca se siente bien.

A — ¡Qué bonito está el día! ¿Quieres ir a hacer ejercicio?

B — Lo siento, pero me duelen mucho las piernas.
o: Pues, no. Tengo un terrible dolor de cabeza.

¿Qué sabes ahora?

Can you:

■ name some parts of your body?

—Tengo dos ___, dos ___ y diez ___.

■ tell how you feel or describe your symptoms?

—¿Cómo te sientes?

— ___.

■ tell how long you have been feeling that way?

—¿Cuánto tiempo hace que te duele el oído?

— ___ dos días ___ me duele el oído.

■ make a suggestion to someone who is feeling ill?

—Me duele la garganta.
—Creo que debes ___.

Perspectiva cultural

Algunas veces, cuando no me siento bien, voy a la farmacia para comprar una medicina. Otras veces tomo algunas hierbas medicinales.

Why do you think these two photos are shown? Why might someone who is sick choose to go sometimes to one of these two places and sometimes to the other?

Imagine this. You aren't feeling well. Your mother talks to some friends, but they can't agree on what your illness is or how to treat it. There is a woman in your community who is not a doctor, but who is known to be able to help people who are sick. You go to see her. She asks about your recent activities. After a while she decides which of her remedies is best for your situation.

In many Hispanic communities, folk remedies have been passed down from generation to generation, largely due to the availability of plants with medicinal value. For example, a tea made from mint (known in Mexico as *yerbabuena*) may be given to someone with a stomachache. A little piece of camphor *(alcanfor)* or the herb rue *(ruda)* wrapped in cotton and put in the ear is said to cure an earache. Other home remedies, such as quinine, have found their way into modern medicine.

Una farmacia en Chetumal, México

Members of many ethnic groups treat an illness in this way. They may consult a doctor, or they may decide the illness can be more easily cured by a long-used folk remedy.

Today scientists are investigating new sources of medicine by consulting ethnic groups that have long used remedies made from local plants.

La cultura desde tu perspectiva

1   What folk remedies are you familiar with? Why might someone choose to go to a folk healer instead of a doctor?

2   If you were living in a different country and your friends and neighbors went to folk healers, would you do the same? Why or why not?

Las hierbas medicinales son importantes en la medicina moderna.

UNIDAD MEDICA DE ESPECIALISTAS

✝ DR. JESUS MANUEL LOZANO G.
PEDIATRA
-ENFERMEDADES DE LOS NIÑOS Y ADOLESCENTES
✝ DR. JUAN MANUEL VILLASEÑOR
TRAUMATOLOGO Y ORTOPEDISTA
-FRACTURAS Y DEFORMACIONES DE LOS HUESOS
ORTOPEDIA PEDIATRICA
✝ DR. JULIAN GARCIA VILLEGAS
MEDICINA GENERAL

CONTAMOS CON SERVICIO DE LABORATORIO Y BANCO DE SANGRE

CITAS
☎ 2-12

CALLE NOGAL
(A UNA CUADRA DE LA IGLE

Gramática en contexto

Look at this article from a health magazine that tells parents how to detect an illness in their children. What kind of information would you expect to find?

¿Cómo puede saber si su hijo tiene mononucleosis?

Ud. debe prestar atención si:

- a su hijo le duele la garganta
- le duelen los ojos y la cabeza
- tiene un resfriado o tiene gripe, y no se mejora
- está siempre cansado o duerme muchas horas
- hace una semana que no puede ir a la escuela
- no tiene energía para hacer ejercicio, aunque le gustan los deportes

Éstos pueden ser síntomas de mononucleosis. Por eso, Ud. debe llevar a su hijo a una clínica para hacerle un examen completo. Mientras tanto, su hijo debe descansar y beber mucho líquido.

A In the article, find the expressions *le duele(n)* and *le gusta(n)*. Why do you think *le* is used instead of *me?*

B Compare the two sentences that use *duele* and *duelen*. When do we use each of these? Find another verb in the article that follows this pattern.

C Look at the sentence *Hace una semana que no puede ir a la escuela. Que* connects two parts of this sentence. The second part tells what the person cannot do. What information does the first part of the sentence give?

El verbo *dormir*

Like *poder*, *dormir* is an *o → ue* stem-changing verb. Here are all its present-tense forms:

(yo)	d**ue**rmo	(nosotros)(nosotras)	d**o**rmimos
(tú)	d**ue**rmes	(vosotros)(vosotras)	d**o**rmís
Ud.(él)(ella)	d**ue**rme	Uds.(ellos)(ellas)	d**ue**rmen

1 Pregunta a un(a) compañero(a) si estas personas duermen bien.

A — *¿Duerme bien Marta?*
B — *No, duerme mal porque todavía tiene dolor de oído.*

Marta

a. Antonio y Pedro   b. Rosita   c. Juanito y Miguel   d. tú   e. Uds.

El complemento indirecto: Los pronombres *me, te, le*

Indirect object pronouns replace indirect object nouns. We use indirect object pronouns with *doler (o → ue)*.

• In Spanish, the part of the body that hurts is the subject of the sentence and the verb agrees with it. The indirect object pronoun tells who hurts:

Me duele **la pierna.** / **Me** duele**n las piernas.**

| (yo) | **me** | (tú) | **te** | (Ud.)
(él)
(ella) | **le** |

- We also use indirect object pronouns with *gustar* and *encantar:*

  Le encanta tocar la guitarra.

- Sometimes we use *a* + a pronoun or a person's name for emphasis or to make it clear who we are referring to.

  Me duelen los pies. Y **a ti,** ¿qué **te** duele?
  A Pablo le duelen los pies.
  A Ud. le duelen los pies, ¿no?

2 Después de hacer ejercicio durante mucho tiempo, te duele todo el cuerpo. Túrnate con un(a) compañero(a) para preguntar y decir qué te duele.

A — *¿Qué te duele?*
B — *Me duele el cuello.*

3 Después de un examen difícil de historia estos estudiantes están cansados. Habla con un(a) compañero(a) y di cómo se sienten.

A —*Veo que José está cansado.*
B —*Sí, y también le duele mucho la cabeza.*

José

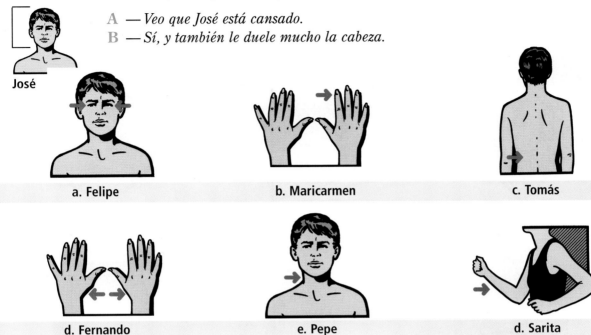

a. Felipe

b. Maricarmen

c. Tomás

d. Fernando

e. Pepe

d. Sarita

4 Pregunta a tus compañeros de clase qué comidas les gustan o no les gustan.

A —*¿A ti te gustan las uvas?*
B —*Sí, a mí me gustan.*
   o: *Sí, a mí me encantan.*
   o: *No, a mí no me gustan.*

Ahora di qué comidas les gustan o no les gustan a tus compañeros de clase.

A Verónica le encantan las uvas.

La expresión *hace . . . que*

To tell how long something has been going on, we use *Hace* + period of time + *que* + present-tense verb.

Hace tres días **que estoy** enfermo.

If we want to ask how long something has been going on, we can use *¿Cuánto (tiempo) hace que* + present-tense verb?

¿Cuánto tiempo hace que Elena **está** enferma?

5 Pregunta a un(a) compañero(a) cuánto tiempo hace que estas personas están enfermas.

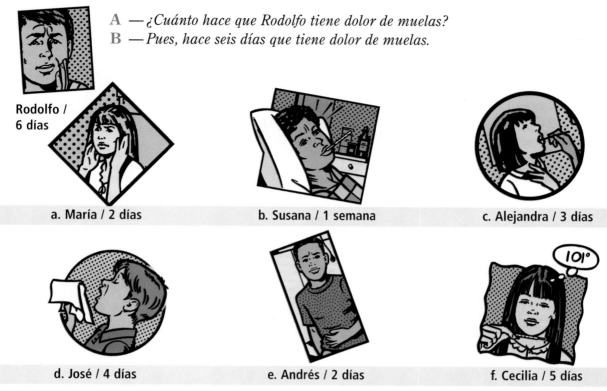

A — ¿*Cuánto hace que Rodolfo tiene dolor de muelas?*
B — *Pues, hace seis días que tiene dolor de muelas.*

Rodolfo / 6 días

a. María / 2 días

b. Susana / 1 semana

c. Alejandra / 3 días

d. José / 4 días

e. Andrés / 2 días

f. Cecilia / 5 días

La sustantivación de adjetivos

Look at how we can avoid repeating the noun in these instances:

> ¿Te duele **la pierna derecha** o **la izquierda?**

> ¿Qué prefieres, **un gorro azul** o **uno amarillo?**

To avoid repetition we drop the noun in the second part of the sentence and put the definite or indefinite article right before the second adjective. Note that the adjective must agree in gender and number just as if the noun were still there. Also note that *un* becomes *uno(a)* when it is not followed by a noun.

We can do the same thing with what we call a "prepositional phrase," or a description that begins with *de*.

> ¿Qué haces, **la tarea de matemáticas** o **la de ciencias?**

> ¿Necesitas marcadores para **la clase de inglés** o para **la de arte?**

6 ¿Qué le duele a tu compañero(a)?

A —¿*Qué tienes?*
B —*Me duele el ojo.*
A —*¿El derecho o el izquierdo?*
B —*El derecho.*

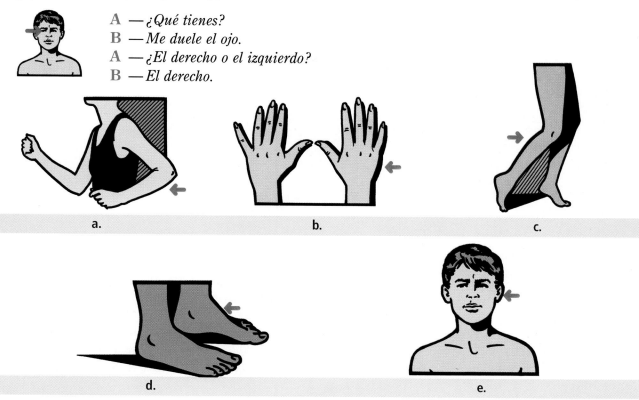

a.

b.

c.

d.

e.

Ahora lo sabes

Can you:

- recommend a way to maintain good health?

  —Debes dormir más. Estás enfermo porque no ___ bien.

- say that a part of the body hurts?

  —___ María ___ la mano derecha.

- tell how long something has been going on?

  —___ tres días ___ Rafael tiene un resfriado.

- avoid repeating a noun?

  —¿Te duele el oído derecho o ___?

Todo Junto

Para decir más

Aquí tienes vocabulario adicional que te puede ayudar para hacer las actividades de esta sección.

**el enfermero,
la enfermera**
nurse

tener mareos
to have dizzy spells

tener escalofríos
to have chills

tener tos
to have a cough

Me duele todo el cuerpo.
My whole body aches.

Me siento débil.
I feel weak.

tomar vitaminas
to take vitamins

el consultorio
the doctor's (dentist's) office

Actividades

Esta sección te ofrece la oportunidad de aumentar tus conocimientos de español al integrar lo que aprendiste en este capítulo con lo que aprendiste en capítulos anteriores.

1 Cada estudiante debe escribir en una ficha *(index card)* un problema de salud imaginario. El (La) profesor(a) recogerá *(will collect)* las fichas y dará *(will give)* una a cada estudiante. Ahora representa *(act out)* el problema de tu ficha. La clase debe identificar el problema y hacer una recomendación.

*A Juan le duele el brazo (izquierdo).
No debe jugar béisbol hoy.
o: Debe descansar esta tarde.*

2 Trae (*bring*) a la clase dos cosas iguales (*two similar things*) pero de color diferente; por ejemplo, una camisa roja y otra amarilla. Inventa un diálogo con un(a) vendedor(a) (*salesperson*) y su cliente. Por ejemplo:

A — *¿Qué desea, señor (señorita)?*

B — *Me encanta esa camisa roja. ¿La tiene en amarillo?*

A — *Sí, aquí la tiene.*

B — *Me queda bien. ¿Cuánto cuesta?*

A — *Treinta y cuatro dólares.*

B — *¡Muy bien! La compro.*

Nadando en la piscina de la Universidad de Caracas, Venezuela

3 Escribe cuatro actividades que te gusta hacer o cuatro cosas que tienes. Puedes usar los verbos y expresiones de la lista u otros. Lee tus frases a un(a) compañero(a). Tu compañero(a) debe averiguar (*find out*) cuánto tiempo hace que haces esas actividades.

A —*A mí me gusta patinar.*
　　 o: *Yo patino.*

B —*¿Cuánto tiempo hace que patinas?*

A —*Hace seis años (que patino).*

nadar
patinar
esquiar
tocar la guitarra
tener un perro
tener un gato
practicar deportes

Corriendo en la playa de Punta del Este, Uruguay

¡Vamos a leer!

Antes de leer

STRATEGY ➤ Using prior knowledge

Look at the pictures. What do you think this article will be about? In two or three sentences, try to summarize what you know about the topic. What new information do you think you might find out?

Mira la lectura

STRATEGY ➤ Using titles and photos to predict

Find the title and the name of the section in the magazine where it appears. Look at the photo and the caption, and read the boldface headings. What cause of headaches do you think will be discussed?

TU SALUD

Cabeza

Hombros

Espalda baja

Pies

CAUSAS DEL DOLOR DE CABEZA

El dolor de cabeza tiene diferentes causas. La mala postura puede ser una de ellas. Diversos doctores y terapistas han hablado sobre la importancia de comprobar la postura de nuestro cuerpo cada vez que nos sentamos. Para eso, hay que considerar varios aspectos:

- **Los pies** deben apoyarse totalmente sobre el suelo mientras estamos sentados.
- **La espalda baja** debe apoyarse contra el respaldo de la silla.
- **La cabeza** debe estar colocada correctamente sobre los hombros.
- **Los hombros** no deben estar tensos.

Sin duda, una buena postura puede evitar que nos duela la espalda, el cuello, los hombros y, por supuesto, la cabeza.

Siéntate derecho y di adiós al dolor de cabeza

Infórmate

 STRATEGY ➤ Coping with unknown words

Remember that you should keep reading when you come across an unknown word. You may find that you do not need to know its meaning, that you can use the surrounding words to figure it out, or that you may have to look it up or ask someone the meaning.

1 Read the entire article several times, without stopping to puzzle over words you do not know. What general body behavior does the author recommend to avoid headaches?

2 Now read the article carefully, paying attention to words you don't know. Can you identify instances where the exact meaning of unknown words isn't important for getting the gist of the sentence?

Use context clues and the diagram to figure out the meaning of each underlined word.

> hombros . . . estar <u>tensos</u>
> pies . . . sobre *(on)* el <u>suelo</u>
> cabeza . . . está <u>colocada</u> . . . sobre <u>los hombros</u>

Para no tener dolor de cabeza, visita al dentista regularmente

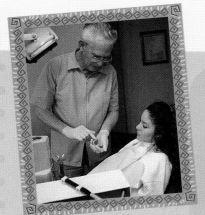

Una visita al dentista

Aplicación

Look at yourself and your classmates right now. Are you following the article's recommendations? If not, try doing the four things that the author advises. Do they feel comfortable or uncomfortable, natural or unnatural? Evaluate the article's recommendations on a scale of 1 to 5 (1 = not at all useful; 5 = extremely useful).

¡Vamos a escribir!

Make a poster in Spanish that might be displayed in a nurse's office or other medical facility. The poster should give information about how to prevent illness or how to take care of yourself when you are sick.

1 First, decide on your theme. Do you want to give suggestions for staying healthy *(Ideas para mantener la salud)*, such as eating healthful foods, exercising, and getting enough sleep? Or do you want to make suggestions for someone who isn't feeling well *(Ideas para sentirte mejor)*, such as staying in bed, drinking a lot of water, and resting?

2 Write the suggestions that you will put on your poster. You may want to use the verbs *debes* or *necesitas*.

3 Show the text of your poster to a partner. Then revise and edit it. Recopy the corrected sentences on your poster. You may want to add a drawing or a picture from a magazine to illustrate your suggestions.

4 Now you are ready to share your work. Here are some ways you can do this:

- Display your posters in the classroom, the hallway, or the nurse's office.
- With your teacher's help, organize a school health fair, and make your posters the main display.
- With your teacher's help, find out if some nearby elementary school or health facility would like to display your posters.

"Me encanta caminar para hacer ejercicio."

¿Lo sabes bien?

This section will help you organize your studying for the proficiency test, where you will be asked to do similar, though not identical, tasks. There will not be any models on the test.

Listening

Can you understand this telephone conversation between Justino and his boss, Señor Donoso? Listen as your teacher reads a sample similar to what you will hear on the test. How is Justino feeling? Mention at least two problems he has. What does his boss suggest?

Reading

Can you read the label on this prescription bottle and use cognates, context, or any other strategy to understand the gist of it? What is the prescription for? Should this medicine be taken on an empty stomach?

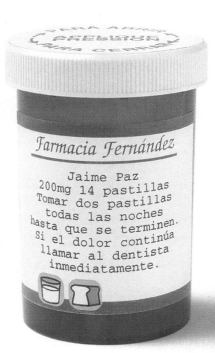

Writing

Can you write a letter to a friend explaining how you are feeling after an accident you have just had? Here is a sample:

> Querida María Marta:
>
> Hace una semana que estoy en la cama. Me lastimé la pierna derecha, los brazos y la espalda. Me siento muy mal. Todavía me duelen mucho los brazos. Pero creo que voy a estar mejor en unos días y voy a poder ir a la escuela.
>
> Tu amiga,
> Maribel

Culture

Can you explain some options for what you could do if you had a stomachache while visiting México?

Speaking

Can you work with a partner to play the roles of a doctor and a patient? Here is a sample dialogue:

A —*Doctor, me siento muy mal. Me duele mucho el estómago.*

B —*¿Cuánto tiempo hace que te duele el estómago?*

A —*Hace sólo unas horas, doctor.*

B —*Pues, creo que comes mucho. Pero, ahora debes ir a tu casa, quedarte en la cama y no comer nada esta noche.*

Resumen del capítulo 9

Use the vocabulary from this chapter to help you:

■ describe how you are feeling

■ tell what parts of your body hurt

■ suggest things you or others can do to feel better

to name parts of the body
la boca
el brazo
la cabeza
el cuello
el cuerpo
el dedo
el dedo del pie
derecho, -a
la espalda
el estómago
la garganta
izquierdo, -a
la mano (f.)
la nariz
el oído
el ojo
el pie
la pierna

to ask how someone is feeling
¿Cómo te sientes?
¿Qué pasa?
¿Qué te duele?
¿Qué tienes?

to describe how someone is feeling
¡Ay!
el dolor
doler (o → ue)
(A mí / ti) me / te duele(n) ___.

(No me duele) nada.
la fiebre
Me siento bien / mal.
Tengo dolor de cabeza.
              estómago.
              garganta.
              muelas.
              oído.
Tengo calor.
       fiebre.
       frío.
       gripe.
       sueño.
       un resfriado.
(Yo) me lastimé ___.
mejor
peor
terrible

to name places to go or things to do when you are sick
la clínica
la enfermería
el hospital
Debo quedarme en la cama.
Debes quedarte en la cama.
llamar
tomar

to name ways to maintain good health
dormir (o → ue)
hacer ejercicio

to name medical professions
el / la dentista
el médico, la médica

to indicate how long something has been going on
¿Cuánto (tiempo) hace que ___?
Hace + *time expression* + que ___.
ahora
todavía
ya no

to express and ask for an opinion
(Yo) creo que ___.
¿no?

CAPÍTULO 10

¿Qué hiciste ayer?

OBJECTIVES

At the end of this chapter you will be able to:

- **name various places in your community**
- **name activities you do or did in your community**
- **identify different means of transportation available in your area**
- **compare and contrast a Hispanic community with a community you are familiar with**

Volcán en Puerto Varas, Chile

¡Piénsalo bien!

Look at the pictures and read the captions.

Think about the many different errands and activities you normally do in your community. Which of the activities in these photos have you done most recently? When?

"Yo fui a ver un partido de béisbol."

Here's a baseball stadium in the Dominican Republic, which has produced many major league baseball players. Do you know the names of any of them?

"Envié una carta a mis tíos."

How is this post office similar to and different from the one in your community?

En Madrid

"¿Y a ti te gusta ir a la biblioteca?"

Estudiantes en la Universidad de Caracas

315

Vocabulario para conversar

¿Adónde vas?

Aquí tienes palabras y expresiones necesarias para hablar de las cosas que puedes hacer en tu comunidad. Léelas varias veces y practícalas con un(a) compañero(a) en las páginas siguientes.

el supermercado

la librería

la biblioteca

sacar un libro

los comestibles

las pastillas (para la garganta)

la farmacia

el champú

la tarjeta de cumpleaños

devolver (o → ue) un libro

el jabón

el regalo

la pasta dentífrica

la tienda de regalos

ir a pasear

ver un partido de béisbol

la tarjeta postal

el banco

el sello

depositar dinero

sacar dinero

el correo

enviar una carta

el dinero

la carta

316   Capítulo 10

doscientos*

trescientos

cuatrocientos

seiscientos

quinientos

setecientos

ochocientos

novecientos

mil

También necesitas . . .

abrir	*to open*	anoche	*last night*
cerrar (e → ie)	*to close*	ayer	*yesterday*
llegar	*to arrive, to get to*	luego	*afterward, later, then*
devolver:	*to return (an object):*	temprano	*early*
(yo) devolví	*I returned*	tarde†	*late*
(tú) devolviste	*you returned*	ya	*already*
enviar: (yo) envié	*to send: I sent*	(Yo) no lo sabía.	*I didn't know that.*
hacer:	*to do, to make:*	si	*if, whether*
(yo) hice	*I did / made*		
(tú) hiciste	*you did / made*		
sacar: (yo) saqué	*to take out: I took out*		
ver: (yo) vi	*to see: I saw*		
(tú) viste	*you saw*		

¿Y qué quiere decir…?
¿Me compras ___?
(yo) deposité

* Note that when a number ending in *-ientos* is followed by a feminine noun, we use *-ientas* instead: *doscientas personas, trescientas cincuenta cartas.*
† Remember that *la tarde* means "afternoon" or "evening."

Empecemos a conversar

Túrnate con un(a) compañero(a) para ser *Estudiante A* y *Estudiante B.* Reemplacen las palabras subrayadas con palabras representadas o escritas en los recuadros. 💡 quiere decir que puedes escoger *(choose)* tu propia respuesta.

1

A — *¿Adónde vas? ¿Al banco?*
B — *Sí, y luego tengo que ir al parque.*
　　 Y ahora Uds.

Estudiante A　　　　　　　　　　　　**Estudiante B**

2

A — *Si vas a la farmacia, ¿me compras pastillas para la garganta?*
B — *Pero ya las compré ayer.*
A — *¡Ah! No lo sabía.*
　　 Y ahora Uds.

¡NO OLVIDES!

Remember that the direct object pronouns are *lo, la, los,* and *las.*

Estudiante A　　　　　　　　　　　　　　　　　**Estudiante B**

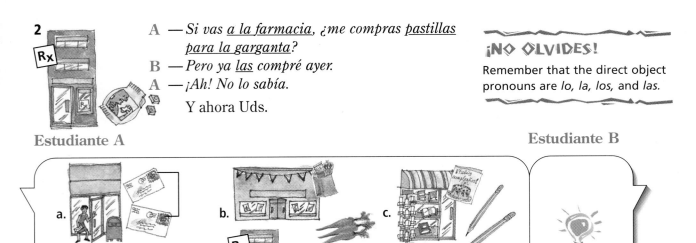

3

A — ¿Qué hiciste ayer? ¿Fuiste _al banco_?

B — Sí, fui y _saqué (deposité) dinero (doscientos dólares)_.

o: No, fui _al parque de diversiones_.

Y ahora Uds.

Estudiante A

Estudiante B

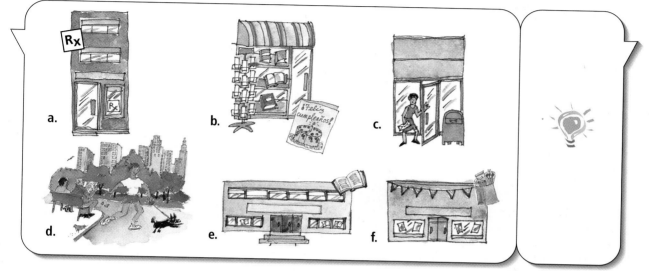

a.

b.

c.

d.

e.

f.

4

A — ¿_La biblioteca_ abre tarde los sábados?

B — _Sí, abre a las diez y cierra temprano por la noche_.

o: No, abre temprano y cierra temprano por la tarde.

Y ahora Uds.

Estudiante A

Estudiante B

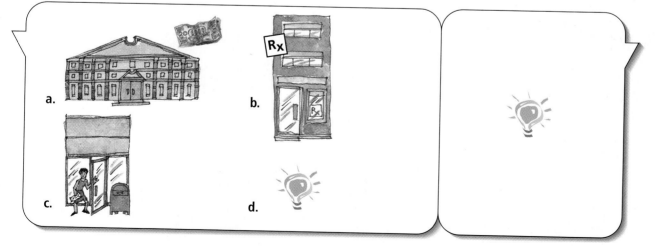

a.

b.

c.

d.

Empecemos a escribir

Escribe tus respuestas en español.

5 ¿Prefieres llegar tarde o temprano a una fiesta? ¿A un partido? ¿Al cine?

6 ¿Ya hiciste todas las tareas para hoy? ¿Las hiciste anoche? Generalmente, ¿las haces por la tarde o por la noche?

7 ¿Adónde fuiste ayer? ¿Y el fin de semana pasado? ¿A quién viste?

8 ¿Qué vas a hacer si recibes *(receive)* mil dólares? ¿Vas a depositarlos en el banco o vas a comprar cosas? ¿Qué vas a comprar?

La Plaza de la
Cibeles en Madrid

Delante del Correo
Central en Madrid

La estación de
trenes Atocha, en Madrid

También se dice

la estampilla
el timbre

la postal

el hipermercado

los correos
la oficina de correos

la botica
la droguería

Vocabulario para conversar

¿Dónde queda el banco?

Aquí tienes el resto del vocabulario necesario para hablar de tu comunidad.

la cuadra

AVENIDA DE

el taxi

el correo

el supermercado

el monumento

la plaza

la estación de policía

el museo

la farmacia

el restaurante

el banco

el hotel

CALLE RIVERA

la estación de servicio

POLICÍA

AVENIDA

JUÁREZ

la esquina

a pie

la estación del tren

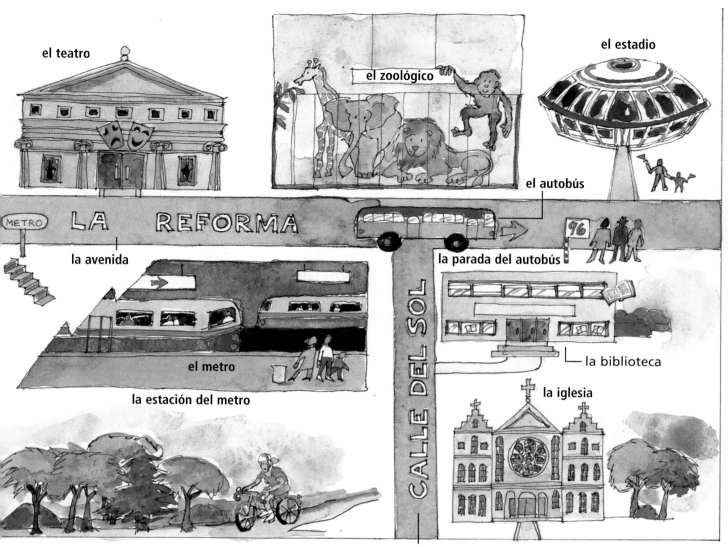

el teatro

el zoológico

el estadio

el autobús

METRO LA REFORMA

la avenida

el metro

la estación del metro

la parada del autobús

CALLE DEL SOL

la biblioteca

la iglesia

la calle

También necesitas...

trabajar	*to work*	enfrente (de)	*facing, opposite, in front (of)*
¿A cuántas cuadras (de ___)?	*How many blocks (from ___)?*	entre	*between, among*
A (cinco) cuadras (de ___).	*(Five) blocks (from ___).*	en + *vehicle*	*by* + vehicle
queda(n)	*is (are) located*	Bueno	here: *OK, fine, all right*
a la derecha (de)	*to the right (of)*		
a la izquierda (de)	*to the left (of)*		
al lado (de)	*next to, beside*		
detrás (de)	*behind*		

¿Y qué quiere decir...?
la comunidad
el templo
(Yo) no sé.

Empecemos a conversar

Para los ejercicios 10–11, usa el mapa en las páginas 322–323.

9

A —*¿Cómo vamos al teatro?*
B —*Pues, no sé. ¿Por qué no vamos en coche?*
A —*Bueno.*

  Y ahora Uds.

Estudiante A   **Estudiante B**

a. b. c. d. e.

10

A —*Perdón, señora (señor / joven / señorita).*
  ¿Dónde queda el banco?
B —*Está en la calle Rivera, entre el restaurante*
  y la estación de servicio.

  Y ahora Uds.

Estudiante A   **Estudiante B**

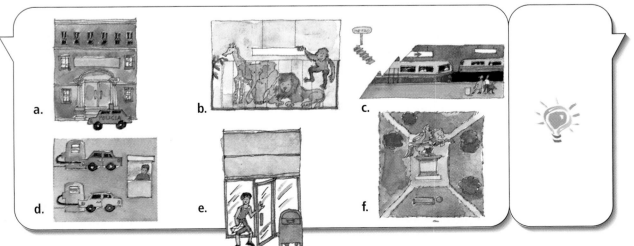

a. b. c. d. e. f.

11

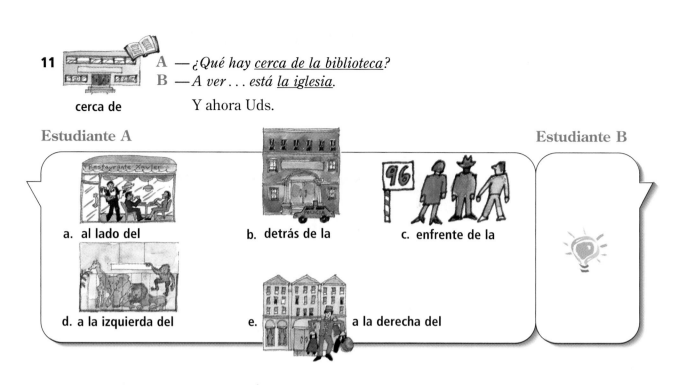

A —¿Qué hay _cerca de la biblioteca_?

B —A ver . . . está _la iglesia_.

cerca de

Y ahora Uds.

Estudiante A

Estudiante B

a. **al lado del**

b. **detrás de la**

c. **enfrente de la**

d. **a la izquierda del**

e. **a la derecha del**

Empecemos a escribir y a leer

Escribe tus respuestas en español.

12 ¿Qué hay en tu comunidad? Por ejemplo:

En mi comunidad hay un monumento en una plaza, un templo, una iglesia, dos bancos, . . .

13 ¿Dónde trabajan tus padres? ¿Trabajan en tu comunidad o en otra comunidad? ¿Y los padres de tu compañero(a)?

14 ¿Dónde queda la estación de policía de tu comunidad? ¿Queda cerca o lejos de tu casa? ¿A cuántas cuadras?

15 Lee la carta y luego cambia _(change)_ las palabras _(words)_ o frases que no tienen sentido _(make sense)_.

> Querida mamá:
> Ayer estuve muy ocupada todo el día. Primero fui al correo y compré unas pastillas para la garganta. Luego fui al teatro y vi un partido de vóleibol. Por la tarde fui al supermercado, donde compré unas tarjetas postales deliciosas. Luego, fui al zoológico para comprar zapatos nuevos. Hoy tengo que ir a la biblioteca porque necesito comprar un regalo para papá.
>
> Tu hija,
> Teresa

También se dice

la gasolinera

el subterráneo (el subte)

el bus
el camión
el colectivo
la guagua
el micro
el ómnibus

¡Comuniquemos!

Aquí tienes otra oportunidad para usar el vocabulario de este capítulo.

1 Con un(a) compañero(a), imaginen que Uds. van a ir de compras.
Primero tienen que decidir qué van a hacer y luego adónde van a ir.

A — *Necesito comprar comestibles y buscar un*
regalo también.

B — *¿Por qué no vamos primero a la tienda de*
regalos y luego al supermercado?

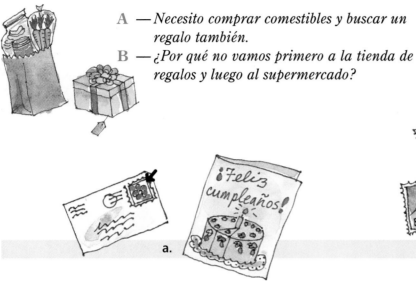

a.

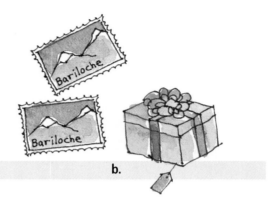

b.

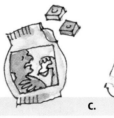

c.

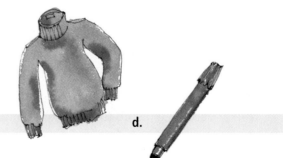

d.

e.

f.

2 Los padres van a visitar tu escuela esta noche, y tú tienes que trabajar de guía *(guide)*. Con un(a) compañero(a), ayuda a los padres a llegar a los lugares correctos.

A — *¿Quién es tu profesor de ciencias?*
B — *Es el señor / la señora ____.*
A — *¿Dónde queda su sala de clases?*
B — *Queda cerca de ____. Es la sala número ____.*

¿Qué sabes ahora?

Can you:

■ **name places in your community?**

—**En mi comunidad hay ___.**

■ **ask about and give the location of a place?**

—**¿Dónde ____ la estación de policía?**

—**Está ____ la librería.**

■ **tell where you go to run errands?**

—**Voy ____ para enviar unas cartas.**

Plaza Morazán en Tegucigalpa
(1969), José Antonio Velásquez

Perspectiva cultural

En esta ciudad hay muchos productos hispanos y servicios en español.

Do you think these photographs were taken in the United States? Why do you think so? Looking at the signs, which language do you think predominates? Why? What do the signs tell you about the community and the people who live there?

Yrma is fourteen and lives in Chicago with her family. When she wants to see a Spanish-language movie at a local theater, she can find the information she needs in any of several Spanish-language papers published in the city. These are the papers that almost one million Hispanic residents in Chicago can read to keep informed, look for a job, or find weekly sales on groceries.

Yrma's neighborhood is called Pilsen. It's one of several large Hispanic communities in Chicago. Most residents of Pilsen are Mexican-American. The Pilsen community offers its residents and the rest of the city a large variety of products and services. Within walking distance of Yrma's home, you can find several small tortilla factories; offices of bilingual doctors, lawyers, and dentists; grocery stores with products from the United States and Mexico; bookstores and record stores with Spanish-language titles; restaurants; and several travel agencies.

(De izquierda a derecha) Del Centro Museo de Bellas Artes Mexicanas en Chicago: la entrada del Museo; un árbol de la muerte en la tienda de regalos; tápiz de madera hecha por una joven mexicana

Tienda de productos latinoamericanos en Nueva Jersey

A few blocks from Yrma's home is the Mexican Fine Arts Center Museum, where works by Mexican and Mexican-American artists are always on view.

People from other areas of Chicago come to Pilsen looking for the special products and services it offers. Where else would you buy the freshest tortillas in town? Or the latest pop hits from Mexico?

Yrma's neighborhood is a good example of how the many Hispanic communities throughout the United States provide unique goods and services to the entire population of the city. Pilsen is part of the diverse mosaic of cultures that make the United States a multicultural society.

La cultura desde tu perspectiva

1 How is Pilsen similar to your own community?

2 Are there communities in your city where the primary language is something other than English? Have you visited them? What products and services do they provide?

Gramática en contexto

Read this story about a reporter and some visiting aliens.

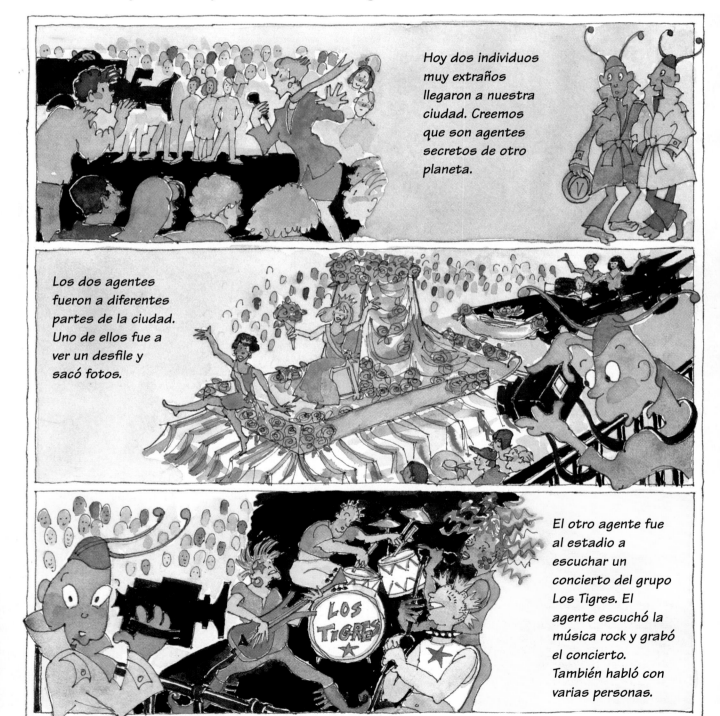

Hoy dos individuos muy extraños llegaron a nuestra ciudad. Creemos que son agentes secretos de otro planeta.

Los dos agentes fueron a diferentes partes de la ciudad. Uno de ellos fue a ver un desfile y sacó fotos.

El otro agente fue al estadio a escuchar un concierto del grupo Los Tigres. El agente escuchó la música rock y grabó el concierto. También habló con varias personas.

LOS TIGRES

Creemos que los agentes llevaron las fotos y otras cosas a su nave espacial y las enviaron a su líder.

No sabemos dónde están en este momento, pero creemos que los agentes ya regresaron a su planeta.

A In the story, the verb forms *llegaron, llevaron, enviaron,* and *regresaron* are used. What do you think they mean? (Remember you already know the meaning of *llegar, llevar, enviar,* and *regresar.*)

B The verbs *escuchó* and *habló* are used to talk about what one of the secret agents did. Can you figure out what these words mean?

C In the second paragraph, find two verb forms that tell where both secret agents went and then where one secret agent went.

La preposición *de* + *el*

When we use the preposition *a* + *el*, we form the contraction *al*. In the same way, when we use the preposition *de* + *el*, we form the contraction *del* ("of the," "from the").

Luisa está enfrente **del** cine.

1 Mira el mapa de abajo. Imagina que buscas varios lugares y tu compañero(a) es un(a) agente de policía. Pregunta y contesta según *(according to)* el modelo. Puedes usar las palabras *(words)* de la lista a la derecha.

A — *¿Dónde está la farmacia? ¿Queda lejos?*
B — *No, no queda lejos. Está al lado del hotel.*
A — *¿A cuántas cuadras de aquí?*
B — *Pues, queda a una (dos) cuadra(s) de aquí.*

cerca (de)
lejos (de)
a la izquierda (de)
a la derecha (de)
detrás (de)
enfrente (de)
al lado (de)
entre

El pretérito de los verbos que terminan en *-ar*

Up to now you have seen verbs in the present tense and a few in the past tense. This past tense is called the preterite. Here are all the forms of *comprar* in the preterite.

(yo)	compr**é**	(nosotros) (nosotras)	compr**amos**
(tú)	compr**aste**	(vosotros) (vosotras)	compr**asteis**
Ud. (él) (ella)	compr**ó**	Uds. (ellos) (ellas)	compr**aron**

- You have already learned that the verb endings tell you who does an action. They also tell you when an action is done (in the present, in the past, or in the future). In the same way that *-o, -as, -a, -amos, -áis, -an* tell you that the action takes place in the present, *-é, -aste, -ó, -amos, -asteis, -aron* tell you that the action took place in the past.

- Notice the accent marks on the endings *-é* and *-ó.*

- Verbs that end in *-gar*, like *pagar, jugar,* and *llegar,* end in *-gué* in the *yo* form. For example:
  —¿Cuándo lle**gaste** al teatro?
  —Lle**gué** a las ocho.

- Verbs that end in *-car*, like *buscar, tocar,* and *sacar,* end in *-qué* in the *yo* form. For example:
  —¿Cuántos libros sa**caste** de la biblioteca ayer?
  —Sa**qué** dos.

- Stem-changing *-ar* verbs do *not* have a stem change in the preterite. For example:
  Generalmente la tienda c**ie**rra a las diez,
  pero anoche c**e**rró a las ocho.

2 Los empleados de este banco tienen que llegar a las 9:00 de la mañana. ¿A qué hora llegaron ayer?

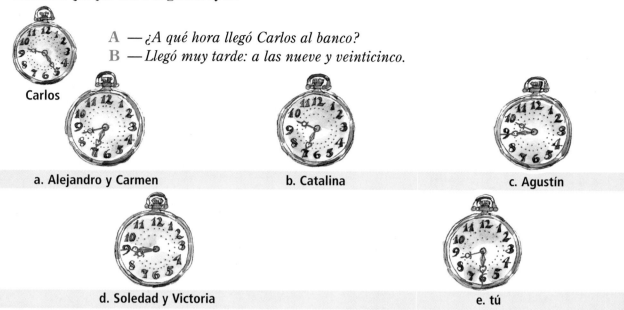

A —¿A qué hora llegó Carlos al banco?
B —Llegó muy tarde: a las nueve y veinticinco.

Carlos

a. Alejandro y Carmen   b. Catalina   c. Agustín

d. Soledad y Victoria   e. tú

3 Escoge *(choose)* cinco de las actividades y di cuándo las hiciste la última vez *(last time)*. Tu compañero(a) va a preguntar con quién las hiciste.

A —*Hace dos días que escuché música.*
B —*¿Con quién escuchaste música?*
A —*Con mi amiga Isabel.*
   o: *Lo hice solo(a).*

4 Josefina sabe *(knows)* que todos tuvieron *(had)* cosas que hacer
ayer. Pero no tiene la información correcta. Con un(a)
compañero(a), pregunta y contesta según el modelo.

A — *Teresa y Julia cocinaron ayer, ¿verdad?*
B — *Creo que no. Ellas escucharon música.*

Teresa y Julia

Estudiante A

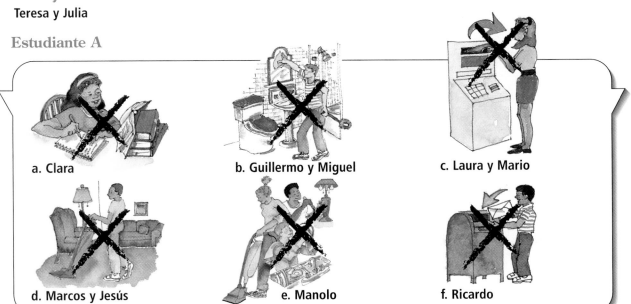

a. Clara

b. Guillermo y Miguel

c. Laura y Mario

d. Marcos y Jesús

e. Manolo

f. Ricardo

Estudiante B

El pretérito del verbo *ir*

You know that we use *fui* and *fuiste* to say that "I went" and "you went" somewhere. They are preterite-tense forms of *ir*. Here are all the forms of *ir* in the preterite.

(yo)	**fui**	(nosotros) (nosotras)	**fuimos**
(tú)	**fuiste**	(vosotros) (vosotras)	**fuisteis**
Ud. (él) (ella)	**fue**	Uds. (ellos) (ellas)	**fueron**

Notice that, unlike regular *-ar* verbs in the preterite, the forms of *ir* do not have accent marks.

5 Con un(a) compañero(a), di adónde y cómo fueron estas personas.

A — *¿Adónde fueron Federico y Esteban?*
B — *Fueron al centro comercial.*
A — *¿Cómo fueron?*
B — *En taxi.*

Federico y Esteban

a. Jorge
b. los Sánchez
c. Adela y Nicolás
d. la Sra. Ochoa
e. Pilar
f. tú y tu hermano(a)

6 Di adónde fueron tú y otras personas, cuándo fueron y qué hicieron *(what you did)* allí.

Mis amigos y yo fuimos al parque ayer y jugamos básquetbol.

a. mis amigos y yo
b. mis padres
c. yo
d. (nombre de un amigo)
e. (nombres de dos amigos)

Ahora lo sabes

Can you:

■ indicate where one person or place is in relation to another?

—El restaurante está al lado ___ hotel. Está ___ la biblioteca.

■ talk about an errand someone ran?

—Mi mamá ___ al banco para ___ dinero.

■ tell where someone went?

—Anoche mis hermanos ___ a la farmacia y nosotros ___ al supermercado.

La estación del metro Universidad, Ciudad de México

Para decir más

Aquí tienes vocabulario adicional que te puede ayudar para hacer las actividades de esta sección.

el maquillaje
makeup

ir de viaje
to take a trip

la estación de bomberos
fire station

Actividades

Esta sección te ofrece la oportunidad de aumentar tus conocimientos de español al integrar lo que aprendiste en este capítulo con lo que aprendiste en capítulos anteriores.

1 Trabaja en un grupo de cuatro personas. En una hoja de papel, cada estudiante debe escribir tres cosas que él (ella) hizo el mes pasado.

> *Compré champú y pasta dentífrica.*
> *Fui al parque de diversiones.*
> *Trabajé en la farmacia.*

Junten *(put together)* las hojas de papel. Luego deben sacar los papeles y preguntar quién hizo qué cosa.

> *¿Quién compró champú y pasta dentífrica?*
> *¿Quién fue al parque de diversiones?*
> *¿Quién trabajó en la farmacia?*

¿Cuántas personas hicieron la misma *(same)* cosa?

> *¿Cuántas personas compraron champú y pasta dentífrica?*
> *¿Cuántas fueron a un parque de diversiones . . . ?*

¿Qué actividades hizo la mayoría de las personas?

Chiles sabrosos de Santa Fe

La catedral de San Francisco, Santa Fe

2 En una tarjeta, escribe una frase sobre cuándo y adónde fueron de vacaciones tú y tu familia.

> *Hace tres años que mi familia y yo fuimos a Santa Fe, Nuevo México.*

Intercambia *(exchange)* tarjetas con tu compañero(a). En una hoja de papel, escribe cinco preguntas sobre lo que hicieron tu compañero(a) y su familia.

> *¿Qué hiciste en Santa Fe?*
> *¿Compraron muchos recuerdos?*
> *¿Sacaron muchas fotos?*

Luego, di a otro grupo lo que hizo tu compañero(a) y su familia cuando fueron de vacaciones.

3 Trabaja en grupos de tres personas. Una persona piensa en un lugar de tu comunidad y dice lo que hizo allí. Otra persona debe repetir esto y añadir *(add)* adónde él (ella) fue y lo que hizo. Sigue *(Continue)* hasta que *(until)* alguien se olvide de *(forgets)* lo que dijeron las otras personas.

A — *Fui a la farmacia para comprar jabón.*
B — *Tomás fue a la farmacia para comprar jabón.*
    Yo fui al correo para enviar unas cartas.
C — *Tomás fue a la farmacia . . . Rosa fue al correo . . .*
    Yo fui . . .

El Museo de Bellas Artes en Santa Fe

¡Vamos a leer!

Antes de leer

STRATEGY> Using prior knowledge

Think of a folktale that you know. Who are the characters? What problems do they have? How is it resolved? How are folktales different from other stories?

Mira la lectura

STRATEGY> Skimming

Skim the reading. What seems to be the problem facing the Tolencianos?

EL PUEBLO DE TONTOS

Hay muchos tontos en la Tierra, pero en el pueblo de Tolencia todos son tontos. Un día don Hortensio Hortalecio, el alcalde de Tolencia, fue a su oficina y vio un hoyo enorme en el camino. "¿Qué pasa?" dijo don Hortensio. "¡Vamos a arreglar este hoyo ahora!"

Don Hortensio llamó a los tolencianos. "¡Tienen que arreglar el hoyo del camino!" Y lo arreglaron.

Después de trabajar don Hortensio fue a su casa. ¿Qué vio en el camino? ¡Otro hoyo! Llamó a los tolencianos y ellos arreglaron ese hoyo también.

Un día después don Hortensio salió de casa. ¿Qué vio delante de su puerta? ¡Sí! ¡OTRO HOYO! El alcalde llamó a los tolencianos y ellos arreglaron ese hoyo también. "¡Ya estamos cansados de arreglar hoyos!" dijeron. Pero esta cosa de los

Infórmate

STRATEGIES➤ Using the dictionary
Scanning

In a dictionary, adjectives and nouns that have masculine and feminine forms are listed under the masculine singular form. Verbs are listed in the infinitive form. Look up these words: *tontos, tierra, alcalde, hoyo, camino, cavaron,* and *llenaron.*

Now read the story thoroughly. How did looking up the words help you?

 1 How did the Tolencianos' problem worsen?

 2 How was it solved?

 3 Do you think the Tolencianos learned from their mistake?

Aplicación

If you had written this folk tale, how would your ending have differed? Get together with a partner and write your own ending for this tale.

---

hoyos ocurría todos los días. Estaban enfrente de la escuela, a la izquierda del banco, a la derecha de la biblioteca, ¡en todas partes!

¿Cómo arreglaron los tolencianos los hoyos? Fueron un poco lejos del hoyo y cavaron tierra. Cavaron y cavaron . . . ¡e hicieron otro hoyo! Después llevaron la tierra al primer hoyo y lo llenaron con la tierra.

Bueno . . . la gente del otro pueblo, al lado, vio los hoyos y el trabajo tonto de los tolencianos. Una noche esa gente fue a Tolencia y llenó los hoyos con cosas viejas: guitarras, teléfonos, radios y equipos de sonido . . . y un niño los llenó con zanahorias y guisantes. ¡Ya no había más hoyos!

Esa mañana don Hortensio Hortalecio salió de su casa. ¡Y no vio hoyos! Todos los tolencianos y él estaban muy contentos.

¡Vamos a escribir!

Every community has places or programs that depend on volunteers. Think about the programs in your community. What kinds of help do they need, and who can help? Make a poster that encourages people to volunteer. Follow these steps.

1 First, think about why community service is important. (*¿Por qué es importante trabajar como voluntario?*) List three reasons. Who can help? (*¿Quién puede ayudar?*)

2 Use your list and the answers to the questions to design your poster.

3 Show the draft of your poster to a partner. Then revise, edit, and make a final copy.

4 Now you are ready to show your poster. In addition to sending it to a Spanish-language newspaper or magazine, you can:

- post your work in the classroom
- submit it to your school newspaper
- include it in a newsletter or other publication that the school sends home
- add it to your writing portfolio

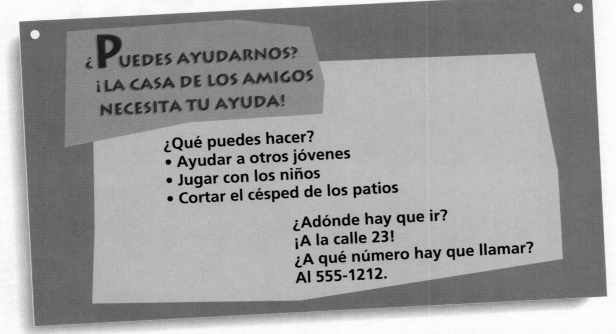

¿**P**UEDES AYUDARNOS?
¡LA CASA DE LOS AMIGOS
NECESITA TU AYUDA!

¿Qué puedes hacer?
- Ayudar a otros jóvenes
- Jugar con los niños
- Cortar el césped de los patios

¿Adónde hay que ir?
¡A la calle 23!
¿A qué número hay que llamar?
Al 555-1212.

Jóvenes guatemaltecos hacen trabajo comunitario.

"¡Hola! Soy Jorge y trabajo en un proyecto escolar en Tegucigalpa."

¿Lo sabes bien?

This section will help you organize your studying for the proficiency test, where you will be asked to do similar, though not identical, tasks. There will not be any models on the test.

Listening

Can you understand when someone talks about what he or she did in different places in the community? Listen as your teacher reads a sample similar to what you will hear on the test. Can you mention two places the person making the statement went to run these errands?

Culture

Can you name some services or products especially offered to meet the needs of the Hispanic community?

Reading

Can you read a passage and know how to look up unknown words in the dictionary?

Ayer vi a Ana en el centro. Ella fue al banco y después a la biblioteca, donde sacó varios libros. Después tomó el autobús y la vi luego cerca del estadio. Por la tarde la vi entrar en una tienda de regalos. Entonces recordé que va a ser el cumpleaños de su esposo dentro de dos semanas. Me gustaría saber qué le compró . . . .

Writing

Can you write a letter about various places in your community and the activities that you did there? There is a sample letter on the right.

Speaking

Can you tell someone the location of a place? Here is a sample:

— *Ud. tiene que tomar el metro porque el correo no está muy cerca de aquí. Queda cerca de la farmacia, en la esquina de la Calle Ocho y Valencia. Enfrente del correo hay un banco y una tienda de ropa. Debe ir rápido; es tarde. El correo cierra a las dos y ya es la una y media.*

Querida Luisa:

Este fin de semana hice muchas cosas. Por la mañana, fui a la librería para comprar un regalo para mi tía, y luego fui al correo para enviarlo. Luego, fui a pasear en el parque y al supermercado para comprar comestibles. Por la tarde, vi un partido de béisbol en la tele.

Cariños,

Rebeca

Una tienda hispana en San Francisco

Resumen del capítulo 10

Use the vocabulary from this chapter to help you:

- name various places in your community
- name activities you do or did
- identify different means of transportation

to talk about places
la avenida
el banco
la biblioteca
la calle
el correo
la cuadra
la esquina
la estación (de policía / etc.)
el estadio
la farmacia
el hotel
la iglesia
la librería
el monumento
la parada
   del autobús
la plaza
el restaurante
el supermercado
el teatro
el templo
la tienda de regalos
el zoológico

to talk about activities or errands in a community
abrir
cerrar
la comunidad
el partido
devolver (o → ue) un libro
ir a pasear

llegar
sacar un libro
trabajar

to talk about things you buy
¿Me compras ___?
los comestibles
el champú
el jabón
la pasta dentífrica
las pastillas (para la garganta)
el regalo

to talk about money
el dinero: depositar / sacar
doscientos ...
quinientos ...
setecientos ...
novecientos
mil

to talk about mailing things
la carta
enviar
el sello
la tarjeta de cumpleaños
la tarjeta postal

to ask and give directions
¿A cuántas cuadras (de ___)?
A (cinco) cuadras (de ___).
queda(n)
del

a la derecha / izquierda (de)
al lado (de) / detrás (de) /
   enfrente (de)
entre

to talk about transportation
el autobús   a pie
el metro   en + *vehicle*
el taxi

to talk about past activities
(yo) devolví, (tú) devolviste
(yo) hice, (tú) hiciste
(yo) vi, (tú) viste

to indicate when an event occurred
anoche / ayer
luego
temprano / tarde
ya

to say you don't / didn't know something
(Yo) no sé. / (Yo) no lo sabía.

to express a condition
si

to express agreement
Bueno.

CAPÍTULO 11

¿Qué te gustaría ver?

OBJECTIVES

At the end of this chapter you will be able to:

- talk about a TV show or movie

- tell when events begin and end, and how long they last

- express and defend an opinion

- compare and contrast Spanish-language TV shows with the TV shows you usually see

Uno de los muchos cines de Madrid

¡Piénsalo bien!

Look at the photos and read the captions.

"Dos entradas, por favor."

Does this movie theater look like the ones you go to? What kind of information do you think appears on the window?

Comprando entradas en un cine en Barcelona

La cantante
Gloria Estefan

"Desde la oscuridad . . . "

Gloria Estefan and the Miami Sound Machine have contributed to the popularity of music with a Latin beat. How many of their songs can you name? What different types of Latin music do you know?

Un grupo de jóvenes ve
la televisión en
Caracas, Venezuela.

"Pero Javier . . . ¿qué nos va a pasar?"

These teens are watching a *telenovela*, a Spanish soap opera. Can you name any *telenovelas* shown on Spanish-language television in your community?

Vocabulario para conversar

¿Cuál es tu programa favorito?

Aquí tienes palabras y expresiones necesarias para hablar sobre la televisión y para expresar o defender una opinión. Léelas varias veces y practícalas con un(a) compañero(a) en las páginas siguientes.

el canal

MISTERIO SIN SOLUCIÓN

el programa de detectives

Televisión

un concierto

cómico, -a

JULIO EN CONCIERTO

el programa musical

EL TÍO PEPITO

la comedia

la actriz
el actor

LOS MEJORES DÍAS

la telenovela

El Mejor

el anuncio

MUNDO DEPORTIVO

el programa deportivo

NUESTROS AMIGOS LOS DELFINES

interesante

el programa educativo

DÍA A DÍA

las noticias

divertido, -a

realista

los dibujos animados

el programa de hechos
de la vida real

el programa de
entrevistas

el pronóstico del tiempo

el documental

También necesitas . . .

dar + *movie or TV program*	*to show*	más	here: *more*
la clase (de)	here: *kind / type (of)*	el / la / los / las mejor(es)	here: *best*
sobre	*about*	el / la / los / las peor(es)	here: *worst*
pensar (e → ie) (que)	here: *to think (that)*	aburrir*	*to bore*
por eso	*that's why,* for that reason, therefore	dar miedo*	*to scare*
¿Cuál(es)?	*What? Which? Which one(s)?*	fascinar*	*to fascinate*
		interesar*	*to interest*
demasiado	*too*		
aburrido, -a	*boring*		
emocionante	*exciting, touching*		
tonto, -a	*silly, dumb*		
triste	*sad*		

¿Y qué quiere decir . . . ?
en blanco y negro
en colores
fascinante

* With the verbs *aburrir, dar miedo, fascinar,* and *interesar* we use the indirect object pronouns *me, te,* and *le,* as we do with *gustar* and *encantar:* **Me fascinan** *los programas de detectives.*

Empecemos a conversar

Túrnate con un(a) compañero(a) para ser *Estudiante A* y *Estudiante B*. Reemplacen las palabras subrayadas con palabras representadas o escritas en los recuadros.  quiere decir que puedes escoger tu propia respuesta.

1   A — *¿Te gustaría ver un programa de entrevistas?*
  B — *Sí, me gustaría mucho.*
    o: *No, esa clase de programas me aburre.*
    Y ahora Uds.

Estudiante A   **Estudiante B**

a.   b.   c.   d.

2   la mejor actriz   A —*¿Quién es la mejor actriz de televisión?*
    de televisión   B —*Para mí, (nombre) es la mejor. Me fascina.*
        Y ahora Uds.

Estudiante A   **Estudiante B**

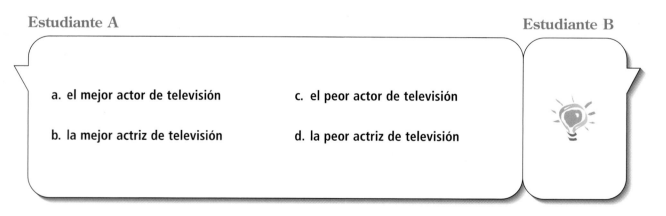

a. el mejor actor de televisión   c. el peor actor de televisión

b. la mejor actriz de televisión   d. la peor actriz de televisión

3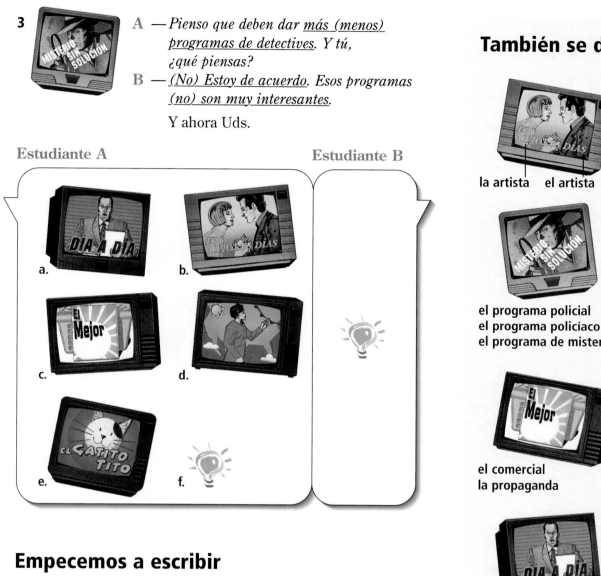

A —*Pienso que deben dar <u>más (menos)</u>*
<u>programas de detectives</u>. Y tú,
¿qué piensas?

B —*<u>(No) Estoy de acuerdo</u>. Esos programas*
<u>(no) son muy interesantes</u>.

Y ahora Uds.

Estudiante A

a.

b.

c.

d.

e.

f.

Estudiante B

También se dice

la artista   el artista

el programa policial
el programa policíaco
el programa de misterio

el comercial
la propaganda

el noticiero
el informativo

Empecemos a escribir

Escribe tus respuestas en español.

4 ¿Ves la televisión después de la escuela? ¿Qué programas de
televisión te interesan? ¿Por qué?

5 ¿Qué piensas tú? ¿Crees que deben dar más o menos programas
de hechos de la vida real en la tele? ¿Más o menos programas
de entrevistas? ¿Por qué?

6 ¿Te interesan las noticias o te aburren? ¿Y los dibujos animados?
¿Y las telenovelas? ¿Por qué?

7 ¿Cuál es tu programa favorito? ¿A qué hora empieza? ¿Qué día
de la semana lo dan? ¿En qué canal?

Vocabulario para conversar

¿Quién es la mejor actriz de cine?

Aquí tienes el resto del vocabulario necesario para hablar sobre el cine y para decir cuándo algo empieza y termina, y cuánto dura.

Cine

la película romántica

ROMANCE DE PRIMAVERA

EL MONSTRUO DE LA MONTAÑA

la película de terror

REBELIÓN EXTRATERRESTRE

la película de ciencia ficción

LA JUSTICIA DEL DESIERTO

la película del oeste

la película de aventuras

la película musical

También necesitas . . .

en punto	*sharp, on the dot*	largo, -a	here: *long* (duration)
de la mañana	*in the morning,* A.M.	corto, -a	here: *short* (duration)
de la tarde	*in the afternoon, early evening;* P.M.	más tarde	*later*
		más temprano	*earlier*
de la noche	*in the evening, at night;* P.M.		
la medianoche	*midnight*		
el mediodía	*noon*		
casi	*almost*		
durar	*to last*		
hasta	*until*		
el tiempo	here: *time*		
un poco	*a little*		

¿Y qué quiere decir . . . ?
media hora
el minuto
puntualmente
todavía no

Empecemos a conversar

8

A — *¿Qué piensas sobre las películas <u>de ciencia ficción</u>?*

B — *Pienso que son <u>interesantes y divertidas</u>. Por eso <u>me gustan</u>.*

Y ahora Uds.

Estudiante A   **Estudiante B**

a.   b.   c.   d.

9

A — *¿Hoy dan <u>una película de terror</u> en el cine?*

B — *Sí, pero empezó a <u>las nueve</u> y ya son casi <u>las nueve y media</u>.*

Y ahora Uds.

¡NO OLVIDES!

You know the word *empezar*. It is an *e* → *ie* verb.

Estudiante A   **Estudiante B**

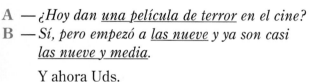

a.   b.   c.

d.

a.   b.   c.

d.   e.

e.

10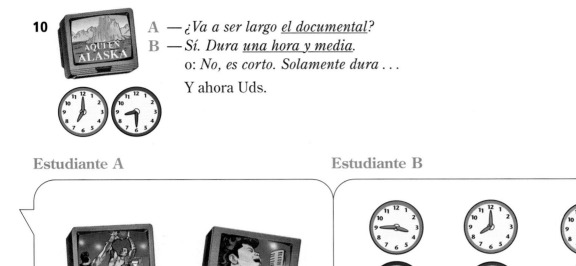

A —¿Va a ser largo *el documental*?

B —Sí. Dura *una hora y media*.

o: *No, es corto. Solamente dura* . . .

Y ahora Uds.

Estudiante A

a.

b.

c.

d.

e.

Estudiante B

a.

b.

c.

d.

e.

Empecemos a escribir y a leer

Escribe tus respuestas en español.

11 ¿Qué clases de películas te interesan? ¿Por qué? ¿Cómo se llama tu película favorita?

12 ¿Cuánto tiempo dura tu programa favorito? ¿Lo dan tarde o temprano? ¿De qué hora a qué hora?

13 ¿Qué prefieres, las películas en blanco y negro o en colores? ¿Por qué?

14 Mariana dice: "El domingo, a las nueve de la noche, dan una presentación especial en el cine Elíseos. Dura tres horas y media. Quiero llegar puntualmente. ¿Quieres venir conmigo?"

¿Termina la película antes de la medianoche?

También se dice

la película de vaqueros

¡Comuniquemos!

Aquí tienes otra oportunidad para usar el vocabulario de este capítulo.

1 Tu amigo(a) y tú están aburridos. Uds. buscan actividades que les gustaría hacer media hora después de la hora indicada *(given)*. Deben usar este calendario.

7:20

A — *Ya son las siete y veinte. ¿Qué podemos hacer?*
B — *En media hora hay una película de ciencia ficción. ¿Quieres ir?*
A — *Sí, vamos.*
    o: Hoy no. A mí me aburre esa clase de películas.

a. 8:00   d. 4:30
b. 3:15   e. 7:20
c. 9:00   f. 3:30

Este sábado en nuestra comunidad

Deportes
Béisbol: Tigres contra Leones
Fútbol: Cachorros contra Medias Blancas   5:00
                                                          3:45

Cine
El detective perezoso
La conquista del Sol   4:00 y 7:50
Aventura en la selva   7:50
                                                          3:45
Teatro
Festival nacional de teatro
La casa de Teresa   7:45
                                                          4:15 y 8:45
Conciertos
La guitarra de Paco Argollas
Orquesta Nacional   5:00
Música folklórica de Honduras   9:30
Museos   8:30
Exposición internacional
Impresionismo mexicano   4:00 y 5:00
                                                          7:15

2 ¿Te gustaría ir al cine? Con un(a) compañero(a) haz *(make)* planes para ver una película este sábado.

3 En una hoja de papel, escribe una descripción corta de tu actor o actriz favorito(a). ¿Es alto(a)? / ¿Bajo(a)? ¿Es joven? / ¿Viejo(a)? ¿Cuál es el nombre de una película o del programa de televisión en el que aparece? No escribas su nombre. En grupos de cuatro, cada *(each)* estudiante lee su descripción. El resto del grupo debe adivinar *(guess)* quién es.

¿Qué sabes ahora?

Can you:

■ tell what kind of television programs and movies you are interested in?

—Los programas ___ me ___.

■ say why you like or dislike certain programs or movies?

—Las telenovelas (no) me gustan porque ___.

■ tell how long something lasts?

—Este programa dura ___; de la(s) ___ hasta la(s) ___ de la ___.

EL MANDO A DISTANCIA INTELIGENTE

tp TELEPROGRAMA

■ Pulsa las páginas de Teleprograma para elegir los programas que más te van. Automaticamente. Porque TP es la guía más completa y manejable de TV. Y con TP la caja tonta se convierte en inteligente.

tp TELEPROGRAMA

N.º 1 en la Tele

Vocabulario para conversar   359

Perspectiva cultural

En estos canales dan programas divertidos. ¿Qué clases de programas son más populares en América del Sur? ¿Son como los que ven tus amigos y tú?

Look at the picture of a Venezuelan household. What does the information in the photo tell you about what room the TV is usually located in and who you would find watching it?

Imagine this: You're an exchange student living in Caracas, Venezuela. You're staying with a family that has two children: Jaime, who is fourteen, and Mariana, sixteen. On your first night there, you sit down with them to watch television and . . . surprise! Bill Cosby pops up speaking perfect Spanish!

What you're watching is the dubbed version *El Show de Bill Cosby.*

Although Jaime and Mariana can also watch other dubbed imports from the United States, those programs are the exception. Venezuela has one of the largest television industries in Latin America.

Some weekend variety shows in Venezuela last several hours. For instance, *Super Sábado Sensacional.* It features performers from all over the world, combining entertainment with mini-interviews. *Super Sábado Sensacional* competes with similar shows from other countries that are also shown in Venezuela, such as Mexico's *Siempre en domingo* and *Sábado gigante,* produced by a Spanish-language station in Miami.

In most of the Spanish-speaking world, teenagers rarely have their own TV, even if the family can afford it. So at night, Jaime and Mariana sit down with the rest of the family to watch TV in the living room. They usually tune in to one of several *culebras.* The word means "snake," which is how Venezuelans jokingly

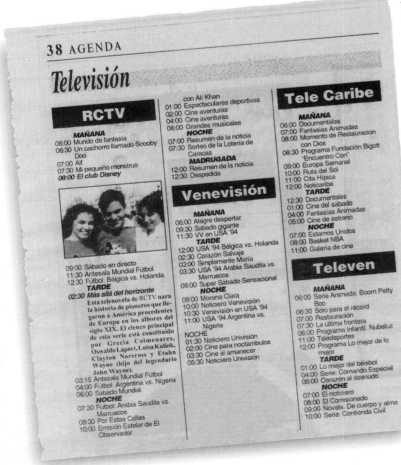

38 AGENDA

Televisión

RCTV

MAÑANA
06:00 Mundo de fantasía
06:30 Un cachorro llamado Scooby Doo
07:00 Alf
07:30 Mi pequeño monstruo
08:00 El club Disney

09:00 Sábado en directo
11:30 Antesala Mundial Fútbol
12:30 Fútbol: Bélgica vs. Holanda
TARDE
02:30 Más allá del horizonte
Esta telenovela de RCTV nara la historia de pioneros que llegaron a América procedentes de Europa en los albores del siglo XIX. El elenco principal de esta serie está constituido por Grecia Colmenares, Oswaldo Laport, Luisa Kuliok, Clayton Norcross y Etahn Wayne (hijo del legendario John Wayne).
03:15 Antesala Mundial Fútbol
04:00 Fútbol: Argentina vs. Nigeria
06:00 Sábado Mundial
NOCHE
07:30 Fútbol: Arabia Saudita vs. Marruecos
09:30 Por Estas Calles
10:00 Emisión Estelar de El Observador

con Ali Khan
01:00 Espectaculares deportivas
02:00 Cine aventuras
04:00 Cine aventuras
06:00 Grandes musicales
NOCHE
07:00 Resumen de la noticia
07:30 Sorteo de la Lotería de Caracas
MADRUGADA
12:00 Resumen de la noticia
12:30 Despedida

Venevisión

MAÑANA
06:00 Alegre despertar
09:30 Sábado gigante
11:30 VV en USA '94
TARDE
12:00 USA '94 Bélgica vs. Holanda
02:30 Corazón Salvaje
03:00 Simplemente María
03:30 USA '94 Arabia Saudita vs. Marruecos
06:00 Super Sábado Sensacional
NOCHE
09:00 Morena Clara
10:00 Noticiero Venevisión
10:30 Venevisión en USA '94
11:00 USA '94 Argentina vs. Nigeria
NOCHE
01:30 Noticiero Univisión
02:00 Cine para noctámbulos
03:30 Cine al amanecer
05:30 Noticiero Univisión

Tele Caribe

MAÑANA
06:00 Documentales
07:00 Fantasías Animadas
08:00 Momento de Restauración con Dios
08:30 Programa Fundación Bigott "Encuentro Con"
09:00 Europa Semanal
10:00 Ruta del Sol
11:00 Cita Hípica
12:00 Noticaribe
TARDE
12:30 Documentales
01:00 Cine del sábado
04:00 Fantasías Animadas
05:00 Cine de estreno
NOCHE
07:00 Estamos Unidos
08:00 Basket NBA
11:00 Galería de cine

Televen

MAÑANA
06:00 Serie Animada: Boom Petty Boo
06:30 Sólo para el récord
07:00 Restauración
07:30 La última frontera
08:00 Programa Infantil: Nubeluz
11:00 Teledeportes
12:00 Programa Lo mejor de lo mejor
TARDE
01:00 Lo mejor del béisbol
04:00 Serie: Comando Especial
05:00 Corazón al desnudo
NOCHE
07:00 El noticiero
08:00 El Comisionado
09:00 Novela: De cuerpo y alma
10:00 Serie: Contienda Civil

refer to their soap operas, because they're long and winding. Venezuela, Mexico, Argentina, and Spain produce many popular soap operas. They usually last several months, then new shows begin, with new characters.

If Jaime and Mariana could watch Spanish-language TV in other countries, they would be surprised to see how many shows from Venezuela are broadcast there. This would give them a sense of how Venezuelan television plays an important role in world communications.

Un programa de noticias en Caracas

La cultura desde tu perspectiva

1 If there is a Spanish-language TV channel in your area, watch a program for at least ten minutes. Make sure you see a commercial break. Write down everything you understood. Which was easier to understand, the program or the commercials? How might watching TV in Spanish benefit you beyond learning the language?

2 If you don't have access to a Spanish-language broadcast, imagine that you are living in Venezuela for an extended period of time. What would be the advantages of watching TV? What could you learn from a Venezuelan program that you could not learn from a dubbed imported program? How might you benefit from watching a dubbed imported program?

"Me gusta ver la televisión con mi familia."

Gramática en contexto

Look at the story boards for this TV commercial for a restaurant delivery service. How is the restaurant using TV to advertise?

Ahora Uds. pueden disfrutar la comida del mejor restaurante de la ciudad sin salir de casa y ¡sin tener que preparar nada!

El Restaurante Taxi

les lleva a sus casas una cena deliciosa. Aquí tienen Uds. los comentarios de algunos de nuestros clientes:

A nosotros nos gustan mucho las enchiladas. Por eso, siempre llamamos al Restaurante Taxi, donde hacen las más sabrosas enchiladas.

Las ensaladas del Restaurante Taxi son más sabrosas y baratas que las ensaladas de otros restaurantes.

El pollo al horno del Restaurante Taxi tiene menos grasa que el pollo frito de los otros restaurantes. A nuestros hijos les encanta.

A You know that we use *me gusta(n)* and *me encanta(n)* when we talk about things we "like" or "love." In the ad, there are similar expressions, but *nos* and *les* are used instead of *me*. Find these expressions. To whom do you think *nos* refers? To whom do you think *les* refers?

B Find the sentence that begins *El pollo al horno del Restaurante Taxi tiene . . .* and the one that begins *Las ensaladas del Restaurante Taxi son . . . .* In each sentence, what foods are being compared? Which words make the comparison? What word do the two comparisons have in common?

Los comparativos

You have learned *más* and *menos* in certain expressions.

Me gusta el tenis pero me gusta **más** el fútbol.

¿Te gustan las manzanas? Sí, **más o menos**.

- We also use *más* / *menos* + adjective + *que* ("than") to make comparisons.

    Las películas de aventuras son **más emocionantes que** las películas del oeste.

    Una telenovela es **menos realista que** un programa de hechos de la vida real.

- The adjectives agree with the nouns they refer to.

- The adjectives *bueno, -a, malo, -a, viejo, -a,* and *joven* have irregular comparative forms. We do not use *más* with them.

ADJETIVO	COMPARATIVO
bueno, -a	**mejor (que)**
malo, -a	**peor (que)**
viejo, -a	**mayor (que)**
joven	**menor (que)**

- *Mejor, peor, mayor,* and *menor* have plural forms ending in *-es.* However, they don't have a different feminine form:

    Las hermanas de Pedro son **menores** que las de Juan.

- *Mejor* ("better") is also the comparative form of *bien* ("well"), and *peor* ("worse") is also the comparative form of *mal* ("badly"). When used in this sense, *mejor* and *peor* have only one form.

    Graciela y Fabián son **mejores que** Susana y Gustavo en tenis.

    Graciela y Fabián juegan tenis **mejor que** Susana y Gustavo.

1 Túrnate con un(a) compañero(a) para comparar estos programas y películas:

Las películas de detectives son más emocionantes que las películas románticas.
o: Las películas románticas son menos emocionantes que las películas de detectives.

a. triste

b. interesante

c. realista

d. aburrido

e. cómico

f. divertido

2 Haz una afirmación *(statement)* falsa sobre cada una de estas personas. Tu compañero(a) te va a dar la información correcta.

A — *Rebeca patina peor que Luisa.*
B — *¡Claro que no! Rebeca patina mejor que Luisa.*
   o: *Luisa patina peor que Rebeca.*

Rebeca

Luisa

A — *Adela y Natalia son mayores que Gabriel y Timoteo.*
B — *¡Claro que no! Adela y Natalia son menores que Gabriel y Timoteo.*
   o: *Gabriel y Timoteo son mayores que Adela y Natalia.*

Adela y Natalia / Gabriel y Timoteo

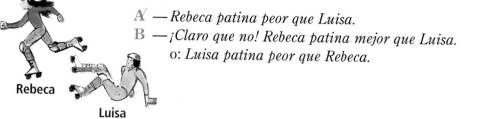

a. Adán / Gerardo

b. Elena / Julio

c. Diana y tú / Fabiola y yo

d. Pepe / Beto

e. yo / Laura

f. Cristóbal / Mateo

Los superlativos

- To say that someone or something is "the most" of a group, we use the definite article + (noun) + *más* + adjective.

  Para mí, *Los tres perezosos* es **el programa más divertido**.

- To say that someone or something is "the best" or "the worst," we use *el / la mejor* and *el / la peor.* These come before the noun.

  Pienso que Gonzalo Ochoa es **el mejor actor**.

- When we say that someone or something is "the most," "the best," or "the worst" in a group or category, we use *de*.

  Para mí, *El día del terror* es **la peor película de todas**.

  Mis amigos los perros es **el mejor programa del domingo**.

  Clara Vega es **la mejor actriz de las telenovelas**.

3 Con un(a) compañero(a), contesta las preguntas.

interesante

A — *¿Cuál es el programa más interesante?*
B — *El programa más interesante es* . . .

a. aburrido   d. tonto
b. divertido   e. 💡
c. emocionante

4 En grupos de cinco o seis, hagan una encuesta *(survey)* para averiguar *(find out)* el / la mejor y el / la peor de estas categorías y por qué. Luego, escribe los resultados de la encuesta.

mes del año

A — *Para ti, ¿cuál es el mejor mes del año?*
B — *Creo que el mejor mes del año es* . . . *porque* . . .
A — *¿Y cuál es el peor mes del año?*
B — *El peor mes del año es* . . . *porque* . . .

a. programa de televisión   d. película del año
b. anuncio de televisión   e. restaurante de la ciudad
c. grupo musical   f. tienda de la ciudad

Ahora, informa a la clase sobre los resultados de la encuesta.
Tres personas creen que . . . *es el mejor mes del año porque* . . .
Cuatro estudiantes creen que . . . *es el peor mes del año porque* . . .

El complemento directo:
Los pronombres y el infinitivo

You know that we use direct object pronouns (*lo, la, los, las*)
to avoid repeating a noun.

* When we use direct object pronouns with infinitives, we
  can either put them before the verb or attach them to the
  end of the infinitive. For example:
  — ¿Vas a ver **las noticias**?
  — Sí, **las** voy a ver.
    o: Sí, voy a ver**las.**

5 Escribe los nombres de cuatro películas y de qué clase es cada una de ellas.
Después pregunta a otros(as) compañeros(as) si quieren verlas.

A — *¿Quieres ver la película* Terror en la noche?
B — *Sí, me gustaría verla. Me encantan las películas de terror.*
  o: *No, no quiero verla. A mí me aburren las películas de terror.*

6 Pregúntale a un(a) compañero(a) si tienes que hacer estos quehaceres en la casa y por qué.

A — *¿Tengo que lavar la ropa?*
B — *Sí, tienes que lavarla. Está sucia.*

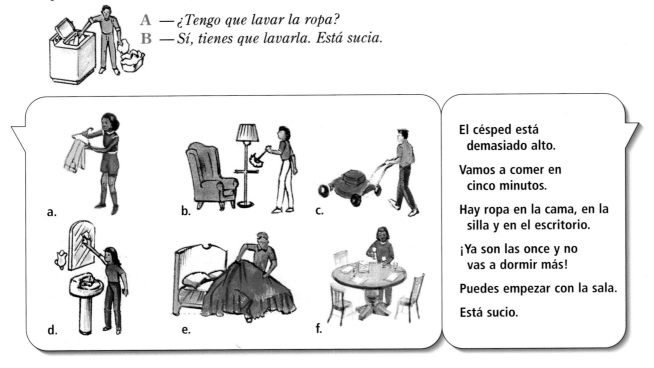

El césped está demasiado alto.

Vamos a comer en cinco minutos.

Hay ropa en la cama, en la silla y en el escritorio.

¡Ya son las once y no vas a dormir más!

Puedes empezar con la sala.

Está sucio.

a.   b.   c.   d.   e.   f.

El pretérito del verbo *ver*

We use *vi* and *viste* to talk about things that we saw. Here are all the preterite-tense forms of the verb *ver*.

(yo)	**vi**	(nosotros) (nosotras)	**vimos**
(tú)	**viste**	(vosotros) (vosotras)	**visteis**
Ud. (él) (ella)	**vio**	Uds. (ellos) (ellas)	**vieron**

7 ¿Qué clase de programa vieron estas personas anoche?

A —¿*Qué clase de programa vieron Rolando y Julia anoche?*

B —*Vieron una comedia.*

Rolando y Julia

a. Juan

b. tú

c. Carmen y Raquel

d. Teresa y tú

e. Carlitos

f. tus padres

8 ¿Qué películas vieron tus compañeros(as) el mes pasado? ¿Dónde? Haz una encuesta para averiguarlo. Escribe la información y comparte *(share)* tus resultados con la clase.

A —*¿Qué película viste el mes pasado?*

B —*Vi* Aladino.

A —*¿Dónde la viste?*

B —*La vi en mi casa.*
    o: *La vi en el cine.*

¿Qué películas vieron tus compañeros(as)?

Dos estudiantes vieron la película Aladino *el mes pasado. La vieron en sus casas.*

El complemento indirecto: Los pronombres *nos* y *les*

We use the indirect object pronouns *me, te,* and *le* with verbs like *dar, doler, encantar, fascinar, gustar,* and *interesar.* Here are all the indirect object pronouns.

¡NO OLVIDES!

Sometimes we use *a* + noun or name to clarify who the indirect object pronoun refers to.

A mis padres les encantan los programas musicales.

me	*(to / for) me*	**nos**	*(to / for) us*
te	*(to / for) you*	**os***	*(to / for) you*
le	*(to / for) you him her it*	**les**	*(to / for) you them*

* The pronoun *os* is used mainly in Spain. We will use it occasionally and you should learn to recognize it.

9 Habla con un compañero(a) sobre los programas de televisión que van a ver estas personas.

Ricardo

A — *¿Qué programa va a ver Ricardo?*
B — Nuestros amigos los delfines.
A — *¿De veras? ¿A él le gustan los programas educativos?*
B — *Sí, le gustan mucho.*
   o: *Sí, le encantan / fascinan / interesan mucho.*

a. el profesor

b. Mario y Eva

c. Uds.

d. Luisita

e. tú

f. Inés y Vicente

g. Santiago y tú

Ahora lo sabes

Can you:

- compare people and things?

  —Las películas de aventuras son ___ emocionantes ___ las románticas.

- tell what is the best or worst in a group or category?

  —(No) me gusta ese programa. Es _____ programa de televisión.

- avoid repeating a noun?

  —¿Cuándo vas a ver la película? Voy a ___ esta tarde.

- tell what you saw?

  —La semana pasada, mis hermanos y yo ___ una película del oeste.

- tell what you and others are interested in?

  —A nosotros _____ las ciencias.

Univisión Despierta Su Apetito Con Un Programa Que Cae Bien.

AL MEDIODIA

Igual que una buena sopa, "Al Mediodía" es el nuevo programa de televisión que cae bien a la hora de almuerzo. María Antonieta Collins y Mauricio Zeilic con Cristina Aceves y Ambrosio Hernández les traen lo mejor en noticias locales e internacionales, lo último en medicina y salud, entrevistas con sus artistas favoritos, segmentos de viajes, moda, cocina y mucho más. "Al Mediodía" contiene todos los ingredientes para convertirse en su programa favorito.

Lunes a viernes 12 pm/11 am Centro.

Univisión

Todo Junto

Para decir más

Aquí tienes vocabulario adicional que te puede ayudar para hacer las actividades de esta sección.

el concurso
contest

el cable
cable

religioso, -a
religious

alegre
merry, lively

infantil
childish

mediocre
mediocre

(yo) recomiendo
I recommend

parecido, -a (a)
similar (to)

la última vez que . . . fue
the last time . . . was

la actuación
acting, performance

la calidad
quality

Actividades

Esta sección te ofrece la oportunidad de aumentar tus conocimientos de español al integrar lo que aprendiste en este capítulo con lo que aprendiste en capítulos anteriores.

1 Prepara una crítica *(review)* de una película. En tu crítica puedes hablar sobre:

- qué película viste y cuándo
- qué clase de película es
- quiénes son los actores y qué piensas de ellos
- algo que uno de los actores hizo *(did)* en la película
- dónde dan la película y a qué hora
- qué piensas de la película

2 ¿Qué programas de televisión te interesan más? Para esta actividad, diferentes lugares de la clase representan clases de programas diferentes. Tu profesor(a) te va a decir el lugar adonde debes ir. En grupo, digan *(tell)* a la clase:

- qué clase de programa de televisión les gusta y por qué
- cuál es el mejor ejemplo de esta clase de programa
- cuándo lo vieron

A —*¿Qué clase de programas les gusta a Uds.?*

B —*A nosotros nos gustan los programas de detectives porque son emocionantes. Son más interesantes que los programas educativos. Rafael Sánchez, detective es el mejor programa de detectives. Lo vimos el martes a las nueve de la noche en el canal 15.*

El cómico mexicano Cantinflas

3 Para esta actividad, necesitas la sección de pasatiempos del periódico. Haz planes con otro(a) estudiante para ir al cine este fin de semana. Necesitas:

- averiguar qué clase de películas le gusta a tu compañero(a)
- buscar en el periódico una película que le va a interesar
- invitarle a ir al cine
- decidir qué día van a ir y a qué hora
- decidir cómo van a ir

La cantante Celia Cruz en concierto

¡Vamos a leer!

Antes de leer

STRATEGY ➤ Using prior knowledge

What kind of information would you expect to find in a page of movie listings? How would you expect it to be presented? Think of a movie you know well and write a movie listing for it.

Mira la lectura

Look at this selection from the Puerto Rican magazine *Vea*. What is the topic of this page? How is the information organized? (Alphabetically? By time sequence? By location?)

Infórmate

STRATEGY ➤ Using cognates

One of the most useful strategies for dealing with unfamiliar words is using cognates. Here are some patterns that might help you recognize them.

- Frequently a double consonant in an English word is represented by a single consonant in the Spanish cognate: *clase, inocente, aceptar.*
- Often words ending in -y in English end in -ia or -ía in Spanish: *historia, geografía, infancia.*
- Many English adjectives ending in -ed end in -ado(a) or -ido(a) in Spanish: *aceptado, -a; permitidos, -as.*

Puerto Rico/televisión

el cine en la tv

DOMINGO 15

11 AM (11)(9)(22) "Alice in Wonderland" con las voces de Kathryn Beaumont y Ed Wynn (1951). Versión animada del clásico de Disney sobre la famosa historia de Lewis Carroll de una niña que al caer en una cueva de conejo entra a un mundo mágico poblado por extrañas criaturas. ★★★

12 PM (2) "First Blood" con Sylvester Stallone y Brian Dennehy (1982). Después de ser arrestado por vagancia, un Boinas Verde veterano de Vietnam escapa a las junglas y emplea la guerrilla en contra de la Policía y de la Guardia Nacional. ★★★

1 PM (11)(9)(22) "The Towering Inferno" con Steve McQueen y Paul Newman (1974). Dramático rescate que comienza justo en el momento en que unos invitados a la inauguración de un rascacielos quedan atrapados en el piso 138 cuando el edificio se enciende en llamas. ★★★

2 PM (2) "Black And White".

3 PM (7) "Caña Brava"

1 PM (6)(3) Película.

7 PM (11)(7)(9)(22) "The Amy Fisher Story".

8 PM (4)(12) "V.I. Warshawski" con Kathleen Turner y Jay O. Sanders (1991). Una atractiva pero ruda mujer policía trata de resolver un caso en el que tiene un interés personal. ★★★

9 PM (11)(7)(9)(22) "The Kansas City Massacre" con Dale Robertson y Bo

con Braulio Castillo.

5 PM (2)(5) "Romancing The Stone" con Michael Douglas y Kathleen Turner (1984). Una solitaria y romántica novelista pasa su tiempo escribiendo y soñando con el hombre perfecto. Pero su vida toma un giro drástico y comienza a parecerse a una de sus novelas cuando vuela a Sudamérica para rescatar a su hermana secuestrada y se encuentra a sí misma buscando un misterioso tesoro con su sueño del hombre perfecto hecho realidad.

6 PM (4)(12) "Oscar" con Sylvester Stallone y Peter Riegert (1991). Un hampón trata de enderezarse y conseguirle esposo a su hija en el Chicago de 1920. ★★

7 PM (2)(5) "Teenage Mutant Ninja Turtles" con Judith Hoag y Elias Koteas (1990). Las adorables máquinas de batalla verdes hacen su debut cinematográfico como amantes del bien, de la gente buena y de las pizzas de pepperoni. ★★★

12 AM (7) "La Devoradora" con María Félix y Luis Aldas.

(11)(9)(22) "Dos Esposas".

LUNES 16

agente a cargo de la oficina del FBI en el medio oeste en los 1930, transporta a un notorio gángster por tren y después por auto hasta la prisión de Levinworth. La movida es la señal para una emboscada en la que los gángsteres rivales tratan de secuestrar al prisionero de la Policía y del FBI. ★★★

(11)(7)(9)(22) "Father of The Bride" con Steve Martin y Diane Keaton (1991). Un padre no puede de lidiar con el anuncio de su hija de que piensa comprometerse y menos con los preparativos para su boda. ★★★

10 PM (2)(5) "Black Magic" con Bud Spenser y Philip Michael Thomas. La misteriosa muerte de una joven causa un sinnúmero de problemas a su novio quien, sin embargo, se canta inocente. Pero la Policía no le cree. Se unen dos detectives para investigar el crimen.

11:30 (4)(12) "Things Change" con Don Ameche y Joe Mantegna (1989). Un sencillo zapatero italiano acepta, a cambio de dinero, pagar los platos rotos por un maleante de Chicago. Pero el hombre asignado a vigilarlo por un fin de semana decide lo imprevisto. ★★

William Shatner (1982). Una periodista de televisión resulta brutalmente atacada en su hogar después de transmitir un editorial a favor de los derechos de la mujer. En el hospital descubre a su asaltante, cuyo torturante pasado le ha transformado en un criminal sicópata masivo que anhela terminar su trabajo. ★★★

(6)(3) Película. (WIPR-

las películas

Semana d (Cualquier defi responsabili

CACIONES: Excelente Regular

MART

go "Po politic vertirse primer suade que e traició bles y mucha

(6)(3) Película. R-TV no sabía el tí-

(7)(9)(22) "Ta- Crime". "Lori" es de citas que tie la oportunidad de r su vida cuando a "Gironda", un ri- nerciante, y su ami-

11 PM (WIP

MIE

Il" c Billy unida la M una con noar ★★

9 PM End 11 PM Co Ale

(12) "Delta Force"

JU

"Caperucita y res Amigos" con Gracia y Manuel Valdez.

Bas nac la Fo cí

(11)(9)(22) "The Purple" con Who- Goldberg y Danny ver (1985). La historia por de dos herma- en 1909 a 1949, quie- eron separadas al ento de su nacimien- reunidas después.

11 P ze Fo For

(6)(3) Película. R-TV no sabía el tí-

(7)(9)(22) "Live!" Death Row" con Cassidy y Bruce

1 Look at the bold-faced headings in the reading.

- When are the most movies shown, in the morning, afternoon, or evening?
- How many channels show movies?
- Read the titles, then classify the movies according to type. See the list on the right. Which category seems to be the most popular?

2 Choose a movie that sounds interesting and read its description several times to get an idea about the plot. Pick out a few cognates that help you understand the description.

3 After reading the description, do you still think the movie belongs to the category suggested by its title? If you have already seen the movie, do you think the description tells what is most important about the plot? Would you change the description? How?

película de detectives
comedia
película musical
película del oeste
película romántica
película de aventuras
dibujos animados

"**En busca del arca perdida** (<u>Raiders of the Lost Ark</u>) es una película emocionante."

Aplicación

1 Which of these movies would you prefer to see? Why?

2 On a piece of paper, list at least ten new words that you learned from this reading selection and ten cognates that you found.

¡Vamos a escribir!

Choose a recent TV show that you enjoyed and write a review of it.

1 First, write out the answers to these questions about the program.

- ¿Cómo se llama el programa?
- ¿Qué clase de programa es?
- ¿Qué día viste el programa? ¿En qué canal? ¿Cuánto tiempo duró?
- ¿Qué artistas participaron? ¿Cómo son?
- ¿Te gustó el programa? ¿Por qué?
- ¿Lo recomiendas? ¿A quién lo recomiendas? (a los niños, a los jóvenes . . .)

2 Now write the review using your answers to the preceding questions as a guide. Show your review to a partner. Ask if there is any other information he or she would want to have or if you should change or rearrange any of your information to make it more helpful to the reader.

3 Decide about the changes you might like to make, and rewrite your review.

El actor Franklin Virguez en una escena de una telenovela

La miniserie "Vida de mi Vida," de Radio Caracas Televisión

4 Check for spelling and accents. Did you use the correct forms of the verbs and adjectives? If necessary, rewrite your review.

5 Now you are ready to share your work. You can:

- collect all the reviews into a class program guide called *Guía de televisión: Los mejores programas,* or
- include it in your writing portfolio

La actriz Marlene Mesada

La comedia "Corte Tropical"

"Kassandra," una telenovela popular

¿Lo sabes bien?

This section will help you organize your studying for the proficiency test, where you will be asked to do similar, though not identical, tasks. There will not be any models on the test.

Listening

Can you understand when someone talks about how long an event will last? Listen as your teacher reads a sample similar to what you will hear on the test. According to the person making the statement, how much time would someone spend watching this, one hour or more than an hour? Would the person watching be at home or at a movie theater?

Reading

Can you read this movie review and use the cognates that appear in it to find out what kind of movie it is?

Con *Tren expreso*, Ud. no puede aburrirse.
Tren expreso es una película divertida, con mucho humor, donde no hay ni fantasmas ni vampiros ni monstruos. Todo es real. Es una emocionante aventura que empieza con el robo de un banco. Los críticos dicen que es la mejor película del año. Véala en el Cine Acuario.

★ ★ ★ ★

Writing

Can you write a letter describing a movie you saw recently? Here is a sample letter:

Hola, Carmelo:

La semana pasada, mi hermano y yo vimos una película bastante buena. Es muy realista. Nos fascinó. En la película hay una familia que no tiene dinero: el padre no tiene trabajo y la hija está enferma. Una persona generosa los ayuda. No es la mejor película del verano, pero es muy interesante.

Saludos, Ana

Culture

Can you explain what is shown on TV in Venezuela, what programs would you choose to watch, and why?

El programa de entrevistas *Cristina*

Speaking

Can you express and defend an opinion about a television program?

—*Para mí, el mejor programa del canal 9 es el programa educativo,* Ambiente. *Es un programa fascinante. Los dibujos animados son demasiado tontos y aburridos. No me interesan. Yo creo que deben dar más programas educativos.*

Resumen del capítulo 11

Use the vocabulary from this chapter to help you:

■ talk about a TV show or movie
■ tell when events begin and end, and how long they last
■ express and defend an opinion

to name types of movies
la clase (de)
la película de aventuras
la película de ciencia ficción
la película musical
la película del oeste
la película romántica
la película de terror

to talk about TV and TV shows
el actor
la actriz, *pl.* las actrices
el anuncio (de televisión)
el canal
la comedia
el concierto
dar + *movie or TV program*
los dibujos animados
el documental
las noticias
el programa deportivo
el programa de detectives
el programa educativo
el programa de entrevistas
el programa de hechos de la vida real
el programa musical
el pronóstico del tiempo
la telenovela

to describe a movie or TV show
aburrido, -a
cómico, -a
¿Cuál(es)?
demasiado
divertido, -a
emocionante
en blanco y negro
en colores
fascinante
interesante
más (here: *more*)
el / la / los / las mejor(es) (here: *best*)
el / la / los / las peor(es) (here: *worst*)
realista
tonto, -a
triste
un poco

to indicate time or duration
casi
corto, -a
de la mañana
de la noche
de la tarde
durar
en punto
hasta
largo, -a
más tarde

más temprano
media hora *(f.)*
el mediodía
la medianoche
el minuto
puntualmente
el tiempo
todavía no

to express opinions or reactions
aburrir
dar miedo
fascinar
interesar
pensar (e → ie) (que)
sobre

to indicate a reason
por eso

CAPÍTULO 12

¡Vamos a un restaurante mexicano!

OBJECTIVES

At the end of this chapter, you will be able to:

- ask politely to have something brought to you
- order a meal
- say what you ate or drank
- compare family dinners in the Spanish-speaking world and in the United States

Haciendo tortillas en el mercado de Chichicastenango, Guatemala

¡Piénsalo bien!

Look at the photos and read the captions.

Think about the Mexican restaurants you're familiar with. What are their names? Are they fast-food places, diners, or fancy restaurants? Which of the restaurants shown in these photos is most similar to those in your community?

"¿Me pasas la sal, por favor?"

En el centro comercial Plaza Flamingo de Cancún

"Este es mi restaurante favorito. Se especializan en enchiladas de toda clase."

Restaurante hispano en Albuquerque, Nuevo México

The people of Mexico eat as wide a variety of foods as we do.

"¿Y qué van a pedir?"

En el patio del restaurante Casa de Pico en San Diego

Vocabulario para conversar

¿Con qué se hacen las enchiladas?

Aquí tienes palabras y expresiones necesarias para hablar sobre algunas comidas mexicanas y con qué se hacen. Léelas varias veces y practícalas con un(a) compañero(a) en las páginas siguientes.

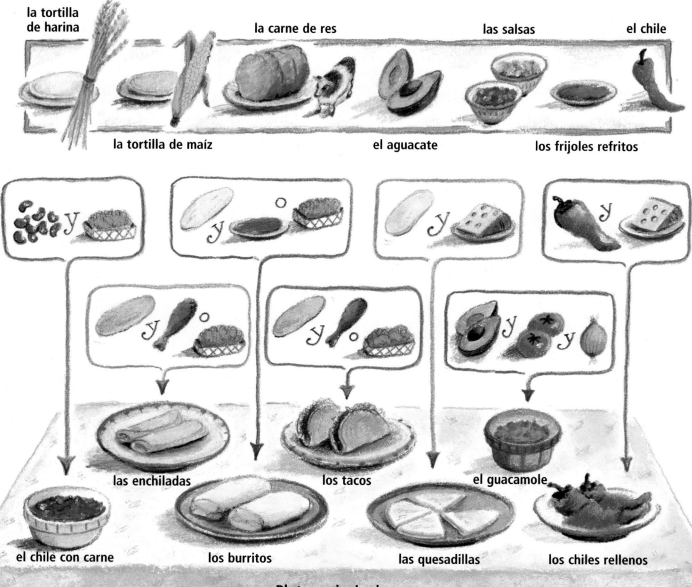

la tortilla de harina

la carne de res

las salsas

el chile

la tortilla de maíz

el aguacate

los frijoles refritos

las enchiladas

los tacos

el guacamole

el chile con carne

los burritos

las quesadillas

los chiles rellenos

Platos principales

el chocolate

los pasteles

el flan

los churros

el helado

la merienda

También necesitas . . .

¿Con qué se hace(n) ___?	*What is / are ___ made with?*
Se hace(n) con ___.	*It's (they're) made with . . .*
pedir (e → i)	*to ask for; to order*
probar (o → ue)	*to try; to taste*
¿Has probado ___?	*Have you tried ___?*
he probado	*I've tried*
una vez	*once*
alguna vez	*ever*
¿Algo más?	here: *Anything else?*
el postre*	*dessert*
de postre	*for dessert*
picante	*spicy, peppery, hot (flavor)*
no picante	*mild (flavor)*
a menudo	*often*
vender	*to sell*
la comida	*food*

> **¿Y qué quiere decir . . . ?**
> de merienda
> muchas veces

* It's not typical in Spanish-speaking countries to have ice cream or cake for dessert. When dining at home, the usual dessert is *queso y fruta*. For your late-afternoon *merienda* you might have sandwiches, pastries, rolls, and *té* or *café con leche*, or *chocolate con churros*.

Empecemos a conversar

Túrnate con un(a) compañero(a) para ser *Estudiante A* y *Estudiante B*.
Reemplacen las palabras subrayadas con palabras representadas o
escritas en los recuadros. 💡 quiere decir que puedes escoger
(choose) tu propia respuesta.

1 plato principal   A — *¿Qué vas a pedir de plato principal?*
                 B — *Quisiera probar las quesadillas.*
                      Y ahora Uds.

Estudiante A   **Estudiante B**

a. de postre   b. de merienda

c. para el almuerzo   d. para la cena

2    A — *¿Has probado chiles rellenos alguna vez?*
                 B — *Sí, una vez. (Sí, muchas veces.)*
                     o: *No, nunca. (No me gustan los chiles rellenos.)*
                     Y ahora Uds.

Estudiante A   **Estudiante B**

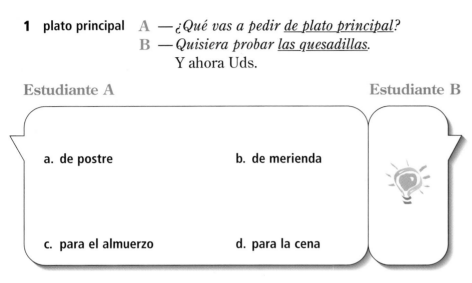

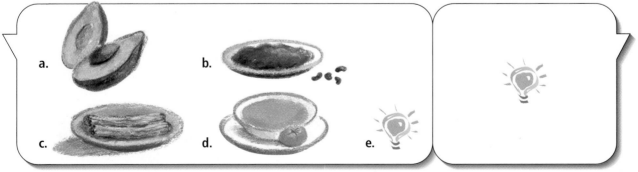

3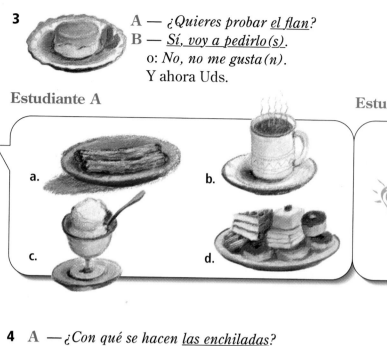

A — ¿Quieres probar *el flan*?

B — *Sí, voy a pedirlo(s)*.

o: *No, no me gusta(n)*.

Y ahora Uds.

¡NO OLVIDES!

Remember that you can attach the pronouns *lo, la, los,* or *las* to an infinitive.

Estudiante A

Estudiante B

a.

b.

c.

d.

También se dice

las masas

4 A — *¿Con qué se hacen las enchiladas?*

B — *Con tortillas de maíz y pollo o carne de res.*

Y ahora Uds.

Estudiante A   **Estudiante B**

el ají

los porotos

Empecemos a escribir

Escribe tus respuestas en español.

5 ¿Cuáles de las comidas de la página 384 has probado? ¿Cuáles te gustaron? ¿Dónde las probaste?

6 ¿Prefieres la comida picante o no picante? ¿Qué restaurantes de tu comunidad sirven comida picante?

7 ¿Cuál es tu comida mexicana favorita? ¿Con qué se hace? ¿Puedes comprar los ingredientes necesarios en el supermercado donde tú vas de compras?

8 ¿Qué comes de postre más a menudo? ¿Pasteles, helado o frutas? ¿Cuál es tu favorito?

la palta

Vocabulario para conversar

¡Me falta una cuchara!

**Aquí tienes el resto del vocabulario necesario para pedir algo,
para pedir una comida y para decir lo que comiste o bebiste.**

el camarero

la camarera

el menú

la cuenta

el plato

el vaso

la taza

el platillo

la mantequilla

la sal

el tazón

la pimienta

el tenedor

el cuchillo

el azúcar

la cuchara

la servilleta

el mantel

encima de

detrás de

debajo de

delante de

También necesitas . . .

Me falta(n)	*I need; I am lacking*
¿Me pasas ___?	*Will you pass me ___?*
traer	*to bring*
¿Me trae ___?	*Will you bring me ___?*
(Le) traigo	*I'm bringing (you)*
beber: (yo) bebí	*to drink: I drank*
(tú) bebiste	*you drank*
comer: (yo) comí	*to eat: I ate*
(tú) comiste	*you ate*
pedir: (yo) pedí	*to order: I ordered*
(tú) pediste	*you ordered*
lo mismo	*the same thing*
en seguida	*right away*

¿Y qué quiere decir . . . ?
a la carta
la especialidad de la casa
el plato del día

Empecemos a conversar

9

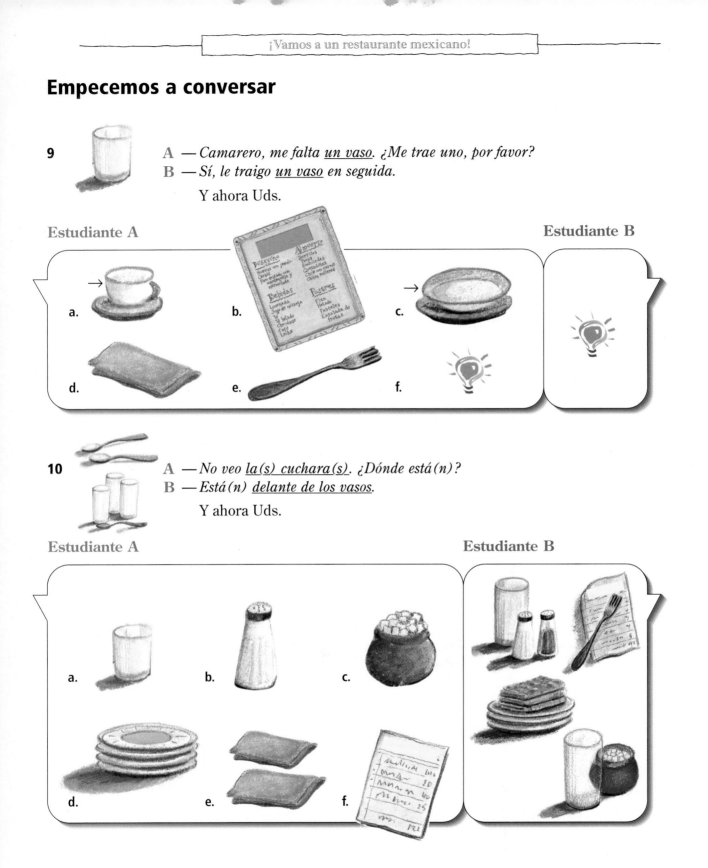

A — *Camarero, me falta <u>un vaso</u>. ¿Me trae uno, por favor?*
B — *Sí, le traigo <u>un vaso</u> en seguida.*

Y ahora Uds.

Estudiante A

Estudiante B

a.   b.   c.

d.   e.   f.

10

A — *No veo <u>la(s) cuchara(s)</u>. ¿Dónde está(n)?*
B — *Está(n) <u>delante de los vasos</u>.*

Y ahora Uds.

Estudiante A

Estudiante B

a.   b.   c.

d.   e.   f.

11 A —*¿Me pasas <u>la sal</u>, por favor?*
　　B —*Sí, aquí <u>la</u> tienes. ¿Necesitas algo más?*
　　A —*Ahora no, gracias.*

　　　　Y ahora Uds.

Estudiante A　　　　**Estudiante B**

Empecemos a escribir y a leer

Escribe tus respuestas en español.

12 ¿Qué bebiste en el desayuno esta mañana? ¿Y ayer?

13 Cuando vas a un restaurante, ¿qué prefieres, el plato del día o la especialidad de la casa? ¿Por qué?

14 ¿Te falta algo ahora? ¿Qué te falta?

15 ¿Es lógico o no? Si no, escribe frases lógicas.

— ¿Con qué se hacen las quesadillas?
— Con tortillas de maíz y queso. Son muy picantes. ¡Me encantan!

— …Y de plato principal pedí chiles rellenos y quesadillas. ¡Me encanta la comida española!

— Javier, ¿me pasas la mantequilla, por favor?
— Sí, en seguida. Está debajo del tenedor.

También se dice

el mesero, la mesera
el mozo, la moza

la carta
la minuta
la lista

¡Comuniquemos!

Aquí tienes otra oportunidad para usar el vocabulario de este capítulo.

1 Usa el menú para pedir una comida completa. Con tu compañero(a) representen *(play the role)* al (a la) camarero(a) y al (a la) cliente.

MENÚ

Desayuno
Huevos con jamón
Cereal
Pan tostado con
   mantequilla y
   mermelada

Bebidas
Limonada
Jugo de naranja
Té
Té helado
Chocolate
Café
Leche

Almuerzo
Burritos
Tacos
Enchiladas
Quesadillas
Chile con carne
Chiles rellenos

Postres
Flan
Helado
Pasteles
Ensalada de
   frutas

A — *¿Qué desea, señor?*
   o: ¿Qué va a comer?
   (¿Y para beber? ¿Y de postre?)
B — *Pan tostado con mantequilla y mermelada.*

2 ¿Qué dirías *(would you say)* en estas situaciones?

Pediste el bistec pero sólo tienes un tenedor y una cuchara.
¿Me trae un cuchillo, por favor?

a. Pediste sopa pero sólo tienes un tenedor y un cuchillo.
b. Te gustaría pedir guacamole pero no sabes con qué se hace.
c. Hay pan pero no hay nada más en la mesa.
d. Pediste agua pero ya la bebiste.
e. Tu tenedor está sucio.
f. Quieres salir del restaurante pero no sabes cuánto tienes
   que pagar.
g. Las enchiladas que comes están demasiado picantes.
   Necesitas beber algo.

3 En este dibujo hay siete errores. ¿Cuántos puedes encontrar?
Trabaja en grupos pequeños para encontrarlos. Después, compartan
(share) con otros grupos los errores que encontraron.

El vaso está debajo del plato.

¿Qué sabes ahora?

Can you:

- describe the ingredients in certain dishes?

  —Los burritos se hacen con ___ y con ___.

- make polite requests to have something brought or passed to you?

  ¿ ___ la salsa, por favor?

- order a meal?

  —Voy a comer ___, y de ___ quisiera un helado.

- tell what you ate or drank?

  —Ayer yo ___ chile con carne y ___ una limonada.

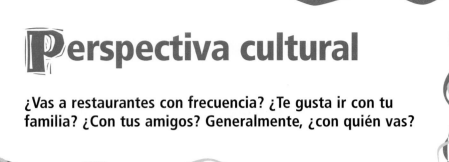

Perspectiva cultural

¿Vas a restaurantes con frecuencia? ¿Te gusta ir con tu familia? ¿Con tus amigos? Generalmente, ¿con quién vas?

What words would you use to describe this restaurant and the people in it? How often do you eat the foods shown on the plate?

The large photo gives you a glimpse of what a family dinner might be like in a restaurant in Mexico. If you lived there, you'd probably be looking forward to seeing your favorite aunt and uncle at the next dinner, because a restaurant meal usually implies a Sunday afternoon dinner, which is an important family event. It is generally a long, leisurely meal that can last for two or three hours. It is an occasion for the whole extended family to get together: brothers, sisters, parents, aunts, uncles, and godparents. Unlike in the United States, where children are often left at home with a baby-sitter, in Mexico even infants are an important presence during a family dinner.

A restaurant dinner can also take place very late at night, especially in a bustling metropolis such as Mexico City. It is common to see an entire family arrive at a restaurant at 10 or 11 in the evening. On Friday and Saturday nights, restaurants often stay open until 2 or 3 in the morning. Some restaurants have entertainment, such as a band.

Many late-night restaurants are inexpensive and the food is very good. They attract people from all walks of life. A man in a work shirt might end up having dinner with his family next to a table of people dressed in suits and expensive fur coats who have just come from the theater.

La cultura desde tu perspectiva

1 What are the similarities and differences between dining out in Mexico and in the United States?

2 You have read about a typical Saturday night and Sunday afternoon in a Mexican restaurant. What values do you think these customs reflect?

Cenando en la Ciudad de México

Un plato típico mexicano: camarones rancheros, arroz, frijoles, guacamole y salsa

Gramática en contexto

Look at this page from a student's travel album and read the captions that she wrote.

El segundo día fuimos a visitar las pirámides de Teotihuacán, cerca de la Ciudad de México.

Nuestro guía nos describió el plano de la ciudad antigua.

Luego, todos subimos la Pirámide del Sol. Yo subí primero y les saqué esta foto a mis amigos en las escaleras.

Cuando bajamos, un vendedor les vendió refrescos a mis amigos. Ellos bebieron los refrescos de unas bolsas de plástico.

A You know that *-aron* is the ending for the *ellos / Uds.* form of *-ar* verbs in the preterite. In the captions, find an *-er* verb that has the *ellos / Uds.* ending in the preterite. How is it similar to the ending for *-ar* verbs? How is it different?

B There are two verbs used in the captions that may be new to you: *describió* and *vendió*. Can you guess their meanings? What do these preterite verb forms have in common?

C Find the sentence that begins *Nuestro guía . . . .* To whom did the guide describe the plan of the city? What word gives you this information?

Verbos con el cambio *e → i*

You know two types of stem-changing verbs: those like *poder (o → ue)* and those like *pensar (e → ie)*. There is a third type in which the *e* in the stem changes to *i* in some of the present-tense forms. *Pedir* is an example of this type. Here are all of its present-tense forms.

(yo)	pido	(nosotros) (nosotras)	pedimos
(tú)	pides	(vosotros) (vosotras)	pedís
Ud. (él) (ella)	pide	Uds. (ellos) (ellas)	piden

- The infinitives of all *e → i* verbs end in *-ir.* Notice that the endings follow the pattern of regular *-ir* verbs.

- Another verb of this type that you know is *servir.*
    En ese restaurante siempre **sirven** arroz con pollo.

1 Dile a un(a) compañero(a) qué piden de postre o de merienda las siguientes personas en un restaurante.

tu profesor
A — *En un restaurante, ¿qué pide de postre tu profesor?*
B — *Generalmente pide flan.*

a. tú
b. tus amigos
c. tu papá / tu mamá
d. Uds.
e. tu hermano / tu hermana
f. tus abuelos

En la Zona Rosa, Ciudad de México

2 Escribe frases para decir qué comida sirven en diferentes ocasiones.

Mis amigos y yo servimos sandwiches y guacamole en la cena.

a. mis amigos
b. mi restaurante favorito
c. mi mamá / mi papá
d. (yo)
e. mis amigos y yo
f. la cafetería de la escuela

en el verano
en el invierno
los domingos
los fines de semana
en las fiestas
todos los días
en la cena
de postre
el 4 de julio

El verbo *traer*

Here are all of the present-tense forms of *traer* (to bring).

(yo)	**traigo**	(nosotros) (nosotras)	**traemos**
(tú)	**traes**	(vosotros) (vosotras)	**traéis**
Ud. (él) (ella)	**trae**	Uds. (ellos) (ellas)	**traen**

- Like *poner* and *hacer, traer* has only one irregular present-tense form: *traigo.* All other forms follow the pattern of regular *-er* verbs.

3 Estás en la playa con un(a) amigo(a). Pregúntale a tu amigo(a)
qué trae al picnic cada *(each)* una de estas personas.

A — ¿*Qué trae Marta?*
B — *Creo que trae los platos y los vasos.*

Marta

a. **Alejandro y Federico**   b. **Uds.**   c. **Paquita**

d. **Elena y Joaquín**   e. **tú**   f. **Diego**

399

El complemento indirecto: Los pronombres

An indirect object tells to whom or for whom an action is performed. You already know the indirect object pronouns *me, te, le, nos,* and *les*. They are used to replace an indirect object noun.

El camarero **nos** sirve enchiladas de queso.	*The waiter serves **us** cheese enchiladas.*
Me trae un refresco.	*He's bringing **me** a soft drink.*
¿**Te** trae el postre ahora?	*Is he bringing **you** dessert now?*

• Because *le* and *les* can have more than one meaning, we can make the meaning clear by adding *a* + pronoun.

Rafael **le** trae el postre **a ella**.	*Rafael is bringing dessert **to her**.*
Les servimos tacos **a ellos**.	*We serve **them** tacos.*

• When we use an indirect object noun, we usually use the indirect object pronoun too.

Le compro naranjas a **mi mamá**.	*I'm buying oranges **for my mom**.*
Les sirvo burritos **a mis amigos**.	*I serve burritos **to my friends**.*

• We can attach an indirect object pronoun to an infinitive or put it before the main verb.

Voy a traer**les** guacamole. } *I'm going to bring **them** guacamole.*

Les voy a traer guacamole.

• Remember that we use indirect object pronouns with verbs like *doler, gustar, encantar,* and *interesar*. This is also true of *faltar*.

4 Tu compañero(a) y tú van a preparar las siguientes comidas. Pídele algo que necesitas. Luego continúa la conversación.

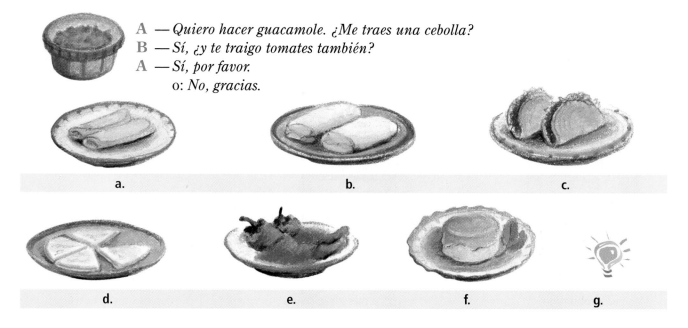

A — *Quiero hacer guacamole. ¿Me traes una cebolla?*
B — *Sí, ¿y te traigo tomates también?*
A — *Sí, por favor.*
  o: *No, gracias.*

a. b. c.

d. e. f. g.

5 El camarero nunca les sirve a Uds. lo que *(what)* piden. Explica la situación con un(a) compañero(a).

Cuando ella pide pollo, el camarero le sirve pescado.

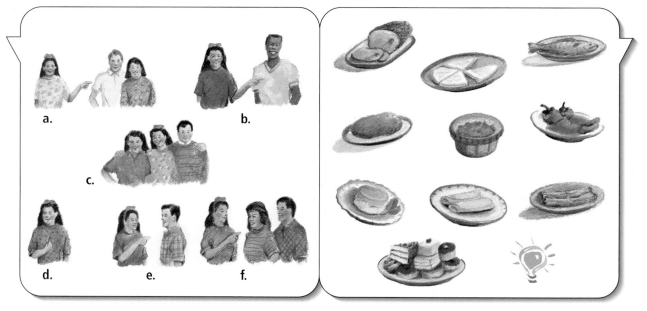

a. b.
c.
d. e. f.

6 Vas al centro *(downtown)* para comprar diferentes cosas. Tu compañero(a) te pregunta adónde vas y por qué vas allí.

A — ¡*Hola!, ¿adónde vas?*
B — *Voy a la tienda de regalos.*
A — *¿Por qué?*
B — *Necesito comprarle un regalo a mi mamá.*

a mi mamá

a. a mi amiga

b. a mis abuelos

c. a mis padres

d. a mi hermano

e. a mi amigo

f. a mis primos

7 Vas a invitar a estas personas a tu casa. Dile a tu compañero(a) qué vas a servirles.

tus abuelos

A — *¿Qué vas a servirles a tus abuelos?*
B — *Voy a servirles arroz con pollo, ensalada, zanahorias y pan.*

a. tu mejor amigo(a)
b. tus primos
c. el Presidente de los Estados Unidos
d. tu profesor(a) de español
e. (nombre de un actor o una actriz)
f. (nombre de un grupo musical)

El pretérito de los verbos que terminan en *-er* e *-ir*

As you know, we use the preterite tense to tell what happened in the past. For *-ar* verbs, we use this pattern of endings: *-é, -aste, -ó, -amos, -asteis, -aron*. The preterite endings for regular *-er* and *-ir* verbs are alike: *-í, -iste, -ió, -imos, -isteis, -ieron*.

Here are all of the preterite forms of *comer* and *salir*:

(yo)	com**í** sal**í**	(nosotros) (nosotras)	com**imos** sal**imos**
(tú)	com**iste** sal**iste**	(vosotros) (vosotras)	com**isteis** sal**isteis**
Ud. (él) (ella)	com**ió** sal**ió**	Uds. (ellos) (ellas)	com**ieron** sal**ieron**

¡NO OLVIDES!

As you learned in Chapter 11, *ver* does not have accent marks on any of its preterite forms: *vi, viste, vio, vimos, vieron.*

- Notice the accent marks on the endings *-í* and *-ió*. These must be included as a part of the spelling.

8 Estas personas salieron de sus casas treinta minutos después de comer. Dile a tu compañero(a) a qué hora comieron y a qué hora salieron.

Pablo / 6:30

A —*¿A qué hora comió Pablo?*
B —*Comió a las seis y media.*
A —*¿Y luego salió?*
B —*Sí, salió a las siete.*

a. Eduardo y Santiago / 7:15
b. Benjamín / 8:20
c. Uds. / 8:45
d. Claudia y Soledad / 6:40
e. María Eugenia / 7:30
f. tú / 💡

9 En cuatro hojas de papel escribe cuatro cosas diferentes que comiste o bebiste la semana pasada. Mezcla *(mix)* tus papeles con los de otros(as) tres compañeros(as). Una persona del grupo va a escoger un papel y preguntar quién comió o bebió esas cosas.

A —*¿Quién comió tacos la semana pasada?*
B —*Yo comí tacos.*
C —*Yo también.*

Lleva un registro *(keep a tally)* de las respuestas de tus compañeros(as) para informar a la clase qué comieron y bebieron las personas de tu grupo.
   Miguel y yo comimos tacos la semana pasada.
   o: *Miguel y Sara comieron tacos la semana pasada.*
   o: *Ricardo no comió tacos la semana pasada.*

Ahora lo sabes

Can you:

- tell what people order and serve?

  —Mis padres siempre ___ pescado cuando van al restaurante.

  —La cafetería de mi escuela ___ hamburguesas a menudo.

- tell what someone brings to a place or to another person?

  —(Yo) le ___ una cuchara a mi hermana.

- tell what someone does or did for you or for someone else?

  —Mis padres no tienen servilletas. Por eso, la camarera ___ trae servilletas.

- tell what someone ate?

  —Federico ___ chile con carne anoche.

Con la familia a la hora de la cena en Madrid

Todo Junto

Para decir más

Aquí tienes vocabulario adicional que te puede ayudar para hacer las actividades de esta sección.

ahumado, -a
smoked

el ajo
garlic

a la parrilla
barbecued

a la plancha
grilled

asado, -a
roasted

salteado, -a
sautéed

la ternera
veal

muy condimentado
spicy

Actividades

Esta sección te ofrece la oportunidad de aumentar tus conocimientos de español al integrar lo que aprendiste en este capítulo con lo que aprendiste en capítulos anteriores.

1 Haz una lista de lo que comiste y bebiste durante los últimos tres días. Si comiste o bebiste algo más de una vez, indica cuántas veces. Con un(a) compañero(a) habla de lo que Uds. comieron y bebieron y escríbanlo en una hoja de papel. Luego informen a la clase o a otro grupo sobre lo que comieron. Pueden hablar sobre:

- lo que comiste y bebiste y cuántas veces
- lo que tu compañero(a) comió y bebió
- si sus dietas tienen algo en común o no
- si comieron y bebieron cosas buenas o malas para la salud

2 ¿Cuál es tu restaurante favorito? ¿Puedes describirlo?
Puedes hablar sobre:

- dónde está
- la clase de comidas que sirve
- qué pides generalmente cuando vas allí
- si el restaurante es caro o barato
- cuándo fuiste allí por última vez y qué comiste

3 Con un(a) compañero(a) prepara una comida para una
fiesta de la escuela. Deben:

- decidir qué comida van a preparar
- hacer una lista de los ingredientes que van a necesitar
- y cuánto van a necesitar de cada uno

Luego, digan a la clase qué comida piensan traer a la
fiesta. También pueden decidir quiénes van a:

- poner la mesa
- lavar los platos
- ser los camareros y las camareras
- sacar la basura

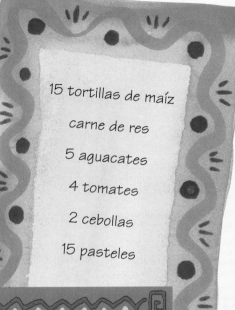

15 tortillas de maíz

carne de res

5 aguacates

4 tomates

2 cebollas

15 pasteles

"Aquí venden los ingredientes que necesito."

Dos jóvenes de compras en la Ciudad de México

¡Vamos a leer!

Antes de leer

STRATEGY ➤ Using prior knowledge

How familiar are you with Mexican food? Do you suppose the menu in a restaurant in Mexico might be different from one found in a Mexican restaurant in the United States? How do you think it might be different?

Mira la lectura

STRATEGY ➤ Scanning

This article compares Mexican food found in Mexico with that found in the United States. It also points out the variety of dishes in three different states in Mexico. What states do the menus come from? Does American cooking vary from one region to another?

EN LA VARIEDAD ESTÁ EL GUSTO

¿Con qué frecuencia comes en restaurantes mexicanos? ¿Te gustan los burritos o el chile con carne? ¿Crees que estas comidas son auténticas? La comida mexicana en los Estados Unidos es diferente a la que se come en México. Los inmigrantes y los mexico-americanos han creado un nuevo mundo de la cocina mexicana. Los burritos y el chile con carne son populares en las ciudades norteamericanas, pero en México son casi desconocidos.

La comida de México es más variada y sustancial. Tiene sus orígenes en las diferentes culturas precolombinas y en España. El chile, el maíz y el tomate son de origen americano, pero la pimienta, la cebolla y el trigo fueron traídos por los españoles. La comida mexicana de hoy usa todos estos ingredientes.

En cada región de México se pueden encontrar diferentes tipos de comidas o platillos. Imagina que haces un viaje por tres estados de México y que en cada estado comes algo distinto. Mira los menús a la derecha.

PLATILLOS DE VERACRUZ, EN EL SURESTE DE MÉXICO

*ensalada tropical
pescado a la veracruzana
arroz verde
dulce de guayaba
café*

Infórmate

STRATEGY Using illustrations to guess the meaning of unknown words

1 Were you able to figure out some of the items in each menu by looking at the pictures? What drinks are offered with each meal?

2 Are there any ingredients you did not expect to find in a Mexican dish? What are they?

3 After reading these menus, explain how the food served in Mexico compares with that served in the United States.

Aplicación

A Mexican exchange student in your class wants to eat at a Mexican restaurant this weekend. What would you tell him about the Mexican food found in the United States? What do you think will surprise him the most?

PLATILLOS DE JALISCO,
EN EL CENTRO DEL PAÍS

ensalada de nopales
carne asada
arroz con leche
agua de horchata

PLATILLOS DE NUEVO LEÓN,
AL NORTE DE MÉXICO

guacamole con enchiladas
huevos con carne de res
dulce de leche
té helado

¿Te gustaría probar alguna de estas tres variedades de comida? ¿Cuál te parece más interesante? ¡Las tres son deliciosas!

¡Vamos a escribir!

Everyone enjoys going out to eat, but it's not always easy to decide where to go. Write a review of a restaurant that you would recommend to your classmates.

1 Think about a restaurant you go to. It can be a fast-food restaurant, a coffee shop, or even the school cafeteria.

- ¿Cómo se llama el restaurante?
- ¿Dónde está?
- ¿A qué hora abre y a qué hora cierra?
- ¿Qué clase de comida sirve?
- ¿Cuáles son sus platos especiales?
- ¿Qué plato te gusta más? ¿Por qué?
- ¿Es caro o barato? ¿Aceptan tarjetas de crédito?
- ¿Es accesible para personas incapacitadas?

2 Use the answers to the questions to write a review of the restaurant. Show your review to a partner. Does he or she think you should change anything? Is there some other information your partner would suggest adding?

3 Rewrite your review, taking into consideration the changes suggested by your partner and any others you might like to make. Check for spelling, accents, verb forms, and adjective agreement. If necessary, write your review again.

4 Now your review is ready to be published. You can:

- submit it to the school paper or Spanish club
- include it in a pamphlet about local restaurants called *Buenos restaurantes*
- add it to your writing portfolio

Buenos Restaurantes

En la Fonda Refugio se cocina la mejor comida mexicana de la ciudad. Allí puede probar la especialidad de la casa: chiles con queso. Son sabrosos, nutritivos y no son muy picantes. Además, en la Fonda Refugio hay una variedad de enchiladas, tacos, quesadillas y burritos.

El restaurante está en la calle Independencia, 4. Abren de 8:00 de la mañana a 11:00 de la noche. ¡Debe visitarlo!

"Y para la merienda, ¿te gustaría pedir unos pasteles?"

Café al aire libre en la Ciudad de México

¿Lo sabes bien?

This section will help you organize your studying for the proficiency test, where you will be asked to do similar, though not identical, tasks. There will not be any models on the test.

Listening

Can you understand when someone talks about a meal? Listen as your teacher reads a sample similar to what you will hear on the test. Is the person planning to eat a snack, a main meal, or a dessert?

Culture

Can you name two similarities and two differences between dining out in Mexico and in the United States?

"El domingo voy al restaurante con mi familia."

Reading

Using the illustration on this recipe, can you figure out how to prepare this dish? What do you think *asar* means? Why is the dish called *carne al carbón?*

CARNE AL CARBÓN

Ingredientes:

carne de res
1 limón verde
sal y pimienta

Diez minutos antes de servirla, pon el jugo de limón verde, la sal y la pimienta sobre la carne. Debes asar la carne tres minutos por cada lado.

Writing

Can you write a letter to a friend describing a meal you ate recently? Here is a sample letter:

Querido Carlos,

Ayer fui a un restaurante que te gustaría mucho.
Pedí dos tazas de chocolate con churros. ¿Has probado los churros? Se hacen con harina, agua y azúcar. ¡Me encantan! ¡Te traigo churros para tu fiesta de cumpleaños el sábado!

Tu amigo,
Berto

Speaking

Can you and a partner play the roles of a waiter and a customer?

A —*Aquí le traigo el menú.*
B —*Gracias. ¿Cuál es el plato del día?*
A —*Enchiladas de pollo, pero no son muy picantes.*
B —*¡Genial! Pero, camarero, me faltan una servilleta y un tenedor.*
A —*¿De veras? ¡Los traigo en seguida!*

Resumen del capítulo 12

Use the vocabulary from this chapter to help you:

- ask politely to have something brought to you
- order a meal
- say what you ate or drank

to name and discuss foods
el aguacate
el azúcar
los burritos
la carne de res
el chile
el chile con carne
los chiles rellenos
el chocolate
los churros
las enchiladas
el flan
los frijoles refritos
el guacamole
el helado
la mantequilla
los pasteles
la pimienta
las quesadillas
la sal
las salsas
los tacos
la tortilla de harina / de maíz

to talk about food
a la carta
la especialidad
    de la casa
la merienda

de merienda
(no) picante
el plato del día
los platos principales
el postre
de postre
beber: (yo) bebí
        (tú) bebiste
comer: (yo) comí
        (tú) comiste
¿Con qué se hace(n) ___?
Se hace(n) con ___.
pedir (e → i)
probar (o → ue):
    (yo) he probado
    (tú) has probado
vender

to describe table settings
la cuchara
el cuchillo
el mantel
el platillo
el plato
la servilleta
la taza
el tazón
el tenedor
el vaso

to talk about eating out
el camarero, la camarera
la cuenta
el menú

to express needs
Me falta(n) ___.
¿Me pasas ___?
¿Me trae ___?
Le traigo ___.
traer: (yo) traigo
        (tú) traes

to indicate time or frequency
alguna vez
a menudo
en seguida
muchas veces
una vez

to indicate position
debajo de
delante de
encima de

other useful expressions
¿Algo más?
lo mismo

CAPÍTULO 13

Para proteger la Tierra

OBJECTIVES

At the end of this chapter, you will be able to:

- describe the natural environment
- list actions to protect the environment
- discuss environmental dangers
- name species in danger of extinction in the United States and the Spanish-speaking world and say what can be done to protect them

Las cataratas de Iguazú, Argentina

¡Piénsalo bien!

Look at this photograph. What do you see that is similar to the environmental efforts in your community?

"Es importante reciclar para proteger la Tierra."

Jóvenes en un centro de reciclaje en Puerto Rico

What do you think the words *reciclar* and *proteger* mean?
What does *centro de reciclaje* mean?

En América Central el jaguar está en peligro de extinción.

What other animals do you
know of that are endangered?

Vocabulario para conversar

¿Cómo podemos conservar energía?

Aquí tienes palabras y expresiones necesarias para discutir peligros del medio ambiente y para hablar sobre qué podemos hacer para protegerlo. Léelas varias veces y practícalas con un(a) compañero(a) en las páginas siguientes.

la luz, *pl.* las luces

la botella

la madera

el plástico

la piel

el cartón

la lata*

el aluminio

el vidrio

montar en bicicleta

la bicicleta

la revista

el periódico

la guía telefónica

También necesitas . . .

apagar	to turn off
proteger*	to protect
recoger*	to pick up
la gente	people
saber: (yo) sé	to know: I know
(tú) sabes	you know
(No) hay que ___ .	It's (not) necessary to___.
(No) vale la pena.	It's (not) worth it.
a la vez	at the same time

¿Y qué quiere decir . . . ?

conservar
la energía
reciclar
reducir†
separar
usar

* Note that to talk about a tin can, a glass bottle, a cardboard folder, a metal table, etc., we use noun + *de* + material.
  For example: *lata de aluminio, botella de vidrio.*
* *Proteger* and *recoger* are regular *-er* verbs with a spelling change in the *yo* form of the present tense: *protejo, recojo.*
† *Reducir* is a regular *-ir* verb in the present tense, except for the *yo* form: *reduzco.*

Empecemos a conversar

Túrnate con un(a) compañero(a) para ser *Estudiante A* y *Estudiante B*. Reemplacen las palabras subrayadas con palabras representadas o escritas en los recuadros. 💡 quiere decir que puedes escoger *(choose)* tu propia respuesta.

1

A —¿*Vale la pena reciclar <u>el aluminio</u>?*
B —*¡Claro que sí* (o: *no*)!
   Y ahora Uds.

Estudiante A   Estudiante B

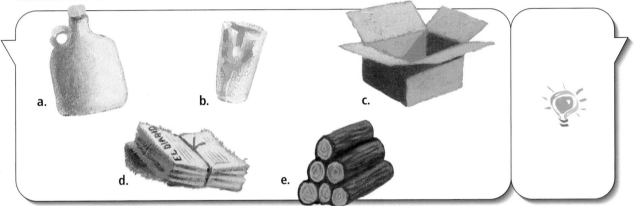

a.   b.   c.   d.   e.

2 conservar energía A — ¿*Cómo puedo <u>conservar energía</u>?*
B — *Puedes <u>usar menos luz</u>.*
   Y ahora Uds.

Estudiante A   Estudiante B

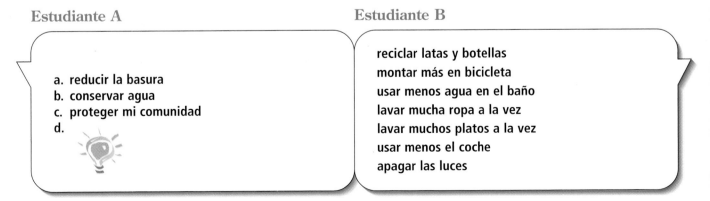

Estudiante A

a. reducir la basura
b. conservar agua
c. proteger mi comunidad
d. 💡

Estudiante B

reciclar latas y botellas
montar más en bicicleta
usar menos agua en el baño
lavar mucha ropa a la vez
lavar muchos platos a la vez
usar menos el coche
apagar las luces

3

A — *¿Sabes si tenemos que reciclar las botellas de plástico?*

B — *Sí, las tenemos que reciclar.*
    o: *No. No hay que reciclarlas.*

    Y ahora Uds.

Estudiante A　　　　　　　　　　**Estudiante B**

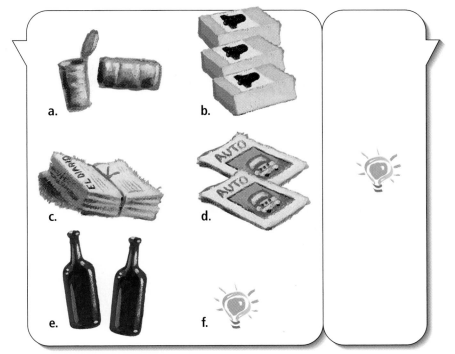

a.　　　　b.

c.　　　　d.

e.　　　　f.

Empecemos a escribir

Escribe tus respuestas en español.

4 ¿Qué puedes hacer con libros que ya no usas? ¿Con ropa que ya no te queda bien?

5 ¿Cómo vas a la escuela? ¿En bicicleta? ¿En autobús? ¿A pie? ¿Por qué?

6 En tu comunidad, ¿qué pueden reciclar que no reciclan ahora?

7 ¿Piensas que la gente debe comprar abrigos u otra ropa de piel o no? ¿Por qué?

También se dice

andar en bicicleta

el directorio
la guía de teléfonos
el listín

Vocabulario para conversar

¿La Tierra forma parte del medio ambiente?

Aquí tienes el resto del vocabulario necesario para hablar sobre el medio ambiente y sus peligros.

Los animales

el jaguar

la vaca

el caballo

el lobo

el oso

el gorila

la ballena

el elefante

el océano

la serpiente

el tigre

el aire

la fábrica

el pájaro

el árbol

el transporte público

la planta

la flor

la Tierra

También necesitas . . .

el medio ambiente	*environment*
la amenaza	*threat*
el mayor peligro	*the greatest danger*
en peligro de extinción	*endangered*
formar parte de	*to be a part of*
decir	*to say*
hacer: hizo	*he / she did, he / she made*
por supuesto	*of course*

¿Y qué quiere decir . . . ?
el centro de reciclaje
contaminado, -a
puro, -a

Empecemos a conversar

8

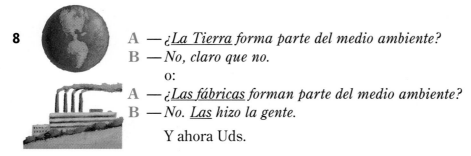

A —¿*La Tierra* forma parte del medio ambiente?
B —*No, claro que no.*

o:

A —¿*Las fábricas* forman parte del medio ambiente?
B —*No. Las hizo la gente.*

Y ahora Uds.

Estudiante A   **Estudiante B**

a.   b.   c.   d.   e.   f.

9

A —¿*Qué es una amenaza para el aire puro*?
B —*Los coches.*

Y ahora Uds.

Estudiante A   **Estudiante B**

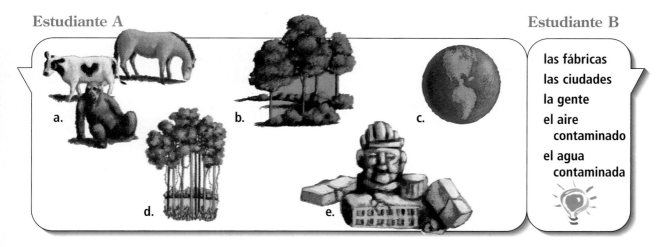

a.   b.   c.   d.   e.

las fábricas
las ciudades
la gente
el aire
  contaminado
el agua
  contaminada

10

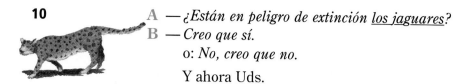

A — *¿Están en peligro de extinción <u>los jaguares</u>?*
B — *Creo que sí.*
    o: *No, creo que no.*
    Y ahora Uds.

Estudiante A   **Estudiante B**

a.   b.   c.

d.   e.   f.   g.

El último retorno del salmón (1988), Alfredo Arreguín

Vocabulario para conversar 425

11

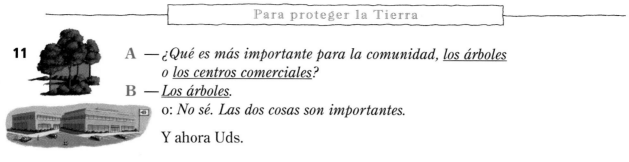

A —¿Qué es más importante para la comunidad, <u>los árboles</u>
o <u>los centros comerciales</u>?

B —<u>Los árboles</u>.

o: *No sé. Las dos cosas son importantes.*

Y ahora Uds.

Estudiante A   **Estudiante B**

a.

b.

c.

d.

Ricky

Si mantienes presente estas tres palabras:

<u>CORRESPONSABILIDAD, CODEPENDENCIA
Y COEVOLUCION</u>

podrás conservar mejor nuestro medio ambiente
y nuestros recursos naturales. ¡Recuerda que tu
comportamiento es importante para que todos
vivan mejor!

RR

"UNETE A LA CAMPAÑA DE:
RICKY EL RECICLADOR

Empecemos a escribir y a leer

Escribe tus respuestas en español.

12 ¿Está contaminada el agua de tu comunidad? ¿Y el aire?

13 ¿Trabaja alguien que conoces en un centro de reciclaje? ¿Quién? ¿Qué hace?

14 ¿Cuántos parques con muchos árboles y flores hay en tu comunidad? ¿Dónde están?

15 En tu opinión, ¿hay suficiente transporte público en tu comunidad? ¿De qué clase? ¿Usa la gente de tu comunidad el transporte público?

16 Lee este párrafo ¿En qué recipiente debemos poner las botellas? ¿Y los periódicos?

Debemos reciclar latas, botellas, plásticos, revistas, periódicos, cartón, vidrio. No olvide que debe poner las revistas, los periódicos y el cartón en el recipiente amarillo. El aluminio, el vidrio y el plástico deben ponerse en el rojo.

YO PROTEJO EL MEDIO AMBIENTE

EN MI CASA USAMOS ENERGIA LIMPIA DE GASCO

¡Comuniquemos!

Aquí tienes otra oportunidad para usar el vocabulario de este capítulo.

1 ¿Qué debe hacer la señora para proteger el medio ambiente?
Observa bien este dibujo. Trabaja con un(a) compañero(a).

Debe reciclar las latas.

2 ¿Están estos animales en peligro de extinción? Si lo están, di por
qué. Tu compañero(a) debe decir qué podemos hacer para protegerlos.

A —*Las ballenas están en peligro de extinción porque los océanos están
contaminados.*

B —*No debemos contaminar el agua de los océanos.*

Estudiante A   **Estudiante B**

a.   b.   c.

d.   e.

3 Dile (*tell*) a tu compañero(a) cómo piensas reciclar
estas cosas viejas.

A — *¿Qué piensas hacer con ese vaso viejo?*
B — *Voy a usarlo para poner lápices.*

Estudiante A

Estudiante B

¿Qué sabes ahora?

Can you:

■ describe the natural environment?

— ___, ___ y ___ forman parte del medio ambiente.

■ describe our responsibilities to the environment?

—Hay que ___ el medio ambiente.

—Debemos ___ energía y ___ la basura.

■ state ways to protect the environment?

—Hay que apagar ___, ___ transporte público y ___ las latas
y las botellas.

Perspectiva cultural

Muchas especies de plantas y animales están en peligro de extinción. Otras ya han desaparecido.

Does anything seem unusual about the animals in these photographs? Explain. What clues do the captions give you about the part of the world they live in?

Can you imagine a three-foot-tall owl or a bird as small as a bee? The giant owl is long extinct, but the *zunzún*, the smallest bird in the world, still lives in Cuba, although it is endangered.

The *Greta cubana* is a very beautiful butterfly with transparent wings. Like the *zunzún*, it lives only in Cuba, and, like so many other species around the world, it is also endangered.

Another very unusual animal from Cuba is the *almiquí.* It has furry feet like a rabbit, the tail of a mouse, and a long snout like an opossum. It's an insect-eating animal about the size of a cat, and one of the few remaining native mammals of Cuba. Catching sight of an *almiquí* is really difficult, because there are so few of them left.

El zunzún, el pájaro más pequeño del mundo

Greta cubana

Why are these species disappearing? It's a long process that started with the first human settlements in Cuba about 7,000 years ago. In recent years, more species have become endangered because of population growth and the redevelopment of the tourist industry, which has again become an important aspect of the Cuban economy.

Learning about these species has been a group effort. A team of Cuban scientists from the Museo Nacional de Historia Natural and U.S. scientists from the American Museum of Natural History in New York, among others, have been researching Cuban animal and plant life. This project is an example of how people around the world are pooling their efforts to study ecology and preserve its biological wonders. The Cuban–U.S. scientific team is also a good example of cooperation between the people of Latin America and the people of the United States.

Este animal, de casi 3 pies de alto, está extinto desde hace más de 7.000 años.

La cultura desde tu perspectiva

1 What endangered species in the United States do you know about? How are the threats facing these animals similar to those facing endangered species in Cuba? How do the threats differ, if they do?

2 How might knowing each other's languages and cultures help experts in Latin America and the United States solve problems more effectively? What problems besides endangered species do you think could be solved by cooperation between the United States and Latin America?

Solenodon cubano

Gramática en contexto

You might see a poster like this at the entrance to a national park. What information would you expect to find there?

A Did the poster contain the type of information you expected?

B You have seen the word *dice* many times in this book. What does it mean? The infinitive is *decir*. Like *pedir* and *servir*, *decir* has an e → i stem change. What would be the *ellos / ellas* form of *decir*? And the *nosotros* form?

C In the poster you can see the following commands: *protege, usa, pide, apaga, lleva, pon.* Do these verb forms look more like present or preterite-tense forms? How does *pon* differ from the others?

El verbo *decir*

The verb *decir* means "to say" or "to tell." Here are all its present-tense forms:

(yo)	**digo**	(nosotros) (nosotras)	**decimos**
(tú)	**dices**	(vosotros) (vosotras)	**decís**
Ud. (él) (ella)	**dice**	Uds. (ellos) (ellas)	**dicen**

- Notice the *e* of the stem changes to *i* in all forms except *nosotros* and *vosotros*.

1 ¿De quién son las opiniones de la lista de la derecha? Túrnate con un(a) compañero(a) para decirlo.

La gente dice que las fábricas no son buenas para el medio ambiente.

a. Los padres
b. Mis amigos(as)
c. Los profesores
d. Nosotros, los estudiantes
e. La gente
f. Muchas personas
g. Nadie
h. Yo

Es importante conservar energía.
Debemos estudiar siempre.
Hay que conservar agua contaminada.
La tarea es una amenaza para la salud.
Las fábricas no son buenas para el medio ambiente.
Vale la pena proteger los árboles.
No hay que estudiar nunca.
El aire contaminado es el mayor peligro de las ciudades.

¡NO OLVIDES!

Remember that we must use *que* after *decir: Dice que . . ., dicen que . . . .*

El mandato afirmativo *(tú)*

When you tell someone to do something, you are giving an affirmative command. Here are some affirmative commands you might give to a person you address as *tú*.

> Pablo, **apaga** las luces por favor.
> Linda, **recoge** la basura.
> Cristóbal, **sirve** la cena ahora.

- Notice that command forms are usually the same forms that we use for *él / ella / Ud.* in the present tense.

- Certain verbs, like *poner, hacer,* and *decir,* have irregular command forms.

> Isabel, **pon** los libros en la mesa.
> Miguel, **haz** tu cama.
> Elena, **di** lo que piensas.

- Object pronouns are attached to the end of affirmative commands. When a pronoun is attached to a command that has two or more syllables, an accent mark is added to the stressed vowel.

> —¿Qué debo hacer con las botellas y latas?
> —**Sepáralas**, por favor.

2 Tus amigos tienen un problema y te piden un consejo *(advice)*. Contéstales usando el mandato del verbo de la lista.

A — *Tengo mucho sueño.*
B — *Pues, duerme un poco.*

a. Tengo catarro.   Llamar a la clínica
b. Me lastimé la pierna ayer.   Comprar unas pastillas
c. Me duele mucho la garganta.   Descansar
d. Tengo gripe y quiero ver al médico.   Hacer ejercicio
e. Quiero ser mejor deportista.   Beber jugo de naranja

3 Túrnate con un(a) compañero(a) para decirles a estas personas lo que *(what)* deben hacer en la casa.

Daniel, corta el césped.

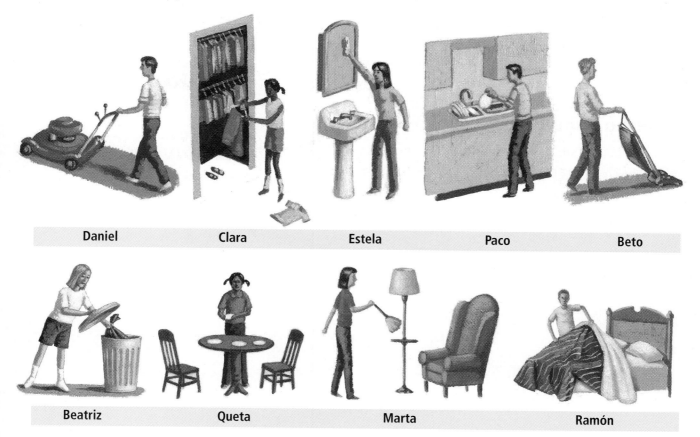

Daniel   Clara   Estela   Paco   Beto

Beatriz   Queta   Marta   Ramón

4 Túrnate con un(a) compañero(a) para leer estas ideas sobre el medio ambiente. Uno(a) de Uds. lee, agregando *(adding) Dicen que* . . . . El (la) otro(a) responde usando el mandato.

Debemos sacar   **A** *—Dicen que debemos sacar la basura.*
la basura   **B** *—Pues, sácala.*

a. Hay que apagar las luces.
b. Debemos conservar energía.
c. Vale la pena proteger el medio ambiente.
d. Tenemos que usar el transporte público.
e. Necesitamos conservar agua.
f. Hay que separar la basura.

5 Pregúntale a tu compañero(a) qué puedes hacer tú para proteger
el medio ambiente. Él(ella) deberá decirte tres cosas que puedes hacer.

A — *¿Qué debo hacer para proteger el medio ambiente?*
B — *Primero, recicla las botellas y las latas.*
    Segundo, conserva agua.
    Tercero, apaga las luces si no las necesitas.

El verbo *saber*

We use the verb *saber* ("to know") to talk about knowing facts or
information. Here are all of its present-tense forms.

(yo)	**sé**	(nosotros)(nosotras)	**sabemos**
(tú)	**sabes**	(vosotros)(vosotras)	**sabéis**
Ud.(él)(ella)	**sabe**	Uds.(ellos)(ellas)	**saben**

¡NO OLVIDES!

Although we can often omit the word "that" in English, in Spanish we must use *que*:
*Mis padres **saben que** voy a ver una película.*

- *Saber* follows the pattern of regular *-er* verbs except for the *yo* form: *sé.*

- When *saber* is immediately followed by the infinitive, it means "to know how to."
  Mis amigos **saben esquiar** muy bien.

6 Pregúntale a un(a) compañero(a) si sabe cómo podemos proteger
la Tierra. Pregunta y contesta con elementos de las tres columnas.

A — *¿Sabes cómo podemos reciclar las latas y las botellas?*
B — *Sí, lo sé. Debemos llevarlas a un centro de reciclaje.*

a. reciclar	el aire contaminado	apagar las luces cuando no las usamos
b. conservar	las latas y las botellas	reciclar revistas y periódicos
c. proteger	la basura	usar menos papel
d. reducir	energía	montar en bicicleta o usar transporte
	los árboles de la selva	público
		llevar(las) a un centro de reciclaje

7 Pregúntale a tu compañero(a) si él(ella), su familia o sus amigos saben hacer estas cosas.

A — *¿Sabes esquiar?*
B — *Sí, sé esquiar bien. Mi amigo Miguel también sabe.*
  o: *No, yo no sé esquiar, pero mis hermanas sí saben.*

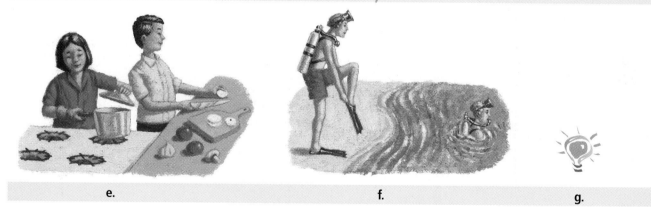

a.
b.
c.
d.

e.
f.
g.

Ahora lo sabes

Can you:

■ **report what people say or tell?**

—Ellos ____ que debemos separar el vidrio y el aluminio.
¿Qué ____ tú?

■ **Tell a friend, a family member, or a child what to do?**

—¿Debo apagar la luz?

—Sí. No la necesitas ahora. _____

■ **say what people know?**

—Mis padres ____ que es importante reciclar.

TODO JUNTO

Para decir más

Aquí tienes vocabulario adicional que te puede ayudar para hacer las actividades de esta sección.

ensuciar
to dirty

purificar
to purify

mantener
to keep, to maintain

lograr
to achieve

la capa de ozono
ozone layer

la mejor manera
the best way

las sustancias químicas
chemicals

talar
to fell, to cut down

la electricidad
electricity

dañar
to harm

Actividades

Esta sección te ofrece la oportunidad de aumentar tus conocimientos de español al integrar lo que aprendiste en este capítulo con lo que aprendiste en capítulos anteriores.

1 En un grupo pequeño, haz un anuncio de radio o de televisión sobre el transporte público de tu comunidad. Estas ideas te pueden ayudar:

> *La gente que sabe usa el metro.*
> *Dicen los pasajeros: ¡El metro es muy rápido!*
> *¡Qué cómodo es!*
> *Úsalo todos los días.*
> *Es la mejor manera de ir a trabajar y a la escuela.*

Presenta tu anuncio al resto de la clase.

Una estación del metro en Buenos Aires

2 Prepara un cartel turístico con fotografías o dibujos de un lugar que te gustaría visitar. Usa mandatos para decirle al turista lo que debe hacer. Puedes incluir esta información:

- qué lugar visitar y cuándo
- cómo llegar
- qué hacer en ese lugar
- qué comprar
- de qué sacar fotos
- qué llevar

Prepara una presentación oral sobre tu cartel para la clase.

3 En grupos pequeños, escriban cada verbo de la lista en una hoja de papel. Luego debes escoger una hoja de papel y dar un mandato a otra persona del grupo. Esa persona debe dar una excusa y no hacer lo que dices. Cada uno debe dar tres mandatos y tres excusas.

—*Haz una ensalada de frutas.*
—*Pero no tengo ni uvas
    ni manzanas.*

—*Limpia el baño.*
—*Pero no está sucio.*

"**Mirar los pájaros es un buen pasatiempo.**"

ayudar	decir	lavar	probar (o → ue)
beber	depositar	leer	sacar
buscar	dormir (o → ue)	limpiar	sacudir
cerrar (e → ie)	empezar (e → ie)	llegar	servir (e → i)
cocinar	escuchar	llevar	terminar
comer	estudiar	pedir (e → i)	traer
comprar	hablar	poner	ver
cortar	hacer	practicar	

¡Vamos a leer!

Antes de leer

STRATEGY ➤ Using prior knowledge

How can you help protect the environment?
Make a list of five things you can do.

Muchacha ayudando
en su comunidad
en Honduras

Mira la lectura

Look over the reading to get an idea about how it is
organized. What is the title? What does the picture tell you?
What is the purpose of the introductory statement?

Cuide el mundo desde casa

¡Ud. puede hacer mucho para proteger el mundo!

Unidos podemos mantener el mundo más limpio y mejor. Cada uno de nosotros debe hacer algo diariamente para protegerlo. Con la ayuda de todos, ensuciando menos el planeta y ayudando a purificar el medio ambiente, lograremos crear verdaderamente un mundo mejor para nosotros y para nuestra familia. ¡No olvide que su participación es muy importante!

¿Qué puede hacer desde su propia casa?

- Ahorre energía. No use innecesariamente electricidad ni gasolina.
- No desperdicie agua.
- Compre alimentos o productos envasados en materiales reciclables.
- No use atomizadores, o cualquier otro producto que pueda dañar la capa de ozono.

- Consuma productos naturales que no contengan demasiadas sustancias químicas alterantes.
- Revise la salida de gas de su vehículo periódicamente.
- Conserve limpios los lugares públicos y privados: calles, parques, plazas, playas, etc.
- No tale árboles innecesariamente.
- Infórmese sobre campañas ecológicas en su comunidad.
- Lea artículos o vea programas de televisión sobre el medio ambiente.

Como ve, hay muchas cosas que puede hacer para ayudar y cuidar el mundo en que vivimos. No se desanime si otras personas no contribuyen. ¡Contribuya Ud. con su ejemplo!

Infórmate

STRATEGY ➤ Recognizing word families

Word families are groups of related words that are used in different ways as nouns, verbs, adjectives, and so on. Often if you know one word in a family you can figure out the meaning of others. Here are some examples from the article:

el día   diariamente

la verdad   verdaderamente

la ayuda   ayudar   ayudando

"Todos debemos ayudar a reciclar."

1 Now read the article carefully. Were any of the suggestions the same as those on your list? Check off on your list the ones they did mention.

2 Find three or four words whose meaning you can figure out because you know the word family they belong to. For example: *sucio / ensuciando*.

3 Divide the suggestions into two groups: those that you do or could easily do and those that don't apply to you.

Aplicación

Make new words out of the following by adding the ending *–mente*. Then use one of the words in a sentence about how you protect the environment. For example: *Reciclo cartón regularmente.*

frecuente
general
rara
regular

Esta niña ayuda a reducir la basura en Buenos Aires, Argentina.

¡Vamos a escribir!

How can we express our concern about the environment? One way is through our writing. Write a poem, on your own or in groups, about an animal or a place that you think needs to be protected. Remember, a poem does not need to rhyme. You can follow a pattern of a diamond poem. For example:

Una ballena gris frente a Baja California, México

 1 Think about an animal or a place that needs protecting, and answer the following questions:

- ¿Cómo te sientes cuando piensas en ese animal o ese lugar?
- ¿Qué vocabulario puedes usar en una descripción del animal o del lugar?
- ¿Por qué debemos cuidarlo?
- ¿Cómo podemos protegerlo?

2 Use your answers to the questions to write your poem. Organize your ideas in the way you think will be most powerful and effective.

3 Show your poem to a partner. Does your partner understand how you feel about the animal or place? Does he or she think you should change, reorganize, or correct anything? Rewrite your poem.

4 Check for accuracy in spelling and the use of accent marks. Did you use the correct forms of the adjectives and verbs? Did you try to use a varied vocabulary? If necessary, rewrite your poem. You may want to add an illustration to make it more eye-catching.

5 Share your poem by:
- submitting it to the school literary magazine or newspaper
- including it in a collection of class poems called *Vamos a proteger nuestra Tierra*
- posting it on a bulletin board in the school library during Earth Day celebration
- adding it to your writing portfolio

¿Lo sabes bien?

This section will help you organize your studying for the proficiency test, where you will be asked to do similar, though not identical, tasks. There will not be any models on the test.

Listening

Can you understand when someone talks about the environment? Listen as your teacher reads a sample similar to what you will hear on the test. According to the person making the statement, what is the problem and what are some suggestions for solving it?

Reading

Can you understand an environmental ad by using word families to guess the meaning of the words you might not know? According to this ad, how can we have a better world?

No corte árboles innecesariamente. No tire papeles en las calles. Recicle. Ayudándonos y trabajando juntos lograremos un mundo mejor.

Writing

Can you write a letter to a friend in which you describe a place you visited while on vacation and what the people there do to protect the environment? Here is a sample letter:

Querida Luisa,

¡Qué aire tan puro tenemos! La gente de esta ciudad sabe que tiene que trabajar mucho para proteger el medio ambiente. Muchas personas montan en bicicleta o usan el transporte público. Por toda la ciudad hay carteles que dicen: Separa la basura, las revistas, las botellas y las latas. La ciudad tiene un parque grande donde hay flores y animales en peligro de extinción.

Tu amiga,
Rebeca

Culture

Can you name two reasons for the gradual disappearance of some species of animals living in the Caribbean region and compare this with other parts of the planet?

Estas ranitas doradas de Costa Rica están casi extintas.

Speaking

Can you and a partner play the roles of a park ranger and a camper in a national park? Here is a sample dialogue:

A —*¿Qué puedo hacer para proteger el medio ambiente del parque?*

B —*Separa la basura para poder reciclarla después y conserva el agua. También puedes proteger las flores y las plantas del parque.*

A —*¿Y si monto en bicicleta . . . ?*

B —*¡Claro que sí! Necesitamos aire puro. No queremos contaminarlo con los coches.*

Resumen del capítulo 13

Use the vocabulary from this chapter to help you:

■ describe the natural environment
■ list actions to protect the environment
■ discuss environmental dangers

to talk about conservation
el centro de reciclaje
la luz, *pl.* las luces
apagar
conservar
proteger
reciclar
recoger
reducir
separar
usar

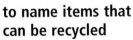

to name items that can be recycled
el aluminio
la botella
el cartón
la energía
la guía telefónica
la lata
la madera
el periódico
el plástico
la revista
el vidrio

to talk about animals
los animales, *sing.* el animal
la ballena
el caballo
el elefante
el gorila

el jaguar
el lobo
el oso
el pájaro
la serpiente
el tigre
la vaca
la piel

to talk about nature and the environment
el aire
el árbol
la flor
el medio ambiente
el océano
la planta
la Tierra

to describe environmental dangers
la amenaza
contaminado, -a
la fábrica
el mayor peligro
en peligro de extinción
puro, -a

to talk about transportation
la bicicleta: montar en bicicleta
el transporte público

to talk about everyday activities
decir
hacer: (Ud., él, ella) hizo
saber: (yo) sé
        (tú) sabes

to give an opinion
(No) hay que ___.
(No) vale la pena.

other useful terms and expressions
a la vez
formar parte de
la gente
por supuesto

CAPÍTULO 14

¡Vamos a una fiesta!

OBJECTIVES

At the end of this chapter, you will be able to:

- make plans for giving or attending a party
- describe gift-giving
- make and acknowledge introductions
- compare parties that Spanish-speaking teenagers go to with those you usually attend

Bailando en la calle durante la feria de Málaga

¡Piénsalo bien!

Look at the pictures and read the captions.

If you were purchasing a birthday gift for a friend, how would you answer the question?

En una tienda de regalos, España

"¿Qué regalo quieres comprar, algo práctico o algo más personal?"

"¿Qué ropa debo comprar para ir a la fiesta?"

En una tienda en la Ciudad de México

At what types of occasions might you need to wear clothes like these?

"Pasamos toda la noche bailando."

En una discoteca en Buenos Aires

Teenagers in the Spanish-speaking world usually attend a wide variety of parties, from family occasions like weddings and baptisms to *quinceañeras* and school dances. What kinds of parties do you usually attend? Are they family occasions, school dances, or get-togethers with friends?

Vocabulario para conversar

¿A quién vas a invitar?

Aquí tienes palabras y expresiones necesarias para hablar
sobre las fiestas. Léelas varias veces y practícalas con un(a)
compañero(a) en las
páginas siguientes.

la fiesta de la escuela

la novia, el novio

bailar

el baile

DICIEMBRE

la fiesta de
fin de año

cantar

la fiesta de cumpleaños

la fiesta de sorpresa

la fiesta de disfraces

También necesitas . . .

la reunión	*get-together*
alguien	*someone, somebody*
algunos, algunas	*some*
conocer: (yo) conozco*	*to know, to be acquainted with:*
(tú) conoces	*I know, you know*
Encantado, -a.	*Delighted.*
el pariente, la parienta	*relative*
Te presento a ___.	*I'd like you to meet ___.*
dar: (yo) doy	*to give: I give, you give*
(tú) das	
recibir	*to receive*
hecho, -a a mano	*handmade*
Depende.	*It depends.*
soler (o → ue) + inf.	*to be in the habit of*

¿Y qué quiere decir . . . ?

elegante
¡Feliz cumpleaños!
invitar
personal
práctico, -a
regalar

* *Conocer* is a regular -*er* verb in the present tense except for the *yo* form: *conozco*.

Empecemos a conversar

Túrnate con un(a) compañero(a) para ser *Estudiante A* y
Estudiante B. Reemplacen las palabras subrayadas con palabras
representadas o escritas en los recuadros. 💡 quiere decir
que puedes escoger tu propia respuesta.

1 A — *¿A quiénes vas a invitar a <u>tu fiesta de cumpleaños</u>?*
   B — *Voy a invitar a <u>quince amigos y a algunos parientes</u>.*
   Y ahora Uds.

Estudiante A   **Estudiante B**

a.   b.   c.

d.   e.   f.

2 padre   A — *¿Qué sueles regalarle a tu <u>padre</u> para su cumpleaños?*
   B — *Depende, pero suelo darle algo <u>práctico</u>.*
      o: *Pues, a veces le doy <u>sólo una tarjeta de cumpleaños</u>.*
      Y ahora Uds.

Estudiante A   **Estudiante B**

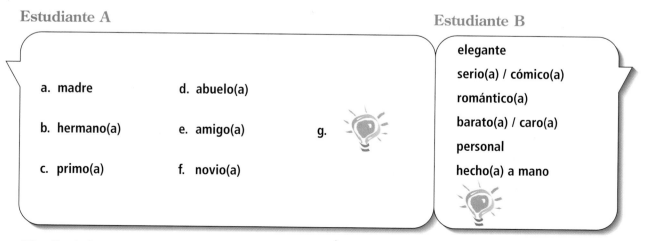

Estudiante A		Estudiante B
a. madre	d. abuelo(a)	elegante
b. hermano(a)	e. amigo(a)	serio(a) / cómico(a)
c. primo(a)	f. novio(a)	romántico(a)
	g. 💡	barato(a) / caro(a)
		personal
		hecho(a) a mano

3 a mi amiga   A — *Te presento a <u>mi amiga Juanita</u>.*
                       B — *<u>Encantado(a)</u>.*

                          Y ahora Uds.

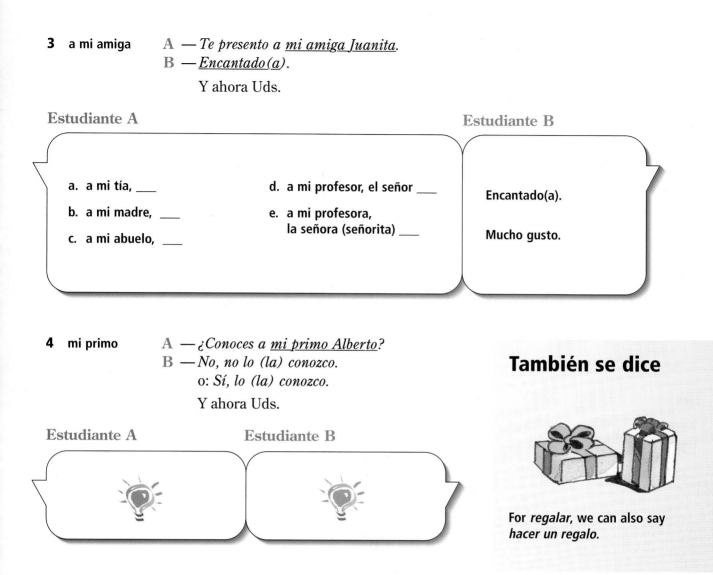

Estudiante A

a. a mi tía, ___

b. a mi madre, ___

c. a mi abuelo, ___

d. a mi profesor, el señor ___

e. a mi profesora,
    la señora (señorita) ___

Estudiante B

Encantado(a).

Mucho gusto.

4 mi primo   A — *¿Conoces a <u>mi primo Alberto</u>?*
                      B — *No, no lo (la) conozco.*
                         o: *Sí, lo (la) conozco.*

                         Y ahora Uds.

Estudiante A   **Estudiante B**

También se dice

For *regalar*, we can also say
hacer un regalo.

Empecemos a escribir

Escribe tus respuestas en español.

5 ¿Qué regalos sueles regalar? ¿Qué regalo te gustaría recibir?

6 ¿Te gustaría dar una fiesta grande? ¿A quiénes te gustaría invitar?
       ¿A toda la familia? ¿A muchos jóvenes? ¿O prefieres las reuniones
       pequeñas?

7 Cuando vas a un baile, ¿qué ropa sueles llevar?

8 ¿Conoces a alguien famoso? ¿A alguien muy viejo? ¿A alguien
       fascinante? ¿Quiénes son? ¿Cómo se llaman? ¿Cómo son?

Vocabulario para conversar

En la fiesta

Aquí tienes el resto del vocabulario necesario para hablar sobre las fiestas y los regalos.

el traje

el vestido de fiesta

los zapatos de tacón alto

la corbata

las joyas

el collar

el reloj pulsera

los aretes (m.)

la pulsera

el lugar: Virrey Arredondo 2553

la hora: 7:00 de la tarde

la fecha: viernes, 2 de julio

la invitación

la invitada

el invitado

las decoraciones (pl.)

la entrada

decorar

También necesitas . . .

el ambiente	*atmosphere*
bailar: bailando	*dancing*
cantar: cantando	*singing*
comer: comiendo	*eating*
hablar: hablando	*talking*
pasarlo bien / mal	*to have a good / bad time*
ver: viendo	*looking*
escoger: (yo) escojo*	*to choose: I choose, you choose*
(tú) escoges	
De ninguna manera.	*Not at all.*

¿Y qué quiere decir . . . ?
la hora
el lugar
escribir
escuchar (la radio, el disco compacto)
preparar
tocar música

* *Escoger* is a regular *-er* verb with a spelling change in the *yo* form of the present tense: *escojo*.

Empecemos a conversar

9 bailando

A —¡Qué fiesta tan aburrida! ¡Nadie está _bailando_!

B —Creo que no les gusta _la música_.

Y ahora Uds.

Estudiante A

a. hablando
b. comiendo
c. cantando
d. pasándolo bien

Estudiante B

la comida
la música
el ambiente

10

A —¿Necesitas comprar algo para llevar con tu _vestido de fiesta_?

B —Sí, _un collar_.

Y ahora Uds.

Estudiante A

Estudiante B

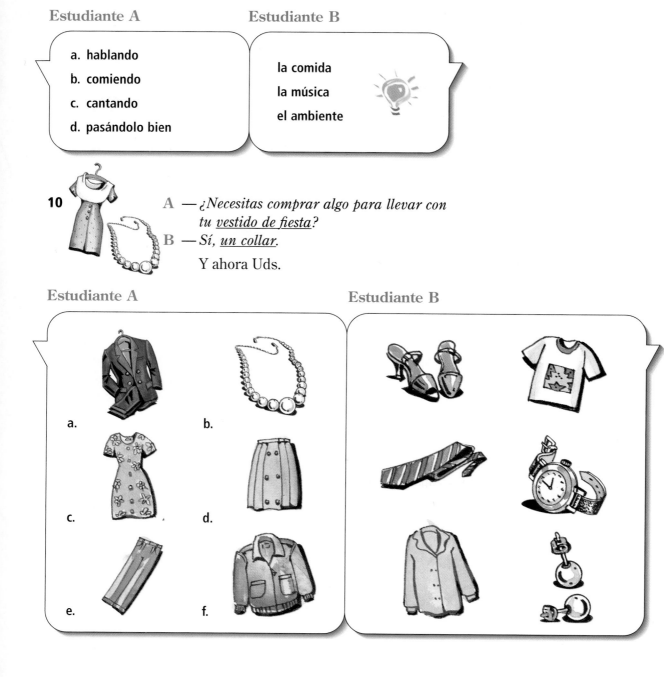

a.
b.
c.
d.
e.
f.

Imagina que vas a dar una fiesta el 2 de junio.

11 decorar
el lugar

A —¿Cuándo vas a <u>decorar el lugar</u> para la fiesta?
B —<u>El 1° de junio</u>.

Y ahora Uds.

Estudiante A

a. escoger la hora y la fecha

b. escribir las invitaciones

c. escoger la música

d. preparar la comida

e. escoger la ropa que vas a llevar

Estudiante B

Empecemos a escribir y a leer

Escribe tus respuestas en español.

12 ¿Llevas aretes? ¿Y reloj pulsera? ¿Cuándo los llevas?

13 ¿Para qué fiestas necesitas comprar entradas?

14 Para dar una fiesta, ¿qué necesitas hacer? ¿Qué música te
gusta tocar?

15 ¿Qué clase de fiesta es? Lee las descripciones y contesta
las preguntas.

a. Alejandro le compró un collar a Anita. Llegó a su casa
temprano con los otros invitados. Cuando Anita entró en la
casa, todos dijeron: "¡Feliz cumpleaños!"

b. María lleva un vestido elegante y zapatos de tacón alto.
Su novio, un traje gris con una corbata azul. La música es
muy bonita y les gusta mucho la fiesta. Pero a medianoche les
duelen mucho los pies.

c. Adela no sabía qué llevar a la fiesta. ¿Jeans, botas y un
sombrero vaquero? ¿Un traje de baño, una toalla, anteojos
de sol y sandalias? Al final, decidió irse de detective.

¿A qué clase de fiesta fue Alejandro? ¿Y María? ¿Y Adela?

También se dice

los aros
los pendientes
los zarcillos

el brazalete

el vestido de gala
el vestido de etiqueta

¡Comuniquemos!

**Aquí tienes otra oportunidad para usar
el vocabulario de este capítulo.**

1   Escoge cinco de tus compañeros(as). ¿Qué ropa llevan hoy?
Toma notas en español para no olvidarlo. Después, describe a
un(a) estudiante. Tu compañero(a) debe adivinar *(guess)* a
quién describes.

A — *Lleva aretes azules, un suéter y jeans. ¿Quién es?*
B — *¿Son blancos los jeans?*
A — *Sí.*
B — *Es Sara.*

2   ¿Conoce tu compañero(a) a las personas de
quienes hablas?

A — *¿Conoces a Mike Smith?*
B — *Sí, lo conozco. Es un estudiante de mi
clase de matemáticas. Es muy simpático.*
    o:
B — *No, no lo conozco. ¿Quién es?*
A — *Es un estudiante de mi clase de arte.*
B — *¿Cómo es?*
A — *Es alto y rubio.*

3 ¡Cuántos regalos! Tu compañero(a) va a comprar regalos para
su familia y sus amigos. Ayúdalo(la) a decidir qué comprar.

A — *El cumpleaños de (mi hermano) es (el 10 de junio).
¿Qué le regalo?*

B — *¿Por qué no le compras (un reloj pulsera)?*

¿Qué sabes ahora?

Can you:

■ discuss preparations for a party?

—Tengo que preparar ___, escoger ___ y escribir ___.

■ tell what kinds of gifts you like to give and receive?

—Me gusta regalar ___. Me gusta recibir regalos ___.

■ tell what you wear to a party?

—Cuando voy a una fiesta de cumpleaños, llevo ___ y ___.

■ introduce people and acknowledge introductions?

—Te ___ a mi amigo Andrés.

— ___.

Perspectiva cultural

¿Qué fiestas especiales hay en tu familia? ¿Y en tu comunidad?

Based on these photographs, what do you think the people are celebrating? What tells you that this is a very special party?

It's 4 o'clock on a Saturday afternoon in Camuy, a town on the northern coast of Puerto Rico. You can hear the approaching sounds of a ten-car caravan blowing their horns. When the caravan arrives in front of the church, Tamaris, a young woman in a white dress, steps out of the first car with her mother and father. Inside the church, Tamaris will receive a blessing from the priest while her mother places a crown on her head.

What might look like a wedding party is actually Tamaris's *quince años*, her fifteenth birthday celebration. It marks the girl's entrance into adulthood.

A *quince años* party can be very lavish or very simple. But one thing they all have in common is that family and friends of all ages join together to make it a memorable success. In Tamaris's case, the caravan was driven by her father's closest friends. They all own similar cars and have formed a car club that meets regularly for fun and to serve as escorts for local parties and celebrations, such as a *quince años*.

The white dress Tamaris is wearing was made by her mother, and her grandparents contributed the crown and white high-heeled shoes. Other family members and friends prepared food and refreshments for the party at her home, where a friend from school will act as deejay. Traditionally, the *quinceañera* starts the first dance with her father and then moves on to her escort. Then other couples will join them. The party will continue late into the night.

Guadalupe Velasco fue Presentada en Sociedad

En el templo de Nuestra Señora de Aránzazu se llevó a cabo solemne ceremonia de acción de gracias, por los quince años de Guadalupe Velasco Cervantes.

A ese acto invitaron con toda oportunidad los padres de la quinceañera: Antonio Velasco Godínez y María del Refugio Cervantes de Velasco, quienes para su satisfacción se vieron acompañados por los familiares y amigos.

A las 19.30, el R.P. Rafael Cervantes, O.F.M., tío de la feliz chica, inició la misa durante la cual un quinteto de cuerdas ejecutó bello programa musical de su amplio repertorio.

Como padrinos de Guadalupe lo fueron: Enrique Sahagún Godínez y María Eugenia N. de Godínez, los que en compañía de sus progenitores acupararon sendos reclinatorios frente al sencillo altar que en el fondo tiene el dórico retablo.

El padre Cervantes con cuánto cariño dirigió a la homenajeada emotivo fervorín para indicarle que, para ser feliz hay que desprendernos del egoísmo e interesarnos siempre por los demás. A continuación le dio a Lupita la Sagrada Eucaristía.

Después de la ceremonia religiosa, los Velasco Cervantes ofrecieron un banquete en honor de la quinceañera que se sirvió en un casino local y al que le acompañaron además de numerosos invitados sus hermanos: Marco Antonio, Marta, Eva, María Elena y Manuel.

Guadalupe Velasco Cervantes. Foto Jesús Preciado Martínez.

Dos quinceañeras celebran su día especial en Austin, Texas.

Another tradition has the girls at the party gathering around the cake to pull ribbons from it. The one who pulls the ribbon with a ring on it will presumably be the first one to get married.

However, not all young girls are interested in having a *quince años* party. Some might ask for a trip or a special gift instead of a formal party and a white dress. Tamaris's friend Loida has asked for a plane ticket so she can spend her summer vacation with her cousins in New Jersey and visit New York City. Loida is looking forward to her first long trip alone. That will really make her feel like an adult.

La cultura desde tu perspectiva

1 Is the party described here similar to any parties you have ever attended? How were they alike or different?

2 What events in the United States are similar to a *quince años?* In what ways are they similar?

Gramática en contexto

¡La peor fiesta de cumpleaños! ¡Pobre Eugenia! ¡Lo está pasando horrible! ¿Por qué?

Nadie está bailando.

Los invitados no están ni comiendo ni bebiendo.

Mi novio no está hablando con nadie.

Algunos invitados están viendo . . . ¡la tele!

Muchas personas ya están saliendo, pero nadie me regaló nada.

¡Nunca voy a tener otra fiesta de cumpleaños!

A The verbs in the first four captions are made up of two words. What ending is used on the -*ar* verbs when they follow *estar*? And on the -*er* verbs? What is the meaning of *están saliendo* in the fifth caption?

B Find all the negative words that Eugenia uses to express her feelings (such as *no* and *nadie*). Do these words come before or after the verbs?

C In which sentences do you find more than one negative word? What word is used before the verb in these sentences?

Construcciones negativas

To make a sentence negative, we put *no* in front of the verb. Some other negative words that you know are: *nada* ("nothing"), *nunca* ("never"), *nadie* ("nobody"), *tampoco* ("neither"), and *ni . . . ni* ("neither . . . nor"). Recall how we use them:

> **Nunca** saco fotos.
> **Nadie** va a ayudarme con las decoraciones.
> **No** me gusta bailar **tampoco.**
> **No** hay **ni** sandwiches **ni** refrescos.
> **No** quiero comer **nada.**

- Sometimes we can put the negative word before the verb and leave out the *no*. However, if the negative word comes after the verb, we must use *no* or another negative word.

> Antonio **nunca** estudia con **nadie.**
> **No** conozco a **nadie** en esta fiesta.

1 Pregúntale a tu compañero(a) qué va a hacer. Usa una palabra *(word)* o una frase de cada columna.

> **leer**
>
> **A** — *¿Vas a leer algo esta tarde?*
> **B** — *Sí, voy a leer una revista.*
>   o: *No, no voy a leer nada.*

a. comer   hoy
b. jugar   esta tarde
c. ver   esta noche
d. beber   mañana
e. escuchar   este fin de semana
f. hacer
g. comprar

2 Quieres hacer una reunión pero nadie quiere llevar nada. Explícale a tu compañero(a) qué problemas van a tener.

A — *¿Alguien va a traer refrescos?*
B — *No, nadie va a traer refrescos. ¡No vamos a beber nada!*

| a. | b. | c. | d. | e. |

3 ¿Cuáles son algunas cosas que no haces nunca? Con un(a) compañero(a), di *(tell)* si siempre, a veces, o nunca haces estas cosas.

llevar aretes

A — *Yo nunca llevo aretes. ¿Y tú?*
B — *Yo tampoco.*
o: *Yo los llevo siempre.*

a. llevar un vestido de fiesta / una corbata
b. escribir cartas / tarjetas postales
c. pasarlo mal en una fiesta
d. regalar algo hecho a mano

e. dar fiestas de sorpresa
f. reciclar botellas de plástico
g. montar en bicicleta
h. ver dibujos animados

El presente progresivo

We use the present tense to talk about an action that always or often takes place or that is happening now.

Ellos **comen** hamburguesas.

*They **eat** hamburgers. (always / usually)*
*They're **eating** hamburgers. (now)*

We use the present progressive tense when we want to emphasize that something is happening right now.

Ellos **están comiendo** hamburguesas.

*They're **eating** hamburgers. (right now)*

The present progressive uses a present-tense form of *estar* + the present participle of another verb. To form the present participle, we drop the ending of the infinitive and add *-ando* to the stem of *-ar* verbs and *-iendo* to the stem of *-er* and *-ir* verbs.

(yo)	**estoy**	bail**ando** com**iendo** escrib**iendo**	(nosotros) (nosotras)	**estamos**	bail**ando** com**iendo** escrib**iendo**
(tú)	**estás**	bail**ando** com**iendo** escrib**iendo**	(vosotros) (vosotras)	**estáis**	bail**ando** com**iendo** escrib**iendo**
Ud. (él) (ella)	**está**	bail**ando** com**iendo** escrib**iendo**	Uds. (ellos) (ellas)	**están**	bail**ando** com**iendo** escrib**iendo**

4 Tienes unas fotos de tus vacaciones en Yucatán. Túrnate con un(a) compañero(a) para explicar qué están haciendo las personas en cada foto.

Aquí nosotros estamos explorando la selva.

nosotros

a. mi papá

b. mi hermana

c. mis padres

d. mi familia y yo

e. unos amigos mexicanos

f. yo

5 Tu amigo(a) está enfermo(a) y no puede ir a la fiesta de fin
de año. Por eso, te llama por teléfono para preguntar qué están
haciendo todos los invitados.

A — *¿Qué están haciendo Raquel y Fernando?*
B — *Están bailando.*

Raquel y Fernando

| a. Paco y Jorge | b. Uds. | c. tú | d. Julia | e. Carlos |

El verbo *dar*

The verb *dar* means "to give." Here are all its present-tense forms.

(yo)	**doy**	(nosotros) (nosotras)	**damos**
(tú)	**das**	(vosotros) (vosotras)	**dais**
Ud. (él) (ella)	**da**	Uds. (ellos) (ellas)	**dan**

- Except for the *yo* form, *dar* takes the same present-tense endings
  as regular *-ar* verbs.

- Because we often say to whom we give something, *dar* is usually
  used with the indirect object pronouns *me, te, le, nos,* and *les.*

  Nuestro profesor **nos da** mucha tarea.
  Nunca **les doy** nada a mis primos.
  Mis abuelos van a **darme** un libro para mi cumpleaños.

6 ¿Qué les regalas a las siguientes personas? Trabaja con un(a) compañero(a) para escoger el regalo apropiado.

**un amigo que
juega béisbol**

A — *¿Qué le das a un amigo que juega béisbol?*
B — *Le doy algunas entradas a un partido.*

a. un amigo a quien le gusta dibujar
b. una amiga a quien le gusta esquiar
c. una amiga que estudia álgebra
d. un amigo que escribe mucho
e. una amiga que ve muchas películas
f. un amigo que va a menudo a la playa
g. una amiga a quien le gusta la ropa

7 Dile a tu compañero(a) quién te da estas cosas.

dinero

A — *¿Quién te da dinero?*
B — *Mi padre me da dinero.*
o: *Nadie me da dinero.*

a. ropa nueva
b. poca tarea
c. regalos hechos a mano
d. los exámenes más difíciles
e. regalos prácticos
f. tarjetas de cumpleaños

Ahora lo sabes

Can you:

■ **express a negative statement?**

—No tengo hambre. ___ voy a comer ___ ahora.

■ **tell what is happening right now?**

—Marta y Rosa ___ unas enchiladas porque tienen hambre.

■ **tell what someone gives to someone else?**

—Yo siempre les ___ regalos a mis amigos.

TODO JUNTO

Para decir más

Aquí tienes vocabulario adicional que te puede ayudar para hacer las actividades de esta sección.

el casco
helmet

el certificado de regalo
gift certificate

el dulce
sweet, candy

el pañuelo
handkerchief, scarf

el perfume
perfume

el sombrero
hat

los esquís
skis

los patines
roller skates

Actividades

Esta sección te ofrece la oportunidad de aumentar tus conocimientos de español al integrar lo que aprendiste en este capítulo con lo que aprendiste en capítulos anteriores.

 Quieres dar una fiesta. Con un(a) compañero(a), decidan:

- qué clase de fiesta va a ser
- cuándo la quieren dar
- dónde
- a quiénes van a invitar
- qué van a servir
- qué ropa llevar
- qué música tocar

Luego escriban una invitación para la fiesta y compártanla *(share it)* con los miembros de la clase.

2 Trabaja con un(a) compañero(a) para crear un anuncio para un regalo. Si quieren, pueden incluir esta información:

- descripción del regalo
- para qué tipo de persona es
- precio
- por qué es el regalo perfecto
- dónde comprarlo

Luego compartan el anuncio con sus compañeros de clase.

3 Escribe en diferentes hojas de papel cuatro cosas que quisieras estar haciendo en este momento.

Estoy tocando el piano.
Estoy bebiendo un refresco.

Pon tus papeles con los de otros tres estudiantes. Después, túrnense para representar lo que dicen los papeles. Los otros estudiantes deben adivinar qué estás haciendo.

¿Estás tocando el piano?
¿Estás bebiendo un refresco?

Luego escojan las mejores representaciones. Háganlas para otro grupo. Ellos deben adivinar lo que están haciendo.

¿Están tocando el piano?
¿Están bebiendo refrescos?

Una muchacha celebra el fin del año escolar en Cuernavaca, México.

¡**V**amos a leer!

Antes de leer

STRATEGY ➤ Using titles and pictures to predict

Look at the title of the story and the pictures to predict who the characters are and what the setting might be.

Uno, dos, tres, ¡rumba!

Roberto es un muchacho cubano que acaba de llegar a Chicago. No sabe una palabra de inglés. Los primeros meses yo le ayudo con las clases y las tareas. También le ayudo con otras cosas. Cada viernes por la tarde, los muchachos tienen que llevar pantalones negros, camisa blanca y una corbata negra para ir a las clases de baile. Nos reunimos en el gimnasio de la escuela por una hora. El primer viernes, Roberto me dice: "Antonio, ¡no sé bailar! ¿Qué voy a hacer? ¡No voy a entender a la profesora y no puedo hablar con las muchachas!"

Mira la lectura

STRATEGY ➤ Skimming

Remember that you can get an overview of a story by skimming it. Skim the story now. Were your predictions correct?

Le digo a Roberto que sólo tiene que observar lo que hacen los otros. Y eso es lo que hace. Cuando baila con las muchachas no puede decirles nada. Pero no importa, porque debe pensar en lo que hace.

Un día la profesora anuncia que va a regalar un disco compacto a la mejor pareja de la clase. Entonces una muchacha llamada Susan le dice: *"Come on, Roberto, we have to win!"*

Infórmate

STRATEGY ➤ Using cognates

Remember that you can use what you know about cognates to figure out the meaning of new words. For example, if you think *observar* means "observe," two facts support that guess. First, if you don't know how to dance, observing the other dancers is something you might do. Second, the phrase *lo que hacen los otros* makes sense after the word *observar*. So *observar* probably means "observe."

 1 What do you think *interpreto* means? What information helps you figure it out?

 2 Which word makes sense in this sentence?

Roberto no sabe ___ sus ideas en inglés.

a. imitar
b. expresar
c. solucionar

 3 How did Roberto solve his problem in the dance class?

"Pero ¿qué me dice?" me pregunta el pobre Roberto. Cuando le explico que la profesora va a dar un regalo a los mejores bailarines y que Susan quiere bailar con él, Roberto está un poco nervioso. "No te preocupes," le digo. "Estás bailando muy bien."

Aplicación

Write an ending for this story in one or two sentences. Compare your ending with that of a partner.

La profesora toca una rumba—¡un baile cubano!—y Roberto empieza a bailar bien. Todos lo miran con sorpresa. ¡Roberto y Susan ganan el disco compacto! Después, Susan dice algo y yo interpreto: "Está preguntando si quieres escuchar el disco compacto con ella después de la clase." Y de esta manera Roberto y Susan se hicieron novios. Él aprendió un poco de inglés y ella un poco de español, y los dos aprendieron a bailar.

¡Vamos a escribir!

You have just been to a party or a prom (un baile de graduación). What do you want to remember about it? Write a diary entry about the party. Follow these steps.

 First, think about the dance and answer these questions.

- ¿A qué hora empezó la fiesta?
  ¿A qué hora terminó?
- ¿Con quién fuiste?
- ¿Qué ropa llevaron?
- ¿Viste a muchos amigos en la fiesta? ¿A quiénes viste?
- ¿Qué comieron?
- ¿Qué tipo de música tocaron? ¿Bailaron?
- ¿Qué te gustó más: la música, la comida, las decoraciones?
- ¿Cómo lo pasaste?

2 Use the answers to these questions to write in your diary. You can start your entry with the words *Querido diario*.

3 Show your entry to a partner. Does he or she think you should add or change anything? Using your partner's recommendations and your own ideas, make the necessary changes and rewrite your entry.

4 Check carefully for accuracy in spelling, the use of written accents, the form and placement of adjectives, and the form of verbs. Rewrite if necessary.

5 Share your entry by

- including it in a collection of writings called *Las fiestas de este año*
- posting it on the bulletin board in your classroom
- adding it to your writing portfolio

Estudiantes mexicanos en el Instituto
Tecnológico en Nuevo Laredo

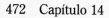

Una celebración en Montevideo, Uruguay

¿Lo sabes bien?

This section will help you organize your studying for the proficiency test, where you will be asked to do similar, though not identical, tasks. There will not be any models on the test.

Listening

Can you understand when someone talks about a party he or she is planning to give? Listen as your teacher reads a sample similar to what you will hear on the test. As a guest invited to this party, what two things should you do and why?

Reading

Can you understand a written description of a party? Here's a written transcription from a radio announcer. What kind of party is described here? Which words or phrases tell you that?

Todos lo están pasando bien y nadie está aburrido. La actriz Manuela lleva zapatos de tacón alto para su disfraz y Kati Rojas lleva joyas y un vestido de fiesta. Está bailando con Enrique Salas, que nunca lleva corbata ni traje. ¡Me encantan las fiestas de ambiente informal!

Writing

Can you write a letter describing the arrangements you need to make for a special occasion? Here is a sample letter:

Querida Susana:

Me gustaría tener una fiesta para nuestra abuelita, una reunión con toda la familia. No me gusta preparar las fiestas grandes. Nunca lo hago. Pero mi mamá dice que tengo que hacerlo. Mi hermana puede ayudar con las decoraciones. (Ella está decorando su cuarto otra vez, pero suele hacerlo bien.) ¿Qué piensas? ¿Me puedes ayudar?

Tu prima, Lina

Culture

Can you describe how girls in Spanish-speaking countries celebrate their fifteenth birthday?

Una muchacha celebrando sus quince años

Speaking

Can you and your partners play the roles of teenagers introducing one another at a party? Here is a sample dialogue:

A —*Laura, ¿conoces al novio de mi hermana?*
B —*No, no lo conozco.*
A —*Pues, Laura, te presento a Jaime Fernández.*
B —*Encantada, Jaime.*
C —*Mucho gusto, Laura.*

Resumen del capítulo 14

Use the vocabulary from this chapter to help you:

- make plans for giving or attending a party
- describe gift-giving
- make and acknowledge introductions

to talk about parties

el ambiente
bailar
el baile
cantar
las decoraciones *(pl.)*
decorar
escribir
¡Feliz cumpleaños!
la fiesta
    de cumpleaños
    de disfraces
    de fin de año
    de la escuela
    de sorpresa
la hora
la invitación
el invitado, la invitada
invitar
el lugar
pasarlo bien / mal
preparar
la reunión

to introduce people

alguien
conocer: (yo) conozco
        (tú) conoces
Encantado, -a.
el novio, la novia
el pariente, la parienta
Te presento a ___.

to talk about what to wear to a party

los aretes *(m.)*
el collar
la corbata
las joyas
la pulsera
el reloj pulsera
el traje
el vestido de fiesta
los zapatos de tacón alto

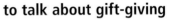

to talk about gift-giving

dar: (yo) doy
   (tú) das
escoger: (yo) escojo
       (tú) escoges
recibir
regalar
el regalo
    elegante
    hecho, -a a mano
    personal
    práctico, -a

other useful terms and expressions

algunos, algunas
De ninguna manera.
Depende.
la entrada
soler (o → ue) + *inf.*

Verbos

INFINITIVE	PRESENT		PRETERITE	

Regular Verbs

estudiar	estudio	estudiamos	estudié	estudiamos
	estudias	estudiáis	estudiaste	estudiasteis
	estudia	estudian	estudió	estudiaron
comer	como	comemos	comí	comimos
	comes	coméis	comiste	comisteis
	come	comen	comió	comieron
vivir	vivo	vivimos	viví	vivimos
	vives	vivís	viviste	vivisteis
	vive	viven	vivió	vivieron

Stem-changing Verbs

(You will learn the verb forms that are in italic type next year.)

cerrar (e → ie)	cierro	cerramos	cerré	cerramos
	cierras	cerráis	cerraste	cerrasteis
	cierra	cierran	cerró	cerraron
costar (o → ue)	cuesta	cuestan	costó	costaron
doler (o → ue)	duele	duelen	dolió	dolieron
dormir (o → ue)	duermo	dormimos	dormí	dormimos
	duermes	dormís	dormiste	dormisteis
	duerme	duermen	*durmió*	*durmieron*
empezar (e → ie)	See *cerrar.*		*empecé*	empezamos
			empezaste	empezasteis
			empezó	empezaron
jugar (u → ue)	juego	jugamos	jugué	jugamos
	juegas	jugáis	jugaste	jugasteis
	juega	juegan	jugó	jugaron
llover (o → ue)	llueve		llovió	
nevar (e → ie)	nieva		nevó	
pedir (e → i)	pido	pedimos	*pedí*	*pedimos*
	pides	pedís	*pediste*	*pedisteis*
	pide	piden	*pidió*	*pidieron*
pensar (e → ie)	See *cerrar.*			

poder (o → ue)	See *Irregular Verbs.*			
preferir (e → ie)	prefiero	preferimos	*preferí*	*preferimos*
	prefieres	preferís	*preferiste*	*preferisteis*
	prefiere	prefieren	*prefirió*	*prefirieron*
probar (o → ue)	pruebo	probamos	probé	probamos
	pruebas	probáis	probaste	probasteis
	prueba	prueban	probó	probaron
querer (e → ie)	See *Irregular Verbs.*			
servir (e → i)	See *pedir.*			
soler (o → ue)	suelo	solemos		
	sueles	soléis		
	suele	suelen		

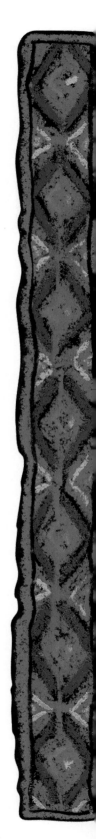

Verbs with Spelling Changes

(You will learn the verb forms that are in italic type next year.)

apagar	apago	apagamos	apagué	apagamos
	apagas	apagáis	apagaste	apagasteis
	apaga	apagan	apagó	apagaron
buscar	busco	buscamos	busqué	buscamos
	buscas	buscáis	buscaste	buscasteis
	busca	buscan	buscó	buscaron
conocer	conozco	conocemos	conocí	conocimos
	conoces	conocéis	conociste	conocisteis
	conoce	conocen	conoció	conocieron
creer	creo	creemos	creí	creímos
	crees	creéis	creíste	creísteis
	cree	creen	*creyó*	*creyeron*
empezar	See *Stem-changing Verbs.*			
escoger	escojo	escogemos	escogí	escogimos
	escoges	escogéis	escogiste	escogisteis
	escoge	escogen	escogió	escogieron
jugar	See *Stem-changing Verbs.*			

leer	See *creer.*			
llegar	See *apagar.*			
pagar	See *apagar.*			
practicar	See *buscar.*			
proteger	See *escoger.*			
reducir	See *conocer.*			
sacar	See *buscar.*			
tocar	See *buscar.*			

Irregular Verbs

(You will learn the verb forms that are in italic type next year.)

dar	doy	damos	*di*	*dimos*
	das	dais	*diste*	*disteis*
	da	dan	*dio*	*dieron*
decir	digo	decimos	*dije*	*dijimos*
	dices	decís	*dijiste*	*dijisteis*
	dice	dicen	*dijo*	*dijeron*
estar	estoy	estamos	*estuve*	*estuvimos*
	estás	estáis	*estuviste*	*estuvisteis*
	está	están	*estuvo*	*estuvieron*
hacer	hago	hacemos	hice	*hicimos*
	haces	hacéis	hiciste	*hicisteis*
	hace	hacen	hizo	*hicieron*
ir	voy	vamos	fui	fuimos
	vas	vais	fuiste	fuisteis
	va	van	fue	fueron
poder	puedo	podemos	*pude*	*pudimos*
	puedes	podéis	*pudiste*	*pudisteis*
	puede	pueden	*pudo*	*pudieron*
poner	pongo	ponemos	*puse*	*pusimos*
	pones	ponéis	*pusiste*	*pusisteis*
	pone	ponen	*puso*	*pusieron*

INFINITIVE	PRESENT		PRETERITE	
querer	quiero	queremos	*quise*	*quisimos*
	quieres	queréis	*quisiste*	*quisisteis*
	quiere	quieren	*quiso*	*quisieron*
saber	sé	sabemos	*supe*	*supimos*
	sabes	sabéis	*supiste*	*supisteis*
	sabe	saben	*supo*	*supieron*
salir	salgo	salimos	salí	salimos
	sales	salís	saliste	salisteis
	sale	salen	salió	salieron
ser	soy	somos	*fui*	*fuimos*
	eres	sois	*fuiste*	*fuisteis*
	es	son	*fue*	*fueron*
tener	tengo	tenemos	*tuve*	*tuvimos*
	tienes	tenéis	*tuviste*	*tuvisteis*
	tiene	tienen	*tuvo*	*tuvieron*
traer	traigo	traemos	traje	trajimos
	traes	traéis	trajiste	trajisteis
	trae	traen	trajo	trajeron
ver	veo	vemos	vi	vimos
	ves	veis	viste	visteis
	ve	ven	vio	vieron

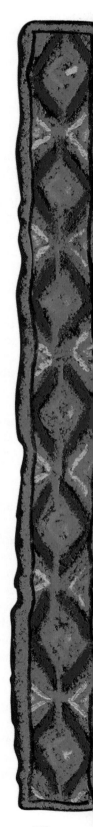

VOCABULARIO ESPAÑOL-INGLÉS

The *Vocabulario español-inglés* contains all active vocabulary from the text, including vocabulary presented in the grammar sections.

A dash (—) represents the main entry word. For example, **pasar la —** after **la aspiradora** means **pasar la aspiradora.**

The number following each entry indicates the chapter in which the word or expression is presented. The letter *P* following an entry refers to *El primer paso.*

The following abbreviations are used: *adj.* (adjective), *dir. obj.* (direct object), *f.* (feminine), *fam.* (familiar), *ind. obj.* (indirect object), *inf.* (infinitive), *m.* (masculine), *pl.* (plural), *prep.* (preposition), *pron.* (pronoun), *sing.* (singular).

a at (2); to (3)
  a la, al *(a + el)* to the (3)
el **abrigo** coat (7)
abril April (P)
abrir to open (10)
el **abuelo, la abuela** grandfather, grandmother (5)
los **abuelos** grandparents (5)
aburrido, -a boring (11)
aburrir to bore (11)
el **actor, la actriz** actor, actress (11)
acuerdo: estar de — to agree (8)
adiós good-by (P)
¿adónde? (to) where? (3)
agosto August (P)
el **agua** *f.* water (4)
el **aguacate** avocado (12)
ahora now (9)
el **aire** air (13)
algo something (4)
  — más something else (12)
alguien someone, somebody (14)
alguna vez ever (12)
algunos, -as some (14)
allí there (2)

  — está there it is (2)
el **almacén,** *pl.* **los almacenes** department store (6)
el **almuerzo** lunch (2)
  en el — for lunch (4)
alto, -a tall (5)
el **aluminio** aluminum (13)
amable kind, nice (1)
amarillo, -a yellow (6)
el **ambiente** atmosphere (14)
  el medio — environment (13)
la **amenaza** threat (13)
el **amigo, la amiga** friend (3)
anaranjado, -a orange *(color)* (6)
el **animal,** *pl.* **los animales** animal (13)
anoche last night (10)
los **anteojos (de sol)** (sun)glasses (7)
antiguo, -a old, traditional (8)
antipático, -a unfriendly, unpleasant (5)
el **anuncio (de televisión)** ad, commercial (11)
el **año** year (P)
  la fiesta de fin de —

New Year's Eve party (14)
  tener . . . —s to be . . . years old (P, 5)
apagar to turn off (13)
el **apartamento** apartment (8)
aprender to learn (2)
aquí here (2)
  — está here it is (2)
  por — around here (6)
el **árbol** tree (13)
el **arete** earring (14)
arreglar to clean up (8)
el **arroz** rice (4)
el **arte** art (2)
artístico, -a artistic (1)
asco: ¡qué —! yuck! that's disgusting! (4)
así, así so-so, fair (P)
la **aspiradora** vacuum cleaner (8)
  pasar la — to vacuum (8)
atractivo, -a attractive (5)
atrevido, -a bold, daring (1)
el **autobús** *pl.* **los autobuses** bus (10)
  la parada del — bus stop (10)

la **avenida** avenue (10)
aventura: la película de —s adventure film (11)
¡ay! ouch! (9)
ayer yesterday (10)
ayudar to help (1)
el **azúcar** sugar (12)
azul, *pl.* **azules** blue (5, 6)

bailar to dance (14)
el **baile** dance (14)
bajo, -a short *(height)* (5)
la **ballena** whale (13)
el **banco** bank (10)
el **baño** bathroom (8)
   el **traje de —** bathing suit (7)
barato, -a cheap, inexpensive (6)
básquetbol: jugar — to play basketball (3)
bastante rather (8)
la **basura** garbage (8)
beber to drink (4, 12)
la **bebida** beverage (4)
béisbol: jugar — to play baseball (3)
la **biblioteca** library (10)
la **bicicleta** bicycle (13)
   montar en — to ride a bike (13)
bien well (P)
el **bistec** steak (4)
blanco, -a white (6)
la **blusa** blouse (6)
la **boca** mouth (9)
el **bolígrafo** pen (P)
bonito, -a pretty (5)
la **bota** boot (7)
el **bote** rowboat (7)
   pasear en — to row (7)
la **botella** bottle (13)
el **brazo** arm (9)
el **bronceador** suntan lotion (7)
bucear to skin-dive (7)

bueno (buen), -a good (P)
bueno OK, fine, all right (10)
la **bufanda** winter scarf (7)
el **burrito** burrito (12)
buscar to look for (6)

el **caballo** horse (13)
la **cabeza** head (9)
   tener dolor de — to have a headache (9)
el **café** coffee (4)
el **calcetín,** *pl.* **los calcetines** sock (6)
la **calculadora** calculator (2)
callado, -a quiet (1)
la **calle** street (10)
calor:
   hace — it's hot (out) (7)
   tener — to be hot *(person)* (9)
la **cama** bed (8)
la **cámara** camera (7)
el **camarero, la camarera** waiter, waitress (12)
la **camisa** shirt (6)
la **camiseta** T-shirt (6)
el **campo** countryside (3)
el **canal** (TV) channel (11)
canoso: pelo — gray hair (5)
cansado, -a tired (3)
cantar to sing (14)
cariñoso, -a affectionate, loving (5)
la **carne (de res)** beef (12)
caro, -a expensive (6)
la **carpeta** pocket folder (2)
   la **— de argollas** three-ring binder (2)
la **carta** letter (10)
   a la — a la carte (12)
el **cartel** poster (8)
el **cartón** cardboard (13)
la **casa** house (8)

el **quehacer (de la —)** household chore (8)
   en — at home (1)
la **especialidad de la —** house specialty (12)
casi almost (11)
castaño: pelo — brown (chestnut) hair (5)
las **cataratas** waterfall (7)
la **catedral** cathedral (7)
catorce fourteen (P)
la **cebolla** onion (4)
la **cena** dinner (4)
el **centro** center (13)
   el **— comercial** mall (3)
   el **— de reciclaje** recycling center (13)
cerca (de) near (8)
el **cereal** cereal (4)
cero zero (P)
cerrar (e → ie) to close (10)
el **césped** lawn (8)
el **champú** shampoo (10)
la **chaqueta** jacket (6)
el **chile** chili pepper (12)
   el **— con carne** beef with beans (12)
   el **— relleno** stuffed pepper (12)
el **chocolate** hot chocolate (12)
el **churro** churro (12)
cien one hundred (5)
la **ciencia ficción** science fiction (11)
las **ciencias** science (2)
   — de la salud health (science) (2)
   — sociales social studies (2)
ciento uno, -a; ciento dos; etc. 101, 102, etc. (6)
cinco five (P)
cincuenta fifty (2)
el **cine** movie theater (1)

ir al — to go to the movies (1)

la ciudad city (7)

claro:

¡— que sí! of course! (3)

¡— que no! of course not! (3)

la clase (de) class (2); kind, type (11)

después de las —s after school (3)

la sala de —s classroom (P)

la clínica clinic (9)

el coche car (8)

la cocina kitchen (8)

cocinar to cook (1)

el collar necklace (14)

el color color (6)

¿de qué —? what color? (6)

en —es in color (11)

la comedia comedy, sitcom (11)

el comedor dining room (8)

comer to eat (4, 12)

los comestibles groceries (10)

cómico comical (11)

la comida meal (4), food (12)

¿cómo? how? (P)

¿— eres? what are you like? (1)

¿— está (usted)? how are you? *formal* (P)

¿— estás? how are you? *fam.* (P)

¡— no! certainly! (12)

¿— se dice . . . ? how do you say . . . ? (P)

¿— se llama(n)? what is his/her/their name? (5)

¿— te llamas? what's your name? (P)

la cómoda dresser (8)

cómodo, -a comfortable (8)

el compañero, la compañera classmate (P)

comprar to buy (6)

¿me compras . . . ? can you buy me . . . ? (10)

compras: ir de — to go shopping (3)

la comunidad community (10)

con with (3)

el concierto concert (11)

conmigo with me (3)

conocer to know (14)

conservar to conserve, save *(energy)* (13)

contaminado, -a contaminated, polluted (13)

contigo with you (3)

la corbata tie (14)

el correo post office (10)

cortar to cut, to mow (8)

corto, -a short *(length)* (11)

la cosa thing (8)

costar (o → ue) to cost (6)

creer to think, to believe (4, 9)

creo que no I don't think so (4)

creo que sí I think so (4)

el cuaderno spiral notebook (2)

la cuadra block (10)

cuadrado, -a square (8)

el cuadro picture (8)

¿cuál(es)? what? which? which one(s)? (11)

¿cuándo? when (P)

cuando when (7)

¿cuánto? how much? (6)

¿— (tiempo) hace que . . . ? how long has it been since . . . ? (9)

¿cuántos, -as? how many? (5)

¿— años tiene . . . ? how old is . . . ? (5)

¿— años tienes? how old are you? (P)

cuarenta forty (2)

cuarto, -a quarter (2); fourth (2, 8)

y — *(time)* quarter after, quarter past (2)

el cuarto room (8)

cuatro four (P)

cuatrocientos four hundred (10)

la cuchara spoon (12)

el cuchillo knife (12)

el cuello neck (9)

la cuenta bill *(in restaurant)* (12)

el cuero leather (8)

de — (made) of leather (8)

el cuerpo body (9)

el cumpleaños birthday (P)

¡feliz —! happy birthday! (14)

la fiesta de — birthday party (14)

la tarjeta de — birthday card (10)

dar to give (14)

— + *movie* or *TV program* to show (11)

— miedo a to scare (11)

de from (P); of **— 's, — s'** (5)

de la, del *(de + el)* of the, from the (10)

— la mañana / la tarde / la noche in the morning / afternoon / evening (11)

— + *material* made of (8)

— nada you're welcome (3)

— postre for dessert (12)

¿— veras? really? (1)

debajo de under(neath) (12)

deber ought to, should (4)

decir to say (13)

  ¿cómo se dice . . . ? how do you say . . . ? (P)

  ¡no me digas! really?, you don't say! (3)

  ¿qué quiere — . . . ? what does . . . mean? (P)

  se dice . . . it is said . . . (P)

la **decoración** *pl.* **las decoraciones** decoration (14)

  decorar to decorate (14)

el **dedo** finger (9)

  — del pie toe (9)

  delante de in front of (12)

  demasiado too (11)

el/la **dentista** dentist (9)

  depende it depends (14)

los **deportes** sports (1)

  deportista athletic (1)

  deportivo: el programa — sports program (11)

  depositar to deposit (10)

  derecha: a la — (de) to the right (of) (10)

  derecho, -a right (9)

el **desayuno** breakfast (4)

  descansar to rest (7)

el **descuento: la tienda de —s** discount store (6)

  desear: ¿qué desea Ud? may I help you? (6)

  desordenado, -a messy (1)

  después de after (3)

  detective: el programa de —s detective show (11)

  detrás (de) behind (10)

  devolver (o → ue) to return *(something)* (10)

el **día** day (P)

  buenos —s good morning (P)

el **plato del —** daily special (12)

  ¿qué — es hoy? what day is it? (P)

  todos los —s every day (3)

dibujar to draw (1)

el **dibujo: los —s animados** cartoons (11)

el **diccionario** dictionary (2)

  dice: ¿cómo se — . . . ? how do you say . . . ? (P)

diciembre December (P)

diecinueve nineteen (P)

dieciocho eighteen (P)

dieciséis sixteen (P)

diecisiete seventeen (P)

diez ten (P)

difícil difficult, hard (2)

digas: ¡no me —! really?, you don't say! (3)

el **dinero** money (10)

disfraces: la fiesta de — costume party (14)

la **diversión: el parque de diversiones** amusement park (3)

divertido, -a amusing, funny (11)

doce twelve (P)

el **documental** documentary (11)

el **dólar** dollar (6)

doler (o → ue) to hurt, to ache (9)

dolor: tener — de . . . to have a . . . ache (9) *see also* **cabeza, estómago, garganta, muelas, oído**

domingo Sunday (P)

  el — on Sunday (3)

¿dónde? where? (3)

  ¿de — eres? where are you from? (P)

dormir (o → ue) to sleep (9)

el **dormitorio** bedroom (8)

dos two (P)

doscientos two hundred (10)

durar to last (11)

la **educación física** physical education (2)

educativo: el programa — educational show (11)

ejercicio: hacer — to exercise (9)

el the *m. sing.* (P, 2)

él he (2); him *after prep.* (3)

el **elefante** elephant (13)

elegante elegant (14)

ella she (2); her *after prep.* (3)

ellos, ellas they (2); them *after prep.* (3)

emocionante exciting, touching (11)

empezar (e → ie) to begin, to start (2)

en in, at, on (P)

  — + *vehicle* by (10)

encantado, -a delighted (14)

encantar to love (5)

  le encanta(n) he/she loves (5)

  me encanta(n) I love (4)

la **enchilada** enchilada (12)

encima (de) on, on top of (12)

la **energía** energy (13)

enero January (P)

la **enfermería** nurse's office (9)

enfermo, -a ill, sick (3)

enfrente (de) facing, opposite, in front of (10)

la **ensalada** salad (4)

enseñar to teach (2)

la **entrada** ticket (14)

entre between (10)

entrevista: el programa de —s talk show (11)
enviar to send, to mail (10)
el **equipo de sonido** stereo (8)
eres you *fam.* are (1)
es it is (P); he/she is (2)
escoger to choose (14)
escribir to write (14)
¿cómo se escribe . . . ? how do you spell . . . ? (P)
el **escritorio** desk (8)
escuchar to listen to (1)
la **escuela** school (1)
ese, -a; -os, -as that; those (6)
eso: por — that's why, therefore (11)
la **espalda** back (9)
el **español** Spanish *(language)* (2)
la **especialidad de la casa** house specialty (12)
el **espejo** mirror (8)
esquiar to ski (7)
la **esquina** corner (10)
la **estación,** *pl.* **las estaciones** season (3); station (10)
el **estadio** stadium (10)
estar to be (3)
¿cómo estás? how are you? (P)
la sala de — family room (8)
este, -a; -os, -as this; these (6)
el **estómago** stomach (9)
tener dolor de — to have a stomachache (9)
el/la **estudiante** student (P)
estudiar to study (1)
la **estufa** stove (8)
explorar to explore (7)
extinción: en peligro de — endangered (13)

la **fábrica** factory (13)
fácil easy (2)
la **falda** skirt (6)
faltar to be lacking, to be missing (12)
la **familia** family (3)
fantástico, -a fantastic (7)
la **farmacia** drugstore (10)
fascinante fascinating (11)
fascinar to fascinate (11)
favor: por — please (P)
febrero February (P)
la **fecha** date (P)
¡feliz cumpleaños! happy birthday! (14)
feo, -a ugly (5)
la **fiebre** fever (9)
tener — to have a fever (9)
la **fiesta** party (3)
el vestido de — party dress (14)
el **fin:**
el — de semana the weekend (3)
la fiesta de — de año New Year's Eve party (14)
física: la educación — physical education (2)
el **flan** flan (12)
la **flor** flower (13)
formar: — parte de to be a part of (13)
la **foto** photo (7)
sacar —s to take pictures (7)
fresco: hace — it's cool outside (7)
el **frijol** bean (12)
los —es refritos refried beans (12)
frío:
hace — it's cold outside (7)
tener — to be cold *(person)* (9)

la **fruta** fruit (4)
fui, fuiste I went, you went (7)
el **fútbol** soccer (3)
el — americano football (3)

la **ganga** bargain (6)
el **garaje** garage (8)
la **garganta** throat (9)
las pastillas para la — throat lozenges (10)
tener dolor de — to have a sore throat (9)
el **gato** cat (5)
el **gemelo, la gemela** twin (5)
generalmente usually, generally (3)
generoso, -a generous (1)
¡genial! great! wonderful! (3)
la **gente** people (13)
el **gimnasio** gymnasium (3)
el **gorila** gorilla (13)
el **gorro** ski cap (7)
la **grabadora** tape recorder (2)
gracias thank you (P)
gracioso, -a funny (1)
grande big (5)
la **gripe** flu (9)
tener — to have the flu (9)
gris *pl.* **grises** gray (5, 6)
el **guacamole** avocado dip (12)
el **guante** glove (7)
guapo, -a handsome, good-looking (5)
el **guardarropa** closet (8)
la **guía telefónica** phone book (13)
el **guisante** pea (4)
la **guitarra** guitar (1)
gustar to like (1)
le gusta(n) he/she

likes (5)
me, te gusta I like, you like (1)
me gusta más I prefer (1)
(A mí) me gustaría I'd like ... (3)
¿(A ti) te gustaría? would you like ...? (3)

hablar to talk (1)
— **por teléfono** to talk on the phone (1)
hablando talking (14)
hacer to do, to make (8)
hace + *(time)* ... ago (6)
hace + *(time)* + **que** it's been *(time)* since (9)
— **ejercicio** to exercise (9)
se hace(n) con ... it's (they're) made with ... (12)
hice/hiciste/hizo did/made (10, 13) *see also* **calor, fresco, frío, sol, tiempo, viento**
hambre: tener — to be hungry (4)
la **hamburguesa** hamburger (4)
la **harina** flour (12)
la tortilla de — flour tortilla (12)
hasta until (11)
— **luego** see you later (P)
hay there is, there are (P)
¿cuántos(as) ... —? how many ... are there? (P)
— **que** it's necessary to (13)
hecho, -a made (14)
— **a mano** handmade (14)

el **hecho** fact (11)
helado: el té — iced tea (4)
el **helado** ice cream (12)
el **hermano, la hermana** brother, sister (5)
los **hermanos** brothers; brother(s) and sister(s) (5)
el **hijo, la hija** son, daughter (5)
los **hijos** sons; sons and daughters (5)
la **hoja de papel** sheet of paper (P)
¡hola! hi!, hello! (P)
el **hombre** man (5)
la **hora** period (2); time (2, 14)
¿a qué —? at what time? (2)
¿qué — es? what time is it? (2)
el **horario** schedule (2)
horrible horrible (4)
el **hospital** hospital (9)
el **hotel** hotel (10)
hoy today (P)
— **no** not today (3)
el **huevo** egg (4)

la **iglesia** church (10)
igualmente likewise (P)
impaciente impatient (1)
el **impermeable** raincoat (7)
incómodo, -a uncomfortable (8)
el **inglés** English *(language)* (2)
el **ingrediente** ingredient (12)
inteligente intelligent (5)
el **interés: el lugar de —** place of interest (7)
interesante interesting (11)
interesar to interest (11)
el **invierno** winter (3)
la **invitación** *pl.* **las**

invitaciones invitation (14)
el **invitado, la invitada** guest (14)
invitar to invite (14)
ir to go (3)
— **a +** *inf.* to be going to + *verb* (3)
— **a la escuela** to go to school (1)
— **a pasear** to take a walk (10)
— **de compras** to go shopping (3)
— **de pesca** to go fishing (3)
izquierda: a la — (de) to the left of (10)
izquierdo, -a left (9)

el **jabón** soap (10)
el **jaguar** jaguar (13)
el **jamón** ham (4)
los **jeans** jeans (6)
joven *adj.* young (5)
el **joven** young man, sir (6)
la **joven** young lady (6)
los **jóvenes** young people (6)
las **joyas** jewelry (14)
las **judías verdes** green beans (4)
jueves Thursday (P)
el — on Thursday (3)
jugar (u → ue) to play (3)
el **jugo** juice (4)
— **de naranja** orange juice (4)
julio July (P)
junio June (P)

la **the** *f. sing.* (P, 2); her, it, you *dir. obj. pron.* (6)
lado: al — de next to,

beside (10)

el lago lake (7)

la lámpara lamp (8)

el lápiz, *pl.* **los lápices** pencil (2)

largo, -a long (11)

las the *f. pl.* (2); them, you *dir. obj. pron.* (6)

lástima: ¡qué —! that's too bad! what a shame! (3)

lastimar to hurt (9)

la lata can (13)

el lavadero laundry room (8)

lavar to wash (8)

le (to) him, her, it, you *ind. obj. pron.* (9)

la leche milk (4)

la lechuga lettuce (4)

leer to read (1)

lejos (de) far (from) (8)

les (to) them *ind. obj.* (11)

la librería bookstore (10)

el libro book (P)

la limonada lemonade (4)

limpiar to clean (8)

limpio, -a clean (8)

llamar to call (9)

¿cómo se llama(n)? what is his /her /their name? (5)

¿cómo te llamas? what's your name?(P)

me llamo my name is (P)

se llama(n) his / her /their name is (5)

llegar to arrive (10)

llevar to wear (6); to take, to carry along (7)

llover: llueve it rains, it's raining (7)

la lluvia rain (7)

lo him, it, you *dir. obj. pron.* (6)

— siento I'm sorry (2)

el lobo wolf (13)

los the *m. pl.* (P, 4); them *dir. obj. pron.* (6)

— + *day of week* on + *day of week* (3)

luego then, afterward, later (10)

el lugar place (14)

— de interés place of interest (7)

lunes Monday (P)

el — on Monday (3)

la luz, *pl.* **las luces** light (13)

la madera wood (13)

de — (made of) wood (8)

la madre mother (5)

el maíz corn (12)

mal:

menos — que . . . it's a good thing that . . . (7)

me siento — I feel ill (9)

la maleta suitcase (7)

malo, -a bad (4)

manera: de ninguna — not at all (14)

la mano *f.* hand (9)

hecho, -a a — handmade (14)

el mantel tablecloth (12)

la mantequilla butter (12)

la manzana apple (4)

mañana tomorrow (P, 3)

la mañana morning (3)

por la — in the morning (3)

el mar sea (7)

el marcador marker (2)

marrón, *pl.* **marrones** brown (5, 6)

martes Tuesday (P)

el — on Tuesday (3)

marzo March (P)

más else (8, 12) more, *adj.* + -er (11)

el / la / los / las — + *adj.* the most + *adj.,* the + *adj.* + -est (11)

— o menos more or less (4)

— tarde later (11)

— temprano earlier (11)

las matemáticas mathematics (2)

mayo May (P)

mayor older (5)

el — peligro greatest danger (13)

me me *obj. pron.* (9)

media:

— hora *f.* half an hour (11)

una hora y — an hour and a half (11)

y — half-past (2)

la medianoche midnight (11)

el médico, la médica doctor (9)

el medio ambiente environment (13)

el mediodía noon (11)

mejor better (9)

el / la (los / las) —(es) the best (11)

menor *pl.,* **menores** younger (5)

menos less (4, 11)

el / la / los / las — + *adj.* the least + *adj.* (11)

más o — more or less (4)

— mal que . . . it's a good thing that . . . (7)

el menú menu (12)

menudo: a — often (12)

la merienda afternoon snack (12)

de — for a snack (12)

el mes month (P)

la mesa table (P)

metal: de — (made of) metal (8)

el metro subway (10)

mi, mis my (3)

mí me *after prep.* (12)

miércoles Wednesday (P)
  el — on Wednesday (3)
mil one thousand (10)
el **minuto** minute (11)
mismo: lo — the same thing (12)
la **mochila** backpack (2)
moderno, -a modern (8)
la **montaña** mountain (7)
montar en bicicleta to ride a bike (13)
el **monumento** monument (10)
morado, -a purple (6)
el **muchacho, la muchacha** boy, girl (5)
mucho, -a a lot of, much (2)
  muchas veces many times (12)
  — gusto pleased / nice to meet you (P)
los **muebles** furniture (8)
las **muelas: tener dolor de —** to have a toothache (9)
la **mujer** woman (5)
el **museo** museum (7)
la **música** music (2)
musical musical (11)
  el programa — music program (11)
muy very (1)

nada nothing (9)
  de — you're welcome (3)
  no me duele — nothing hurts (9)
  no me gusta — . . . I don't like . . . at all (1)
nadar to swim (1)
nadie nobody (5)
la **naranja** orange (4)
la **nariz** nose (9)
necesitar to need (2)

negro, -a black (5, 6)
  en blanco y — in black and white (11)
nevar: nieva it snows, it's snowing (7)
ni . . . ni neither . . . nor, not . . . or (1)
la **nieve** snow (7)
ninguna parte nowhere, not anywhere (7)
no no, not (P)
  creo que — I don't think so (4)
  ¿no? don't you?, aren't I . . . ? (9)
la **noche** evening (P)
  buenas —s good evening, good night (P)
  de la — at night (11)
  por la — in the evening (3)
el **nombre** name (5)
nos us *obj. pron.* (11)
nosotros, -as we (2); us *after prep.* (3)
las **noticias** news (11)
novecientos nine hundred (10)
noventa ninety (5)
noviembre November (P)
el **novio, la novia** boyfriend, girlfriend (14)
nuestro, -a our (8)
nueve nine (P)
nuevo, -a new (6)
el **número** number (P)
nunca never (4)

o or (P)
el **océano** ocean (13)
ochenta eighty (5)
ocho eight (P)
ochocientos eight hundred (10)

octavo, -a eighth (2)
octubre October (P)
ocupado, -a busy (3)
el **oeste: la película del —** western (11)
el **oído** ear (9)
  tener dolor de — to have an earache (9)
el **ojo** eye (9)
once eleven (P)
ordenado, -a neat, tidy (1)
el **oso** bear (13)
el **otoño** fall, autumn (3)
otro, -a another, other (6)

paciente patient *adj.* (1)
el **padre** father (5)
los **padres** parents (5)
pagar to pay (6)
el **país** country (7)
el **pájaro** bird (13)
el **pan** bread (4)
  el — tostado toast (4)
los **pantalones** pants (6)
las **pantimedias** pantyhose (6)
la **papa** potato (4)
  la — al horno baked potato (4)
  la — frita French fry (4)
el **papel** paper (P)
  la hoja de — sheet of paper (P)
para for (2)
  — + *inf.* to, in order to (7)
la **parada del autobús** bus stop (10)
el **paraguas** umbrella (7)
el **pariente, la parienta** relative (14)
el **parque** park (3)
  el — de diversiones amusement park (3)
el **partido** game, match (10)
pasado, -a last, past (7)

el **pasaporte** passport (7)
pasar to pass (12)
  — la aspiradora to vacuum (8)
  —lo bien (mal) to have a good (bad) time (14)
  ¿qué pasa? what's the matter? (9)
el **pasatiempo** pastime, hobby (3)
pasear:
  ir a — to take a walk (10)
  — en bote to row (7)
la **pasta dentífrica** toothpaste (10)
el **pastel** cake, pastry (12)
la **pastilla** tablet, lozenge (10)
patinar to skate (1)
pedir (e → i) to order, to ask for (12)
la **película** film, movie (11)
el **peligro** danger (13)
  en — de extinción endangered (13)
pelirrojo, -a red-haired (5)
el **pelo** hair (5)
pensar (e → ie) to think (11)
  — + inf. to plan (7)
peor worse (9)
  el / la (los / las) —(es) the worst (11)
pequeño, -a small, little (5)
perdón excuse me (6)
perezoso, -a lazy (1)
el **periódico** newspaper (13)
pero but (1)
el **perro** dog (5)
la **persona** person (5)
personal personal (14)
pesca: ir de — to go fishing (3)
el **pescado** fish (4)
picante spicy, peppery, hot *(flavor)* (12)
  no — mild *(flavor)* (12)
el **pie** foot (9)

a — walking, on foot (10)
  el dedo del — toe (9)
la **piel** fur (13)
la **pierna** leg (9)
la **pimienta** pepper (12)
la **pirámide** pyramid (7)
la **piscina** pool (3)
el **piso** story, floor (8)
la **pizarra** chalkboard (P)
la **planta** plant (13)
el **plástico** plastic (13)
  de — (made of) plastic (13)
el **plátano** banana (4)
el **platillo** saucer (12)
el **plato** dish, plate (12)
  el — del día daily special (12)
  los —s principales main dishes (12)
la **playa** beach (3)
la **plaza** town square (10)
poco: un — (de) a little (11)
poder (o → ue) can, to be able to (3, 7)
la **policía** police (10)
el **pollo** chicken (4)
poner to put, to place, to set (8)
  — la mesa to set the table (8)
por for (6)
  — aquí around here (6)
  — eso that's why, therefore (11)
  — favor please (P)
  — la mañana / la tarde / la noche in the morning / afternoon / evening (3)
  ¿— qué? why? (4)
  — supuesto of course (13)
porque because (4)
el **postre** dessert (12)
  de — for dessert (12)

practicar to practice (1)
práctico, -a practical (14)
preferir (e → ie) to prefer (4, 8)
preparar to prepare (14)
presentar to introduce (14)
  te presento a . . . I'd like you to meet . . . (14)
la **primavera** spring (3)
primero (primer), -a first (P, 2, 8)
el **primo, la prima** cousin (5)
probar (o → ue) to try, to taste (12)
el **profesor, la profesora** teacher (P)
el **programa** program, show (11)
el **pronóstico del tiempo** weather forecast (11)
proteger to protect (13)
prudente cautious (1)
puedo, puedes *see* **poder**
la **puerta** door (8)
pues well *(to indicate pause)* (1)
la **pulsera** bracelet (14)
  el reloj — wristwatch (14)
punto: en — sharp, on the dot (11)
puntualmente on time (11)
el **pupitre** student desk (P)
puro, -a pure, clean (13)

que that, who (5)
qué what (2)
  ¡— + adj.! how + *adj.!* (6)
  ¿— tal? how's it going? (P)
quedar to fit (6); to be located (10)
  me queda(n) bien it fits (they fit) me well (6)
  —se (en la cama) to stay (in bed) (9)

el quehacer (de la casa) household chore (8)

querer (e → ie) to want (3, 7)

¿qué quiere decir . . . ? what does . . . mean? (P)

(yo) quisiera I'd like (7)

la quesadilla quesadilla (12)

el queso cheese (4)

¿quién(es)? who? whom? (2, 5)

quince fifteen (P)

quinientos five hundred (10)

quinto, -a fifth (2)

quisiera *see* **querer**

quitar la mesa to clear the table (8)

razón: (no) tener — to be right (wrong) (8)

real real (11)

realista realistic (11)

recibir to receive (14)

el reciclaje: el centro de — recycling center (13)

reciclar to recycle (13)

recoger to pick up (13)

el recuerdo souvenir (7)

redondo, -a round (8)

reducir to reduce (13)

el refresco soft drink (4)

el refrigerador refrigerator (8)

regalar to give (a gift) (14)

el regalo gift (10)

la tienda de —s gift shop (10)

la regla ruler (2)

regresar to come back, to return (7)

regular so-so, fair (P)

el reloj pulsera wristwatch (14)

el resfriado cold (9)

el restaurante restaurant (10)

la reunión, *pl.* **las reuniones** get-together (14)

la revista magazine (13)

rojo, -a red (6)

romántico, -a romantic (11)

la ropa clothes (6)

rosado, -a pink (6)

rubio, -a blonde (5)

las ruinas ruins (7)

sábado Saturday (P)

el — on Saturday (3)

saber to know (13)

(yo) no lo sabía I didn't know that (10)

sabroso, -a delicious, tasty (4)

sacar to take out (8)

— dinero to withdraw money (10)

— fotos to take pictures (7)

— un libro to check out a book (10)

sacudir to dust (8)

la sal salt (12)

la sala living room (8)

la — de clases classroom (P)

la — de estar family room (8)

salir to leave (7)

la salsa sauce (12)

la salud health (4)

el sandwich sandwich (4)

sed: tener — to be thirsty (4)

seguida: en — right away (12)

segundo, -a second (2, 8)

seis six (P)

seiscientos six hundred (10)

el sello stamp (10)

la selva forest (7)

la — tropical rain forest (7)

la semana week (P)

el fin de — on the weekend (3)

el semestre semester (2)

sentir:

¿cómo te sientes? how do you feel? (9)

lo siento I'm sorry (2)

me siento bien / mal I feel well / ill (9)

señor Mr. (P); sir (6)

señora Mrs. (P); ma'am (6)

señorita Miss (P); miss (6)

separar to separate, to sort (13)

septiembre September (P)

séptimo, -a seventh (2)

ser to be (5)

serio, -a serious (1)

la serpiente snake (13)

el servicio: la estación de — gas station (10)

la servilleta napkin (12)

servir (e → i) to serve (12)

sesenta sixty (5)

setecientos seven hundred (10)

setenta seventy (5)

sexto, -a sixth (2)

si if, whether (10)

sí yes (P); do *(emphatic)* (1)

siempre always (4)

siento, sientes *see* **sentir**

siete seven (P)

la silla chair (8)

el sillón, *pl.* **los sillones** armchair (8)

simpático, -a nice, friendly (5)

sobre about (11); on (12)

sociable outgoing (1)

el sofá *m.* sofa (8)

el sol sun (7)

   los anteojos de — sunglasses (7)

   hace — it's sunny (7)

   tomar el — to sunbathe (7)

   soler (o → ue) + *inf.* to be in the habit of (14)

   solo, -a alone (3)

   sólo only (5)

   son (they) are (4)

   — las it is . . . *(in telling time)* (2)

   sonido: el equipo de — stereo (8)

la sopa soup (4)

la sorpresa: la fiesta de — surprise party (14)

el sótano basement (8)

   soy I am (1)

   su, sus his, her (5); your *formal,* their (8)

   subir to climb (7)

   sucio, -a dirty (8)

la sudadera sweatshirt (6)

   sueño: tener — to be sleepy (9)

el suéter sweater (6)

el supermercado supermarket (10)

   supuesto: por — of course (13)

   tacaño, -a stingy (1)

el taco taco (12)

   tal: ¿qué —? how's it going? (P)

   también also, too (1)

   a mí — me too (1)

   tampoco either, neither (1)

   tarde late (10)

la tarde afternoon (P)

   buenas —s good afternoon, good evening (P)

   por la — in the afternoon (3)

la tarea homework (2)

la tarjeta card (10)

   la — postal post card (10)

el taxi taxi (10)

la taza cup (12)

el tazón, *pl.* **los tazones** bowl (12)

   te you *fam. obj. pron.* (9)

el té tea (4)

   el — helado iced tea (4)

el teatro theater (10)

el teléfono telephone (1)

   hablar por — to talk on the telephone (1)

   el número de — phone number (P)

la telenovela soap opera (11)

la tele(visión) television (1)

   ver la — to watch television (1)

el templo temple (10)

   temprano early (10)

el tenedor fork (12)

   tener to have (2, 5)

   ¿qué tienes? what's wrong? (9)

   — que + *inf.* to have to (8) *see also* **año, calor, dolor, fiebre, frío, gripe, hambre, razón, sed, sueño**

el tenis tennis (3)

los tenis sneakers (6)

   tercer, tercera third (8)

   terminar to end (2)

   terrible terrible (9)

   terror: la película de — horror film (11)

   ti you *fam. after prep.* (12)

el tiempo weather (7); time (11)

   hace buen, mal — the weather is nice, bad (7)

   el pronóstico del — weather forecast (11)

   ¿qué — hace? what's the weather like? (7)

la tienda store (6)

   la — de ropa clothing store (6)

la Tierra Earth (13)

el tigre tiger (13)

el tío, la tía uncle, aunt (5)

   los tíos uncles; aunts and uncles (5)

   típico, -a typical (12)

   tocar to play (1)

   todavía still (9)

   — no not yet (11)

   todos, -as all; everyone (5)

   — los días every day (3)

   tomar to take (9)

   — el sol to sunbathe (7)

el tomate tomato (4)

   tonto, -a silly, dumb (11)

la tortilla (de harina, de maíz) (flour, corn) tortilla (12)

   tostado: el pan — toast (4)

   trabajador, -a hard-working (1)

   trabajar to work (10)

   traer to bring (12)

el traje suit (14)

   el — de baño bathing suit (7)

el transporte público public transportation (13)

   trece thirteen (P)

   treinta thirty (P, 2)

el tren train (10)

   la estación del — train station (10)

   tres three (P)

   trescientos three hundred (10)

   triste sad (11)

   tu, tus your *fam.* (2, 3)

   tú you *fam.* (2)

un, una a, an, one (P, 2)

   es la una it's one o'clock (2)

único, -a only (5)

uno one (P)

unos, -as a few, some (4)

usar to use (13)

usted (Ud.) you *formal sing.* (2)

ustedes (Uds.) you *formal pl.* (2)

la **uva** grape (4)

la **vaca** cow (13)

las **vacaciones** vacation (7)

   ir de — to go on vacation (7)

   valer: (no) vale la pena it's (not) worthwhile (13)

el **vaso** glass (12)

   ¡vaya! my goodness! gee! wow! (7)

   veinte twenty (P)

   veintiuno (veintiún) twenty-one (P)

   vender to sell (12)

la **ventana** window (8)

   ver to see, to watch (1)

     a — let's see (2)

el **verano** summer (3)

   veras: ¿de — ? really? (1)

   ¿verdad? isn't that so?, right? (4)

   verde green (5, 6)

las **verduras** vegetables (4)

   sopa de — vegetable soup (4)

el **vestido** dress (6)

   el — de fiesta party dress (14)

   vez, *pl.* **veces:**

     a la — at the same time (13)

     a veces at times, sometimes (1)

     alguna — ever (12)

     dos veces two times (twice) (12)

     muchas veces many times (12)

     una — one time (once) (12)

   vi, viste *see* **ver**

la **vida** life

   el programa de hechos de la — real fact-based program (11)

la **videocasetera** VCR (8)

el **videojuego** video game (3)

el **vidrio** glass *(material)* (13)

   de — (made of) glass (13)

   viejo, -a old (5)

el **viento** wind (7)

   hace — it's windy (7)

   viernes Friday (P)

   el — on Friday (3)

   visitar to visit (7)

   vivir to live (8)

el **vóleibol** volleyball (3)

   vosotros, -as you *pl.* (2)

y and (1)

ya already (10)

   — no no longer, not anymore (9)

yo I (2)

la **zanahoria** carrot (4)

la **zapatería** shoe store (6)

el **zapato** shoe (6)

   los —s de tacón alto high-heeled shoes (14)

el **zoológico** zoo (10)

ENGLISH-SPANISH VOCABULARY

The *English-Spanish Vocabulary* contains all active vocabulary from the text, including vocabulary presented in the grammar sections.

A dash (—) represents the main entry word. For example, — **party** following **birthday** means **birthday party.**

The number following each entry indicates the chapter in which the word or expression is presented. The letter *P* following an entry refers to *El primer paso.*

The following abbreviations are used: *adj.* (adjective), *dir. obj.* (direct object), *f.* (feminine), *fam.* (familiar), *ind. obj.* (indirect object), *inf.* (infinitive), *m.* (masculine), *pl.* (plural), *prep.* (preposition), *pron.* (pronoun), *sing.* (singular).

a, an un, una (2)
able: to be — poder
  (o → ue) (3, 7)
about sobre (11)
ache el dolor (9)
actor, actress el actor, la
  actriz (11)
ad el anuncio (de televisión)
  (11)
adventure film la película de
  aventuras (11)
affectionate cariñoso, -a (5)
after después (de) (3)
  — school después de las
  clases (3)
afternoon la tarde (P)
  — snack la merienda (12)
  good — buenas tardes (P)
  in the — por la tarde (3)
ago hace + *(time)* ... (6)
to **agree** estar de acuerdo (8)
air el aire (13)
all todo, -a (5)
  — right bueno (10)
almost casi (11)
alone solo, -a (3)
already ya (10)
also también (1)
aluminum el aluminio (13)
always siempre (4)

amusement park el parque
  de diversiones (3)
amusing divertido, -a (11)
and y (1)
animal el animal, *pl.* los
  animales (13)
another otro, -a (6)
anywhere: not — ninguna
  parte (7)
apartment el apartamento
  (8)
apple la manzana (4)
April abril (P)
arm el brazo (9)
armchair el sillón, *pl.* los
  sillones (8)
around here por aquí (6)
to **arrive** llegar (10)
art el arte (2)
artistic artístico, -a (1)
to **ask for** pedir (e → i) (12)
at en (P); a (2)
athletic deportista (1)
atmosphere el ambiente (14)
attractive atractivo, -a (5)
August agosto (P)
aunt la tía (5)
  —s and uncles los tíos (5)
autumn el otoño (3)
avenue la avenida (10)

avocado el aguacate (12)
  — dip el guacamole (12)

back la espalda (9)
backpack la mochila (2)
bad malo, -a (4)
  that's too —! ¡Qué
  lástima! (3)
banana el plátano (4)
bank el banco (10)
bargain la ganga (6)
baseball el béisbol (3)
basement el sótano (8)
basketball el básquetbol (3)
bathing suit el traje de baño (7)
bathroom el baño (8)
to **be** estar (3); ser (5)
  — from ser de (P)
  to — able to poder
  (o → ue) (7)
beach la playa (3)
beans los frijoles (12)
  green — las judías verdes (4)
  refried — los frijoles
  refritos (12)
bear el oso (13)
because porque (4)
bed la cama (8)
bedroom el dormitorio (8)

beef la carne (de res) (12)

to **begin** empezar (e → ie) (2)

behind detrás (de) (10)

to **believe** creer (4)

beside al lado (de) (10)

best el / la mejor (11)

better mejor (9)

between entre (10)

beverage la bebida (4)

bicycle la bicicleta (13)

  to ride a — montar en bicicleta (13)

big grande (5)

bill (*in restaurant*) la cuenta (12)

binder (3-ring) la carpeta de argollas (2)

bird el pájaro (13)

birthday el cumpleaños (P)

  — card la tarjeta de cumpleaños (10)

  — party la fiesta de cumpleaños (14)

  happy —! ¡feliz cumpleaños! (14)

black negro, -a (6)

  in — and white en blanco y negro (11)

block la cuadra (10)

  how many —s (from . . .)? ¿a cuántas cuadras (de . . .)? (10)

blond rubio, -a (5)

blouse la blusa (6)

blue azul, *pl.* azules (5, 6)

body el cuerpo (9)

bold atrevido, -a (1)

book el libro (P)

bookstore la librería (10)

boot la bota (7)

to **bore** aburrir (11)

boring aburrido, -a (11)

bottle la botella (13)

bowl el tazón, *pl.* los tazones (12)

boy el muchacho (5)

boyfriend el novio (14)

bracelet la pulsera (14)

bread el pan (4)

breakfast el desayuno (4)

  for — en el desayuno (4)

to **bring** traer (12)

brother el hermano (5)

  —(s) and sister(s) los hermanos (5)

brown marrón, *pl.* marrones (5, 6); *(hair)* castaño (5)

burrito el burrito (12)

bus el autobús, *pl.* los autobuses (10)

  — stop la parada del autobús (10)

busy ocupado, -a (3)

but pero (1)

butter la mantequilla (12)

to **buy** comprar (6)

by por (6)

  — + *vehicle* en + *vehicle* (10)

cake el pastel (12)

calculator la calculadora (2)

to **call** llamar (9)

camera la cámara (7)

can poder (o → ue) (3, 7); la lata (13)

cap el gorro (7)

car el coche (8)

card la tarjeta (10)

cardboard el cartón (13)

carrot la zanahoria (4)

carte: a la — a la carta (12)

cartoons los dibujos animados (11)

cat el gato (5)

cathedral la catedral (7)

cautious prudente (1)

center:

  recycling — el centro de reciclaje (13)

  shopping — el centro comercial (3)

cereal el cereal (4)

chair la silla (8)

chalkboard la pizarra (P)

channel el canal (11)

cheap barato, -a (6)

to **check out a book** sacar un libro (10)

cheese el queso (4)

chestnut(-colored) castaño, -a (5)

chicken el pollo (4)

  — soup la sopa de pollo (4)

chili pepper el chile (12)

chocolate: hot — el chocolate (12)

to **choose** escoger (14)

chore: household — el quehacer (de la casa) (8)

church la iglesia (10)

churro el churro (12)

city la ciudad (7)

class la clase (de) (2, 11)

classmate el compañero, la compañera (P)

classroom la sala de clases (P)

clean limpio, -a (8); puro, -a (13)

to **clean** limpiar (8)

  — up arreglar (8)

to **clear the table** quitar la mesa (8)

to **climb** subir (7)

clinic la clínica (9)

to **close** cerrar (e → ie) (10)

closet el guardarropa (8)

clothes la ropa (6)

coat el abrigo (7)

coffee el café (4)

cold frío, -a (7)

  it's — out hace frío (7)

  to be (very) — tener (mucho) frío (9)

  to have a — tener (un) resfriado (9)

color el color (6)

  in — en colores (11)

  what —? ¿de qué color? (6)

comedy la comedia (11)

comfortable cómodo (8)

comical cómico -a (11)

commercial el anuncio (de televisión) (11)

community la comunidad (10)

concert el concierto (11)

to **conserve** *(energy)* conservar (13)

contaminated contaminado, -a (13)

to **cook** cocinar (1)

cool: it's — out hace fresco (7)

corn el maíz (12)

  — tortilla la tortilla de maíz (12)

corner la esquina (10)

to **cost** costar (o → ue) (6)

costume party la fiesta de disfraces (14)

country el país (7)

countryside el campo (3)

course: of — ¡Claro que sí! (3); por supuesto (13)

  of — not ¡Claro que no! (3)

cousin el primo, la prima (5)

cow la vaca (13)

cup la taza (12)

to **cut** cortar (8)

daily special el plato del día (12)

dance el baile (14)

to **dance** bailar (14)

danger el peligro (13)

daring atrevido, -a (1)

date la fecha (P, 14)

  what's today's —? ¿cuál es la fecha de hoy? (P)

daughter la hija (5)

day el día (P)

  every — todos los días (3)

December diciembre (P)

to **decorate** decorar (14)

decoration la decoración *pl.* las decoraciones (14)

delicious sabroso, -a (4)

delighted encantado, -a (14)

dentist el / la dentista (9)

department store el almacén, *pl.* los almacenes (6)

to **depend** depender (14)

to **deposit** depositar (10)

desk el escritorio (8); el pupitre *(student)* (P)

dessert el postre (12)

  for — de postre (12)

detective show el programa de detectives (11)

dictionary el diccionario (2)

difficult difícil (2)

dining room el comedor (8)

dinner la cena (4)

  for — en la cena (4)

dirty sucio, -a (8)

to **disagree** no estar de acuerdo (8)

disgusting: that's — ! ¡qué asco! (4)

dish el plato (12)

  main — el plato principal (12)

to **do** hacer (8)

doctor el médico, la médica (9)

documentary el documental (11)

dog el perro (5)

dollar el dólar (6)

door la puerta (8)

dot: on the — en punto (11)

to **draw** dibujar (1)

dress el vestido (6)

  party — el vestido de fiesta (14)

dresser la cómoda (8)

to **drink** beber (4, 12)

drugstore la farmacia (10)

dumb tonto, -a (11)

to **dust** sacudir (8)

ear el oído (9)

  —ache el dolor de oído (9)

early temprano (10)

earring el arete (14)

Earth la Tierra (13)

easy fácil (2)

to **eat** comer (4, 12)

educational show el programa educativo (11)

egg el huevo (4)

eight ocho (P)

eighteen dieciocho (P)

eight hundred ochocientos (10)

eighth octavo, -a (2, 8)

eighty ochenta (5)

either tampoco (1)

elegant elegante (14)

elephant el elefante (13)

eleven once (P)

else más (8)

  anything — algo más (12)

enchilada la enchilada (12)

to **end** terminar (2)

endangered en peligro de extinción (13)

energy la energía (13)

English *(language)* el inglés (2)

environment el medio ambiente (13)

evening la noche (P)

  good — buenas noches, buenas tardes (P)

  in the — por la noche, por la tarde (3)

ever alguna vez (12)

every day todos los días (3)

everyone todos, -as (5)

exciting emocionante (11)

excuse me perdón (6)

to **exercise** hacer ejercicio (9)

expensive caro, -a (6)

to **explore** explorar (7)

eye el ojo (9)

facing enfrente (de) (10)

fact el hecho (11)

  — **-based program** el programa de hechos de la vida real (11)

factory la fábrica (13)

fair regular, así, así (P)

fall el otoño (3)

family la familia (3)

  — **room** la sala de estar (8)

fantastic fantástico, -a (7)

far (from) lejos (de) (8)

to **fascinate** fascinar (11)

fascinating fascinante (11)

father el padre (5)

February febrero (P)

to **feel** sentir

  how do you —? ¿cómo te sientes? (9)

  I — well / ill me siento bien / mal (9)

fever la fiebre (9)

  to have a — tener fiebre (9)

few: a — unos, unas (4)

fifteen quince (P)

fifth quinto, -a (2, 8)

fifty cincuenta (2)

film la película (11)

finger el dedo (9)

first primero (primer), -a (P, 2, 8)

fish el pescado (4)

  to go —ing ir de pesca (3)

to **fit** quedar (6)

five cinco (P)

five hundred quinientos (10)

flan el flan (12)

floor el piso (8)

flour la harina (12)

  — **tortilla** la tortilla de harina (12)

flower la flor (13)

flu la gripe (9)

  to have the — tener gripe (9)

folder la carpeta (2)

food comida (12)

foot el pie (9)

  on — a pie (10)

football el fútbol americano (3)

for para (2); por (6)

forest la selva (7)

  rain — la selva tropical (7)

fork el tenedor (12)

forty cuarenta (2)

four cuatro (P)

four hundred cuatrocientos (10)

fourteen catorce (P)

fourth cuarto, -a (2)

French fries las papas fritas (4)

Friday viernes (P)

  on — el viernes (3)

friend el amigo, la amiga (3)

friendly simpático, -a (5)

front: in — of enfrente de (10); delante de (12)

fruit la fruta (4)

funny gracioso, -a (1); divertido, -a (11)

fur la piel (13)

furniture los muebles (8)

game el partido (10)

garage el garaje (8)

garbage la basura (8)

gas station la estación de servicio (10)

gee! ¡vaya! (7)

generally generalmente (3)

generous generoso, -a (1)

get-together la reunión (14)

gift el regalo (10)

  — **shop** la tienda de regalos (10)

girl la muchacha (5)

girlfriend la novia (14)

to **give** dar (14)

  to — a gift regalar (14)

glass el vaso (12); *(material)* el vidrio (13)

  (made of) — de vidrio (13)

glasses los anteojos (7)

glove el guante (7)

to **go** ir (3)

  — **on!** ¡vaya! (7)

  to be —ing to + *verb* ir a + *inf.* (3)

  to — fishing ir de pesca (3)

  to — on vacation ir de vacaciones (7)

  to — shopping ir de compras (3)

  to — to school ir a la escuela (1)

good bueno (buen), -a (P)

  — **afternoon** buenas tardes (P)

  — **evening** buenas noches (P)

  — **morning** buenos días (P)

  — **night** buenas noches (P)

  it's a — thing that . . . menos mal que . . . (7)

good-by adiós (P)

good-looking guapo, -a (5)

goodness: my —! ¡vaya! (7)

gorilla el gorila (13)

grandfather el abuelo (5)

grandmother la abuela (5)

grandparents los abuelos (5)

grape la uva (4)

gray gris, *pl.* grises (5, 6)

— **hair** pelo canoso (5)

great! ¡genial! (3)

green verde (5, 6)

— **beans** las judías verdes (4)

groceries los comestibles (10)

guest el invitado, la invitada (14)

guitar la guitarra (1)

gymnasium el gimnasio (3)

habit: to be in the — of soler (o → ue) + *inf.* (14)

hair el pelo (5)

half:

— **an hour** media hora (11)

— **-past** y media (2)

ham el jamón (4)

hamburger la hamburguesa (4)

hand la mano (9)

—**made** hecho, -a a mano (14)

handsome guapo, -a (5)

hard difícil (2)

hard-working trabajador, -a (1)

to **have** tener (2, 5)

to — a good (bad) time pasarlo bien (mal) (14)

to — to tener que + *inf.* (8)

he él (2)

head la cabeza (9)

—**ache** dolor de cabeza (9)

health la salud (4); *(class)* las ciencias de la salud (2)

hello! ¡hola! (P)

to **help** ayudar (1)

may I — you? ¿qué desea (Ud.)? (6)

her su, sus (5); *dir. obj. pron.* la (6); *ind. obj. pron.* le (9)

here aquí (2)

around — por aquí (6)

— **it is** aquí está (2)

hi! ¡hola! (P)

high-heeled shoes los zapatos de tacón alto (14)

him *dir. obj. pron.* lo (6); *ind. obj. pron.* le (9)

his su, sus (5)

hobby el pasatiempo (3)

home: at — en casa (1)

homework la tarea (2)

horrible horrible (4)

horror movie la película de terror (11)

horse el caballo (13)

hospital el hospital (9)

hot *(flavor)* picante (12)

it's — out hace calor (7)

to be — *(person)* tener calor (9)

hotel el hotel (10)

house la casa (8)

— **specialty** la especialidad de la casa (12)

household chore el quehacer (de la casa) (8)

¡how! qué + *adj.* (6)

how? ¿cómo? (P)

— **are you?** ¿cómo está (usted)? ¿cómo estás (tú)? (P)

— **long has it been since** . . . ¿cuánto (tiempo) hace que. . . ? (9)

— **many?** ¿cuántos, -as? (5)

— **much?** ¿cuánto? (6)

— **old are you?** ¿cuántos años tienes? (P)

— **old is . . . ?** cuántos años tiene . . . ? (5)

—**'s it going?** ¿qué tal? (P)

hundred cien (5); ciento (6)

hungry: to be — tener hambre (4)

to **hurt** doler (o → ue) (9); lastimarse + *part of body* (9)

I yo (2)

ice cream el helado (12)

iced tea el té helado (4)

if si (10)

ill enfermo, -a (3)

I feel — me siento mal (9)

impatient impaciente (1)

in en (P)

— **order to** para + *inf.* (7)

inexpensive barato, -a (6)

ingredient el ingrediente (12)

intelligent inteligente (5)

interest: place of — el lugar de interés (7)

to **interest** interesar (11)

interesting interesante (11)

to **introduce** presentar (14)

invitation la invitación *pl.* las invitaciones (14)

to **invite** invitar (14)

it *dir. obj.* lo (6)

jacket la chaqueta (6)

jaguar el jaguar (13)

January enero (P)

jeans los jeans (6)

jewelry las joyas (14)

juice el jugo (4)

orange — el jugo de naranja (4)

July julio (P)

June junio (P)

kind amable (1); la clase (11)
kitchen la cocina (8)
knife el cuchillo (12)
to **know** saber (13); conocer (14)

lacking: to be — faltar a (12)
lake el lago (7)
lamp la lámpara (8)
to **last** durar (11)
last pasado, -a (7)
— **night** anoche (10)
late tarde (10)
see you —r hasta luego (P)
laundry room el lavadero (8)
lawn el césped (8)
to mow the — cortar el césped (8)
lazy perezoso, -a (1)
to **learn** aprender (2)
least el / la / los / las menos + *adj.* (11)
leather el cuero (8)
(made of) — de cuero (8)
to **leave** salir (7)
left izquierdo, -a (9)
to the — (of) a la izquierda (de) (10)
leg la pierna (9)
lemonade la limonada (4)
less menos (4, 11)
more or — más o menos (4)
letter la carta (10)
lettuce la lechuga (4)
library la biblioteca (10)
life la vida (11)
light la luz, *pl.* las luces (13)
to **like** gustar (5)
he / she —s le gusta(n) (5)

I / you — (a mí) me / (a ti) te gusta(n) (1)
I'd — quisiera (7)
likewise igualmente (P)
to **listen** escuchar (1)
little pequeño, -a (5)
a — un poco (de) (11)
to **live** vivir (8)
living room la sala (8)
located: to be — quedar (10)
long largo, -a (11)
to **look for** buscar (6)
lot:
a — mucho (1)
a — of mucho, -a (2)
to **love** encantar (5)
he / she —s le encanta(n) (5)
I — me encanta(n) (4)
loving cariñoso, -a (5)
lunch el almuerzo (2)
for — en el almuerzo (4)

ma'am señora (6)
made hecho, -a (14)
— of de + *material* (8)
magazine la revista (13)
to **mail** enviar (10)
to **make** hacer (8)
mall el centro comercial (3)
man el hombre (5)
March marzo (P)
marker el marcador (2)
match el partido (10)
mathematics las matemáticas (2)
matter: what's the —? ¿qué pasa? (9)
May mayo (P)
me *obj. pron.* me (9); *after prep.* mí (1, 12)
meal la comida (4)
to **meet:**
I'd like you to — te presento a… (14)

pleased to — you mucho gusto (P); encantado, -a (14)
menu el menú (12)
messy desordenado, -a (1)
metal el metal (8)
(made of) — de metal (8)
midnight la medianoche (11)
mild *(flavor)* no picante (12)
milk la leche (4)
minute el minuto (11)
mirror el espejo (8)
miss la señorita (P, 6)
miss: to be —ing faltar a (12)
modern moderno, -a (8)
Monday lunes (P)
on — el lunes (3)
money el dinero (10)
month el mes (P)
monument el monumento (10)
more más (4, 11)
— or less más o menos (4)
morning la mañana (3)
good — buenos días (P)
in the — por la mañana (3)
most: the — el / la / los / las más + *adj.* (11)
mother la madre (5)
mountain la montaña (7)
mouth la boca (9)
movie la película (11)
— theater el cine (1)
to go to the —s ir al cine (1)
to show a — dar una película (11)
to **mow the lawn** cortar el césped (8)
Mr. (el) señor (P)
Mrs. (la) señora (P)
much mucho, -a (2)
how —? ¿cuánto? (6)

museum el museo (7)
music la música (2)
  — **program** el programa
    musical (11)
musical film la película
  musical (11)
my mi, mis (3)

name el nombre (5)
  his / her / their — is se
    llama(n) (5)
  my — is me llamo (P)
  what's your —? ¿cómo te
    llamas? (P)
napkin la servilleta (12)
near cerca (de) (8)
neat ordenado, -a (1)
necessary: it's — to hay
  que (13)
neck el cuello (9)
necklace el collar (14)
necktie la corbata (14)
to **need** necesitar (2)
neither tampoco (1)
  — ... nor ni ... ni (1)
never nunca (4)
new nuevo, -a (6)
New Year's Eve party la
  fiesta de fin de año (14)
news las noticias (11)
newspaper el periódico (13)
next to al lado (de) (10)
nice amable (1); simpático, -a
  (5)
night noche
  at — de la noche (11)
  good — buenas noches (P)
  last — anoche (10)
nine nueve (P)
nine hundred novecientos
  (10)
nineteen diecinueve (P)
ninety noventa (5)
no no (P)
  — longer ya no (9)

nobody nadie (5)
noon el mediodía (11)
nor: neither . . . — ni ... ni (1)
nose la nariz (9)
not no (P)
  — anymore ya no (9)
  — at all nada (1); de
    ninguna manera (14)
  — yet todavía no (11)
notebook el cuaderno (2)
nothing nada (9)
November noviembre (P)
now ahora (9)
nowhere ninguna parte (7)
number el número (P)
  phone — el número de
    teléfono (P)
nurse's office la enfermería
  (9)

ocean el océano (13)
October octubre (P)
of de (5)
  — course ¡Claro que sí!
    (3); por supuesto (13)
  — course not ¡Claro que
    no! (3)
often a menudo (12)
ok bueno (10)
old viejo -a (5); antiguo, -a (8)
  how — are you? ¿cuántos
    años tienes? (P)
  how — is . . . ? ¿cuántos
    años tiene . . . ? (5)
older mayor (5)
on en (P); sobre (12)
  — the dot en punto (11)
  — time puntualmente (11)
  — top (of) encima (de)
    (12)
once una vez (12)
one uno (un), -a (P)
  it's — o'clock es la una
    (2)
onion la cebolla (4)

only sólo (5)
  — child el hijo único, la
    hija única (5)
to **open** abrir (10)
opposite enfrente (de) (10)
or o (P)
  not . . . — ni ... ni (1)
orange *(color)* anaranjado, -a
  (6)
orange la naranja (4)
  — juice el jugo de naranja
    (4)
to **order** pedir (e → i) (12)
other otro, -a (6)
ouch! ¡ay! (9)
ought to deber (4)
our nuestro, -a (8)
outgoing sociable (1)

pants los pantalones (6)
pantyhose las pantimedias (6)
paper el papel (P)
  sheet of — la hoja de
    papel (P)
parents los padres (5)
park el parque (3)
  amusement — el parque
    de diversiones (3)
part: to be a — of formar
  parte de (13)
party la fiesta (14)
to **pass** pasar (12)
passport el pasaporte (7)
past pasado, -a (7)
  half- — y media (2)
  quarter — y cuarto (2)
pastime el pasatiempo (3)
pastry el pastel (12)
patient *adj.* paciente (1)
to **pay** pagar (6)
pea el guisante (4)
pen el bolígrafo (P)
pencil el lápiz, *pl.* los lápices
  (2)
people la gente (13)

pepper la pimienta (12)
   stuffed — el chile relleno (12)
peppery picante (12)
period la hora (2)
person la persona (5)
personal personal (14)
phone el teléfono (1)
   — book la guía telefónica (13)
   — number el número de teléfono (P)
photo la foto (7)
physical education la educación física (2)
physician el médico, la médica (9)
to **pick up** recoger (13)
picture el cuadro (8)
pink rosado, -a (6)
place el lugar (14)
   — of interest el lugar de interés (7)
to **place** poner (8)
to **plan** pensar + *inf.* (7)
plant la planta (13)
plastic el plástico (13)
   (made of) — de plástico (13)
plate el plato (12)
to **play** jugar (u → ue) (3); tocar (1)
please por favor (P)
pleased to meet you mucho gusto (P); encantado, -a (14)
pocket folder la carpeta (2)
police la policía (10)
   — station la estación de policía (10)
polluted contaminado, -a (13)
pool la piscina (3)
post card la tarjeta postal (10)
post office el correo (10)

poster el cartel (8)
potato la papa (4)
   baked — la papa al horno (4)
   French-fried — la papa frita (4)
practical práctico, -a (14)
to **practice** practicar (1)
to **prefer** preferir (e → ie) (4, 8)
   I — me gusta más (1); prefiero (4)
to **prepare** preparar (14)
pretty bonito, -a (5)
program el programa (11)
to **protect** proteger (13)
public transportation el transporte público (13)
pure puro, -a (13)
purple morado, -a (6)
to **put** poner (8)
pyramid la pirámide (7)

quarter cuarto, -a (2)
   — past y cuarto (2)
quesadilla la quesadilla (12)
quiet callado, -a (1)

rain la lluvia (7)
to **rain** llover (o → ue) (7)
   it's —ing llueve (7)
raincoat el impermeable (7)
rain forest la selva tropical (7)
rather bastante (8)
to **read** leer (1)
real real (11)
realistic realista (11)
really? ¿de veras? (1); ¡no me digas! (3)
to **receive** recibir (14)
to **recycle** reciclar (13)
recycling center el centro de reciclaje (13)
red rojo, -a (6)

   — -haired pelirrojo, -a (5)
to **reduce** reducir (13)
refrigerator el refrigerador (8)
relative el pariente, la parienta (14)
to **rest** descansar (7)
restaurant el restaurante (10)
to **return** regresar (7); devolver (o → ue) (10)
rice el arroz (4)
right? ¿verdad? (4)
right derecho, -a (9)
   — away en seguida (12)
   to be — tener razón (8)
   to the — (of) a la derecha (de) (10)
romantic movie la película romántica (11)
room el cuarto (8)
round redondo, -a (8)
to **row** pasear en bote (7)
rowboat el bote (7)
ruins las ruinas (7)
ruler la regla (2)

sad triste (11)
salad la ensalada (4)
salt la sal (12)
same: the — thing lo mismo (12)
sandwich el sandwich (4)
Saturday sábado (P)
   on — el sábado (3)
sauce la salsa (12)
saucer el platillo (12)
to **save** *(energy)* conservar (13)
to **say** decir (13)
   how do you — . . . ? ¿cómo se dice . . . ? (P)
   it is said . . . se dice . . . (P)
   you don't — ! ¡no me digas! (3)

to scare dar miedo a (11)

scarf: winter — la bufanda (7)

schedule el horario (2)

school la escuela (1)

after — después de las clases (3)

science las ciencias (2)

science fiction la ciencia ficción (11)

sea el mar (7)

season la estación, *pl.* las estaciones (3)

second segundo, -a (2, 8)

to see ver (1)

let's — a ver (2)

to sell vender (12)

semester el semestre (2)

to send enviar (10)

to separate separar (13)

September septiembre (P)

serious serio, -a (1)

to serve servir (e → i) (12)

to set poner (8)

— the table poner la mesa (8)

seven siete (P)

seven hundred setecientos (10)

seventeen diecisiete (P)

seventh séptimo, -a (2)

seventy setenta (5)

shame: That's a —! ¡Qué lástima! (3)

shampoo el champú (10)

sharp en punto (11)

she ella (2)

sheet of paper la hoja de papel (P)

shirt la camisa (6)

T- — la camiseta (6)

shoe el zapato (6)

high-heeled —s los zapatos de tacón alto (14)

— store la zapatería (6)

shopping:

— center el centro comercial (3)

to go — ir de compras (3)

short *(height)* bajo, -a (5)

— *(length)* corto, -a (11)

shorts los pantalones cortos (6)

should deber + *inf.* (4)

show el programa (11)

to show *movie or TV program* dar (11)

sick enfermo, -a (3)

I feel — me siento mal (9)

silly tonto, -a (11)

since: it's been *(time)* **—** hace + *(time)* + que (9)

to sing cantar (14)

sir señor (6)

sister la hermana (5)

sitcom la comedia (11)

six seis (P)

six hundred seiscientos (10)

sixteen dieciséis (P)

sixth sexto, -a (2, 8)

sixty sesenta (5)

to skate patinar (1)

to ski esquiar (7)

ski cap el gorro (7)

to skin-dive bucear (7)

skirt la falda (6)

to sleep dormir (o → ue) (9)

sleepy: to be — tener sueño (9)

small pequeño, -a (5)

snack *(afternoon)* la merienda (12)

for a — de merienda (12)

snake la serpiente (13)

sneakers los tenis (6)

snow la nieve (7)

to snow nevar (e → ie) (7)

it's —ing nieva (7)

soap el jabón (10)

— opera la telenovela (11)

soccer el fútbol (3)

social studies las ciencias sociales (2)

sock el calcetín, *pl.* los calcetines (6)

sofa el sofá (8)

soft drink el refresco (4)

some unos, unas (4); algunos, -as (14)

someone, somebody alguien (14)

something algo (4)

— else algo más (12)

sometimes a veces (1)

son el hijo (5)

—s; —s and daughters los hijos (5)

sorry: I'm — lo siento (2)

to sort separar (13)

so-so así, así, regular (P)

soup la sopa (4)

souvenir el recuerdo (7)

Spanish *(language)* el español (2)

special: daily — el plato del día (12)

specialty: house — la especialidad de la casa (12)

spell: how do you — . . . ? ¿Cómo se escribe . . . ? (P)

spicy picante (12)

spoon la cuchara (12)

sports los deportes (1)

— program el programa deportivo (11)

spring la primavera (3)

square cuadrado, -a (8)

stadium el estadio (10)

stamp el sello (10)

to start empezar (e → ie) (2)

station la estación, *pl.* las estaciones (10)

to stay (in bed) quedarse (en la cama) (9)

steak el bistec (4)

stereo el equipo de sonido (8)

still todavía (9)

stingy tacaño, -a (1)

stomach el estómago (9)
  —ache el dolor de estómago (9)
store la tienda (6)
  clothing — la tienda de ropa (6)
  department — el almacén, *pl.* los almacenes (6)
  discount — la tienda de descuentos (6)
story *(of a building)* el piso (8)
stove la estufa (8)
street la calle (10)
student el / la estudiante (P)
to study estudiar (1)
subway el metro (10)
  — station la estación del metro (10)
sugar el azúcar (12)
suit el traje (14)
  bathing — el traje de baño (7)
suitcase la maleta (7)
summer el verano (3)
sun el sol (7)
to sunbathe tomar el sol (7)
Sunday domingo (P)
  on — el domingo (3)
sunglasses los anteojos de sol (7)
sunny: it's — hace sol (7)
suntan lotion el bronceador (7)
supermarket el supermercado (10)
surprise party la fiesta de sorpresa (14)
sweater el suéter (6)
sweatshirt la sudadera (6)
to swim nadar (1)
swimming pool la piscina (3)

table la mesa (P)
  to clear the — quitar la mesa (8)
  to set the — poner la mesa (8)
tablecloth el mantel (12)
tablet la pastilla (10)
taco el taco (12)
to take llevar (7); tomar (9)
  to — out sacar (8)
  to — pictures sacar fotos (7)
  to — a walk ir a pasear (10)
to talk hablar (1)
  to — on the phone hablar por teléfono (1)
  — show el programa de entrevistas (11)
tall alto, -a (5)
tape recorder la grabadora (2)
to taste probar (o → ue) (12)
tasty sabroso, -a (4)
taxi el taxi (10)
tea el té (4)
  iced — el té helado (4)
to teach enseñar (2)
teacher el profesor, la profesora (P)
teeth las muelas (9)
telephone el teléfono (1); *see also* **phone**
television la tele(visión) (1)
  to watch — ver la tele(visión) (1)
temple el templo (10)
ten diez (P)
tennis el tenis (3)
  — shoes los tenis (6)
terrible terrible (9)
thank you gracias (P)
that ese, esa; (6); que (5)
  isn't — so? ¿verdad? (4)
  —'s too bad! ¡qué lástima! (3)
  —'s why por eso (11)

the el, la, los, las (P, 2)
theater *(movie)* el cine (1); el teatro (10)
their su, sus (8)
them *after prep.* ellos, ellas (3); los, las *dir. obj. pron.* (6); les *ind. obj. pron.* (11)
then luego (10)
there allí (2)
  — is / are hay (P)
  — it is allí está (2)
therefore por eso (11)
these estos, estas (6)
they ellos, ellas (2)
thing la cosa (8)
to think creer (4); pensar (e → ie) (11)
  I don't — so creo que no (4)
  I — so creo que sí (4)
  to — about pensar en (11)
third tercer, -a (2, 8)
thirsty: to be — tener sed (4)
thirteen trece (P)
thirty treinta (P)
this este, esta (6)
those esos, esas (6)
thousand mil (10)
threat la amenaza (13)
three tres (P)
three hundred trescientos (10)
three-ring binder la carpeta de argollas (2)
throat la garganta (9)
  sore — el dolor de garganta (9)
  — lozenges las pastillas para la garganta (10)
Thursday jueves (P)
  on — el jueves (3)
ticket la entrada (14)
tidy ordenado, -a (1)
tie la corbata (14)
tiger el tigre (13)

time la hora (2, 14); el tiempo (11); la vez (12)

   at the same — a la vez (13)

   at —s a veces (1)

   at what — ¿a qué hora? (2)

   many —s muchas veces (12)

   on — puntualmente (11)

   to have a good (bad) — pasarlo bien (mal) (14)

   what — is it? ¿qué hora es? (2)

tired cansado, -a (3)

to a (3)

   in order — para + *inf.* (7)

toast el pan tostado (4)

today hoy (P)

   not — hoy no (3)

toe el dedo del pie (9)

tomato el tomate (4)

   — soup la sopa de tomate (4)

tomorrow mañana (P, 3)

too también (1); demasiado (11)

   me — a mí también (1)

toothache el dolor de muelas (9)

toothpaste la pasta dentífrica (10)

tortilla la tortilla (12)

touching emocionante (11)

town square la plaza (10)

train el tren (10)

   — station la estación del tren (10)

tree el árbol (13)

to try probar (o → ue) (12)

Tuesday martes (P)

   on — el martes (3)

to turn off apagar (13)

twelve doce (P)

twenty veinte (P)

twice dos veces (12)

twin el gemelo, la gemela (5)

two dos (P)

two hundred doscientos (10)

type la clase (11)

typical típico, -a (12)

ugly feo, -a (5)

umbrella el paraguas (7)

uncle el tío (5)

uncomfortable incómodo, -a (8)

under(neath) debajo de (12)

unfriendly antipático, -a (5)

unpleasant antipático, -a (5)

until hasta (11)

us *after prep.* nosotros, -as (3); *obj. pron.* nos (11)

to use usar (13)

usually generalmente (3)

vacation las vacaciones (7)

   to go on — ir de vacaciones (7)

to vacuum pasar la aspiradora (8)

vacuum cleaner la aspiradora (8)

VCR la videocasetera (8)

vegetable la verdura (4)

   — soup la sopa de verduras (4)

very muy (P, 1)

video game el videojuego (3)

to visit visitar (7)

volleyball el vóleibol (3)

waiter, waitress el camarero, la camarera (12)

walk: to take a — ir a pasear (10)

walking a pie (10)

to want querer (e → ie) (3, 7)

to wash lavar (8)

to watch ver (1)

water el agua (4)

waterfall las cataratas (7)

we nosotros, -as (2)

to wear llevar (6)

weather el tiempo (7)

   the — is nice (bad) hace buen (mal) tiempo (7)

   — forecast el pronóstico del tiempo (11)

   what's the — like? ¿qué tiempo hace? (7)

Wednesday miércoles (P)

   on — el miércoles (3)

week la semana (P)

weekend el fin de semana (3)

welcome: you're — de nada (3)

well bien (P); *(to indicate pause)* pues (1)

went fui, fuiste (7, 10)

western la película del oeste (11)

whale la ballena (13)

what qué (2); cuál(es)? (11)

when ¿cuándo? (P); cuando (7)

where? ¿dónde? (3); donde (7)

   from —? ¿de dónde? (P)

   (to) —? ¿adónde? (3)

whether si (10)

which? ¿cual? (11)

   — ones ¿cuáles? (11)

white blanco, -a (6)

   in black and — en blanco y negro (11)

who que (5)

who? whom? ¿quién(es)? (2, 5)

why ¿por qué? (4)

   that's — por eso (11)

wind el viento (7)

windy: It's —. Hace viento. (7)

window la ventana (8)

winter el invierno (3)

   — scarf la bufanda (7)

with con (3)
  — me conmigo (3)
  — you contigo (3)
to withdraw *(money)* sacar (10)
wolf el lobo (13)
woman la mujer (5)
wonderful fantástico (7);
  ¡genial! (3)
wood la madera (13)
  (made of) — de madera
  (8)
to work trabajar (10)
worse peor (9)
worst el / la (los / las)
  peor(es) (11)
worthwhile: it's (not) —
  (no) vale la pena (13)
wow! ¡vaya! (7)
wristwatch el reloj pulsera
  (14)

to write escribir (14)
wrong:
  to be — no tener razón (8)
  what's —? ¿qué tienes? (9)

year el año (P)
  New —'s Eve party la
  fiesta de fin de año (14)
  to be . . . —s old tener . . .
  años (P, 5)
yellow amarillo, -a (6)
yes sí (P)
yesterday ayer (10)
yet: not — todavía no (11)
you *fam.* tú *; formal* usted
  (Ud.), *pl.* ustedes (Uds.)
  (2); lo, la, los, las *dir. obj.*
  pron. (6); te *fam. dir. obj.*

pron. (8); le, les *ind. obj.*
pron. (9, 11); ti *fam. after*
prep. (1, 12)
young *adj.* joven (5)
  —er menor *pl.* menores (5)
  — lady la joven (6)
  — man, sir el joven (6)
  — people los jóvenes (6)
your tu (2); tus (3); su, sus
  (8)
yuck! ¡qué asco! (4)

zero cero (P)
zoo el zoológico (10)

Índice

In almost all cases, structures are first presented in the *Vocabulario para conversar*, where they are practiced lexically in conversational contexts. They are explained later, usually in the *Gramática en contexto* section of that chapter. Light-face numbers refer to pages where structures are initially presented or, after explanation, where student reminders occur. **Bold-face numbers** refer to pages where structures are explained or otherwise highlighted.

ACKNOWLEDGMENTS

Illustrations Kaz Aizawa: pp. **346-347, 439;** Andrea Baruffi: pp. **90-101, 104-108;** Mark Bender: pp **470-471;** Jennifer Bolten: pp. **148, 397;** Margaret Carsello: pp. **63, 343;** Mark Charlier: pp. **67, 77, 147;** Rick Clubb: pp. **30-44, 210-211, 252-259, 261-271, 276-277, 281;** Tim Foley: pp. **340-341;** Joe Fournier: pp. **304-305;** Elissé Jo Goldstein: pp. **316-326, 330-332, 334-336, 345;** Chuck Gonzales: pp. **150-151;** David Gothard: pp. **274-275;** Patti Green: pp. **78, 142, 144-145;** Donna Ingemanson: pp. **40, 46, 51;** Iskra Lettering Design: Hand lettering on cover and pp.**I-XIII, 1, 3, 27, 55, 87, 119, 151, 181, 217, 249, 283, 313, 347, 381, 415, 447;** Paul Jermann: pp. **118-119;** Mike Kasun: pp. **376-377;** Hiro Kimura: pp. **350-357, 362-371;** Mapping Specialists Limited: pp. **XIV-XVII, 11;** James Mellett: pp. **58-62, 64, 66-67, 71-72, 74-76, 85, 210-218, 224-227;** Susan Melrath: pp. **408-409;** Jane Mjolsness: p. **443;** Lori Osiecki: pp. **184-193, 195-196, 201-203, 205-207, 215;** Donna Perrone: pp. **49, 69, 243;** Rob Porazinski: pp. **173, 307, 308;** Karen Pritchett: pp. **154-163, 167-170;** Mike Reed: pp. **418-429, 432-437;** Javier Romero Design: p. **46;** Sandra Shap: pp. **286-295, 299-303;** Scott Snow: pp. **7-23, 450-459, 462-467;** Mark Stearney: pp. **414-415;** Stephen Sweeny: pp. **468-469;** Susan Williams: pp. **175, 240;** Elizabeth Wolf: pp. **122-130, 135-137, 139, 141; 149, 384-396, 398-405, 413.**

Photographs **Front and back covers,** II, XVIII-1: Suzanne L. Murphy/FPG. All rights reserved.; **IV:** Otis Imboden ©National Geographic Society; **VI, 19:** David Ryan/DDB Stock Photo; **VII**(t), 28, 54-55, 63, 71, 219(t), 251(t): ©Peter Menzel; **VII**(b), 57(b), 77, 133, 152, 165(b), 173(tl), 189(b), 361(b): ©Ulrike Welsch; **VIII**(t), 89(t): James K. Hackett/Leo de Wys, Inc.; **VIII**(b), 40, 48(b), 51, 56, 136, 148, 182, 188(r), 238(br), 241(t), 244(l), 245(b), 284(t): David R. Frazier Photolibrary; **XI**(t),57(t), 79, 81, 86-87, 89(b), 102, 125, 131, 133(t), 175, 177(b), 183(t), 183(b), 189(b), 216-217, 231(r), 238(cr), 250, 260, 279(t), 321(t), 321(c), 380-381, 446-447, 448(b): Frerck/Odyssey/Chicago; **IX**(b), **XI**(b), 189(t), 189(c), 194, 265, 315(t), 328-329, 346-347, 397, 407, 416, 438, 441(t), 473: ©Beryl Goldberg Photographer; **X**(t), 230-231: ©1989 Glenn Randall; **X**(bl), 50(bl), 173(br), 273(l): Owen Franken/Stock Boston; **X**(br): M. Díaz Vélez/DDB Stock Photo; **XI**(t), 343: ©K. Preuss/The Image Works; **5**(t): Gerardo Ramírez/Photography by Vicki Lee Ragan; **6**(tl): Tom McCarthy/PhotoEdit; **6**(tr), 166, 307: Tony Freeman/PhotoEdit; **6**(bl): Richard Hutchings/PhotoEdit; **6**(br), 26-27, 29(b), 47(t), 48(t), 50(br), 52, 80, 120(b), 173(bl), 188(l), 198(l), 232(t), 232(c), 238(t), 238(cl), 238(bl), 241(b), 305(b), 337, 395: Chip & Rosa Maria de la Cueva Peterson; **14:** Otis Imboden ©National Geographic Society; **18:** ©David Lavender; **29**(t), 348, 449: ©Owen Franken; **41, 47**(b), 265(inset), 361(t): Stuart Cohen/Comstock; **42:** ©Carl Toth; **46:** ©Sven Martson/Comstock; **50**(t), 339: ©Jack Parsons; **69, 120**(t): ©Nancy D'Antonio; **81**(t),199(t), 261(t), 279(b), 349(b), 405: Joe Viesti/Viesti Associates; **86-87**(t), 88-89(t): Adamsmith Productions/Westlight; **88:** ©Diane Joy Schmidt; **103**(t), 118-119, 180-181, 219(c): ©Wolfgang Kaehler; **103**(b), 111(b), 116, 411:** ©D. Donne Bryant; **104:** Pete Seaward/Tony Stone Images; **109:** ©M. Algaze/The Images Works; **110:** ©Jack Vartoogian. All rights reserved.; **111**(t), 382(t): Robert Fried/Stock Boston; **112:** Courtesy Paramount Pictures/United International; Pictures, Madrid; **121:** ©Martha Cooper/Viesti Associates; **133**(c): Steve Vidler/Leo de Wys, Inc.; **138:** Focus On Sports; **150-151:** Viesti Associates; **152:** Bohdan Hrynewych/Stock Boston; **165**(t): Randall Hyman/Stock Boston; **171:** Museo Nacional de Historia, Castillo de Chapultepec, Mexico City; **174**(l): David Young Wolff/PhotoEdit; **174**(r): Mary Kate Denny/PhotoEdit; **176**(t): Ilene Perlman/Stock Boston; **176**(b), 343, 460, 469: Bob Daemmrich/Stock Boston; **177**(t): ©R.S. Wagner; **177**(c): Spencer Grant/Stock Boston; **199**(b): Courtesy the Puerto Rican Tourism Company; **200:** Superstock; **214:** Peter Menzel/Stock Boston; **218:** Eric Lessing/Art Resource; **219**(b): Max & Bea Hunn/DDB Stock Photo; **231**(l),232(b): ©David Wells/The Image Works; **243**(t): The Bettmann Archive; **243**(b): Randy G. Taylo/Leo de Wys, Inc.; **244**(r): Ray Pfortner/Peter Arnold, Inc.; **245**(t), 245(c): Comstock; **248-249:** Chris R. Sharp/DDB Stock Photo; **251**(b): Rhoda Sidney/PhotoEdit; **261**(b): Vince Dewitt/DDB Stock Photo; **272:** Cahlus Goldin/DDB Stock Photo; **273**(r): M. Díaz Vélez/DDB Stock Photo; **278:** Ken Ross/Viesti Associates; **282-283:** Schalkwijk/Art Resource; **284**(b): Jeff Greenberg/PhotoEdit; **285:** ©Victor Englebert; **296:** Jeff Greenberg/The Image Works; **297:** Alyx Kellington/DDB Stock Photo; **305**(t), 315(b): M. Antman/The Image Works; **309:** Bob Daemmrich/The Image Works; **312-313:** Rob Crandall/Stock Boston; **314:** Algaze/The Image Works; **321**(b): Charles Kennard/Stock Boston; **327:** Art Museum of the Americas/Organization of American States; **329:** Alan Landau for ScottForesman; **343**(inset), 440, 472: Bob Daemmrich Photography; **349**(t): ©Maler/Retna Ltd., NY; **373**(t), 375: Kobal Collection; **373**(b): Imapress/Archive Photos; **376-377:** Courtesy Coral Picture Corporation/Radio Caracas Televisión, Venezuela; **378:** Jack Demuth for ScottForesman; **382**(b): ©1990 Chase/PhotoBank, Inc.; **383:** ©Billy E. Barnes/PhotoEdit; **395**(inset): Robert Fried/DDB Stock Photo; **412:** ©Gary A. Conner/PhotoEdit; **415:** ©Wayne Lynch/DRK Photo; **417:** Gerard Lacz/Animals, Animals; **430:** ©Robert A. Tyrrell/Animals, Animals; **430**(inset): Richard La Val/Animals, Animals; **431**(r): American Museum of Natural History/Courtesy Eduardo Aparicio; **431**(l): J.A. Hancock/Photo Researchers; **434:** ©Alfredo Arreguín; **439:** Gerry Ellis Nature Photography; **441**(b): Courtesy Waste Management, Inc.; **442:** ©Betsy Blass/Photo Researchers, Inc.; **444:** ©Michael Fogden/DRK Photo; **448**(t): David Simpson/Stock Boston; **474:** ©Robert Fried.

Realia Page 112: From "Calendario" from EL DIARIO DE JUÁREZ, July 16, 1993, p. 7. Reprinted by permission.